ANCESTORS

...And The Seeds Still Grow....

To Tina
with many thanks
+ love
Myrtle Rose

April 2011

Ancestors and The Seeds Still Grow
Written and Compiled by Myrtle Rose Leggett Emerson

Copyright © 2011
First Edition - First Printing April 2011
Library of Congress Number pending
ISBN # 978-1-934615-52-2
          1-934615-52-8

Published by Main Street Publishing, Inc., Jackson, TN.
Copy Editing by Shari B Hill and Melissa Drummonds
Cover Design by Shari B Hill
Cover Picture by Myrtle Rose Leggett Emerson
Edited by Pat Little
House Illustrations by Myrtle Rose Leggett Emerson
Printed and bound by NetPub, Poughkeepsie, NY.

For more information write Main Street Publishing, Inc.,
206 East Main St., Suite 207, P.O. Box 696, Jackson, TN 38302
Phone 1-731-427-7379 or toll free 1-866-457-7379.
E-mail: editor@mainstreetpublishing.com for managing editor and
               mspsupport@charterinternet.com for customer service.
Visit us at www.mainstreetpublishing.com and www.mspbooks.com.

ANCESTORS

Gentian Book Basic
2 8

...And The Seeds Still Grow....

18

A JOURNEY OF MY FAMILY

Myrtle Rose Leggett Emerson

Email: myrtle007@bellsouth.net

On the Back Cover

The back cover of this book is a section of a painting I commissioned a Mrs. Viers from Brownsville, Tennessee, to paint for me. The bride and groom represent the marriage of the houses and buildings included in this piece. The old Fruitvale Store, men playing cards, cows, the fruit shed, train track, the "yellow house" Joe and I lived in for fourteen years.

In the foreground is a quilt with our Milly there, our Jody standing by the old truck we have, and our lovely dog Poo Doo, making this so special to us. It represents so many happy days together. The whole painting is included inside this book and represents so much of not only mine and Joe's family, but the lives of our ancestors before us.

The Whole Painting

This is the whole of the painting on the previous page. The houses represent his family and mine. This is our livelihood represented here. There is the house where we lived when all four of our children were born; Grandpa Archie is making sorghum molasses; the tombstone in the graveyard for our beautiful Mame' Lou; the schools we attended; the Fruitvale train tracks; our great barn the tornado took; our own Cypress Church; the log house Grandma Annie was born in; the store and crossing; the dreaded squash patch; two of our great-grandparents homeplaces; and clusters of people with houses representing actual people that lived there.

This painting may not be an old master, but to me it is a wonder of feelings and living of families so dear to me.

Myrtle Rose Leggett Emerson

The dear lady that I commissioned to paint this was 88 years old and would not agree to paint for you until she had interviewed you and liked what she heard. She told me she was too old to do anything she did not want to do...Well, *Grandma Moses* was 88, so wake up, people,...there is still a road ahead and living to do!

IN LOVING MEMORY

Of OUR LOVELY DAUGHTER

None knew her but to love her

Mame' Lou Emerson

Born August 8, 1961

Died May 21, 1977

Table of Contents

Acknowledgements

Special Thanks

Special thanks to family members who wrote memories they have of our family and church.

To Tina Gray for her insight and many words of encouragement. For her hard work and for never giving up on me. I am one to hit the high places, and she loves the detail in the valleys, and together we seem to cover all the bases.

To Billy Neal Webb, my cousin, for his inspiration he never knew he had given with his own wonderful book he wrote.

James Blanks for his help with early information about the Baileys, and discovering he is, indeed, one of us.

To Sister Mary Frances Cates for her words and help with the Webb family and her great story she wrote of our Aunt Bettie.

For my parents, grandparents and lovely daughter who have gone before me and left me with love and appreciation for life.

To my husband Joe, my life back to childhood and is still to this day.

My son Jody Van, daughters Milly Ann and Elizabeth Shane, and grandchildren Maggie Leigh, Chelsey Harris, Kayley Mame', Silas Austin, Olivia Rose, Rebecca Emerson, John Fenner, Jr. and Flora Elizabeth, who delight me to no end.

To Bailey Photography, whose photos of my paintings grace the front and back covers of this book.

And last, to Shari B Hill and Main Street Publishing for their advice and help, but most of all, for their patience. Believe me, it took us all to get the "Seeds all Sown."

Myrtle Rose Leggett Emerson

Note to the reader...

I would like to make a note here to clarify the spelling of some names in this book. As years go by the spelling of a person's name gets misspelled on different documents, schools, or just plain mistakes that "stick" to their original spelling. In this book the most versatile name is Dilifate, Dilyfate, Delafate, etc. Also a nickname of Charlonas Ann Leggett, sometimes spelled "Aunt Loonie" and sometimes "Aunt Lony." Sometimes the birth certificate will be one way and the marriage license another.

Sybela Lewis is yet another. It graduated to Syble on some documents confusing her with her daughter that was named Syble.

Prologue

A Journey of Our Family

"When this you see, remember me, and bear it in your mind
What others say when I'm away, speak of me as you find."

I had started out writing down a few notes about my family and life shortly after the death of my oldest daughter, Mame' Lou. Her death triggered some need for records of life, as I know it and what it has meant to me. I wrote most about the children and their antics of childhood. This did not amount to much at the time, but I kept the little black notebook in my desk and every five years or so, I took it out and jotted down some more things that I wanted to remember and that I thought might be of interest to my children and eventually grandchildren.

I tried to get more information about my ancestors about fifteen years ago from an older aunt that I knew was a walking history book. This aunt was Bettie Elizabeth Bailey and she is a very prominent part of this book. However, there was not a lot that I could get from her.

I went to see Granny Bailey where she was living at the time and took my notebook and pencil and felt very much "the reporter." However, I soon saw that this interview was not going anywhere anytime soon. She was blind and I was almost deaf. She held her head down and talked softly that to my weak ears, it sounded much like a whisper or a mumble. We both had good intentions and this was a setback, but this is where determination sets in and takes over for anyone to finish what they have started.

After the children all married and moved out, I once again got out the little black book and started jotting down a few words when I got a chance. The push and shove that really got the ball rolling was about five years ago when my doctor told me that I was not going to be able to communicate much longer using my ears.

The things I had written through these years were family stories that Joe and I had lived through in our married life and some of them were of our life, as children. These are a majority of this book. After I had sorted through all these rambling pages, I had a Bailey Family Reunion at my house after Homecoming at the church. I gave each guest a blank page and asked him or her to write some memories of Bailey life they would like recorded. I did get a few and was so happy to have these in my book. Then my children and nephews wrote several pages for me about their feelings, and these were quite useful and entertaining. This gave a wider view of our families' thoughts and what had impressed them through the years.

I added another extension to my project when Joe and I took our family to Europe. On the plane when things were getting pretty quiet and the children were getting restless, I gave each grandchild a few blank pages and a pen and told them to write some things they remembered about growing up in the Emerson family. They kept sending pages after pages back to me, and I was so amazed and thrilled at what they had to offer in the line of family history and their thoughts on growing up. We should really ask for our children's opinion more often, and we just might get some good advice and knowledge.

I had so much of the genealogy of families connected to Joe and me just literally thrown in my lap. I know I had tried to get some information on the Forsythe side of my family. This was Granny Bailey's side. At a family gathering the night before Homecoming, there was a Forsythe cousin that had traced the family back to the Revolutionary War and through the Civil War all in book form. This was just too good to be true. Then one day a cousin called from Tullahoma to talk and I had known him slightly twenty years. He wanted to come and meet some of us. We were expecting the Baileys from Texas at the time, so I told him to come on over. He did come over and stayed almost a week and brought so much information on the Bailey side of my family back to 1620! Would you believe we were Yankees for three generations? (But don't tell anyone this.)

Joe had a cousin who wrote a book on the Emerson family that we have had for many years and traced this family back to Ireland and England, and I have included some of this information for anyone that may be connected or interested in genealogy. We are at this time still working on the Leggetts but have not had a lot of success so far. But as Scarlett O'Hara says, "...after all, tomorrow is another day!"

> *When soon or late, we reach that coast*
> *O'er life's rough ocean driven*
> *May we rejoice, no wanderers lost*
> *A family in Heaven.*

CHAPTER 1

Fruitvale Community

Watercolor by Judy Grant

Fruitvale in the 1900's

Fruitvale in earlier times was called Jackson Hollow. The old schoolhouse there was also called Jackson's School. Mr. Frank Raines was a much admired member of our community for some time. He was born in 1905 and remembered so much about the community at the beginning or close to that. He taught in some of our schools around Bells and Fruitvale and was interested in many things. Among the things he did was tell stories of his youth and environment while growing up. He was an upright gentleman, very intelligent, spry, and an inspiration to young and old. Most of the information in this section came through him on down to me. I hope you enjoy these facts as much as I did. He related some interesting information about the little town.

The name change from Jackson's Hollow to "Fruitvale" is reputed to have come from (of all things) a hobo that came through and said that the name should be Fruitvale instead. The "vale" suggested because it sat in a small level space between Bells and Gadsden and both sat on low hills. The "Fruit" part of the name because of all the fruits and vegetables that were shipped out from the shed on the railroad tracks behind the store. The little station shipped strawberries, sweet potatoes, cabbage, tomatoes and every conceivable, edible thing that these country farmers could raise in bulk to help supplement their meager incomes. Timber logs were also cut and shipped from this station. These foods had to be shipped on ice and this had to be bought in Brownsville and brought back in sawdust on the floor of wagons to keep it from melting. This was a good distance to travel with melting ice being 13 miles with mules pulling the wagon.

Another "occupation" for the townsmen were geese. The family would kill the geese and pull the feathers off and womenfolk would make small pillows from the pluckings and ice down the birds to be shipped on the train to Chicago, etc. Mr. Frank would take these small head pillows his mother made to the tracks and sell them through the train windows to the weary travelers to rest their heads on. One tale that Mr. Frank loved to tell was that he knew that Ollie Boyd owned the store and surrounding land and he was just a little tyke; and when the train left the station and the conductor called out, "All aboard, all aboard," he thought the man was calling, *"Ollie Boyd, Ollie Boyd."*

In 1910-1915, Fruitvale had three stores plus a sawmill and blacksmith shop. The stores were owned by Boyd, Jackson, and Kenner-Evans. They built a new school and raised money by having box suppers and making and selling quilts. These quilts were plentiful in those days because in wintertime the women spent so much time inside keeping the fires blazing to keep the family warm and had time for this endeavor. These old country quilts now would bring very high prices, and these women that made them would not be able to believe the amount of dollars their efforts would command.

Around this time there were only two cars in Fruitvale. One was owned by a man named Bob Jackson, the other owned by Zab Williams. Mr. Zab Williams owned the only wheat thrashing machine in town, and all the men in surrounding areas would follow this machine and help harvest the wheat from one farm to the other. When the day was done and the wheat on one farm finished, the lady of the house would have supper ready and hot for all the men. The menu usually consisted of fried chicken, because of its availability and blackberry or other fruit made into cobblers. These men were well fed because it was harvest time and a time when the womenfolk had access to good nourishing foods and no fast foods nor boxed mixes. These things were unknown to these farm folks or anyone else at that time.

School lunches at the Jackson School were usually brought in pails instead of sacks and certainly not the time of lunchrooms and cafeterias. The pail usually contained a Johnny Cake because store bread was hard to come by and too expensive for the country people to buy. You were not allowed to swing your pail in any way because this would cause your food to scramble. (A Johnny Cake is made of cornmeal and buttermilk and fried in round pones.)

At the end of each school year, the children were rewarded with stick candy and only on this one day. They used to swing on the many saplings in the thick woods that surrounded the school. They also had a nearby stream that they waded and splashed each other in.

Another story related to Mr. Frank was one told about his grandfather who ate with a dog on one side of him and a cat on the other. This older man rode a horse named Richard. Wherever old Richard and Grandpa went, the Shepherd dog named *Taso,* was always by his side. Grandpa carved his own casket out of poplar boards and left it on the side porch. He also had an apple orchard and when the children wanted an apple they knew where Grandpa kept them. You guessed, didn't you? The apples were stored in Grandpa's hand-hewed casket.

The trains that came through Fruitvale were as regular as a clock. In fact, it was one way that local folks set their clocks and kept good time by doing so. The morning train would come through at 10:45, and this meant to all of us in the fields that it was almost dinnertime. It was a joyous sound to all the children and adults alike. The afternoon train came through at six. Mail sacks were filled with letters and cards in the post office and hung on a tall pole with an iron hook on the end; and when the train came along it would use another "arm" and swoop the sack to the train and just keep on going. The incoming mail to the junction would be thrown out the back of the passing train. (Better not send Grandma's glass vase by mail in those days.) The impact of the bag flying through the air and flopping to the ground would sometimes burst the sack, and letters, etc. would go flying in the wind. I guess you could say this was an "early air mail!"

FRUITVALE, TENN. _____ 19__

IN ACCOUNT WITH

O. N. KENNER

DEALER IN GENERAL MERCHANDISE

ALL KINDS OF COUNTRY PRODUCE

BOUGHT AND SOLD

From the Crockett County Centinel
1874 - 1974
Fruitvale & Mason Grove

time.

Mr. Dorse Leggett rane a store for a long time up on the highway. This store is now operated by his daughter, Mrs. Nathalie Yearwood. The store is known as Leggett's Grocery.

Mr. Clarence Nelson ran a store on the south side of the highway for many years, but has now retired and the store is vacant.

Like all other country communities in the county, Fruitvale has lost its school. The children go two ways, some to Bells, and some to Gadsden. The old school building now serves as a community center for community meetings.

1974
FRUITVALE
by
Mrs. C. C. James

Early settlers of Fruitvale were the Williams families from North Carolina by way of Wilson County, Tennessee. The exact date of their arrival is not known, but Nathaniel and Jeremiah Williams bound themselves to pay Edward Williams two barrels of corn per acre on all the ground they planted in corn and cotton, and one dollar per acre for all the small grain planted. This was in March of 1836. Nathaniel Williams purchased 635 acres in District 9 of Madison County. The center of this tract is located about one and one-fourth miles east of Fruitvale.

Nathaniel's wife was Gilley Cooley. Her sister, Malinda, married Gray B. Medlin and they, too, came to Crockett County. Many Medlin descendants still live in the county.

By 1850, three of Nathaniel's children had married, and seven remained at home. A daughter, Wealthy, married Henry Blurton. Sons of Nathaniel were: Wesley, Winfield, Wyat, Woodson, Wilson, Whitfield, W. D. "Dock," W. P. "Pony," W. S. "Shug." Those directly descended and still living in Fruitland are Carl Wayne Williams, Edward Williams, Hiawatha Williams, Leon Williams, Jim Williams, and Mrs. Earl Dunlap.

Nathaniel's son, W. P. "Pony," married first Julia Ann Eliza Edwards, and his second wife was Almedia Louise Jackson, daughter of Elisha Jackson, also one of the first settlers. Pony's children by the first marriage were Tiny and Lemuel Ammen. By the second wife the children were Dena, Lizzie, Zab, Ernest, Ethel, Cora, Allie, Otto, Laudell, Lurline, Claude, and Chester. Many descendants remain today in Fruitvale, across the county and other states. Pony Williams cared for many victims during the small pox epidemic soon after the Civil War. Many of the victims were attended in a one-room log house on the southeast corner of the original Nathaniel Williams 635 acre tract. When a victim died, Mr. Williams and an elderly colored man would carry them out for burial, Mr. Williams riding along in front to warn people to move away from the road. Crockett County later had another epidemic for the County Court called a meeting on Monday, Feb. 19, 1900, to take action relative to small pox.

Direct descendants of W. P. and Almedia Louisa Jackson Williams totaled 169 in 1971, and in 1971 there were 139 still living. Dan Williams, son of Claude, has written a booklet on the Williams family and much of our information has come from him. There are more people carrying the name of Williams in Crockett County today than those bearing any other name.

The first Crockett County magistrates from the Fruitvale community were John E. Pearson and T. B. Casey.

Henry Blurton, b. 1813 married Wealthy Williams, b. 1819. They were married in Wilson County and came west with her parents. Their children married into the Kenner, Medlin, Faulkner, Permenter, and Mayfield families. You will find their descendants all over the county. Those bearing the Blurton name are mostly in the southeast portion of the county. Mrs. Idella, widow of Gale Blurton, is among the oldest members of the family. She is now eighty-seven, a wonderfully interesting person to talk with, and an artist of some note. She has painted many pictures, and done art work for several churches.

Joseph A. Bodwell came from Carroll County in 1899 to Crockett County. He boarded with Mr. Clinton Scarborough and taught school. He taught for many, many years, and today there are many teachers in the family. His daughter, Erin, married Dorse Leggett of the Fruitvale Community. "Miss Erin has written many articles for the newspapers and at least one book. The Leggett children were Garland, Nathalie, Joe Leonard, Merlin, Clifton, Madeline, and Bennie Faye. Most of them still live in Crockett County or in nearby counties.

An ad in the "Alamo Sentinel" in 1900 says that T. P. Taylor has moved to Fruitvale and will deal in drygoods notions, boots, shoes, a full line of staple groceries, and will take country produce in exchange for groceries. He must not have remained long for his name is missing from the businesses listed in the 1903 city directory. This 1903 list included these businesses: Marlow Bros. Grocery; Nelson, Raines, & Scarborough Groc.; J. R. Jackson and Co. Dry Goods and Groceries; W. Z. Williams, blacksmith; R. N. Raines, express agent; R. W. Riggins & Co., Sawmill.

In 1903, a telegraph office was open during the June and July fruit season, and there was telephone connection with all parts of the county and the country at large.

It seems that Fruitvale has had three names. It was first called Jackson Hollow, for Elisha Jackson, one of the earliest settlers. Later it bore the name of "The Switch." In 1874, a post office was commissioned there and the name seems to have been changed to Fruitvale at that time. The name must have come from the fact that so many vegetables and fruits were shipped from there.

A list of all those who have served as postmaster is not available to us at this time, but in 1906, Mr. J. O. Boyd was appointed postmaster. He served continuously as postmaster for forty-five years, until his retirement. Mr. Boyd began business with his brother, Oscar Boyd, in Fruitvale in 1906. They were related to the Boyds who came very early to the Center Community. When World War II began, Mr. Oscar Boyd entered the armed service. When he returned from the war, he did not again re-enter business with his brother.

Mr. J. O. Boyd seems to have bought and sold everything — hardware, groceries, dry goods, fertilizer, coal, and in modern times he added electrical appliances. He had several warehouses filled with goods. He bought produce, cabbage, tomatoes, berries, beans, and sweet potatoes. That area seems to have been the sweet potato capital of Crockett County. He shipped all these things in carload lots. All the people of the community must have helped during the peak of the shipping season each summer. As many as eight railroad cars of green wrapped tomatoes have been shipped in a single day in years past. Mr. Boyd also acquired a vast amount of land and raised many cattle and hogs. His niece, Mrs. Merlin Leggett, began working for him when she was about twelve years old and worked for about nine years. Her sister, Mrs. Geneva Emerson, also worked for him and continues to work for Mr. O. W. Boyd, his successor. Cecil Stewart, of Alamo, got a lot of experience working there in the summers. Mrs. Lonnie Boyd was also a clerk for a long time. Elmer Brassfield was a clerk for many years, and people still remember his piano playing. Probably the one who worked the longest was Mrs. Malcom Emerson. She was both clerk and bookkeeper.

Mr. Boyd died July 4, 1971, at the age of ninety. Relatives still in Fruitvale include Bill Emerson and his family, Joe Emerson and his family, Mrs. Geneva Emerson. Mrs. Lonnie May Leggett is a niece living in Gadsden.

Mr. O. W. Boyd assumed ownership of the business after Mr. Boyd died. The business still has anything you would need to buy, almost. They still sell dry goods, groceries, well supplies, hardware, and fertilizer. Mrs. Geneva Emerson is still working as a clerk for Mr. Quentin.

After Mr. J. O. Boyd retired as postmaster in 1951, Mr. Malcom Emerson became the poastmaster, and has held the office to the present time.

Mr. Dorse Leggett rane a store for a long time up on the highway. This store is now operated by his daughter, Mrs. Nathalie Yearwood. The store is known as Leggett's Grocery.

Mr. Clarence Nelson ran a store on the south side of the highway for many years, but has now retired and the store is vacant.

Like all other country communities in the county, Fruitvale has lost its school. The children go two ways, some to Bells, and some to Gadsden. The old school building now serves as a community center for community meetings.

MASON'S GROVE
by
Artelia Humphreys

Mason's Grove was settled in the 1820s and named for the Mason family, Ezekiel Brownlee (Lee) Mason, Isaac H. (Ike) Mason, and Green Hill (Hill) Mason being prominent among the first settlers. They were the sons of Abram Mason b. 10/22/1778 in Revet County, Delaware, m. 10/28/1800 in Williamson County, Tennessee to Margaret Curry (b. 7/15/1774 in North Carolina d. 9/29/1858 at Mason's Grove, Tennessee) d. 8/29/1862 at Mason's Grove. Ezekiel Brownlee (Lee) Mason was b. 10/18/1802, Williamson County, Tennessee, m. 2/26/1822 to Camden Hubbard Walden, (dau of John and Sarah Walden, b. 12/26/1793 in Mecklenburg County, Virginia, d. 4/13/1873 at Mason's Grove, Tenn.) d. After 1886. Isaac Hall (Ike) Mason b. 7/1/1806 Williamson County, Tennessee m. 10/26/1830 Rebecca Ann Ferguson d. 4/13/1873 at Mason's Grove, Tennessee. Green Hill Mason b. 10/14/1807, Williamson County, m. 1/17/1835 to Frances Wood. These Masons are the forebears of many of the people still living in and around Mason's Grove and prominent in Crockett County history. Some descendants are the McLearys, Bennetts, Collinsworths, Powells, Dungans, Watkins, Adams, Coxes, Craddocks, Dunlaps, Gregorys, Griggses, Jameses, Jettons, Kincaids, Lanes, Metchells, Raineses, Powells, Senters, Deloaches, Warmaths, Warrens, Williamses, Willoughbys, and many, many related families. It grew rapidly into one of the centers of activity in Madison County and by the mid 1800s was relatively thickly settled and prosperous. It was laid out in lots, streets, etc., and had two churches, a well known secondary college, an inn, a cabinet and casket maker, a doctor and various businesses, a Masonic Lodge, a Grange, and several cemeteries in the vicinity. The churches were the Christian and the Methodist Episcopal South, the college was Mason's Grove Masonic Academy, a coed school for boarding as well as local students and was under the capable professorship of Prof. I. B. Day. A reunion held at Mason's Grove Thursday, September 8, 1910 was attended by more than fifty former pupils and several hundred guests. Mason's Grove was on the main stage coach road between Jackson, Tennessee and Dyersburg, Tennessee and was a stop over point for the mail. The two story, frame Inn had a large corral for accommodating the horses and a dining room reported to be 20 by 30 feet. The Masons were the original Inn keepers and a popular jingle inspired by the frequency of a certain menu item ran "Mason's Inn, Mason's Out, Mason's Hotel, Plenty of Kraut." Mr. J. S. Watkins (Uncle Jack) was the Cabinet and Casket maker and many of his articles of furniture are in homes in the community. It is told that Uncle Jack, when he had an unusually heavy demand for caskets, would tie a note on his dog and send the dog across the field to the home of Mr. Tom McCord who would then come to help him out. The pulpit stand in use today in the Church of Christ in Gadsden, Tennessee is said to be the handiwork of Uncle Jack. In the 1850 Census of Madison County, listing No. 320 is for J. S. WATKINS, Cabinetmaker 34 years old, born in North Carolina, Jane L. 25 years old born in Tennessee, Tabitha L 6 years old, born in North Carolina and Nancy J., 2 years old, born in

Tennessee, Tabitha married Bob Cox, Nancy married John Willoughby and later John B. Tatum. About 1860, business men J. B. Boykin, R. W. Sims, W. W. Williams, and William Richardson moved their business to Gadsden to have the advantage of the L & N Railroad which had come through there. After this, Gadsden outgrew Mason's Grove but the latter remained a populous and prosperous community with Mr. Robert Buchanan Griggs (Mr. Bob) one of its leaders. Mr. Griggs, son of Robert and Susan Collins Griggs, was born 7/20/1856 and died 5/04/1923 at Mason's Grove. On 12/12/1876, he was married to Miss Mary Susan Cox b. 4/3/1855 in Madison County, died 5/26/1938 at Mason's Grove. She was the daughter of Margaret Elizabeth Collinsworth and James Alexander Cox and a great granddaughter of Isaac Mason. A large country store run by the Griggs family for many years is no longer open but extensive farming interests, a cotton gin and a dealership in agricultural chemicals and fertilizers, along with modern, well-kept residences insures Mason's Grove a continued vital spot in Crockett County. The first cotton gin in this community was owned by Lemuel E. Humphreys and located on the Mason's Grove Road just above the present Lem Humphreys (grandson of Lemuel E.) residence. This was a horse powered gin and following a serious accident to Lemuel E. Humphreys was sold to Mr. Bob Griggs who moved the equipment to Mason's Grove and operated it by windmill power, later converting to the modern equipment in use today. In the late 1800s, following the coming of the L&N Railroad and the introduction of strawberries as a commercial crop, a place known as Pomona, Land of Fruits, came into being, roughly halfway between Humboldt and Gadsden at the intersection of the railroad and Temperance Road. A siding for loading berries was put in, a large shed with platforms and ticket office was soon erected and during Strawberry Season Pomona was a scene of unusual activity. Mule drawn wagon loads of 24 quart berry crates made a procession from early until late, often having to wait to be checked and unloaded, and agents from Commission Houses in far away places like St. Louis were inspecting and bidding. Many carloads were sent out on consignment and during the season thousands of crates were handled at Pomona. The major growers, such as W. Z. Raines & Son, planted acres and acres in berries and shaking and setting new plants, hand hoeing and picking, field supervision during picking, pack shed work at the field, ticket giving and cashing, and various other jobs provided more work than could be handled by local labor and pickers were hauled in from miles away. These were housed in make shift accommodations near the station and these living quarters were the scene of socializing, singing, guitar and banjo picking, fighting, etc., until far in the night. A store was operated during this season but many would ride the train to Humboldt or Gadsden to spend their berry money in town. During the early days of the railroad, passenger trains would stop to pick up or discharge passengers and a familiar sight was a man standing in the middle of the tracks and flagging a train to stop. A large white handkerchief or cloth was used in the day and a lighted lantern at night. It was a fearsome sight to watch the flagger standing there while the train bore down on him until he was seen by the crew and given a whistle signal. Improved road systems, refrigerated trucks, and local competitive buying brought an end to railroad shipping of berries and gradually the facilities at Pomona fell into disuse. Today there are only a very few small plantings of strawberries in the vicinity and these are harvested mainly by pick-your-owners for home consumption.

Following are a few early settlers whose descendants remain in Mason's Grove. Robert Thomas McCord (b. 1842) married Claudia E. Hardy. Their children were; George Robert, Minnie N., Cora Belle, Mary Elizabeth, William Henry, and James Eugene.

Another old settler was R. S. Matthews (b. 1839) and married to Nannie L. Hart. Their children were; Julia E., Susan F., Willie L., Mary B., Robert L., James I., Lillie A., George F., Sarah Alma, Martha P., Annie D., and Allie C.

Sponsored by: Mr. & Mrs. Jerry Wells, Phara Leight, Joe, John & Jason

Fruitvale School Organization

Copy of a letter of the organization of the Fruitvale School.
(Typed as written)

Fruitvale, June 20, 1913

Mr. B.G. Fullinsbee, Pittsborough, Pa.

My dear Brother Fullinsbee, Your contribution of Mar, 1912 continues to do good. I beg to refer you to my letter of May 20, 1912 in which I told you of the S. School which I organized for you in the town of Fruitvale in Crockett Co. Tenn. on Sun, May 19,1912 a sermon had never been preached in a S. School organized or a literary school ever existed in this town.

Your S. School was organized in an old two room discarded residence with 4 classes and 33 students, and a building committee selected on this same day for the purpose of collecting funds and building a house in which the S School could be operated in which they hoped to secure a literary public free school and in which they could have preaching, hold elections, hold political meetings and all other purposes for which it was desired to use it.

The young S. School needed encouragement which I often returned to give. A preacher was secured for one Sunday in each month. In the summer of 1912 a protractor meeting was held during which the ????of the S. School was converted and baptized.

The building committee became active from the time they were chosen. They secured a 2- acre lot in the corner of a large beautiful woods lot. This 2 a. lot was fine on three sides leaving it open at the front. Enough of the trees were cleared away to give room for the building, leaving a number of massive oaks nearby for shade. Then they went to work gathering funds for the building Again I beg to refer you to a post card picture which I sent to you in Feb.20, 1913 of the old house in which his school was organized and operated till the new building was ready. The section of the school standing in front of this old building became leaders in helping the building committee. R. N. Raines, J.P. secured $500.00 from the county school funds. The ladies organized themselves into a society known as "Willing Workers". An initiation fee of 10 cents was paid by each lady who joined. They quilted quilts for the public at $1.00 each. They gave a box supper out of which $22.00 was charged and afterward, an ice cream supper out of which $20.00 were made. A fine of 10 cts. was collected from any man who imposed his presence on their regular meetings. To May 20,1913 these dear ladies had raised $75,00.

To be brief, the necessary funds were raised and the beautiful $2000.00 building now stands without incumbency buried back amid those monarchs of the forest, a picture good to look upon, a centennial to the integrity of the young in the vicinity of Fruitvale and her future welfare as a town. The "Willing Workers" have lately paid $40 on the painting and furnished the house with beautiful swinging lamps and wall lamps.

While visiting this little trown on June 12,1913 a citizen said to me "Our s school is moving right on with 42 attending. We have our literary school and our house to hold it in. We have preaching twice per month and preparations are being made for a protracted meeting this Summer" Another citizen said: ======" A new 22 ft. road is opening up leading out east of this new building, and another leading out west, making it and the town approachable from all directions. Then, too, our roads are all to be widened and graded this summer and then we will have as good roads as are to be found in the county. All we needed was a start in the right direction and you gave us that start+++++++++I wish I could write a good letter. I would write a good one to that brother in Pennsylvania. The good result coming from that little lift he gave us - No telling where it will end."

The good people of Fruitvale have worked nobly for all these things and have gained every point. As this brother said your contribution enabled many to make the start for them, and they appreciate it. May God bless and prosper you abundantly as He has our kindly contribution.

Yours in Christ,

A.L. Jernigan
Mis. Am. S.S Union

Fruitvale School 1979

Fruitvale Sunday School

Writer of article unidentified. It was copied from writings of someone years ago and never completed. *Myrtle Rose Leggett Emerson*

Fruitvale Sunday School was organized in the year 1911 by Journagan. The Sunday School Missionary who was sent out by the "American Sunday School Union" of Philadelphia. The school was first held under a temporary tent erected by the men of Fruitvale for the purpose to hold a revival. The covering was of sheets that had been used for covering tomato plants in the cold frame. The seats were of planks, which rested on blocks of wood or stove-wood blocks. The stand or rostrum was constructed in like manner and a table was used for a book-board and at the close of this series of meetings. Sooner or later the school was organized as above stated by the Sunday School Missionary. The first superintendent was brother B—, a member of the Methodist church and the Sunday school seemed to move nicely. But as every movement for good has hindrances, so had this Sunday School, and they came in this shape. After the school had enjoyed its first few sessions, it happened so that an appointment was made for a minister of a different denomination and in the course of his sermon, he made some strong points in favor of his particular faith and order, which conflicted with the favorite opinions of the superintendent and after the benediction was said they locked horns and it was reported by some present that there was visible anger on both sides.

Let that be as it may, Brother B.——would have no more to do with school as superintendent, or otherwise. There must be another superintendent or the school would stop. Another one was chosen. This second was brother G. He was a Methodist also but he would not belittle himself to even go. So the Sunday School that started with a promising outlook was so soon doomed by those who should have nourished it.

It was reported by all, that Fruitvale Sunday School had died in its infancy and it's reason was being sung on every corner, especially by the enemies of such movement that does not go their way. But after all there was a half dozen or more good women who were not dead. I might say here, but for the zeal and faithfulness of the few women above mentioned, the Sunday school might never have been revived. They solicited help from other points and that help re-opened readily, and consequently an appointment was made for the purpose of reviving the school. The first appointment was to meet in a vacant dwelling belonging to Mrs. J. R. Jackson on a Sunday afternoon. And there were only eleven attending the meeting including the speaker. And a part of that number came through curiosity, thinking they would witness another failure and have more bones to pick. But in this they were disappointed, for there was a handful there who was in dead earnest, for where there are as many as three for God, he will make the fourth one and that will always count for victory.

At the stated hour for the meeting the little crowd assembled in the south room of the house above mentioned and the speaker took a position near the center at that part of the room which would face the crowd and stated the purpose of the meeting in a few sentences, stating that he had been solicited by some to head the service. They had a song, a short prayer and after reading or quoting a few verses from the 12th

Chapter of the letter to the Romans, proceeded with a short exoneration and stressing more particular on the fifth verse calling attention to the fact the Sunday School is a Union school and that there was no room for denominational bias. As we are all one in Christ and under obligation one to another.

It was announced by someone how W. Z. Williams had offered to the Sunday school, the use of a tenant house which was just a short distance out of what was understood as the limits of Fruitvale and the offer was accepted. And the next Sunday the school was re-established in the tenant house with its different classes and the teachers also with literature.

At this meeting of the Sunday school, there were signs of interest being manifested by the people and there was a much larger crowd than on the previous Sunday.

Morals

This paper below is written just as I received it and has not been altered in any way. Author unknown. *Myrtle Leggett Emerson*

It might not be out of place to mention the morals of the little town. At this particular time, and note the difference in those morals a few years later. I might add however that there is room yet for improvement along the line of morality. But I will speak more particularly of the years before and at the time the Sunday School was started. I think I am not using any hyperbole when I say, morals in Fruitvale were superlatively bad. It was as the little boy had it when he first began to study grammar. It was "bad, badder and baddest." Altogether, they were, that is to say, a greater part of the men and boys, white and black, was engaged in some way that did more to desecrate the Sabbath than otherwise. They were generally drinking whisky, shooting craps, playing cards, using profane and vulgar language, and in a general way profaning the Lord's day. but from the day that the few women had the meeting in the vacant dwelling above mentioned, the school began to grow and develop and before long, people began to stand up and take notice. The school in a short time grew too large for the tenant house and was forced to seek more roomy quarters and fortunately for the school the Fruitvale school house was being built near. It was finished and we were tendered the use of it and we moved there.

The Sunday School at the school house in considering the Sunday school from now on. We will be less tedious and leave off to some extent minor details. After the school was housed in this spacious quarters, it began to show in the morals of the community.

Fruitvale

Through the years the Fruitvale store was the hub of things happening all around the community. The people from Cypress, Walnut Hill, Liberty Hall, Gum Flat and surrounding communities came to J.O.Boyd's store for food, clothing, dishes, gas, farming tools, fertilizers, plants, nails and even socks and brooms. Anything useful on the farm could be purchased there. The Post Office was there for you to get mail and stamps. They sold appliances, iron stoves, towels and sheets; you could get yard goods for quilts, dresses, and even a pair of shoes or boots. The kids could purchase toys, candy bars and ice cream sticks. If they did not have it, you did not need it! There were three owners of this store before J.O. Boyd was the sole owner. They were: O.N. Kenner; the Marlowe Brothers; brothers, Ollie and Oscar Boyd.

The old fruit shed was also a busy place. It was a shipping center for Chicago and Memphis and other cities, a storage place for crates, shipping supplies, and was also a meeting place for the children and men. The men played cards on Saturday and Sunday afternoons and when there was a lull on work days. They sat together and laughed and talked and "chewed the cud." I have a picture of the men at their game and the children playing all around them. Age seemed not to make any difference; they were all in the same boat, so to speak.

I remember we had strawberries and sweet potatoes that we gathered, and Daddy took them to the fruit shed in Fruitvale for shipping. I remember Daddy saying, "These berries are going north to Chicago." We were paid 5 cents a quart for picking and 10 cents a quart for capping them. It took a lot of workers to do all the work there. Anyone who was willing to work could find something to do in Fruitvale in its *heyday*.

The colored and white men would sit on the benches in front of the store each morning and wait to see if Ollie could hire them that day. He never seemed to be short on workers and always got the produce out on time.

Back in earlier times before Ollie bought his own pea sheller, there was a man who came through in pea-picking time with a sheller and he would park behind the shed in front of the store and shell peas all day for the women in the community. He had some shade under the big walnut tree there. Lots of peas were shelled to eat and to can in jars for the long winter months. This was a staple food for these country people then and now.

Two of the Norville brothers had the small brick building next to the store and they had groceries there for a long time. It was later converted it into a TV shop. This building was not destroyed by the tornado that wrecked the big building, housing Ollie's store. It destroyed the store and moved the blacksmith shop off its foundation and several smaller buildings when the big one hit in 2002.

The Butler boys came home from the war to the store, feeling good and were so glad to be back home in Fruitvale. Their family had been living there for years and were welcomed back by the community. What a service these boys did for us, and now we have other boys there who are still doing us a great favor by serving in the U.S. Forces. We owe them all a great deal of appreciation for what they endured and for what they are still enduring for our safety...Go SOLDIERS!!!!!!

FRUITVALE, Tn 38336

Card game in the Fruit Shed, Fruitvale, TN 1951 (standing – Malcolm Emerson, Clif McSlothin, Ray Woodson, W.H. Woodson, Russell Emerson, Ben Emerson)

James Ollie Boyd (Center) – Inside his store (Quentine Boyd [on right], Ada Boyd and Malcolm Emerson)

James Ollie Boyd

Ollie Boyd in his
Strawberry Field
below

The fruit shed and house where Joe and Myrtle Rose lived when first married

Postmasters of Fruitvale

Fruitvale, Crockett County, Tennessee.
Established on May 6, 1893.

Appointment Dates Thru
September 30, 1971

Postmasters

Robert N. Raines   May 6, 1893
Silas E. Emison   September 3, 1901
Willie Ida Bedwell   July 1, 1905
James O. Boyd   June 7, 1909
Malcolm H. Emerson   September 30, 1950 (assumed charge)
                                October 12, 1950 (acting)
                                November 16, 1960 (confirmed)

We can furnish for a total cost of $2.00 electrostats of site location
reports relating to this office.

Ancestors and The Seeds Still Grow

Crockett County Sentinel   **50¢**

:ory closes its doors

dried peas and rice. They bought bolts of printed cloth and wooden spools of colored thread. And they came, perhaps, hoping to snatch a few tidbits of gossip, and to steal a rare few moments away from their hot stoves and their ironing boards.

Three or four clerks were always on hand, Boyd said, to climb the two rolling ladders to the topmost shelves to retrieve their customers' orders. They wrapped the goods neatly in brown paper bags and tied them with lengths of string hanging from cone-shaped spools near the ceiling.

The children of Fruitvale came too. They came with their hoarded pennies and nickels to buy a few minutes of sweet pleasure....candy, lined up on the counter in their glossy wrappers, just at a kid's eye-level. Boyd particularly remembers Baby Ruths, Three Musketeers and Mounds, his favorites. For a nickel you could buy a whole bag of small candies to share with your friends....or a Hershey's chocolate bar to savor greedily in front of them.

The sharecroppers and the "hired hands" came to escape the hot rays of the sun for a few minutes, and maybe to spend a nickel on an ice-cold Coca-Cola and a sandwich of cold cuts and cheese.

Everybody came back then, remembers Boyd. And business stayed good for many years after Boyd starting running the store in 1959. The store even survived the Depression years of the '30s. So, when did the long, downward spiral begin from the heyday of the 'teens and twenties and the prosperous '40s and '50s?

Boyd noticed his business slowing about a decade ago. "I remember my business slacking

off, I guess eight or 10 years ago," he said.

"It got too slack for me. But I was old enough to stop anyway."

The faithful few

Now, it's a busy day if more than a handful of customers come in. And some of those may be coming to pick up their mail at the post office located just inside the store, said Boyd.

Oh, there are still a faithful few who come in to "loaf" as Boyd calls it. People like 84-year-old Malcolm Emerson who stopped by last Saturday.

"I got no place to loaf (after the store closes)," lamented Emerson. "I need to get out of my wife's hair every now and then."

> *"It's going to be a big void in our community. People have gathered here for a long time......for fellowship, visiting and news."*
> *Lavanda Williams, Fruitvale Postmaster*

Emerson's own history is tied closely to that of the old Fruitvale store. He worked for Boyd's uncle from 1934 to 1950, waiting on customers and working in the produce shed. He remembers that once, he and other workers loaded 5,050 bushels of sweet potatoes on the L & R for shipment.

He was postmaster in the small post office in the front corner of the store from 1950 to 1978. His father, Silas Emerson, was the Fruitvale postmaster at the turn of the century.

Emerson chatted with his long-time friend for a while and offered information on the history of the Fruitvale store. After a while he left, but returned shortly to say: "Be sure to say

that I'm 84 years old and I just came off the golf course. My buddies will get a kick out of that."

Other faithfuls include Boyd's brother Fred, Edward and Randy Williams, John Hart, John Lee, David Lee, Luther Norville and Joe Emerson.

Business is too slow

Unfortunately, the faithful few and the rare "happen-bys" will not be enough to keep Boyd in business.

The old Underwood cash register on the counter just doesn't ring enough. The once stocked-full shelves are more empty than not.

The long, oblong antiquated Pepsi cooler is almost empty. Soon, it will stop humming altogether.

A wall will probably be built just inside the front door, Boyd guesses, to partition off the store and make an entry way to the post office. Postmaster Lavanda Williams will still be in her usual place, taking care of incoming and outgoing mail.

Boyd and his store will be missed

"It's going to be a big void in our community," said Williams of the store's closing. "People have gathered here for a long time......for fellowship, visiting and news."

Boyd and his store will be missed by many; perhaps by more people than he knows.

As Boyd pulls each string on the six single light bulbs that hang from the rafters for the final time, he will leave in shadow what remains of many familiar objects of 54 years of his life.

And as he closes the doors behind him, he will be closing the doors on an important part of the history of an entire community.

Fruitvale: 1979

ABOVE: Store owner Q.W. Boyd, left, and his cousin Geneva Emerson remember when people bought everything at the store in Fruitvale. **BELOW LEFT:** Fruitvale held many memories for Erin Bedwell Leggett, 89. **BELOW RIGHT:** Retired postmaster Malcolm Emerson said the town was dead. **BOTTOM:** Memories of yesterday cling to the Main Street of old Fruitvale on Aug. 6, 1979.

The Jackson Sun file photos

24

CENTENNIAL CELEBRATION – Postmaster Lavada Williams raises the flag at the Fruitvale Post Ofice on its 100th anniversary, May 6. The facility has been housed in Boyd's Grocery since 1917.

Fruitvale Post Office serves county for 100 years

The Fruitvale Post Office marked its 100th anniversary last week.

On May 6, 1893, a post office was established in the community that formed around the railroad track.

The area was originally called Jackson Hollow because the Jackson family was first to settle there.

When the railroad came through during the 1800s, the name changed to Switch.

As business grew at the fruit stand beside the tracks, the name was changed to Fruitvale.

The first office was in a grocery across the tracks from the current location.

In 1917, the original equipment was moved to Boyd's Grocery. The facility hasn't changed much since then.

In addition to being a century old, the Friutvale post office is the smallest in the state.

Postmaster Lavada Williams serves 30 regular customers from an 8' by 10' cubicle in the front corner of the store.

No rent is charged for the post office boxes, and customers have no key. Lavada has to be there to hand them their mail.

If one of her customers is sick, Mrs. Williams will deliver.

Mrs. Williams is the eighth postmaster in Fruitvale's 100 years. Others who served were:

Robert N. Raines, 1893
Silas Emerson, 1901
Willie Ida Bedwell, 1905
James O. Boyd, 1909
Malcolm H. Emerson, 1951
A.N. Antwine, 1978
Charlotte H. Cooke, 1982
Lavada Williams, 1984.

May 12, 1993
120TH YEAR, No. 50

50¢

© Copyright

ALAMO, TENNESSEE   Tri-County News &

A piece of local hist

HISTORICAL FRUITVALE STORE CLOSES- Q.W. Boyd (right) is closing his store, "Q.W. Boyd's General Merchandise," in Fruitvale. Malcolm Emerson (left) worked in the store for several years and was Fruitvale postmaster from 1950 to 1978.

by Rachel Brown

The faded black lettering on the rusted sign above the entrance of the old brick store building is barely legible. But look closely and it reads: "Q.W. Boyd Gen. Mchdse."

But Boyd is closing his store permenantly because business is too slow to pay the bills.

The store has been an integral part of the tiny community of Fruitvale (population about 125 currently, and double that 50 years or more ago), for 79 years. First as "J.O. Boyd General Merchandise" when it was built in 1917, and beginning in 1959 as "Q.W. Boyd's General Merchandise" when the younger Boyd took the business over from his uncle.

The store has been at the center of Q.W. Boyd's life for most of his 76 years. He worked for his uncle beginning in 1937, until 1942 when he joined the army and traveled overseas during World War II. When he returned in 1945, his uncle hired him on again.

There was plenty of work to be done back then, in the store and in the big produce shed out back, where home-grown fruits and vegetables from J.O. Boyd's 1,200-acre farm were stored. Later, wooden crates full of the Irish potatoes, snap beans, cabbage, sweet potatoes, tomatoes and strawberries would be shipped by train across the country for sale. With the L & R Railroad just a few hundred yards from the shed, the items

might wind up on grocers' shelves in distant cities or even other states.

Boyd raised cattle, sheep and pigs, as well, that would be slaughtered, packed on ice and shipped.

Customers aplenty

In those days, said Boyd, as many as 30 or 35 people might come through the front doors of the store in a day's time.

Fruitvale farmers came to buy gear for their mules and their wagons, seeds for planting, hoes, rakes and plow points. And they came to swap news about crops and weather.

Women came to stock up on coffee, sugar, flour, dried beans,

Boyd Homeplace

The old Boyd Homeplace stood in the exact spot where Ken and Gaye Jordan have built their lovely country home. The old house stood in this spot for many, many years. There was a very pretty winding road going into the yard off the main road, and Gaye and Ken still use this same road.

I remember going into this home several times when growing up. Gaye and Donna Thomas have always been great friends of mine and their Aunt Rene (Flora Lorene Boyd, Ollie's sister)lived there and we would go visit her. She would always meet us with open arms being the warm, loving woman that she was.

The house was a two story structure with front porch and high ceilings. Typical house of the times for people that could afford one this big. J.D. Boyd and his wife, Margaret Emison, had ten children. They were James Ollie, Rosa Ella, William Lonzo, Elbert L., Oscar, Hosea Herman, Minnie Azalee, Lillie Mai, Flora Lorene, and a baby who did not survive; I do not have the name to record.

J.D. was a stern father and raised the children with a no nonsense attitude toward fatherhood. Ollie left at an early age to move to Fruitvale into the house with Francis Marion Leggett. (Details on another page in this book.)

Bobby Hampton Stories
As told to Myrtle Leggett Emerson

We lived in a few places when I was a boy, and I remember when I was seven years old we lived in the house where James and Blanche Clark live. Back then it only had two rooms and a porch, and through the years it has been added onto, making a much larger house. I lived in a house between Malcolm Emerson and Ollie Boyd's office most of my growing up years. I lived here until Faye Kail and I married, and we then lived in the house behind where Joe and Myrtle Rose lived after they married. This house sat on the north side of the railroad track only a little way from it and the trains were very loud and distracting until you got used to them. At one time earlier, this same house was used as a camp house for the migrant workers that stayed there while the jobs they were doing were in season.

Behind our house in Fruitvale when I was a boy, there was a huge red water tank that furnished water for all the surrounding houses, the store, and the fruit shed that washed all the sweet potatoes, etc. before they were shipped out.

Bobby remembers when he was a boy Ollie had given the boys for Christmas a sheep, and he was a pet and stayed around the store all the time. Some colored boys that lived up the road in front of the store were afraid of this big animal and would not come to the store by themselves. This animal had some mysterious circumstances connected with his death. Could this be a story for *Unsolved Mysteries* on TV?

Bobby also had a pet dog named, "Snowball." (Evidently a white dog or one born in a snowstorm). This pet was noted for his meanness and ability to keep stray dogs from coming around the area. He simply would not let the other canines enter his territory. Another mean dog was the one Ollie kept in the store to keep out burglars. During store hours he was tied in the yard in back of the store, but he did not last long because Joe's parents were afraid he would bite some of the children playing close by. He had the unlikely name of *Sun*. Sun was a German Shepherd dog.

There were several houses around that were used as camp houses for seasonal workers. As machines took over the manual jobs, these people were no longer needed; the houses were then used by the laborers that had steady jobs there all year long and were permanent residents.

Faye Hampton said she remembered that sometimes Ollie would sleep in the store if he thought someone had an idea to rob it. There was a lot of this going on in the old days. So many people really did not have everything they needed.

I remember an old plank walk that Ollie had put down from his house to the office and the store. This was a luxury for the times and was really nice because of the mud and holes in the roads.

Fruitvale Colored School House and Macedonia Church

The colored school house in Fruitvale sat on what is known as the Morris Farm. Joe had bought the farm; and when the school closed, he bought the land it sat on and, in turn, donated the land for the new church to have room for a gymnasium added to it.

Macedonia Church burned in 1996 and was a great loss to the community. It is said to have been set on fire deliberately. About this time there were several churches that burned and was a time of much speculation. This person must have had much hostility and hatred inside. When you think of churches, you should think of peace, forgiveness and good will, not destruction.

After this fire, the whole community joined together to rebuild this House of God. Both black and white had a hand in this rebirth. The new Macedonia Church is a beautiful brick building and is thriving with worshipers each Sunday.

The old school house had closed years before it was torn down and was typical of all school houses of the day and much like Emerson School in the Cypress community and Fruitvale School in Fruitvale.

I am fortunate to have one of the original church benches that came from the first church here. L. V. White sold it to me many years ago. It came out of the old church that was there before the one that burned was built.

7 hours of hope

Clinton, Gore bring message of unity to congregations of burned West Tennessee churches

By DIANA BRANUM
The Jackson Sun

There are cheaper ways to get a little drywall hung than having the president and vice president do it.

And given the crack between pieces that President Bill Clinton and Vice President Al Gore attached to the front altar of Salem Missionary Baptist Church in Fruitland on Monday, there certainly are more expert workmen.

But members of the rural, black Gibson County church, claimed by an arsonist in December, wouldn't have it any other way.

"This is a great day in the life of Salem and in the life of the community," the Rev. Daniel Donaldson said as he introduced Clinton to a crowd of 500 to 800 people on the church grounds just after 2 p.m.

Clinton told the crowd assembled at Salem that he is putting emphasis on rebuilding burned churches because he believes that America must be an example to the world.

"I have spent a lot of time on this because I think it is a test of the character of the American people," Clinton said. "Part of what we're dealing with today, folks, is not only how we live our faith, but how we manage our differences."

The event at the church was part of a 7-hour stay that Clinton, Gore and their families made in West Tennessee Monday. In addition to helping with Salem's rebuilding, the Clintons and Gores shook hands at nearby New Shiloh United Methodist Church in Gibson, ate a meal at Madison's Restaurant in Jackson, and greeted more than 4,000 people at McKellar-Sipes Regional Airport before they departed.

The Clintons and Gores worked a little over an hour

Please see 7 HOURS, 3D

Fruitvale Store now after tornado

Ollie's-Post Office (current picture)

The Blacksmith Shed now

Storage Sheds

Pea Shed

Tractor and Truck Shed

The Shop
Had tools and was used for repairing equipment

Fruitvale through Joe's Adolescent Years
Around 1945

I know this sounds spacey, but remember I did not live there then and was living in the Cypress community two or three miles away. I also remember my chief way of transportation was a bicycle and did not have that until I was 12 years old.

Some of the people that I know lived in Fruitvale back then were Lily and Andy Hampton, J.C. Selph and Blondell, James and Louise Hart, L.V. and Belle Bonds White, Hautie and Milton Nelson, Edward and Mott Williams, Malcolm and Maggie Lou Emerson, Mary and Earl Dunlap, Laudell Williams, Erin and Doss Leggett, Oscar and Tiny Crossnoe Boyd, Tom Phillips, Jim and Mary Williams, the Shutes family, the Walter Nelson family, Bill and Rosette Nichols, Robert and Polly Arnold, Bill Kail, Otto Emison, Madge and Elmer Brasfield, Dalton Odell, Leon and Martha Williams, Annie and Minnie Norville, Carl Hughes, Stenson Hughes, Neil and Maggie Wilson, and the Blurton family.

The Fruitvale Store was the hub of things for so many families. The people from Cypress, Walnut Hill, Liberty Hall and surrounding communities came to J.O. Boyd's Store for food, clothing, dishes, gas, farming tools, fertilizers, plants and mail. The Post Office was in the front of the store. They sold appliances, nuts and bolts, iron stoves, towels, sheets, and fabric by the yard and even toys for the kids.

The old fruit shed was a busy place. It was a shipping center for Chicago and Memphis and other cities, storage place for crates and shipping supplies, and was also a meeting place for the children and men. The men played cards on Sunday afternoon and when there was a lull on a workday. (I have a picture of the men at their game and the children playing all around them.) They shipped out strawberries, sweet potatoes, cabbage, turnips, tomatoes and any vegetable the farmers in the area were producing at the time. I remember we had strawberries and sweet potatoes that we gathered, and Daddy took them to the fruit shed in Fruitvale for shipping. It took a lot of workers to do all the work here. The colored and white men would sit on the benches in front of the store and wait and see if Ollie could hire them to work that day. He never seemed to be short on workers and always got the produce out on time. Malcolm Emerson and Bobby Hampton usually drove the big truck with long benches hauling pickers to and from the fields.

Boys in Fruitvale (Harry Kail, Ray Woodson, Joe and Bill Emerson, Leon and Wesley Wilson)

Joe and playmates (Cleo McLemore, Junior Bonds, Joe Emerson)

Paw Paw's (Malcolm) Money Jar

Paw Paw, Joe's dad, worked in the Fruitvale Post Office for several years and during all this time, saved all the Indian Head Nickels and Wheat Pennies that came through the office. He had quite a collection in jars that he had kept there with him. Someone stole his entire collection and he was so distraught that he never saved another nickel or dime that came through the office.

I have seen the prices on these old coins lately in magazines and papers and there is no telling how much these would bring in today's market. I have a feeling that if he still had those before he died, he would not have exchanged them for dollars.

He enjoyed looking for them and seeing the jars slowly fill up. The thief not only stole the money, but stole a dream from my father-in-law and this crime is the greater of the two.

"Fruit Basket Turn Over" with Houses in Fruitvale

Stories by: *Lonnie Maie Boyd Leggett*

Francis Marion Leggett was living in the white house in front of the sheds in Fruitvale when Ollie came to live with him there. Ollie moved into the bigger house next door toward the store when he began to make some money and wanted his own place. When Ollie moved and Francis Marion and Charlonas died, (they called her Aunt Loonie), Madge and Elmer Brasfield moved into the F.M. Leggett house. Madge and Elmer having moved from the Boyd farm, where they lived in a small house next door to the Boyd Homeplace.

Rosa Belle and Walter Leggett – Another story I heard from Lonnie Maie was that Rosa Belle and Walter Leggett would come to visit their son Doss and made the trip from Cypress to Fruitvale in a wagon with mules. She remembered seeing them after she had married their grandson, Merlin Leggett.

One of the things she tells about Rosa Belle is that one time they were visiting and someone asked her if she had "put up" any green tomato relish and she replied in a very country dialect, "God, I made a whole wagon bed loaded full of it!" She was known for her country accent and crude words. They called it the "Old Country Talk."

Lonnie Boyd lived on a farm he owned across the road from Dewayne Dove with his wife Ada. They had two girls, Lonnie Maie and Geneva. Lonnie had back trouble and could not work the farm and knew he would not live long, so Ollie took his nieces into his home to care for in Fruitvale. Lonnie died in 1924 and by then Maggie Lou Goldsmith had moved in also. They all lived like this together for about 17 years. Lonnie Maie and Maggie Lou worked in the store and office for Ollie during this time. Lonnie Maie worked after she married until she was expecting her third child. Geneva worked after she married Ben Emerson until the store closed.

At one time Maggie Lou dated Russell Emerson and Hiram Henderson and a few other boys before marrying Malcolm Hooper Emerson. Ollie ran Hiram off for some reason. Malcolm farmed until he married Maggie Lou and worked in the store and became Postmaster for several years. The Boyd girls still lived with Ollie until Maggie Lou was expecting Joe and they all lived together, but one more baby seemed to be "the straw that broke the camel's back." Ollie gave the house next door on the hill (back from his house) to the girls and their mother to live in, leaving the Malcolm Emerson's.

Stanback

Funny thing about this old colored man. He was one of those people that you could not tell within 25 years of his age. He was an old man when I first saw him and looked the same the last time I saw him and that was years and years later. He wore the same clothes winter and summer and always looked the same.

He rented the old shabby house from us that was near Quentin Boyd's, and Joe knew he had no money so he set the rent at thirty dollars a month. I'm sure he drew a check from somewhere but there was no evidence of it. He was a very gentle man and laughed readily. He knew how to talk well and what to say and what not to. He would feel bad about not paying the rent, and he knew that I loved old things and would bring me old double trees, blue fruit jars, iron wash pots, etc.

I knew nothing really about antiques then, only that I loved things that I remembered from childhood at home. Who knows where he found these things but they steadily came through. He wandered around a lot and knew everyone and their cousins.

There is a good story about an old white enamel bathtub that he brought to me. How he ever got the thing in his old beat-up relic of a Ford is beyond me. Joe was not pleased with this find because it was so heavy and took four men to carry it. Instead of feet like a regular tub, it had a "skirt" that was of the same enamel and raised it up off the floor very high up. I finally got Joe to put it in the shed so it would not rust, for it was in almost perfect condition. I soon forgot about the relic until I saw one just like it in an *Architectural Digest* used in an enormous beautiful house. When Shane built her house on the lake in Mississippi, I gave it to her and yes, Joe got to move it yet again, but all were pleased with the "new" tub in the master bath. "Thank you very much, Stanback!"

Belle Bonds

I did not know Belle Bonds until after Joe and I married. She was a woman of color that had been with his family for years and years. She reminded me so much of Mammy in *Gone with the Wind.* She was indeed, one of the family. She helped raise Joe and his brother: cooked, washed, cleaned and generally did most anything that needed to be done. Now you would call her a nanny. She was a large woman that shifted her feet when she walked and always wore an old apron and always had a ready laugh. She shuffled around the kitchen with a wet mop and hummed as she worked. She stayed with the family long after she was really able to do much, but that seemed to come from habit more than anything.

Belle was married to L.V. White, who worked for Ollie at the store and in the fields. He was a wiry small black man and did not have much to say. He was quiet and went on about his business and stayed pretty much to himself. He drove the field trucks, helped feed the cows and cleaned up around the office and Fruitvale Store. When Belle died, they buried her in the cemetery by the Macedonia Church. After she had been buried a few years, L.V. came to the house and told Joe that he did not have the money to have a stone put on her grave; Joe had one put there for her. She was like one of the family and greatly missed.

Do You Cast Stones?

There is a true story that happened in our little hamlet of Fruitvale. I saw in it an opportunity to maybe bring a surge of feelings to anyone reading this saga. I know this to be a true story and a sad one too.

There was an older couple that lived here and the wife died and left her husband all alone. They were known to have a little money and the widower took up with a younger woman. She took his money from him; he shot her in her car and then turned the gun on himself. When it came time to bury the neighbor, no one showed up to dig this grave. It was raining, but it had to be done and my husband Joe, his dad Malcolm, his brother Bill, and Bobby Hampton took up the task to dig the grave in the bad weather. This was the Christian thing to do. These other people were being judgmental of the dead man.

Under circumstances like these, we would need to think of the Biblical story of Stephen. He was condemned to die by stoning. When time came to kill him, Jesus said, "Let he who is without sin cast the first stone." These people were "throwing stones" at the dead man by not digging his grave and mourning him.

Aunt Belle and Aunt Broxie Goldsmith Marlowe

The two sisters of Joe's mother were named Belle and Broxie. They married twin brothers, Ewell and Earl Marlowe. They were always together. They built their houses a few feet apart and worked gardens and fields together. You never saw Belle without Broxie or Ewell without Earl. When Milly was small and I worked in the fields with Joe, Aunt Belle kept her for me. I left here early in the mornings and she stayed all day until late afternoon. As soon as I left, the two would go out to the hen house and Milly would pick out the egg she wanted for breakfast, sometimes eating two just to get to pick the "best ones" off the nests. She learned not to be afraid of the hens lying on the nests and boldly stuck her little hands under the fouls and pulled out her breakfast. These two bonded and loved each other dearly. They would pick the tomatoes and shell the beans and then cook it all up for lunch. Happy days!

The twins were Deputy Sheriffs here in Crockett County and were no-nonsense in their personalities. They were tall men and very impressive with their uniforms, not to mention the holsters and guns they carried. I was supposed to be the self-assured married woman, but those guns were a show stopper to me! I did not know it at the time, but my dad had pistols at home that I never saw. He had his hunting guns on a rack and that was about all I knew about fire arms.

Aunt Belle was such a gentle woman in her talking, walking and her personality, and Aunt Broxie was a sweet, fun-loving woman that sometimes loved little tricks and jokes and kept the family laughing. It is strange how two sisters that grow up together can be so different. This happened with my children. With four, I did not have two with even similar personalities or interests. The important thing here is that the sisters loved each other and so did my four offspring. A good pie has lots of different ingredients but mix them together and you have something good and wonderful!

F.M. Goldsmith & Molly

The Goldsmith Family
(Back: Belle and Ewell
Marlowe, Joe Emerson,
Earl Marlowe, Malcolm
Emerson.
Front: Archie Goldsmith,
Addie Goldsmith, Louise
Marlowe, Bobby
Marlowe, Broxie
Marlowe, Maggie Lou
Emerson)

Archie Goldsmith

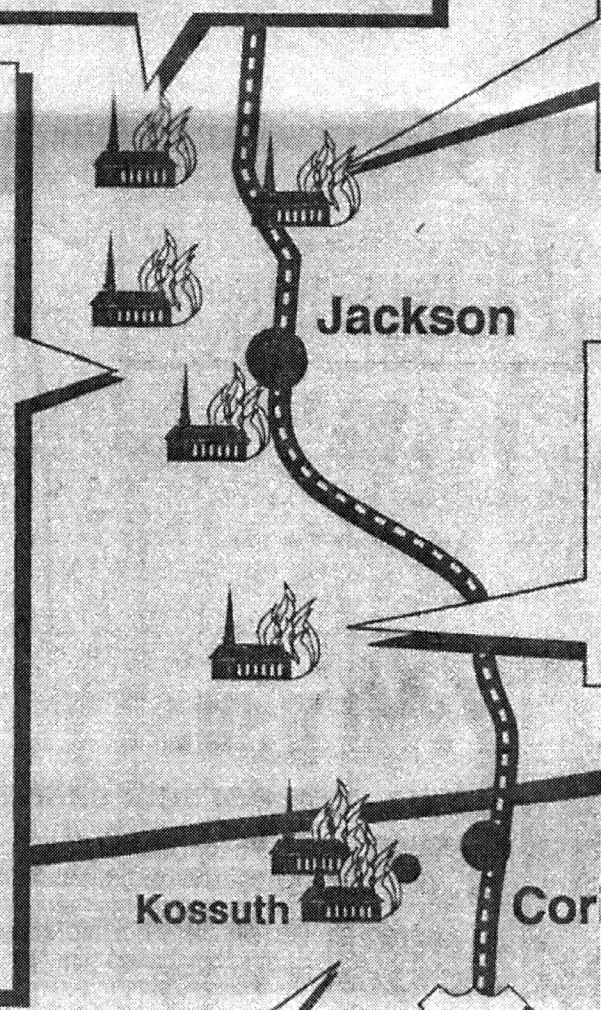

Mount Pleasant Missionary Baptist Church

- Tigrett, Dyer County.
- 25 miles from U.S. 45.
- Burned May 14 at 12:55 p.m.
- Church destroyed; fire ruled suspicious.
- No arrests have been made.

Macedonia Missionary Baptist Church

- Fruitvale, Crockett County
- 10 miles from U.S. 45.
- Burned Jan. 13, 1995 at 4:30 a.m.
- Church destroyed; fire ruled arson.
- No arrests have been made.
- The same accelerant was used at Johnson Grove Missionary Baptist Church, which burned 14 miles away on the same night.

Johnson Grove Missionary Baptist Church

- Rural Madison County
- 10 miles from U.S. 45.
- Burned Jan. 13, 1995 at 5:30 a.m.
- Church destroyed; fire ruled arson.
- No arrests have been made.
- The same accelerant was used at Macedonia Missionary Baptist Church, which burned 14 miles away on the same night.

Jackson

Kossuth

Cor

CHAPTER 2

Local Stories of Surrounding Communities

History of Bells

Bells Depot, Haywood County, was founded in 1855 and was named in honor of William Bell, who built the first dwelling in the town. It is shown as District 11 on the early Haywood County Census.

He purchased one thousand acres from Daniel Cherry for $1 per acre. This land is where Bells stands and extended to the Forked Deer River.

The first merchant was C. C. Clay, who moved from Cherryville to Bells Depot and began selling goods in 1859. The following year, Harrell & Wood opened a dry goods store; A.C. Allen, a family grocery; A.M. Anker, a bakery; and Tom Evans, a saloon, where the Corner Drug Store stood.

The town of Bells was completely closed during the Civil War. There were no military annals from the county during the war, but a full company was organized at Bell's Depot. The company joined the 27th Regiment of the Tennessee Infantry as Co. G. There were 107 men in this company and after the surrender of the Confederate Army in 1865, only three men out of 107 were accounted for. Captain Francis J. Wood was one of these three. He had assisted in the organizing of Co. G.

After the war, he was elected Crockett County's first County Court Clerk in 1872.

Bells Depot was incorporated in 1868 with Hardy L. Winburn as first mayor. Others who have served as mayor are J.J. Farrow, Dr. A.G. Hicks, Dr. S. H. Thomas, J.C. Best, L.F. Walker and C. Rex Mehr, Sr.

Crockett County was organized in 1872 and was formed from portions of Haywood, Dyer, Madison and Gibson Counties.

After its organization in the 1880's by an act of the government, "Depot" was eliminated and the town became Bells and part of Crockett County instead of Haywood.

Bells in the Early 1900's

Bells was the place to be in the early 1900's. On Saturday everyone that could walk or ride a horse showed up on the streets of this mini-town. There were so many horseback riders, their dogs, cats and stray animals, that it was called an animal path in those days. Bells had two or three dry goods stores, six grocery stores, two gins, two banks, a restaurant and a tavern or two. It was said that the walkways would be full on Saturday, and you had to be careful crossing the road or a horse could trample you. These sideways were wooden boards laid in the dirt to cross the road.

Now you can see that those times were so different then. Not any of these people had access to stores in towns like Jackson or Memphis. The only time they went to these big towns was for business, funerals, etc. and this left the town of Bells flooded on Saturday. As I said, "Everyone went to town on Saturday, even in the 1940's and 50's when I was young." It was the social, economic center of everyone's life. If you could not find it in Bells, you most likely did without it.

Crockett County:

Area First Settled In 1824; Formed In 1871

Crockett County is bounded on the south by Gibson County on the east by Madjson County, on the south by Haywood County, and on the west by Lauderdale and Dyer Counties, and has an area of about 284 square miles. The county is situated between the south and middle forks of Forked Deer River, and the surface is level or gently undulating, with rich, fertile soil, being a yellow loam, of an average depth of about two feet.

The country around the county seat is level from three to five miles in every direction. Going north from Alamo the country is level to the county line; going south the same; going west, level for about three miles, and thence it is hilly and broken to the county line; going east it is level until the Madison fraction is reached, about three miles from Alamo, when the surface becomes quite hilly. There are no hard rocks to be found on the surface, or under it, and in most sections sand is reached at a depth of about thirty-five feet. The best lands are found in the Eighth, Tenth, Twelfth and Thirteenth Districts. The color of the soil in these districts is very dark, and has no mixture of sand. The poorest lands are found in the eastern districts, near the town of Gadsden, the soil found there being a reddish color. The lands of the districts numbered above, are better than those of the eastern part, and yield very well. The products of the county are corn, wheat, cotton, sweet and Irish potatoes, the grasses and fruits and strawberries; of this last product upward of $80,000 worth were shipped from the county in 1885 of which $60,000 worth were shipped from Gadsden, and $20,000 from Bell's Depot. In 1886 the shipment from berries from the county to upward of $100,000 of which $75,000 worth were shipped from Gadsden and $25,000 from Bells. The streams of the county are as follows: The south fork of Forked Deer River forms the southern boundary line of the county, and the middle fork of Forked Deer River forms the northern boundary line. Pond Creek rises about 300 yards north of Alamo, flows southwest and empties into the main Forked Deer River, at about twenty-five miles from that town. Cypress Creek rises in Madison County, flows northwest, and empties into Forked Deer River, about ten miles north of Alamo. Other streams of the county are Beech, Elliott Sugar, Mill, Nelson, Beaver Dam and Black Creek. There are but few springs in the county, and cut one mineral spring exists, and that, situated two and one-half miles west from Alamo, is of small consequence.

It was not till about the year 1824 that the territory now embraced within Crockett County was first settled. At about that time a settlement was made near the Haywood County line, south of the present town of Bells by a number of Middle Tennesseans and North Caroliantans, who were attracted to the county by the large growth of yellow poplar, hickory and oak timber. Among the above settlers were Francis M. Wood and Charles Wortham, the former coming from North Carolina and the latter from Middle Tennessee. At about the same time, Gen. Blackman Coleman, who lived at Murfressboro, purchased a tract of land in the neighborhood of what afterwards became Lanefield, and sent out a party of laborers in charge of Thomas Ferguson, to open up a farm and put in a crop. The following year William Johnson and son, Issac and Timothy Parker, came from Rutherford County, Tenn. and settled in the same neighborhood. Other settlers of the neighborhood were Wyatt Kavanaugh. In 1826 Thomas Ferguson moved from the Lanefield neighborhood and settled what afterward became Ferguson's Landing on Forked Deer River, and in a short time James Wylie and Abram Eason came from North Carolina and settled near him. A few miles farther down the river, a settlement was formed by Cornelius and Albert Buck, Edwards Williams and Capt. Moody, and at about the same time David Nunn, Parson Koonce, William Antwine and Henry Powell settled about five miles north of the Lanefield settlement. Other pioneers of the county were John F. and C.H. Felts, Stephen Booth, Spencer Payne, John Burnett, Tho-Young, Solomon Hunter, David Wilson, Zachariah Hobson, Richard Coop, Miles Jennings, Dinwiddie, Solomon Shaw, Samuel Wilkins, Newton Mayfield, Thomas Tucker, Wilson Wyann, James Carter, B. G. and H. B. Avery, Moses Cox, John Tatum, Levin James, Le-B.F. Collingsworth, Robert Edmundson, James McClary, Sugars McLemore, J.B. Boykin, Henry Pearson, H.B. Wilson, R.W. Sims, G.H. Mason, E.B. Mason, Anthony Swift, John McFarland, Solomon Rice, Joseph Clay, John Bowen, Issac H. Mason, Hugh Raines, John Hill and Bently Epperson.

The face of the country, when first fiewed by these hardy pioneers, was most beautiful to behold. The woods stretched away into vast forests of poplar, hickory, oak and ash timber, while in the river and creek bottoms the cypress and tall cane were seen. The face of the earth was covered with the pea vines, so high and thick that man or beast could be easily followed by their trail through it. The woods abounded with deer, bear, wolves, catamounts, panthers, wild turkey and the smaller game, and upon this game the first settlers were, to a great extent, compelled to subsist, as food was indeed a scarce article. For a number of years afterwards, in fact, until they were all killed off, the stock of the settlers was destroyed, in fact, until they were all killed off, the stock of the settlers was destroyed to an alarming extent by the wolves and bears, scarcely a night passing but that a young calf or shoat was carried off.

The first settlements were in the nature of small clearings. One pioneer, more bold than the others, would push forward into the forest, make a clearing and build a cabin, and in a short time others would follow and settle near him. The homes of the settlers were small log cabins, notched up a little higher than a man's head and covered with oak boards. Each cabin, when sufficiently high, received a cave-bearer, on which rested the butting poles for the boards to rest against as well as the knees to hold the weight poles to their places, on of which was put on each course of boards. An opening of six or seven feet made in the end of the roof for a chimney, which was built of sticks and clay, the back jambs and hearth being made out of dirt dug up and pounded with a maul till it became sŏlid. The floor was a poplar puncheons, and the cracks of the house were daubed with mortar made of dirt and water. The house consisted of but one room, and that answered for parlor, bedroom and kitchen. The furniture was usually of the settler's own make, but little, if any, articles being brought from the old State. In those days the settlers were more neighborly and sociable than now, and would think nothing of walking six and eight miles to help a neighbor build a house or roll logs, asking nothing in return but a similar lift in time of need.

There was no such thing as mills in the county at that time, and the grain was crushed for bread and hominy by means of the mortar and pestle. A few years later, however, John Warren put up a horse-power mill in Dyer County, to which a great many went from Crockett County for grinding, paying one-sixth of their grain for toll. One of the first mills built in Crockett County was a water-power corn mill on Middle forked Deer River, at the crossing of the Brownsville and

The Crockett Times 50th Anniversary Edition Wednesday, March 2, 1983 Page 9A

Trenton road, which was owned by Solomon Shaw. Several years afterwards, Mr. Shaw built a large steam spinning factory, at what was known as Quincy, in the Seventh District, to which he subsequently added flour and corn attachments. The mills was in active and successful operation until during the late war when Mr. Shaw was murdered, and the property destroyed by fire. Other early mills were owned by Charles Clay, Squire McDonald and William Harpole. The mills and cotton gins of the county, at the present, outside of the town, are as follows: First District, Bunker Sherrod's steam saw mill; Third District, J.R. Bowle's gotton gin; Fourth District, R.J. Williams' steam corn and saw mill and cotton gin combined, and Patterson Bros. steam corn mill and cotton gin; Seventh District, W. A. Cooper's and Cooper & Nance's cotton gins; Eighth District, David Mayo's cotton gin and John Tipkin's steam corn and saw mill. Ninth District, E.L. Jetton's and G. W. Vaughn's steam corn mills and cotton gins; Eleventh District, John Brewer's cotton gin; Twelfth Disctrict, Wm. King's, Obedah Vernon's and A.T. Fielder's cotton gins; Thirteenth District, J.L. Parker's and J.H. Farmer's corn, saw mill and cotton gins; Fourteenth District, James Ward's steam saw and grist mill, wool factory and cotton gin, W.W. Sharron's steam saw mill and cotton gin and Bailey & Bros. steam saw mill.

The inconvenience of reaching their respective county seats induced the people living in the fractions of Haywood, Gibson, Madison and Dyer Counties, lying between the Middle and South Forks of Forked Deer River, to take steps looking to the formation of a new county as early as 1832-33, and a petition was circulated, and receiving numberous signatures, was forwarded to the constitutional convention of 1834, praying that body to grant them authority to form a new county out of the above fractions. The petition, however, was not presented to the convention, and consequently nothing came of the efforts, much to the disgust and dissatisfaction of the people.

The agitation of the question was continued, however, and resulted in the passage on December 20, 1845, of an act by the General Assembly, entitled as follows: "An act entitled and act to establish the county of Crockett in honor of and to perpetuate the memory of David Crockett, one of Tennessee's distinguished sons." The act provided that the county Madison and Dyer, and appointed Isaac H. Johnson, David Whitaker, Joel Nunn, Willis L. Rivers, Kinchen Hathaway, Isaac H. Mason, Alfred T. Fielder and Noah Perry as commissioners to run the boundary lines, designated the house of Isaac M. Johnson, near where the county seat now stands, as the place of holding the various courts, until the selection of a county site and the erection of a court house.

In the spring of 1846 the above commissioners marked off the boundary lines of the county and selected the present county site, where a town was laid out and named Cageville, in honor of Lycurgus Cage, one of the first merchants of that vicinity.

The magistrates of the new county met at the designated place in June, 1846 and organized the county. Officeers were elected as follows: clerk, Isaac M. Johnson; sheriff, John R. Jelks; register, N. W. Mayfield; trustee, Joel Nunn.

In October of the same year the circuit court met in session at Mr. Johnson's house. The court was presided over by Judge J.C. Reed, and John Manning was appointed clerk. The new county had its enemies among the citizens of the old counties, who sought to throw every obstacle in the way of and prevent, if possible, its organization. The question of the new county's constitutionality was raised, and being presented to Judge Reed, that gentlemen decided adversely to the county, adjourned his court and returned to his home. This action on the part of Judge Reed, in whom the people had great confidence, demoralized the citizens and friends of Crockett County, and the organization, then completed, was abandoned, the several fractions returning to the parent counties. Thus matters rested for awhile, but it was not long before the people began anew their effort to secure a new county, and their incessant labors resulted in the enactment of a similar law to the one of 1845, granting them the desired new county. This second act was passed by the General Assembly November 23, 1871 and authorized the formation of Crockett County out of fractions of the counties of Haywood, Gibson, Madison and Dyer, the same territory before incorporated in the new county.

The act appointed William N. Beasley and John F. Sinclair of Dyer County; J. Frank Robertson and David H. James of Gibson County; Thomas J. Hicks and John C. Pearson of Madison County; Asa Dean and Fancis J. Wood of Haywood County as commissioners to survey and mark off the boundary lines of the new county, locate the county seat and hold an election for county and district officers.

The act further provided for the naming of the county seat, Alamo, in commemoration of the spot where fell the illustrious Crockett, for whom the county was named. The commissioners met at Cageville on December 19, 1871 and were sworn in, in accordance to law, by Isaac M. Johnson, acting justice of the peace in Haywood County. They then organized by unanimously electing John F. Sinclair as president and F. J. Wood, secretary. On motion, the commissioners were ordered to take the census of the qualified voters of their respective fractions, and report the same on January 15, 1872, after which the commissioners adjourned, to meet again on that date. On the above day the commissioners met at Cageville and received the following report of the census: Madison County fraction, 374 votes; Haywood County fraction, 799 votes; Gibson County fraction, 354 votes; Dyer County fraction, 403 votes. The commissioners then ordered an election held in the several fractions of the counties, to take the census of the voters upon the question of the proposed new county. The election was held on February 17, 1872 and resulted in more than two-thirds rate in favor of the new county.

Cageville was selected as the county seat, and the name changed to that of Alamo in accordance with the provisions of the act. The commissioners met with much opposition in the organization of the county from E. B. Mason, Esq. of Madison County, who filed an injunction suit in the chancery courts of Haywood Gibson, Madison and Dyer. While the suit was pending, however, the organization was proceeded with, and an election for county and district officers was called, and held on March 9, 1872, at which the following officers were elected.

Sheriff, R. G. Harris; circuit court clerk, William Best; county court clerk, R. J. Wood; register, R.T.D. Fouchee; trustee, Asa Dean, tax collector, John Smothers; surveyor, W. H. Johnson; coroner, A. G. Norville; magistrates, John E. Pearson, Thomas B. Casey, F. M. Thompson, Robert W. Mason, Samuel S. Watkins, John R. Roseman, David H. James, Shady D. Harper, John J. Farron, Lewis W. Daniel, Issac M. Johnson, George W. Bond, John C. Cook, Noah F. Stallings, John C. Best, Zachary P. Warren, John F. Robertson, Dennis Tatum, Henry Buck, Henry Wyse, Benjamin H. Harmon, James H. Perry, Jonathan H. Davis, John F. Sinclair, Isaac H. Nunn and William H. Beasley.

The sessions of the courts were held in the Odd Fellows and Masonic Hall until sometime in 1873, when the records were removed to a large frame carriage factory on the corner of West Main Street, where they were held until the completion of the court house in 1875. This building is a large two-story brick, with four entrances and cross halls. On the first floor are the offices of the county court clerk, sheriff, register and two additional offices. On the second floor are the offices of the circuit court clerk and the clerk and master of the chancery court, and also the building is surmounted with an observatory, guarded by iron railings, the same having been constructed with a view of placing them in a tower clock. The court house cost about $25,000 and is claimed to be the finest building of the kind in West Tennessee.

The county jail was completed in 1874 at a cost of about $10,000. The building is of brick, two-story, and is a sheriff's and jailer's residence and jail combined. The jail is fitted up with substantial cells, and considered as safe as any in the country.

In 1879 the county court purchased ninety acres of land in the Sixth District, two miles west from Alamo, and converted the same into an asylum for the poor. The farm and frame buildings thereon cost the county about $2,000.

/1.7

Crockett County Postmasters

Bell's, Crockett County, Tennessee

Established as Harrisburgh in Haywood County on April 1, 1826
Name changed to Cherryville sometime during 1835
Name changed to Bells Depot on February 11, 1859
Located in Crockett County sometime during 1869
Name changed to Bells on May 12, 1894

Postmasters	Appointment Dates Through September 30, 1971
Daniel Cherry	April 1, 1826
Edward J. Read	December 8, 1843
Calvin M. Cherry	December 21, 1843
Norman T. Cherry	December 9, 1847
Hiram A. Partee	August 22, 1848
Benjamin H. Pyland	October 27, 1860
Hardy L. Wenburn	August 12, 1868
Thomas J. Smothers	April 24, 1869
John J. Farrow	April 20, 1877
A. W. Brooks	January 13, 1879
Mrs. S. C. Winburn	May 21, 1885
Mrs. Mary B. Freeman	April 15, 1889
Mrs. Josephine B. Walker	April 5, 1893
John H. Smith	April 12, 1897
Clayton J. Montgomery	May 16, 1900
William R. William	April 21, 1910
G. W. Bell	June 5, 1914
Clayton M. Hunn	February 24, 1912
Alson C. Patton	March 18, 1918
William R. William	September 1, 1918
Guy W. Mobley	May 24, 1934 (Confirmed)
Russell M. Emerson	March 20, 1959 (Assumed charge)
	March 25, 1959 (Acting)
Warren D. Blackburn	August 19, 1960 (Assumed charge)
	August 26, 1960 (Acting)
Charles A. Whitaker	February 3, 1961 (Assumed charge)
	February 6, 1961 (Acting)

We can furnish for $2.00 electrostats of the site location reports relating to the Bells Post Office.

Crockett County Districts
1872

Crockett County became a county in 1872. It was made up of Madison, Gibson, Haywood and Dyer Counties. Below is a list of the districts and counties that Crockett County was taken from.

Crockett County		Town or Community	County of Origin	
District	1	Pearson's Mill	Madison	9
District	2	Mason's Grove	Madison	18
District	3	Gadsden	Madison	18
District	4	Mabley/Coxville	Gibson	16
District	5	Bells, Bellville	Haywood	11
District	6	Cageville/Alamo	Haywood	13
District	7	Thorpe Crossroad/Quincy	Gibson	4
District	8	Lanesfield/Maury City	Haywood	12
District	9	Crockett Mills/Robertsonville	Gibson	20
District	10	Fosters Farm	Haywood	14
District	11	Crossroads/Maury Junction	Dyer	1
District	12	Friendship	Dyer	2 & 14
District	13	Chestnut Bluff	Dyer	3

The photograph on the facing page is of the first automobile in Alamo, owned (and driven in the picture) by Dr. Robert Fleming. The exact date is not known; however, Dr. Fleming died in 1908. This photograph is a part of the collection of the Crockett County Historical Society, and was donated by Jerry Pittman.

1st Car–Alamo, History of Bells write up

Civil War Times

The 1860's were times of great conflict for the country but also tough times for communities, churches and most of all, families. There were families that were split on their beliefs about slavery and landowners. Such a big gap existed between the classes of people that there were few inhabitants that were completely satisfied with their lot in life, and these few groups usually consisted only of the upper class that owned large plantations or were successful in businesses. The sharecroppers were barely getting by with their meager share of the farm products, and the slaves were struggling just to stay alive and many had their families sold off to farms great distances from them and sometime not even knowing which direction they had gone. We were becoming a country divided. We all know the old saying, "Together we stand and divided we fall," seems like it was proving its content at this time.

All five Bailey brothers fought in the Civil War. Some were for the North and some for the South. When the fighting got really rough, the boys that fought for the North saw they were winning and let their fighting southern brothers go and get out safely.

Indian Mounds
On Family Farm

What is there about an Indian mound that is so fascinating? They have always intrigued me even when I was young in school. The first I heard about one being close was on the farm that Betty inherited from Mama and Daddy Jim in "Black Bottom." I was amazed there was one so close. The mound was there when Betty and I were small. There was an old shack on the property right by the mound. Through the years when Daddy Jim was getting older, the people that lived in the old house began slowly digging in the relics and pulling out pottery and arrowheads, etc. The family knew about it, but I suppose that no one felt they had the authority to do anything about it; and really, I don't think that too many of the adults at the time really cared or realized the importance of these things they were digging up or the seriousness of destroying something that some of the natives would consider Holy things. It would be right up there with grave robbers in my estimation and would be something that should have been stopped but was not really noticed by many. I was small and did not know this until I was much older and have grieved over this since I heard of it. These people moved off but the whole mound was more or less flattened. I saw this when I was about ten years old and have not seen it since, but the memory is embedded in my mind.

There are other mounds that are closer to home, and I found out about them only after I had been researching things for several years. Actually about three years ago, I was thrilled that one was on one of our farms at Cypress not far from the church. It was out in the middle of the fields that were farmed and has been reduced to a gentle rise. It was located north of where Clinton Moore had his house and about halfway to the levee road toward Liberty Hall. This is the land that the Leggetts once farmed and then belonged to Ollie and then to Joe and me.

Behind Jody's house, close to the fence row and the creek, was another one. This is on the old Emerson Homeplace and was probably a definite hill when they settled in this house. The clay to form this mound was brought from the hill across the road from Jody on the Renshaw Emerson land. The clay was used to make a strong hill that would not wash away and would stick together. The Emerson family raised peas on this place because peas will grow good in clay dirt and do not like much loose, loamy soil. This clay came from where Julia and Robert Skelton live now.

There was also one behind Charlotte Naylor's house. I do not know much about this one but do know that it is very close to where the Emisons had a cotton gin in the late 1800's.

These Indian mounds are a vanishing part of America's history, and we do not realize the things that have been happening here for centuries. The Chickasaw Indians signed a treaty in 1800, and most had left this area before the settlers started arriving in the early 1800's. The Chickasaw Indians were an agricultural and hard working people; they were tall, straight, well-formed, active, hardy and strong. They had brownish rust skin or (copper color), black hair and eyes. They were the friendliest tribe toward the white people more than any other tribe, and taught the white settlers how to plant corn.

Can you imagine Indians roaming around where we live and having teepees in our cotton patches and killing rabbits with bows and arrows? Goes to show you we cannot visualize what we cannot see. We can see Indians in Hollywood easier than we can see them here, simply because we thought we saw them in the western movies with cowboys chasing them on the big screen, when these mounds here are more real than anything we have seen at the movies.

Emerson Schoolhouse

The old Emerson Schoolhouse was a little over a mile from our house in the Cypress community. It sat on the lot across the road from where Charlotte Naylor lives now. I started to school there in the first grade and through the second. Miss Florence Hayes was my teacher and, as a matter of fact, everyone's teacher... One big room, one big student body and one teacher. I was the only one in the second grade so Miss Florence put me in the third grade with Joe Wayne and his classmates. The next year I started to the big school in Bells, and they put me in the third grade and this really bummed me out. So I skipped the second grade and took the third grade twice and was mortified at the very idea!

The Emerson School was a typical school of the day. One large room that could be separated by a folding wall. The walls were the regular old beaded ceiling and it was high. There was a small vestibule when you came in and a cloak space on either side of the entrance. We each had a hanger to hang our coats and store our lunches. There was a stage at one end for our chapel programs and a huge canvas "curtain" with a cylinder pipe-like piece that it rolled up on when you pulled the ropes behind the stage. The canvas had advertisements painted on it. The different stores and individuals had paid to have the artist put their names and slogans on it. This is where the saying, "the curtain goes up;" comes from. The old curtains did indeed go up.

We all took our lunches in buckets or paper bags or anything that could be found at the time. We had peanut butter and jelly mostly. In summer we had tomato sandwiches. Egg sandwiches were common and sometimes we had fried potatoes or cold chicken if we were lucky.

At recess we played in the woods across the road and swung on the trees like monkeys and played in the creek behind the building down the lane to Uncle Doode's house. We would bend small saplings and swing up and down on them. We loved those trees! The favorite pastime under the bridge was catching the big pinch bugs and throwing them on each other. Mostly, the boys throwing them on the girls. We played Red Rover, Kick Ball, and Hide and Seek. The area around the school was all woods. We had to walk to school, which was a pretty good hike. The roads were dirt with no gravel, just ruts from the rains and mud when it did rain. Betty and I would start out early and stop at Aunt Olive's and get Sarah and Joe Wayne.

My two best friends went to the big school in Bells in the second grade and I missed them so much. Of course, I saw them at church on Sunday and played with them on weekends, but I couldn't help but feel left behind.

We used to swap lunches at noon. It was a favorite pastime, and I would swap my lunch with someone even though I knew they had something that I didn't particularly like. Friends do things for each other, right?

I have a picture of the old Emerson School. I have seen so many of the same print so I am assuming that a photographer that took school pictures also made one of the building for each family to have.

The old Emerson Schoolhouse sat where Laverne Spitzer lives. It was cut in half, where the folded wall was, and half of it stayed there and Laudell built his house around that part. Horace Reasons moved the other half and lived in it until he built the new brick house.

Emerson Schoolhouse Cypress Community 1939

Old Schools and Houses of Cypress and Fruitvale
Illustrations by Myrtle Rose (Leggett) Emerson
Schools

Midway School – There were several old school buildings in the area at one time. There is one old school that sat on the opposite side of the road from the Joe Edwards' house, down closer to the little creek. Was this the original Midway School? I can remember one school house by this name that sat on the road where you come from Joe Edwards house on the left; about one hundred feet. It was brick and today there is a pile of old bricks and brush right on the site where it sat.

Fruitvale School – The old Fruitvale School that we all remember still stands as an apartment building today. Years before this building, there was one that was built near Fred Boyd's house on the same side of the road. This was down the road a little toward Highway 79. This was before our time but Joe's dad, Malcolm Emerson, told him

44

about this one.

Jackson School – The school with a lot of history is the old Jackson School that sat on the very spot that Milly Hart (my daughter) has her log house. The road leading to her house is the same lane that led to this school. Her log house was originally Mr. Zab Williams house that was moved to the school site. The kitchen on this house was reported in some church records as being the original Walnut Hill Baptist Church that the congregation sold to Mr. Zab and he attached it on the back to use as a kitchen.

Mr. Frank Raines went to school there and wrote that his teacher was Bettie Bailey. He said it had the usual Pot-bellied stove in the middle for warmth, and on the last day of school, they got stick candy. They used to swing from limbs and play in a nearby creek. If the older boys were not back inside in time, Miss Bettie would call, "Books" to remind them it was time to resume their studies. The schoolhouse did not have a bell.

Houses and Church

Casey House – There once sat an old house on the old *Casey Place* in Fruitvale and some of the timbers are still there today. Francis Casey (a childhood friend of Joe's mother) once lived there. The old *Casey Cemetery* is up from the house on a hill with a beautiful view of the fields, a pond and country roads. On around this field road on the left of a big curve is where another old house sat. The Clarkie Johnson family lived there for a while. There is still an old cistern well there today. This well was between two houses.

Willie Butler (father's) house – Continue on down this old road around another curve on the right. This is where a Mr. Emerson moved to live. The house belonged to Willie Butler's father.

Macedonia Church (original) – Sat in a corner lot across the road from where the old school and the old Macedonia Church that burned sat. The newer church now is sitting on the same ground.

George and Clara Cooke house – Is where Greg Spraggins now lives. Two older people lived here.

Pearl and Miss Etta Evans' house – Is across the road from Jo and Joe. Four room house with pointed roof and front porch all the way across.

Don and Rosa Pierce house – Where the Wilson family live now. Charles and Don Crossnoe lived here later.

Aubrey Webb house – In a field between David Williams and Charlotte Naylor, back away from the road.

Cotton Gin – In Charlotte Naylor's yard. A little to the left of her house. Heavily wooded.

Yose's house – Down the lane in front of Buster Leggett, on the right on top of the hill. Across from Lisa and Danny Marbury. (Helen Yose had two thumbs on one hand.)

Leggett house – Old house where Vince McGee now lives. Old house with front porch all across. Walter Leggett and Rosa Belle lived here.

Neal and Elizabeth (Tookie) house – Lived in a small pointed top house on the road to Alamo on right, across the road from Cypress Church.

Florence Hayes' house – Lived on the same side of the road as Dalton Jones, down in the flat just past his house. It was a small salt box type house and she had lots of beautiful flowers in her yard.

Smith house – Lived down the road from Florence Hayes on the same side of the road right on the corner lot. Almedia Spitzer and W.H. lived there with her awhile. She always wore long black dresses down to her ankles and black shoes, stockings and bonnet.

Crossnoe house – On the corner before you get to Doris Crossnoe now. The large two-story house burned in the 1950's.

Silas Emerson house – Is where Jody Emerson now lives in the exact same spot. Old frame house with a front porch across the whole front on the hill. Always had guineas and cats.

Dalton Jones house – His mother lived where he now lives

McKnight House – Julia and Robert Shelton now live here. This is the woman that brought the Emerson family from England. Then Renshaw and Vera Emerson lived there. Vera was the sister of Carrie Selph McNeely. Carrie married Mr. Lee Selph. Their brother was Dib McNeely. This is one of the three locations that are said to be where the house was.

Paul Edwards and Miss Alton house -- They lived here when first married. The house is on a lane in front of Virginia Leggett. The Pigues lived there after that. There were two old houses on down from there across the canal.

Elmer and Madge Brasfield house – They lived in a house between Ada Boyd and Emerson homeplace on down toward the store. Malcolm lived there before he built the new house in 1970. Francis Marion Leggett lived here too. (my great-grandfather) Betty Bailey also lived in this old house. Front was turned toward the Emerson house and had a long front porch. It was a small house with 2 or 3 rooms only.

Joe and Myrtle Rose Leggett Emerson first house – On Highway 79 where you turn off this highway to go to Fruitvale. Mr. John Ed Castellaw lived here before us. Others that I know lived there at some time are Merlin and Lonnie Mae Leggett, Carolyn Williams, Rose Hampton.

W. H. and Louise Woodson house – They lived down from the store on the corner on the right where you turn to Bill's on the right. J.C. Selph lived here a long time also.

Clinton Moore house – It was near where he built the new brick house. It sat behind the new house and to the left. Old three-room house with porch all the way across and back porch also. Ollie sold him the lot to build a new house. Francis Marion lived here before that.

Reggie Spraggins house – An old house with a wraparound porch. Across the road from Ira Webb on the little triangular patch just as you turn to go to Liberty Hall from Cypress on the left.

Daddy Jim's bottom house – A man was drunk one freezing, cold, winter night and fell into a ditch and froze to death. This house sat on the left side of the road on the first corner coming from Cypress to Liberty Hall, where Betty Cooke has a farm. Just before you leave her line.

Bailey house – Behind present Bailey house. It was then moved down the road east and on the left side of the road.

Norville Family house – (Center Church Bunch) The home was on a lane that went from the lane that connected my house to Uncle Doode's. This lane went on a straight line to Charlotte Naylor's house. It is on the right about half–way down.

Bobby Hampton (Grandfather's) house – They lived on the lane by where Donna Cleek Thomas lived. On down the lane on the left side on John Hart's farm.

Andy Hampton house – By Malcolm's old house closer to the store. It sat on the hill back from the road in Fruitvale.

Ben and Frances house – They lived in Fruitvale in a house by the railroad, just as you go up from the store on the left.

Francis Emerson house – Old house on the road in front of store on the right in front of Bobby and Faye's new house. Francis Emerson lived there. Geneva sold it to Bobby and Faye to build their new house.

Raines house – A log house where Bill built his new house. The old Raines house with dogtrot. Mr. Raines sold this place to Ollie and moved to Cross Roads.

Emerson house – Aunt Ruth Emerson said there was an old house just off the back entrance to our house, on the left of the drive just as you go in. Some of the Emerson's lived there.

Arthur and Jewell Bailey house – They lived in an old house that sat where Lucille Bailey now lives. Had a front porch and sat right on the road.

Lee Selph house – They lived in an old house across the road from Lucille's house on the corner on left from the bottom road. He married Carrie McNeeley.

Theron Spraggins Tenant house – Between his house and our house on the same side of road. Was covered with red roofing on sides and front with a tin roof. Two small rooms. They had a baby girl named Christine that I played with often. This was a black family.

48

Another black family lived on the other side of Theron and Olive. This was another tenant house. A black family and the man's name was Robert and wife was a great cook. Joe Wayne and I loved her cornbread made on the wood stove.

Butler house – On Highway 79 on the right just before you get to Jones Road, where we live.

Another old house – Old house sat in front of Gerald Skelton down the drive from Doris Crossnoe, in front of where Finis Crossnoe's house was and on Joe's farm about half-way to the creek.

Finis Crossnoe house – Near Doris Crossnoe to the right facing the highway. Tornado got this house.

Clarkie Johnson house – Where the dump is now at Jones Road entrance opposite side. The house was moved out of the field to this place. Elgie Butler lived there at one time. The house came from Macedonia Church road. Off 70, go over the railroad, pass one corner and go up another and there is a barn on the right. House sat on the left across the road from the barn. Old Cistern well still there.

Frances Casey house – Old house in Bill's pasture by the pond. Frances Casey lived there. Between Casey Cemetery and the road. She is in lots of pictures with Joe's mother and dad.

Willie Mae Butler (father's) house – Turn down the road from #41 on right. Close to colored cemetery and opposite side of road. Mr. Emerson came from Bolivar and moved this house between Bill and the church.

Hughes house – The house across the road from Bill on hill back toward Macedonia Church. Mr. and Mrs. Hughes lived here and had 8 or 9 children. Doode Leggett lived here when Gretta and I were very small.

W. H. and Louise Woodson house – House in front of Bill's down toward the store to the corner on the left at the crossing. Ray was small.

W. H. Woodson (Father) house – Passed Ray's house first road to the right and on down this road on the left before you get to the cemetery.

*Walter Leggett hous*e – In Bells where the ballpark was and now where the freezer for the plant is.

Kail Farm house – Just as you go in the drive to Kail farm on the left. Bettie Bailey and John lived there. Elizabeth Kail and James lived there later.

Cypress Pond - Germans lived at the crossing on down in the farm where the farm road turns right on the left at this crossing. They had the Hitler swastika painted on their door. Another house on further down from this one by the fencerow and not on the second field road.

Ballentine house - They lived across the first bridge going into Cypress Pond and right at turn off place on the highest spot there.

Cypress Pond #3 - Farm road turn right and house on left. Pond between the house and the German house. No name for this one. Husband shot and killed his wife in this house.

Buster Leggett house - First house on left after going straight in front of Cypress Church.

James Clark house - Permenter Road on left before you get to where Emerson School was.

Dalton Odell house - Sat across road up the road right past Malcolm Emerson house.

McKnight house - Drawn by description only. Sat somewhere close to Wilson, David Clark and Julia Skelton's houses. I have been told 3 places where this house sat.

Lonnie Boyd house - Sat right where the Malcolm Emerson house sits.

J.A. Bailey Homeplace – On Bailey Road. Still standing.

Ollie Boyd house in Fruitvale – Malcolm Emerson house.

Old Water tank – by Boyd house

J.D. Boyd Homeplace – Sat on exact spot where Ken and Gaye Jordan have their new house now.

EMISON FAMILY, NEW HAMPSHIRE? THOMAS A. EMISON lived in Laconia?
N.H. His father, Edward J. Emison, was born in 1829 on Leinster
Road in Dublin. He published "Footprints of the Emison Family",
1172-1881. The Emisons came from Denmark to Ireland in the Danish
invasions during 1172, when Ireland was subjected for five years.
Four Emison brothers in that army remained in the community which
is now Dublin. There were three Emison migrations to America.
(1) William, Thomas, Henry and John Emison came to Baltimore.
(2) Three Emison brothers came to America and intended to land at
Baltimore, but were shipwrecked and landed further south. This is
believed to have been the family which later settled in Kentucky.
(3) The third Emison migration landed at Baltimore about 1800.
NOTE by JWE: There are some unusual similarities in the foregoing,
but nothing has been identified from Irish or American records.

*Final Supplement 1969 to The
Emison Families [1954] & [1962]
by James Wade Emison Vincennes,
Indiana 1069. Copyright 1969
James Wade Eimson, Jr. Library of
Congress Number CS71.E536:1969
lithographed in U.S.A. by EB
Edwards Brothers Incorporated
2500 South State Street/ Ann
Arbor Michigan 48104*

JASPER DAVID EMISON and his family, with his father-in-law,
Berry Williams, moved to Paris, Texas, late in 1887. They lived
there for 10 years and returned to Alamo, Tenn December 23, 1897.
The return trip required 28 days in a group of nine covered wagons
--- standing guard each night through Indian territory, and ford-
ing all streams except the White and Mississippi Rivers. Mr Emison
was Tax Assessor of Crockett Co. Tenn., for two terms. Both his
wife Sarah Frances and he were buried in the Cypress Cemetery.
He was a Baptist and a Democrat.

DAVID LEE EMISON (above) relates the following family hearsay,
handed down by the immigrant forebear JOHN EMISON to his son Wm
E. Emison,(1827-1900); to his grandson David Edgar, born 1884; and
thence to the nephew David Lee. "The original JOHN EMISON, age 12
and an older brother (unnamed) age 14, came to west Tennessee via
the Mississippi River (presumably from the area of Bristol, Tenn.,
via the Cumberland or Tennessee Rivers) and landed at Cottonwood
Point near Dyersburg. John settled in Crocket County and his brother went somewhere to the north, and they had no further contact
in life". See version of JOSEPH ELDRIDGE,(1892-1952) on page 104.12

*Malcolm, Maggie Lou, Joe,
and Bill Emerson*

CHAPTER 3

Emerson Family

Emerson and Jones Connections

The original ancestor that we have with the Jones' family is John Emerson, who with his brother, (name unknown) was first found in Northern Ireland and then later in Yorkshire, England. Somewhere in this time zone the parents of said brothers died and were left in the care of an aunt, Rebecca McKnight. I do not know if they were legally adopted or just handed down to her being a close relative. Papers to this effect have not been found. John was born in Northern Ireland in 1799. After leaving Ireland and England, they came to America, later coming through North Carolina to Tennessee. They were in Eastern Tennessee (Bristol) in 1823. Their next move was to Cotton Grove. In 1832 they were living in Madison County, what is now Crockett County, Tennessee, since 1872.

John married Margaret Boals in about 1820 in Moore County, North Carolina. Margaret was born in 1799 in Scotland, evidently immigrating about the same time as John.

One of the first sons born in America was named Benjamin Emison, born on September 15, 1837, and later married Mary Helen Permenter and they had a son named Silas. When Benjamin died, Mary Helen married S. A. Jones and had a son, Arthur Jones, thus making Silas and Arthur half-brothers. When Mary Helen and S. A. died, they left the land equally between these half-brothers. The Jones family taking the western side, and Emisons, the eastern side of the farm. These two families, still to this day, own the land that their forefathers left them.

The place where Rebecca McKnight had her log house is not proven to one certain spot. I have been told three possible places where this home stood. One is in the spot where David Clark lives now; another is where Leon Wilson's house is and a little toward Joe Emerson's house. I learned from Dalton Jones that he remembers his father telling him that it stood east of Julia Skelton's house on that hill or close by.

When Rebecca was older, she asked Jim Boyd (Ollie's daddy) to take care of her until she died and promised to give him her house and land. Jim Boyd took care of her, and she left him her belongings in a will. Two deeds to the Emerson land was never recorded or burned in the Court House fire.

Arthur Jones's wife, Mamie, was mistreated and lived in Texas. Mr. Don Pierce went to Texas and brought her home by train later going back to Texas and bringing all her belongings back to Tennessee in a covered wagon. Can you imagine the hardships of such a trip? One of the pieces he brought back in that wagon was a very big and bundlesome organ that Dalton and Jewell Jones have kept and recently given to their daughter Judy Tarvis. When Mamie left Texas, she had some money and she bought 20 acres of land; this lies right in front of the Joe Emerson home.

Dalton Jones's mother and sister were killed on the railroad track crossing over toward the Fruitvale store. This was sudden and very tragic for all the family. J.D. Boyd came to find Arthur and a small Dalton in the field by Cypress Church on Neil Webb's farm. He had to tell them that their mother and sister were dead. The family was distraught. Mr. Don took Dalton and dressed him for the night and put him to bed.

When Silas married Annie, he took his mother, Mary Helen, to live with him and his wife. Mary helped Annie in the house until she died November 23, 1913, and was buried in the Cypress Church Cemetery.

Benjamin Emison's daughter Frances Marions Leggett's wife, Charlonas Ann

Emerson Family Connections

I had not realized the many, many connections that one family could have until I started looking into these families that I am directly connected to. I will take the Emerson families and try to connect as many as I can. I have had many people tell me, "this is so and so's great-granddaddy," etc. and have jotted them down through the years and am astounded at the connections there. I am sure I don't have even a fraction of the possible ones. One could take a lifetime and never make a dent in the number of limbs that are involved in one family tree if all the branches were explored. John Emison, Sr. from Ireland and England surely left a legend behind that we know nothing of. Cousins by the dozens abound in these faraway countries. His wife Margaret Boals from Scotland also adds quite a number of lost family there.

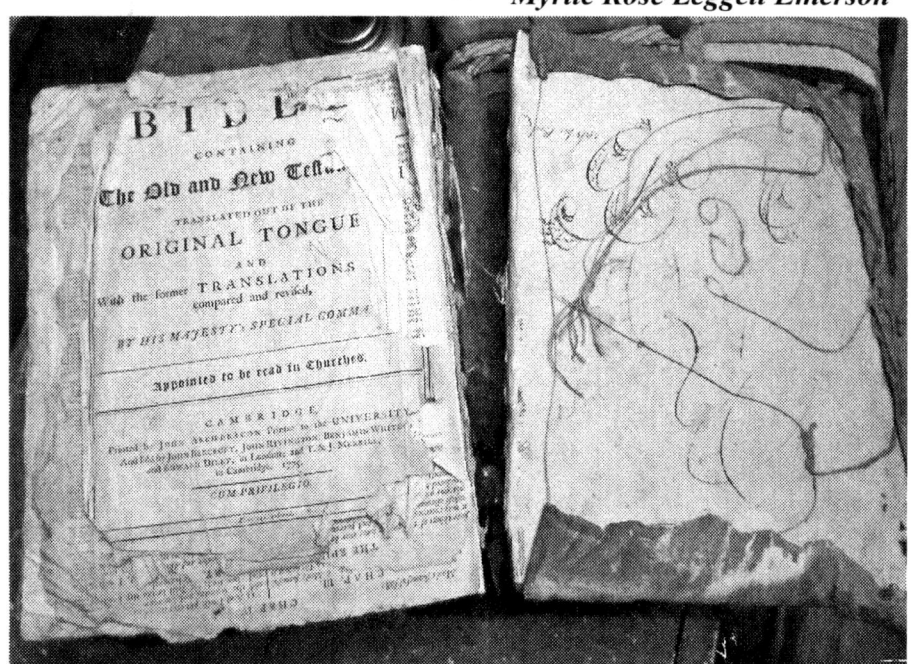

S.A. Jones (Made from old tin type)

Emerson Bible
Front page of 1775 Bible, covered in skin. Samples of calligraphy.

Silas' mother:

Mary Helen Permenter Emison Jones

Silas and Annie Emison with baby Ruth

Mary Ann Emison

The children of this first American John Emison/Emerson are listed with what little information I have of them so these facts may be recorded and not lost with time:

James – Renshaw Emerson's grandfather

Susan – Grandma Addie Goldsmith's grandmother

Rebecca – No information on her

Robert – Ewell and Earl Marlow's grandfather

William E – No information on him

Mary Ann – Small woman and smoked a pipe. Aunt Ruth Emerson saw her before she died, and she last visited the old homeplace in 1922.

Jane (Sarah?) – No information on her

Margaret – Her daughter married old Mr. Ketchum. Margaret Laman Goldsmith used to write to her. (Margaret Norville has her picture.)

Benjamin – Joe Silas Emerson's ancestor. (Lineage listed later)

Joseph – Theo Emison's lineage came from him

John Jr.– Ollie Boyd's maternal grandfather. Miss Viola Rust married his grandson

Nancy Ann – Married Francis Marion Leggett, who was my father's grandfather, thus connecting me with Joe's. When Nancy Ann died, he married Charlonas Ann (Nancy's niece) thus connecting the families again.

Information on Robert Emison Family:

Carol Elizabeth Emison – (adopted)

Levi Emison – Grandma Addie Goldsmith's father.

Martha J. Emison – Mr. William Stewart's mother or grandmother (not sure which).

Margaret Emison – Ollie Boyd's mother.

Arena (Rena) – Viola Rust's husband's mother.

Information on William E. Emison's line:

Mary Jane Emison – Carrie Mayfield's mother

Sarah Deliphate Emison – Jim Bailey's mother and my great-grandmother. (She was the first dead person I ever saw.)

Grandpa Archie Goldsmith

Archie Goldsmith, my husband's maternal grandfather, was a character. By this I mean that he had character by being a very religious man who knew his Bible and lived by it. He was considered by many to be a common man, but he reached heights above the common man. His religion took him to church every Sunday and to raising his three girls by the book. Their names were Maggie Lou (Joe's mother), Clara Belle, and Broxie May. Maggie Lou was the oldest of the three, and I have written in another section about her two sisters and their husbands. Grandpa, as we all called him, made sorghum molasses. I saw him many times; I saw the horse pulling the wooden "tongue" with the spatulas in the big iron pot full of sorghum liquid, going round and round, stirring the sweet, sticky gum until it turned a certain amber color, indicating that it was the right thickness to cool. He made brooms in a barn by the sorghum mill and the barn had many early tools and relics in it. The brooms were made from rushes in the field. How I wish I had saved one of these wonderful handmade pieces.

Grandpa was also good with a plane and a hammer. He made many pieces of furniture in their humble house. I remember one particular piece I loved that sat right by the door going into the main room on the right by the door. It was a desk on legs that had a wide top that rose and exposed the inside for papers and the top down for writing.

The kitchen was a marvel to me. Grandpa had made shelves down one side of the kitchen and Grandma Addie had made a curtain of some old cotton fabric to cover it, making a fabulous pantry that was out of sight or maybe just out of range of flies and bugs. On top of this pantry was a fantastic array of old churns, dishes, etc., but the thing that caught my eye was this wonderful lamp with a glass shade, etched with a scene on it. I remarked how pretty I thought it was, and later Grandpa brought it to me and I still cherish this lamp today.

Grandma Addie's domain was the kitchen, of course, and she had one of those iron and porcelain wood stoves. The stove had warming ovens protruding over the "eyes" that she kept food warming before meals. When these two doors were opened, some of the most amazing food appeared both to our eyes and to our noses. Her biscuits were golden brown and her chicken would win first prize in anyone's contest. She was older in her looks than she actually was for her age. For one thing, her face was so wrinkled that it went from one wave of wrinkles to another. Another was her back was so humped that she had to raise her head to look forward. I had a great aunt on the Leggett side that had this same hump back and head going forward. This aunt was only 65 years old and looked at least ninety.

On a brighter side, Grandpa would eat whole green hot peppers with his peas or butter beans. He would lift his head and pop that pepper in his mouth and munch on it like it was a piece of uncookedspaghetti. He had a great sense of humor and was always kidding around with people and walked like he was in a dance contest. He was never "down."

Tuesday morning
Maggie Lou I am
getting along fine
this beautiful morning
hope you are still
getting along fine at
school I havent started
your doillies yet Bell
ordered a new book
yesterday I am going
to wait till that comes
they may be the prettiest
I will get your dress
made before many days
hope Lonnie is better
Brooksie wasent able to
go to school yesterday
with her throat she

didient get up till
dinner but she is gone
this morning I am
afraid it will give her
lung truble again I
will close hope to hear
from you soon
Your mother

Letter from Addie Goldsmith to her daughter Maggie Lou Emerson

Maggie Lou Emerson on Railroad Boxcar

John Seth Emison

When the parents of John Seth Emerson died in 1924, he did not have the money to pay for the farm they lived on and someone else bought the land. There were 80 acres at the cost of four dollars an acre. When this happened, he lived with Aubrey Webb and his family and paid them four dollars a month for a room and three meals a day. These four dollars also included for the Webb women to wash and clean his clothes. He finally saved enough money to buy back the farm, but by this time the land had gone up to seven dollars an acre, but he somehow managed it. The old log house where the Webbs lived was John Seth Emison's house. He lived in one side and they lived in the other side. I wonder how much increase in cost this acre of land would bring today?

John Seth got sick one night about 12:00 pm. They got his daddy word to come and see about him. His daddy was a barber in Bells. The father went back to Bells and got Dr. McDonald, who came and gave him some medicine, but he died the next day anyway. Whatever he had moved very fast and he had such a short illness.

At this time, the Emison family had a cotton gin that sat where Charlotte Naylor now lives. The family also spelled their name with an (I) until the 1920's or 30's. No one in the family seems to know why this change was made. All the very old records of the Emersons today were descended from the Emisons before branching out with a new name.

Silas Emerson

Silas Emerson was Joe's granddaddy and lived in the old homeplace, where Jody's house is today. Jody built his house on the terraced rise in the exact spot where the Emersons were all raised. When the new house was finished, it looked like it had always been there because all the plantings and trees were right in place, and even the buttercups and flowers that came up were right around the house.

The old homeplace burned in the nineties and must have been a cigarette thrown out of a car. We do not know why it burned. The electricity had been gone for years and there was no storm to set it off with lightning. The grass was dry and tall and could have easily caught fire from the road with fire climbing the hill to the house—one of life's mysteries!

Silas was sick and died in 1920. He had contacted a cold that got worse and worse and developed into pneumonia, which back then was almost a certain death sentence. Oh, what a little modern medicine could have done for so many people back then. Dr. Harris (the old doctor from Bells) came to see him and when he started to leave, his wife Annie asked the doctor if he could back the next morning around 9:30 or 10 o'clock to check on him. She knew that Silas was very sick indeed. Dr. Harris was very direct with Annie and told her he did not think that he would be of any use to Silas tomorrow because he did not think he would live that long. Annie lost control and was so very upset but had a little time to compose herself and prepare for it before he died that afternoon around 4:30. Dr. Harris had come to see Silas on his way from seeing a family that lived in front of the Fruitvale store on the left, and his car would not make it through the mud over the hill. Paw Paw and his brother got a mule and pulled him over the hill and was finally on his way back to Bells. He saw lots of people down this road in front of the store. Where the road forks now going to the Williams' home once went north on a narrow farm road that a few people live on. When he drove on these back roads, he often had to call on men in Fruitvale to come and get him out or sometimes just carry him and bring him out after seeing his patient. When you saw the doctor around the community, you knew that someone was very, very sick or he would not have been called.

Silas was 52 when he died and Paw Paw (Joe's father) was eight at the time. Grandma Annie was forty. She was considered to be fairly old back then and now she would be a woman in her prime. Silas died in the front room to the right of the front door and was lain out there to receive visitors before burial. This was a very difficult time for the Emerson family. There was no electricity, running water nor gravel on the roads that were impassable in winter and spring. A horse drawn hearse came from Gadsden to pick Silas up and carry him to the Cypress Church Cemetery.

When Silas was on his death bed, Arthur Jones took the baby, Dalton Jones, to see him. Silas always wanted to see the baby Dalton. It is time proven that everyone loves a baby and that they convey a message of hope and happiness and innocence.

Silas and Ollie Boyd were both born in 1880.

Emerson Homeplace

Silas Emerson and sisters

Annie Taylor Emison at home

Lonnie Emerson, Silas' sister 1902

Malcolm Emerson In front of fruit shed

Cotton Growers Associations Nov. 21, 1931 – Annie Taylor Emerson (right)

79

State of Tennessee, Crockett County.

To any Regular Minister of the Gospel having the care of Souls, or to any Justice of the Peace for said County—GREETING:

These are to Authorize you to solemnize the Rite of Matrimony between *Silas Emison* and *Annie Taylor* of your County, agreeably to an Act of Assembly in such cases made and provided; Provided always, that the said *Annie Taylor* be an actual resident of this County; otherwise these shall be null and void, and shall not be accounted any license or authority to you, or either of you, for the purpose aforesaid, more than though the same had never been prayed or granted.

Given under my hand, at the Clerk's office, this 27 day of *Dec* 1901

D B Dotson
Clerk of Crockett County.

Know all Men by these Presents, That we *Silas Emison* all of the County of Crockett, and State of Tennessee, are held and firmly bound unto the State of Tennessee in the sum of Five Hundred Dollars, which payment, well and truly to be made, we bind ourselves, our heirs, executors, and each and every one of us and them, jointly and severally, by these presents.

Witness our hands and seals, this 27 day of *Dec* 1901

The Condition of the above Obligation is such, That whereas, the above named *Silas Emison* has this day prayed and obtained a license to marry *Annie Taylor* Now, if the said *Annie Taylor* be an actual resident of the aforesaid County, and there shall not appear any lawful cause why the said *Silas Emison* and *Annie Taylor* should not be joined in Holy Matrimony as Husband and Wife, then this obligation to be void; otherwise, to remain in full force and virtue.

Silas Emison [SEAL]
J S Emison [SEAL]

I solemnized the Rite of Matrimony between the within named parties on the 30 day of *Dec* 1901 *N C Bailey J.P.*

Silas & Annie Taylor Emerson's Marriage Certificate

CERTIFICATE OF MEMBERSHIP AND IDENTIFICATION CARD
Mid-South Cotton Growers Association

This Certifies That **MRS ANNIE EMERSON**

CONTRACT No. **105 140**

of **FRUITVALE**, **CROCKETT** County

in the State of **TENNESSEE**, is a member of the Mid-South Cotton Growers Association; that he has executed the application of membership and the marketing agreement of the Association; that he is doing his share to abolish speculation and waste, and stabilize cotton markets in the interest of the growers of cotton of the South. Dated at Memphis, Tenn., this the 21 day of **NOV 1931**.

President   Secretary

(OVER)

Don N. Emerson
Born–September 17, 1909. Died–October 13, 1991
By: Donna K. Emerson,, daughter

"Daddy"

Don Neal Emerson was the third child, and second son, born to Silas and Annie Taylor Emerson, on September 17, 1909. He grew up on the Emerson farm on Cypress Creek in Crockett County, Tennessee, near the community of Fruitvale. In addition to older sister, Ruth, and older brother, Russell, he also had a younger brother, Malcolm. Don had black hair and hazel brown eyes, generally with a twinkle in them. He had an olive cast to his skin tone, which allowed him to tan easy, which was the envy of his daughters, and led one of them to ask if he had any Indian blood, to which he replied in the affirmative. *(My somewhat slapdash genealogical research has never indicated that this is true, but perhaps a more in depth search might lead to the veracity of this affirmation.)*

Don's father, Silas Emerson, died in 1920, when Don was 11, leaving Miss Annie as the head of the family. Daddy never said much about Mr. Silas, except to say that he was a stern man. As an example of this, Daddy talked about a much-anticipated trip to Jackson to visit Miss Annie's brother. They were to take the train from Fruitvale to Jackson, where his uncle would pick them up. Daddy said they 'lived in fear' that Mr. Silas would decide they could not go, until the time that they actually got on the train. (Russell, the oldest boy, did not get to go, because he had to help on the farm.)

At the age of 12, Don was diagnosed with tuberculosis. By that time, the (possibly log) house the Emersons lived in had been replaced with a wood frame house with a large porch or veranda across the front. As part of the therapy the doctor ordered, Daddy had to sleep out on the porch during all kinds of weather. It is highly probable that that is the point at which the porch was screened in, to keep the farm animals off of it. While Daddy survived the tuberculosis, it is probably why he had severe allergies as an adult.

Education was important to the Emersons (*whether this came from the Emersons or the Taylors, I don't know.*) There were always books and magazines in the house, and all of the children took advantage of the one-room schoolhouse that served the local community. Miss Annie would often walk across the fields to bring a hot can of beans to the children so that they could have a warm, mid-day meal. Daddy mentioned that, once they had read all of the books in the school library, and, I assume, the ones at home, they were allowed to visit "the German" who had a log house/cabin in one of the fields, whose walls were lined with shelves full of books. They were allowed to borrow those books to read, on the conditioned that once completed, they would be returned.

Church going was another important part of the weekly schedule. The Emerson family had been instrumental in the establishment of Cypress Methodist Church, where Miss Annie and her children attended when weather permitted. *I always wondered why Daddy never needed a hymnal in church on Sundays, until he talked about going to shaped-note singing school periodically.* He, along with many of his contemporaries, had memorized the hymns of their childhood and learned to sing using the shaped-note method. Music was also important to the Emerson family. Aunt Ruth took piano lessons as a child and then was supposed to teach the boys how to play the pump organ that always sat in the center hall of the house. It used to fascinate me, as a child, when we would visit Miss Annie and Uncle Pete (Russell), when Daddy would sit down at the organ and play, generally hymns, but also other popular songs of his childhood. Sandra, my older sister, inherited her musical abilities from the Emersons, I'm sure, as she could play any instrument she picked up!

Don graduated from the local school at the age of 16, and, in 1925, following in Aunt Ruth's footsteps, traveled to Milligan College in upper East Tennessee to continue his education. He was always stylishly dressed, as Miss Annie and Aunt Ruth made all of his clothes, from bell bottom trousers with button fronts, to three-piece suits, to heavy, hand-knitted sweaters. Even as an adult, I was horrified to learn that when Daddy left for school in the fall, he did not return to West Tennessee until school was out in the spring! Before he left Fruitvale for Milligan, the greatest distance from home he had traveled was to Jackson, and that very infrequently!

Interestingly enough, while doing my slapdash genealogical research, I had discovered that the Emerson name was originally spelled Emison, and both spellings are still found in Crockett County. Several of Daddy's freshman textbooks at Milligan were inscribed with the name "Don Emison," while later texts and his diploma had the spelling of "Don Emerson," indicating that the spelling change came between 1925 and 1929, when Don completed his undergraduate work.

The United States was on the brink of the Great Depression in 1929, when Don completed his degree at Milligan, putting an end to his hopes of becoming a doctor. His other career interest was in sports writing! He had served as a correspondent with the Johnson City newspaper while in school, writing and reporting on the results of Milligan's athletic endeavors. But jobs were scarce so Don returned to Fruitvale and taught in the one room schoolhouse he had gone to school in for several years. In 1934 Don accepted a teaching position at Maury City High School, on the other side of Crockett County, where he taught math, chemistry, and coached girls' basketball. In the fall of '34, at the instigation of several of his students, Don met LaVergne Riddick, who had graduated from the high school the previous spring. In November 1935, after a year-long courtship, they were married and set up housekeeping in Maury City.

Following a tenure of several years in Maury City, by 1938 Don and LaVergne Emerson had moved to Middle Tennessee. Don had accepted a position as principal of Hillsboro School. In 1940, their first child, Saundra Ellen, was born in April. After several years in rural Hillsboro, a community not much larger than Fruitvale, the Emersons moved on to Culleoka in Maury County, where Don was principal of Culleoka School, a 1st through 12th grade school. In 1944, a second daughter, Donna Kay, was born to the Emersons. *(Interestingly enough, when I was working as a historic preservationist in Columbia, in the mid 80s, many of the people I met had parents that had been Daddy's students at Culleoka and who had fond memories of Momma, Daddy, and Sandra. In one instance where I had been invited to discuss the restoration of a home in Culleoka, I glanced at a class picture hanging in the parlor, and there was Daddy! Further inquiry brought the information that the gentleman whose home I was in had left school in 1944 to join the army. Prior to leaving school, his woodworking class had built a cabinet for Momma to put my baby clothes in! I still have that cabinet.)*

In 1945, the Emersons left Culleoka for Franklin, Tennessee, where Don became, first the principal of the elementary school, and, ultimately, the superintendent of the Franklin Special School District, a position he held for ten years. In 1947 a son, David

Neil, was born, to round out the family at five. During Don's tenure at FSSD, the educational program he helped put in place gained a reputation as one of the premier school districts in the State of Tennessee. He worked at securing a living wage for his teachers, built a junior high school, and preserved a "separate but equal" educational system for the African-American population of Franklin. I was surprised to learn from my mother, years later, that one reason Daddy left the teaching profession was because he was a strong supporter of segregation! I never had the opportunity to ask him why he felt that way but wonder if he foresaw the impact that integration would have on both the white and the black communities.

Upon leaving the teaching profession, Don became associated with Encyclopedia Britannica as an educational representative, selling Britannica and its educational products and aides to schools and libraries across the state. He worked in the 'book business' for the next 30 years, until his retirement at the age of 72. *He told me once that retirement was the worst thing that could happen to a person.* My mother, Lavergne Riddick Emerson, told me once, "Old men are the biggest gossips around!" And I guess it is true. Daddy used to love to be the first person to carry news of happenings at one county school system or library to their friends and colleagues in the next county. Hirings, firings, promotions, marriages, deaths, and babies were his stock in trade. He kept up with the needs of schools and libraries, never pushing them to purchase new encyclopedias, etc., until it was his "turn." Having been in the school business for 20 +/- years, he understood the funding cycles and was always ready to help his school friends get the products they needed. And because he was a great source of stories and anecdotes, he was always welcomed wherever he went.

One of the reasons that Daddy liked the traveling life was because he was pretty much in charge of his own schedule. If it was Election Day, or our local high school was playing in a big game, whether it was football or basketball, he could arrange his schedule so he was there to take us to the game. Sports was one of his loves that he never lost interest in, although he was never an athlete. He did not even play golf! But he loved baseball, football, and basketball. I recall times when Daddy and I would sit out in the rain to watch a college football game, or the (several) times when it was "March Madness" time, and the family would have a newer, bigger, better TV. In fact, if I recall correctly, our first color TV was bought and installed in time for the basketball tournament.

Momma and Daddy never traveled much. But Daddy was an "armchair" traveler. He generally had a subscription to a travel magazine and/or *National Geographic*, and he read them cover to cover, a characteristic I guess I inherited. We even read the advertisements! But he and Momma did go to Hawaii with David and Delta to celebrate their wedding anniversaries, which were both in November.
We always were involved in church wherever we lived. In Murfreesboro, where we moved in 1956, we belonged to St. Mark's Methodist Church. The couples Sunday School class is named in Daddy's honor, having taught the class for over 20 years. We were expected to go to Sunday School and church every week, unless we were sick or out-of-town.

Other continuing influences in our lives were music and books. As previously mentioned, Sandra was a talented musician, starting with the clarinet in junior high school and on through high school and college. She won many "contests" she competed in, consistently scoring at the top of the ranks. When she determined that she wanted to be a band director, she was given an expensive clarinet as a high school graduation present. Daddy promised me that if I ever could play saxophone like Sandra played the clarinet, he would get me a good sax, too! Unfortunately, I could have cared less. We always, from when I remember, had a good radio and record player. Many Sunday afternoons were spent sitting together in the living room listening to Pete Fountain, Benny Goodman, Louis Armstrong, and Wayne King! I can almost promise you, Daddy would have had an IPod!

Books/education was another strong influence in our lives, and that is an influence that carries on through Laura's children, whose favorite gift is a Barnes and Nobles gift card, and through Neile and Ashley, though Ashley was slow in getting to that point. One of my lingering memories of Daddy is the winter he read *The Rise and Fall of the Third Reich*. It took him all winter long to read it, because he sat beside the encyclopedia, and if a person, place, or battle was mentioned that he did not fully know about or understand, he would stop and read about it in the encyclopedia. He would have loved the Internet and Wikipedia! There were many nooks and corners in our house that had bookshelves stuffed with books.

Don retired in 1981, when LaVergne was diagnosed with ovarian cancer. The next ten years were spent battling a series of health problems, both his and hers. He died in 1991 from liver cancer. In 1993 LaVergne died, also of liver cancer.

DESCENDENTS:

Saundra Ellen Emerson Arnold White (Sandra; Sandi) b. April 8, 1940, d. May, 1984

Janet Niele Arnold, b. April 19, 1964

Laura Taylor Arnold Isolani, b. Feb. 19, 1970; m. Rodney James Isolani, Dec. 10, 1994

Nicholas Patrick Isolani, b. Sept. 19, 1997

Megan Taylor Isolani, b. Oct. 19, 1999

Lucas James Isolani, b. Feb. 24, 2001

Donna Kay Emerson, b. November 16, 1944

David Neil Emerson, b. April 5, 1947, m. Delta Ann Little, Nov. 23, 1983

Ashley Grace Emerson, b. July 12, 1986

MEMORIES:

Sunday afternoon drives in the country and stopping at a general store for soft drinks, etc. Momma, Sandi, David and I would get cokes, 5 cents a bottle, and Daddy would get an Orange Crush in a brown bottle. All of us kids had to have a taste, and then Daddy would go in and get himself another one! We also generally got some kind of peanut butter candy, 2 each. The whole adventure, probably including gas, probably cost 50 cents or less.

One memorable Sunday drive, when we came to a fork in the (dusty) road, and we always got to choose. This time we chose to go left. The road went on and on and on...only to end up in someone's yard! And the occupants of the house were on the front porch...wondering who their company was! To this day, long roads with no ends are "long driveways."

Spending summer weeks at Milligan, where Daddy taught education classes in summer school. Sandi was probably 10, I was 5 or going on 5, and David was 3. We lived in the girls' dormitory and generally ate our meals in the cafeteria in the basement. Knowing now that students generally stayed at Milligan from beginning of fall semester until ending of spring semester, I understand that the main floor of the girls' dorm was probably the campus living room. It had sofas, easy chairs, card tables and chairs, and a piano around which everyone would gather to play and sing. There were books and magazines, and everyone, to my memory, got along. I think we did this for 2 years. There were some other families there also. I assume that their fathers were teaching summer classes also. Since they had children the general ages of David and me, we had a grand time fishing in the goldfish pond and playing dolls in the rose arbors. The "courting couples" generally had to show the girls out of the arbor, which we thought was a great place for us to play house with our dolls, and built just for us!

I remember when I was in the second or third grade, always being the student that the teacher would send down to the office to find out what time it was. I couldn't read the clock, but I could always get Daddy or Joyce, his secretary, to come out and tell me what the clock said. So the teacher always knew I would bring back the correct time.

Daddy was a great storyteller. Our favorite one was the story of "The Preacher and the Bear." Today I couldn't tell you what the story was about, other than that the bear chased the preacher up a tree, I think. It is a classic story, told at many storytelling sites. But we thought it was just Daddy's story! At visitation after Daddy's death, one of his cronies, who was the superintendent of schools for Rutherford County, said he generally asked him to tell him the story every few months when they would meet for some reason, because Daddy always told it differently, with new embellishments, so it was always different.

When we lived in Franklin, we always had a big garden. It took up the whole back half of the lot our house sat on. It was great fun to help Daddy plant corn, although David and I could not really understand why we weren't putting a fish in each hole, along with the pieces of corn! Sandi and I were always so envious of Daddy's tan. If he was outside for an hour or so, in a short-sleeved shirt, when he would take his watch off, you could see tan lines! Sandi's skin type was closer to Daddy's than mine. I always burned. The garden was also the cemetery for the cats and kittens we had and where we had numerous burial ceremonies.

When I was in college, I took French as my foreign language. One evening, I came into the living room, and in my terrible accent, I asked Daddy if he spoke French. You can imagine my surprise when he answered me in a long, flowing sentence, with an accent equal to that of my French professor, who was from France! Momma later told me that when he graduated from high school, Daddy read, wrote, and spoke French as fluently as he did English. I wonder who was teaching French in that one room schoolhouse in Fruitvale?

When I was in high school, my friends and I decided that we needed to learn how to play bridge. The primary reason for this was because my best friend had a crush on a college-age boy who lived next door, and he had promised to teach us how to play. David and some of his friends learned how to play, too. The girls used to play while we listened to the college basketball games. (Crushes on 'older' men that came to play here, also.) Playing bridge also helped while away the time on those snow holidays that sometimes went on for days and days at a time. I never really got into bridge much, so one day when I didn't want to play, Momma suggested that the boys ask Daddy to play. I had never even seen Daddy pick up a card before, but he wiped the table with his skill. Momma later told us that playing bridge was the only thing she had ever heard of that Daddy stayed up all night to play, while he was in college!

Daddy's last granddaughter, Ashley, was born in 1986. We have pictures of Momma and Daddy holding Ashley when she was a newborn baby and later of her sitting in Daddy's lap while he read her a book. One of my favorite memories revolving around Daddy and Ashley was on a family trip to Colorado in June 1988. Ashley's home was a one-story house, so at 18 months old she was fascinated by the enclosed stairs to the second floor and wanted to go up and down them frequently. Several time, when she was just fixing to take her first step up, Daddy asked her, "Will you be back, Miss Emerson?" Ash's reply was "I be back." Thereafter, when she was getting ready to go upstairs, she would either wait for Daddy's question, in order to reassure him she would be back, or she would tell him she would be back, before he would have a chance to ask.

Although Laura's children were not born until years after Daddy's death, I often think of him in relationship to one of my early memories of Nick, Laura's oldest son. Nick is a great athlete and plays baseball and soccer and runs cross-country track. But he also has a great love for football. I spent some of my winter break, from teaching in Kansas, with Laura and Nick, while Rodney visited a friend living in Phoenix and going to the Fiesta Bowl, where UT won the 1998 National Championship. At one point, when the announcer yelled, "Touchdown, Tennessee," and Laura and I were cheering, Nick's arms flew up in the signal for a touchdown, and he yelled touchdown! (He was about 15 months old.) Daddy would have loved it!

A memory that others shared with David and me, after Daddy's death, was about his thoughtfulness and caring for others. Several different young couples from our church, St. Marks United Methodist Church in Murfreesboro, whose parents were friends and associates of Momma and Daddy's, told us that several times, after their marriages but while still in school, that Daddy would call them when he knew he would be in the same town they were in and invite them to dinner. All of them said that he would take them to a nice restaurant, somewhere they could not have afforded to go at all, and what a treat it was for them.

Grandma Annie (Taylor) Emison

I only met Grandma Annie officially to talk to etc. after I married Joe. She was one of the most gentle, agreeable persons I had ever met, and I instantly liked her.

Her family never seemed to have material things, but neither did mine nor many other families around. What she did seem to have and had instilled in her children was a sense of pride in them and an air of respectfulness. Anyone knowing this little lady would not think of saying or doing anything that would be considered out of place or ugly. She never said any of this, but I picked up on it by just being around her and her demeanor.

Although they were farmers like probably 85 percent of the community, she somehow got her son Don and her daughter Ruth through college. Malcolm was farming and postmaster of the Fruitvale Post Office for many years, and Pete held the same position in Bells for some years. You could tell the family valued their education.

Grandma loved her cats, and she usually had quite a few in the house and around in the yard. If she was sitting, she had one of her beloved cats in her lap. If she was walking, one was in her arms with a few following her every step. She always had a yard full of guineas. They stayed around the house there for several years after she died. They were as staple as the boards on the house. They just belonged there, so there they stayed.

Her garden and yard were important to her also. She raised most of their food and had a profusion of flowers to beautify her yard that was on a hill and terraced that gave it a very unusual look.

You did not see Grandma out much in the surrounding country or in town. Pete went to the Fruitvale Store every morning and got the mail and what they needed in the house each day. She was homebound, so to speak, of her own accord.

Grandma was a small woman with wire glasses and curly gray hair and very neat in her appearance. She looked like the "All American Grandmother" that everyone seems to want. She loved her family, and showed this in a million ways. She was particularly close to her daughter Ruth, and the feeling was mutual.

Who says you have to be seen and heard to make a difference? Certainly Grandma did not. She made her mark on this world right in her own space!

Grandma Annie Emerson, her cat & chicken

Reginal (Reggie) Buckingham and Beatrice (Taylor) Buckingham

Born 1887 – Died 1954   Born 1908 – Died 1952

Both are buried in the Young Cemetery in Crockett County

Beatrice was the daughter of Abraham Price Taylor and Mary A. Jernigan and sister of Anna M. Taylor, who married Silas Emison. This family line is included in the back of this book.

Abraham Taylor
(Courtesy of Donna Loyd Mansfield)

Abraham Prince Taylor was born 22 Sep 1850 in Madison County, Tennessee to Nathan T. Taylor (born 1820 NC) and Jane Prince (born 1832 NC). Abraham married Mary A. Jernigan on 23 Feb 1876 in Crockett County. They had the following children: **Annie Taylor,** who was born in 1876 and died in 1964 in Crockett County. She married Silas Emison on 30 Dec 1906 in Crockett County. Silas was born in 1868 and died in 1921 in Crockett County. They are buried in the Cypress Church Cemetery. Their children were Ruth, Russell, Don Neil, and Malcolm Hooper,

William Latta Prince Taylor, who was born in 1878 and died in 1952 in Crockett County. He married Bessie Lewis on 7 Aug 1904 in Crockett County. Bessie was born in 1887 and died in 1975.They both are buried in the Young Cemetery. Their children were Hazel, George Penn, Betty L., Camelia, and Neil Brown.

Beatrice Taylor was born in 1883 and died in 1952 in Crockett County. She married Reggie Buckingham on 21 Jun 1908 in Crockett County. Reggie was born in 1887 and died in 1954. They both are buried in the Young Cemetery. Their children were Elijah Prince, Maylon, Mary A, and Annie M.

Cordova (Dovie) Taylor was born in 1886 and died in 1981 in Chester County. She married Virgil Hopper on 22 Oct 1904 in Crockett County. Virgil was born in 1883 and died in 1960 in Chester County. They both are buried in the Bethel Baptist Church

Cemetery. Their children were Burdon, Bonnie, Mayo, Owen (Twin), and Oscar (Twin).

Olive V. Taylor was born in 1889 and died in 1975 in Crockett County. She married Alsie Raines Reasons on 19 Aug 1907 in Crockett County. Alsie was born in 1888 and died in 1951 in Crockett County. They both are buried in the Salem Church Cemetery. Their children were Truman, Douglas, Abbot, Marshal, Genrose, D.W., Gladys, and Doris.

Elizabeth Taylor was born in 1892 and died in 1974 in Crockett County. She married John Nelson on 20 Jan 1920 in Crockett County. John was born in 1895 and died in 1972. They both are buried in the Young Cemetery. Their children were A.J., Paul, Juanita, Mary E., Charles, Herman, and Jerry.

Alta B. Taylor (Daughter) was born in 3 Jan 1898 and married Cleveland (Joe) Lloyd on 19 Apr 1914 in Crockett County. Joe was born 30 Nov 1894 and died 14 Mar 1969. Their children were Blondell, Jimmie, Steven, Ernest, Mary, Betty, Bobby, Jessie Vernell, Abraham, and Wendell.

Annie Taylor Emerson
3 years - Made from tin-type

Abraham Prince Taylor and wife, Mary Asenath Jernigan Taylor

William Prince Taylor

Log house where Annie Taylor was born. Still standing outside Gadsden

The Emerson Family

Joe Lloyd, Blondell and Jimmy

The Emerson family was as different to me as my family was to Joe. The Leggett family was clannish and the Bailey family always going here and there together.

Joe's family stayed pretty close to home but made yearly trips to St. Louis to see the Cardinals play or to Pensacola to see Joe's Aunt Ruth that taught school there. Their friends were all ball fans or fishing buddies. Malcolm (Joe's dad) had two brothers, Don and Pete, and one sister, Ruth. Uncle Don was a schoolteacher and later a school principal and later in life he sold encyclopedias. We did not see them often. Uncle Pete was a farmer on the old Emerson Home-Place and was a postmaster in the Bells Post Office for a short time.

Joe's grandmother, Annie Taylor Emerson, had a reunion every summer and they all came to this along with Grandma's sisters and their families. I remember they always had fried salmon patties. There were many Yucca plants in the yard that still survive, down the side of the road past the hill toward our house. Grandma Emerson was a very sweet and gentle woman. She was short with pretty gray hair and always neat in her pretty cotton dresses and very well-groomed. It amazes me, as I look back, how these women accomplished their good looks without all the makeup and cosmetics we have now. Makes me wonder if all the paint and scents are completely necessary when we have perfectly good soaps and lotions.

Uncle Pete, her son, lived with her until he married. He drove an old green Ford car while he was there and would drive to the store every day to pick up the mail and chat awhile with all the men. The old car was slow going but could make it to the store and back.

In the 1930's FDR signed a "New Deal" program that included the CCC (Civilian Conservation Corps) as a means to provide useful employment for the many young men caught in the depression with no work available, and be put to work conserving the country's natural resources under army officers and forest rangers. Pete signed up and was sent to military posts and then to various states where the camps were set up. He was sent to Middle and East Tennessee, planting trees as an environmental exercise and also to give the unemployed at the time a job and thus, as the story goes, "killing two birds with one stone," which meant better environment and employed citizens.

The Emerson homeplace had a front porch that went all the way across and was screened in. There was a back porch also where the clothes were washed and tubs were stored. Five rooms and a hall made up the floor plan. There were two bedrooms on the left of the front door and a living room, dining room and kitchen off the right of the door.

The entire Emerson family went to Natchez Trace each summer together and rented one of the lodges there with the Merlin Leggett family. We fished, swam, went boat riding and really enjoyed these days together.

The family owned a farm close to Jackson that had a very large pond on it. The farm is called the Epperson Farm, named after the family that Ollie Boyd bought it from. We would go there on Sunday afternoons and walk through the woods and fish some. The old road from Jackson to Bells went through this farm, and you can still see evidence of this old road now. By the pond there is an old slave cemetery in the woods. The trees have grown up in there in later years. The pond, old road and the cemetery are all there right together with the woods and made for an interesting and wonderful place for afternoon outings.

Hazel Comelia, Penn Taylor, Annie Taylor Emison (Bailey)

Annie Taylor Emison

Latt Taylor and his sisters, Bee Buckingham, Lizzie Nelson, Donie Hopper, Annie Emerson, and Darbie Reasons (below)

Epperson Farm Secrets

The Epperson Farm that is almost to Jackson from our house holds many secrets from its past, and we have uncovered a few of them. The old slave cemetery is one. It sits just a few feet away from the big pond where we spent so many summer days. The stones are almost covered completely over with vines and underbrush, and some are turned topsy turvy and some with the inscription completely washed away, but a few still whisper their secrets to us with a word here and there. The snakes are abundant here because of the underbrush and the pond furnishing water nearby, but in the winter when the leaves are all gone and snakes snuggly in the ground, it is an interesting place.

The old road bed is still visible in a few places. This road went from Jackson to Bells when the buggies and horses were the only transportation available. Of course, there are no gravel deposits because there was none back then. Only dirt roads that turned into mud tracks from fall on through the spring.

My grandniece found clues in a small form on this farm too. While walking, she saw two or three small round objects that looked like marbles, but they were brown and not shiny with lots of color, etc. They were, indeed, marbles made from clay and were a staple toy for earlier children. They knew many games that could be played with these tiny, hard-baked pieces of clay.

If we look closely at most any place, we can discover things from our past that are interesting. If we just knew the exact place to dig—well, who knows what might "turn up!"

By the old slave cemetery, slave cabins were on the west side of the burial plot. The black slaves were buried on the north side of the cemetery and the white people were buried on the south side. The slave cabins were on the side of the old roadbed going from Bells to Jackson. Joe's dad told him this story when he was young. All this was on the Epperson Farm near Jackson. The Epperson family lived close to the old Jackson blacktop in the corner where you turn at the big cow barn that curves to a gravel road between the farm and this cow barn, and the gravel road is the border of the Epperson farm. This made the house sit right where the gravel road and the black top meet just off the road on the right.

Ollie bought this farm from the family on a tip from Squire Mathews that the farm was soon going up for sale and asked Ollie if he wanted to put in a bid for it. Of course, he did! Land was a passion with this man, and he did very well with his love of the land and on his instinct directing him as he went. So Ollie put in a bid for the land and gave it to Mr. Mathews and it was accepted. Joe remembers the price of an acre as being thirty-seven dollars. What a buy that was!

A year or two later, the Bond-Jones farm came up for sale that adjoined the Epperson farm and Ollie bought it also, making the two farms as one and a sizeable lot at that. Joe thinks that this farm went for forty three dollars an acre. I suppose that by it being near the other farm they assumed, and rightly so, that the new land would be worth more since it merged.

John Emison, Jr.

John Emison, Jr. was the sixth child of John Emison, Sr. and Margaret Boals. He was born in (Cotton Grove), Madison County, Tennessee on 8 May 1829 and died in El Paso, White County, Arkansas, on 25 Jan1890, and is buried in Cypress Valley Cemetery in Vilonia, Arkansas.

He married Mary A Bowlton about 1851 and was living in Lauderdale County, Tennessee in 1870 The 1870 census shows they were living with some of his brothers and sisters that eventually moved to Arkansas after this census. They had 8 children.

John Emison Jr. – One of first Emison sons born in America

James Wesley Emison
b. 7-21-1853   d. 10-22-1922

Joe's Mother, called Mimi, and Events 1964

Joe's mother, we all called Mimi, had a breathing problem similar to asthma. It was a very rare type of illness. For years and years she could not climb stairs or walk far without resting because her breath would get so short. I remember in 1964 when I was carrying Jody and Joe was in bed with hepatitis, they carried Mimi to Memphis to Baptist Hospital and thought she would not live through the night, but she pulled through and came home.

This was a very difficult time for Joe and me. Everyone was afraid to come in to help me for fear they would contact the dreaded disease. Wouldn't you know that with Joe down and his mom seriously ill, me carrying a child with one two-year-old, and the well went dry or broke, I don't remember exactly what happened, but I do know we didn't have a drop of water. There was one true friend that came and brought me water in five gallon buckets that sat with Joe and talked to him and made his days brighter. That friend was Bobby Hampton. He is one of the group of boys that grew up together in Fruitvale. We will never forget this kindness he showed us when we really needed it. When Bobby 's wife Faye was having their second child, their oldest one stayed with us and slept between us and we were so glad to have her with us.

Joe's mother and her two sisters were very close and loved each other dearly. They visited often and did things to help each other out. Aunt Belle Marlowe was very quiet and easy-going, very loving and was like everyone's grandmother when I knew her. Aunt Broxie Marlowe was the youngest of the three and very spry and jolly. She kept things going and laughed at almost anything. Joe's mother, Maggie Lou, was a mixture of the two. She was easy-going and always had a smile for anyone, and she loved to primp and dress up. The three of them together were a whole. You knew in an instant that they were kin and probably sisters. We need more of these women in our world today. They knew what was important in life and lived accordingly.

Flora Goldsmith was a cousin of Joe's mother. She lived in Milan and had a beauty parlor there and June, my sister-in-law, and I would go to her shop when we were all first married and we had our hair done. Often Flora would invite us to her house for awhile and she would play her Baby Grand piano. Her favorite song being "Indian Love Call." I can still hear her singing this song even today. It was a great treat for me to get my hair done because I was not used to such luxuries. This was before half the females in the country were blondes and did not know what a manicure, let alone, a pedicure was.

Emersons During Joe's Grandmother's Time

The Old Emerson Homeplace was sitting right where Jody has his house now. When we first married, I remember going there and having family reunions and getting to know the family. We did not go to see Grandma as much as my family visited each other, but we were close enough (right across the road a little) that we kept up with them. The food was very different from what I was used to eating at home but was very good.

Uncle Pete was still living there at this time until he married.

It took Joe a long time to get used to my family. His was so different from mine. We were all so busy and talking and running from one house to the other for meals

together and fishing together, etc.
(I guess you could call most of us hyper.) His family was all quiet and serious. They did not spend the night with each other, and never a week at a time. I remember Uncle Dutch and Aunt Louise coming
to see us for the day, and the weather got bad so they just stayed a week. This was not unusual. Joe's family was more educated and worldly than mine. Does the term "Redneck" come to mind here when I talk about my family? Don't you dare think that! Anyway, I've always heard that opposites attract and this may have some truth in it. It's something to think about anyway.

Ollie with Our Children

Ollie was a man of few words. He didn't know how to express himself like a lot of people. We always knew that he loved the children because he would watch them and Bill's with affection on his face and in his eyes. One way he had of saying "I love you" to the kids was at Christmas time. He would give them all a ten dollar bill and have Joe's mother pin it on their clothes, and he watched every move they made with this special gift. The kids thought they were rich and entertained much to his delight. Ollie loved to have his picture made with the children and the money pinned to their clothes.

*Malcolm, Don, and Pete Emerson
1918*

Malcolm Emerson

Joe and Bill Emerson

*Ollie Boyd with Vince, Lori and Baby Mame' –
with their Christmas money pinned on them.*

Joe Silas and Mac Boyd Emerson
with twin calves

Joe and Bill Emerson with pet lamb

Lori Dawn, Vince, Mame',
John, and Jody Emerson –
Emerson first cousins

Joe Emerson can
walk! – A happy
moment in time

Joe Emerson and Ray Woodson

78

John and Molly Emerson
The Casket Makers

John and Molly Emerson lived where the home of Blanche Clark is now. The house was described to me by Erin Leggett and was so similar in description that it could possibly be the same house. They made coffins for people near and far. They branched out and also made furniture (table, chairs, etc).

This was told to me by Aunt Erin Leggett, and she was noted for her accuracy and interest in family records. According to the time frame here and the time frame of the unmarked graves on the north of the Cypress Church, professional people were brought in to verify if there were people buried in the empty spaces. In about 2002, holes were dug at intervals to find if graves were actually there. This proved there were more graves than had been expected. They were close together and very definitely marked by the texture of squares lined up one right after the other in shapes of coffins. If things are what they look and what seems logical to me, these coffins, or at least some of them, were made by John and Molly Emerson. I had heard about the "Coffin Makers" several times from older people in the community. I had also heard there were Bailey, Emerson and Forsythe families buried in these unmarked graves. Wooden or thin tin markers were often used and through the years were either discarded or gone with age.

There was a Henry Arnette that lived either here or close by that made caskets too. He owned land behind Emerson School and led singing at church. Bud and Molly Permenter lived behind the school right on the hill there.

The parents of Sterling Permenter had a big clapboard house that was unusual for the times. Sterling and Doss Leggett were good friends. Sterling married Lois Cates and he and Lois lived in the house with his daddy. J.D. Boyd owned the farm and Erin and Doss bought it from him. This farm was located where Erin and Doss lived most of their married life. When they had Jesse living with them, they lived in a log house behind Pearl Evans' house, similar to the Gaba house before they built the big clapboard one. Jessie lived with Erin until he married. Erin had five children born in this house.

Ollie's Farm Workings

On the farm that Ollie owned and managed, there were always cows that were his main love where animals were concerned. There was a time though when he raised sheep on the land too. These animals were not too common to this part of the country, so when time came to shear the sheep, he hired a man to do this. The sheep shearer went from farm to farm to do his job. This job was not practiced much around this area. When Ollie had him come to help him, the man stayed in the house with Ollie, Joe and his family. He came to Fruitvale by train. All I have found out about him was that he was an agreeable, middle-aged man.

Another crop that made Ollie bring in help was when the strawberries ripened. These berries had to be harvested quickly and shipped out immediately because they ruined fast. When picked and crated, they were shipped out from the fruit shed here in Fruitvale. He paid 5 cents a quart for picking and 10 cents a quart for capping them.

Ollie sent a big truck to Brownsville (and sometimes other places) to pick up pickers to gather the berries. Malcolm Emerson and Bobby Hampton usually drove the big truck with long benches lining the sides along the sideboards that enclosed the bed of the truck. The pickers sat on these benches for the ride to Fruitvale and back home. They stayed here about three weeks and slept in various buildings around the store. There were men, women, and children of all ages. Some of the children were big enough to help pick the berries. There would always be a baby or two along. Usually the young girls took care of them and brought water to the workers as well. There were whole families there and all had their own job.

The berry fields were around the store and some were at the Buttermilk Farm, so called because of the dairy cows that were kept there at one time. This farm was in Madison County close to Jackson. This farm also had a huge barn and two big silos to house the feed for the cows raised there on the cattle operation. I picked strawberries in this field when the barn and silos were still there and I loved looking at the old buildings. I was so sad when they were destroyed, making room for more acreage for row crops. This was located where the intersection of 412 and Interstate I-40 are now on the left going into Jackson from Bells.

Emison and Taylor Berry Tickets

I can just taste those lush berries when I look at the tickets I found with Joe's ancestor's names on them. I can remember very vividly how proud I was walking up to the fruit shed in the fields with my hand carrier full of strawberries to get my "tickets" to put in my pocket so at the end of the day I would have a handful of nickels and dimes! I never picked any raspberries, though I love eating them today. The flavor is so tart and sweet.

The tickets in the picture are for strawberries with Silas E. Emison's name on it and the raspberry ticket has Abraham Prince Taylor's name on it. What a find! These tickets belonged to Joe's grandfather and his great-grandfather and were given to field hands to turn in and collect their money for berries picked.

This shows you that whatever you have does not have to be big and expensive for you to love and cherish it. The best things in life are free and sometimes small.

Ollie's Office (Across Road from Store)

Ollie had his office in the small square building across the road from the store. It had a small bathroom and storage area behind a wall in the main room. This is where he hired men to work on the farm and around Fruitvale doing anything from plowing, harvesting, mowing, driving trucks or tractors and a variety of things every day that had to be done to keep his operation going. Some days, there would be men lined up, both black and white, trying to get a job for a day or longer if they could. The work was hard and long, but these were rugged men, used to the heat or cold or whatever the day brought to them.

The office had been used for different things through the years. I know it was a barber shop at one time, and I have a set of ice cream chairs that came out of this building, so it could have been an ice cream shop?

Ollie kept dogs in the store overnight to keep people from breaking in and stealing things. These dogs were mean, and Joe's mother did not approve because she was afraid that one would get out or the boys would go into the store for something and get bitten. They both had good reasons for their differences of opinion and don't know who won out on this one. I do know whose side I would have been on! Well, I'm a Mama too!

Strawberry tickets were from Silas E. Emison - Raspberry ticket was from Abraham Prince Taylors

Tithe with Chickens

You know that stories from years ago sometimes sound so unreal and hard to believe when we live like we do today. They seem so silly and made-up, but I have been assured that this little tidbit is true. In the Emerson household, things were tight when it came to finances, much like most of the people in their community and the rest of the country. Back in the 1920's, it was hard to find pennies to live on, not counting free offerings, and the church was no exception. Families believed more in tithing back then than they do now, even though money is more abundant and often spent carelessly. When the Emerson family went to church, they wanted to do their part with finances. When they had no change to spare to tithe, they often took chickens to church for their offering. You know, this seems so unreal to me, but when I think about it, it really is an offering even more than we give when we put in several dollars at a time. Reminds me of the Bible story of the woman that washed Jesus' feet with expensive oils when that was all she had. If we give with our hearts, we have truly given a gift. A hen in church really sounds like a good idea when seen from this perspective.

John Ollie Emerson

John Ollie Emerson was the third child born to Bill (Joe's brother) and June Emerson. He was an all-around boy loving sports, family, and friends. His love for the mountains and outdoor life was a very important part of his active short life. He spent many weeks and months in the western states camping out in the mountains and being quite the outdoorsman. He was married to a longtime girlfriend from Sweden. They were expecting their first child when he was diagnosed with cancer and did not live long enough to see his lovely daughter, Annie Sophie Emerson. This tragic story was a shock to his family and the community and his friends scattered far and wide.

His wife Otti, and daughter Annie live in Sweden today but are still very close to the Emerson family. They come to visit at least once a year and sometimes more, making sure to be here for the Christmas Holidays with John's family, so Annie can keep a close relationship with them. John is sorely missed by us all.

Emersons in the 50's

My information and stories have basically been the older ones and I am counting on this generation to have one or two interested persons that will keep this updated and add to the theories I have written down so it will be completed as close as we can all get it.

I am ending the Emerson episode with photo of the 50s on down through the present time. Sort of a curve line to put a point on the end of the heavier writings and add a little humor at the end too. As the old movie goes "It's a wonderful Life."

John Ollie Emerson

Front: John, Kay, Vince, Milly, Jody and Shane
Back: Lori, John Nelson, June, Bill, Jill, Malcolm, Joe and Myrtle

Maggie Jill Emerson, Elizabeth Shane French, John Ollie Emerson, Malcolm Hooper-Emerson, Jody Van Emerson, Milly Ann Emerson, and Stephen Vincent Emerson

Hooper Emerson Newspaper Article

Self-taught organist, 88, plays every Sunday at Cypress UMC

By CATHY FARMER
Associate Director, Program Ministries Team

During the Great Depression, there wasn't much to do if you lived out on a farm near Bells, TN.

The dirt roads made even the shortest trips an ordeal, but really, without money, there wasn't much reason to go anywhere anyway.

"I was bored," confesses Mr. Malcolm Emerson who was born on the farm his family settled in the early 1840s. "So I decided to learn how to play the organ. At that time, we had an old pump organ at home."

A woman in the neighborhood offered organ lessons for fifty cents a lesson.

"But I couldn't afford that," Mr. Malcolm said. "In those days, a grown man got fifty cents a day for plowing; a youngster like me only got forty cents."

Far from giving up, the man who grew up to be a farm manager and then Fruitvale, TN postmaster, determined to learn on his own.

His older sister Ruth showed him how to find middle C. Everything else, he learned from a book.

While the intent youngster was struggling with the old pump organ, he was also going to church every Sunday at Cypress Methodist Church, only four miles from his home if you stayed on the roads, three miles if you cut across the fields.

"Going to this church is one of my earliest memories," said the 88-year-old. "I've lived here all my life. Really never been nowhere else."

Around 1950, Mr. Malcolm started playing the organ at the little red brick church. Fifty years later, he's become an institution.

"I don't play by ear," he said firmly. "And I don't pick the music. They usually tell me what we're going to sing when I get here Sunday morning."

The enthusiastic choir, which includes his son, Bill Emerson, and his grandson, Jody, counts on the accompaniment provided by Mr. Malcolm and pianist Annette Wheeler.

"We play together so if one of misses a note, the other one will get it," Mr. Malcolm said with a mischievous smile.

The Rev. Jim Bittner, Cypress pastor, said he expects Mr. Malcolm, who's really devoted to the church, to continue as organist as long as he can.

"Or until we get a new organ," Bittner added with a chuckle. "He told me he doesn't have enough energy to learn to play a new one. Unfortunately, we can't get parts for the one he's using now. It's a 1950s vintage."

You know something? That old organ suits Mr. Malcolm right down to the ground. It might be a rare old vintage, but so is he.

Above: Mr. Malcolm carefully turns the pages in the sheepskin-covered family Bible that came with the Emersons from England in 1801.

Every Sunday morning at Cypress UMC, the combined tones of Mr. Malcolm's organ and Jeannette Wheeler's piano undergird the choir.

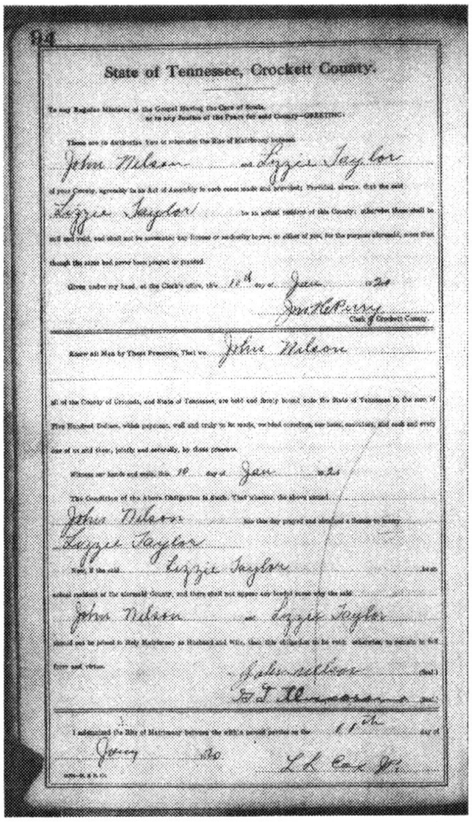
94

State of Tennessee, Crockett County.

John Nelson and Lizzie Taylor

Lizzie Taylor

Given under my hand, at the Clerk's office, this 10th day of Jan 1920

Jno H. Perry
Clerk of Crockett County.

Know all Men by These Presents, That we John Nelson

Witness our hands and seals, this 10 day of Jan 1920

John Nelson
Lizzie Taylor
Lizzie Taylor

John Nelson and Lizzie Taylor

John Nelson
G. T. Thomason

I solemnized the Rite of Matrimony between the within named parties on the 11th day of Jany 1920 L L Cox J.P.

TENNESSEE STATE MARRIAGES, 1780-2002

Spouse: Lizzie Taylor & John Nelson
Marriage Date: 11 Jan 1920
Marriage County: Crockett
Marriage State: Tennessee

Source Information: www.Ancestry.com Database: Tennessee State Marriages, 1780-2002

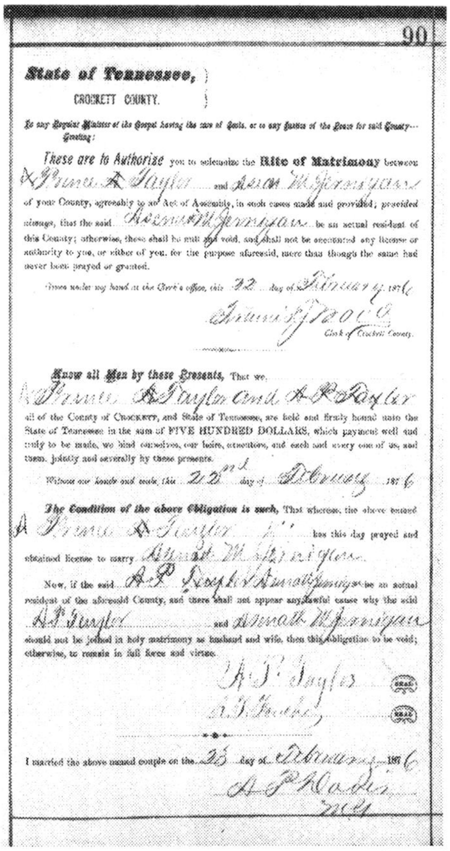
90

State of Tennessee,
CROCKETT COUNTY.

To any Regular Minister of the Gospel having the care of Souls, or to any Justice of the Peace for said County—Greeting:

These are to Authorize you to solemnize the **Rite of Matrimony** between A Prince A Taylor and Asian M Jernigan of your County, agreeably to an Act of Assembly, in such cases made and provided; provided always, that the said Asian M Jernigan be an actual resident of this County; otherwise, these shall be null and void, and shall not be construed any license or authority to you, or either of you, for the purpose aforesaid, more than though the same had never been prayed or granted.

Given under my hand at the Clerk's office, this 22 day of February 1876

Clerk of Crockett County.

Know all Men by these Presents, That we, A Prince A Taylor and A P Taylor all of the County of Crockett, and State of Tennessee, are held and firmly bound unto the State of Tennessee in the sum of FIVE HUNDRED DOLLARS, which payment well and truly to be made, we bind ourselves, our heirs, executors, and each and every one of us, and them, jointly and severally by these presents.

Witness our hands and seals, this 22nd day of February 1876

The Condition of the above Obligation is such, That whereas, the above bound A Prince A Taylor has this day prayed and obtained license to marry Asnath M Jernigan

Now, if the said A P Taylor & Asnath Jernigan be an actual resident of the aforesaid County, and there shall not appear any lawful cause why the said A P Taylor and Asnath M Jernigan should not be joined in holy matrimony as husband and wife, then this obligation to be void; otherwise, to remain in full force and virtue.

A P Taylor (SEAL)
(SEAL)

I married the above named couple on the 23 day of February 1876
A P Hodges
M G

TENNESSEE STATE MARRIAGES, 1780-2002

Spouse: Asion M Jearigan & A. Prince Taylor
Marriage Date: 23 Feb 1876
Marriage County: Crockett
Marriage State: Tennessee

Source Information: www.Ancestry.com Database: Tennessee State Marriages, 1780-2002

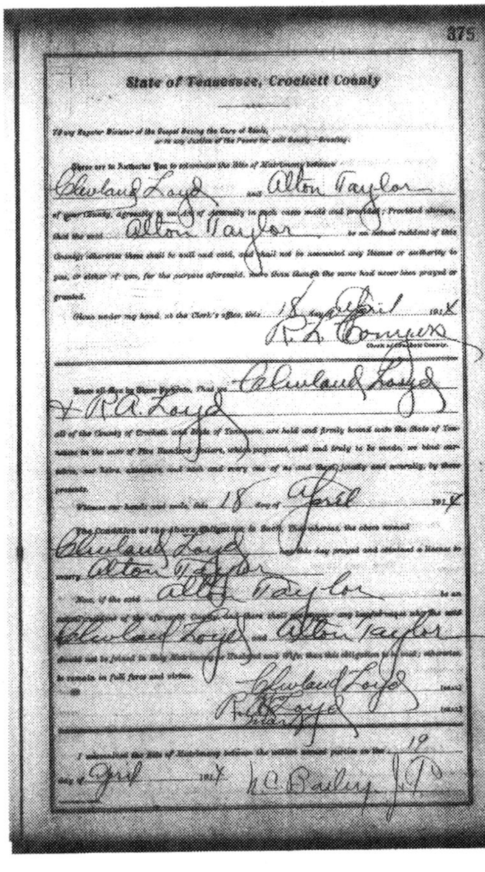
375

State of Tennessee, Crockett County

Cleveland Loyd and Alton Taylor

Alton Taylor

Given under my hand, at the Clerk's office, this 18 day of April 1914
R. L. Cowper

Know all Men by These Presents, That we Cleveland Loyd & R.A. Loyd

Witness our hands and seals, this 18 day of April 1914

Cleveland Loyd
Alton Taylor
Alton Taylor
Cleveland Loyd and Alton Taylor

Cleveland Loyd
R.A. Loyd

I solemnized the Rite of Matrimony between the within named parties on the 19 day of April 1914 W C Bailey J.P.

TENNESSEE STATE MARRIAGES, 1780-2002

Spouse: Alton Taylor & Cleveland Loyd
Marriage Date: 19 Apr 1914
Marriage County: Crockett
Marriage State: Tennessee

Source Information: www.Ancestry.com Database: Tennessee State Marriages, 1780-2002

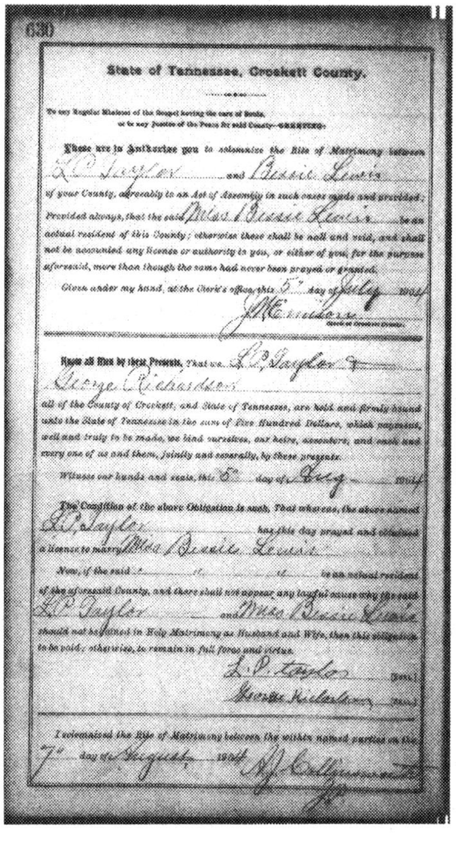
630

State of Tennessee, Crockett County.

To any Regular Minister of the Gospel having the care of Souls, or to any Justice of the Peace for said County—GREETING:

These are to Authorize you to solemnize the Rite of Matrimony between L P Taylor *and* Bessie Lewis *of your County, agreeably to an Act of Assembly in such cases made and provided; Provided always, that the said* Miss Bessie Lewis *be an actual resident of this County; otherwise these shall be null and void, and shall not be accounted any license or authority to you, or either of you, for the purpose aforesaid, more than though the same had never been prayed or granted.*

Given under my hand, at the Clerk's office, this 5th *day of* July 1904
J M Emison

Know all Men by these Presents, That we L P Taylor & George Richardson *all of the County of Crockett, and State of Tennessee, are held and firmly bound unto the State of Tennessee in the sum of Five Hundred Dollars, which payment, well and truly to be made, we bind ourselves, our heirs, executors, and each and every one of us and them, jointly and severally, by these presents.*

Witness our hands and seals, this 5th *day of* Aug 1904

The Condition of the above Obligation is such, That whereas, the above named L P Taylor *has this day prayed and obtained a license to marry* Miss Bessie Lewis

Now, if the said " " " *be an actual resident of the aforesaid County, and there shall not appear any lawful cause why the said* L P Taylor *and* Miss Bessie Lewis *should not be united in Holy Matrimony as Husband and Wife, then this obligation to be void; otherwise, to remain in full force and virtue.*

L P Taylor (Seal)
George Richardson (Seal)

I solemnized the Rite of Matrimony between the within named parties on the 7th *day of* August 1904 A J Collingsworth
J.P.

TENNESSEE STATE MARRIAGES, 1780-2002

Spouse: L P Taylor & Bessue Kews
Marriage Date: 7 Aug 1904
Marriage County: Crockett
Marriage State: Tennessee

Source Information: www.Ancestry.com Database: Tennessee State Marriages, 1780-2002

CHAPTER 4

THE LEGGETTS

Leggett History and Stories

Walter Columbus Leggett was the man I always thought was my grandfather, and I was not told any different until I was almost grown. He was my real grandfather's brother that had died with three small children. At the time, the oldest living unmarried brother was expected to marry the man's wife and raise up his children. So when Granddaddy (Homer Cyrus) died and left his three children, Walter Columbus married his widow, Rosa Belle Webb Leggett, and had five children of his own by her. So in my stories Walter will be Uncle Walter and Granddaddy will be Homer Cyrus.

Francis Marion Leggett was my great-grandfather. He was a strong and upright man with a good heart and a straight-laced religious mind. His family and friends looked up to and regarded him as a good example to follow for the good life with Christ. He provided his family with all basic necessities and guidance and love. Although they did not have luxuries in life, they did not seem to notice this. I guess they went by the saying as I have said before, "If you never had it, you don't miss it."

His family consisted of Ella, Walter, Ben, Doss, Florence and Irene and a baby that died. They are named in order of their birth. They were a big and happy family. Florence played the piano, furnishing music for entertainment and for the many gospel songs they all sang together. They did not own the homeplace. It literally took all they could make just to feed and clothe the family. They were a very religious family, and Francis Marion had daily devotions and knew his Bible well. He wrote pages and pages of notes and thoughts about the Bible and what it meant to him and his life. These writings were passed down to the family, and I was fortunate to have read them when Aunt Florence Culp had them. I have some copies of them on file here. They were written on the old Blue Horse tablets in pencil.

After the death of his first wife Nancy, Francis Marion married Charlonas Emison, daughter of Benjamin Emison and Mary Helen Permenter, from Joe's family tree, and they had the aforementioned children. Charlonas Ann Emison had a spinal problem that resulted in a severe humped back that is evident in her pictures. Could this have been corrected today? Possible.

The old Leggett homeplace had a cafe swinging door going into the kitchen, and Tommy came running through the door and did not know that his grandmother was on the other side. He knocked her down on the floor. This was very upsetting to Tommy because she was very old at the time this happened.

Homer Cyrus Leggett was my grandfather; he married Rosa Belle Webb. She was 20 years old and he was only sixteen. Francis Marion told Rosa Belle she was too young to get married, but she kept seeing Cyrus and he was not fast enough on the marriage draw for her, and so one day she said to him, "God, Cyrus! It's now or never!" They got married soon after this. Rosa Belle's mother (Mary McMillin) died young and her father (James Thomas Webb, Jr.) broke up the family. Rosa Belle, Mose, and one more stayed with the parents of Lou Myrtle Forsythe Bailey (Syble Lewis and Thomas Jefferson Forsythe) for a while.

Cyrus and Rosa Belle had three children: Raymond, Mary Jewell and Cyrus Liburn. When Cyrus died, she had five children by Walter Columbus; they were Louise, Clarence, Evelyn, Lydia Belle and Howard Thomas.

Homer Cyrus died in the old house that stood by the Clinton Moore house and left three small children. He farmed the land that was around this old house. This house was still standing when Joe and I inherited the land, and I remember visiting Clinton Moore and Bessie in this house and going into the attic and seeing old things there and wondered whose they were, never suspecting at the time that it could have been my grandfather's house. No one had told me by then that he had ever lived there. Cyrus never was in bed sick. The night he died he ate a big supper and drank a lot of water and was so thirsty and was sick from it. He told Rosa Belle the next morning that he was gone. He died early that morning during Christmas. Cyrus had sores on the lower part of his leg and did not know how to treat it. He was 21 years old and died in 1922 of a diabetic coma. Cleve Rust brought the children's Christmas to them because their dad had died on Christmas Eve. No insulin at the time, patients just went into a coma and died with no help for their illness. Homer had been standing over the water bucket a long time and did not know that this was a sign he would not live long. His son (my dad) died at 40 with the same illness. More on this in another story.

Homer Cyrus had a small brother that was helping burn off some corn stalks in the field when his clothes caught fire and he burned to death; his name was Liburn, too.

Walter Columbus Leggett

Raymond Leggett, Cyrus Liburn Leggett, Mary Jewell Leggett – Daddy is the smallest, he was not old enough for pants yet and was still in his little dress.

Walter Columbus Leggett and wife,
Rose Belle Webb Leggett

Francis Marion Leggett and Charlonas Ann
Emison Leggett "Aunt Loonie" (age 65)

Buster Leggett, Roy Clide, and
Raymond Leggett

Homer Cyrus Leggett –
Died at 21 from
diabetes

Back: Doode or Buster, Evelyn, and Raymond
Front: Tommy, Lydia, Louise and Walter – Early
cart with ox

Uncle Ben Leggett, wife,
Elsie, and daughter

Front: ___, Joe Spraggins, Sarah Spraggins, Forsythe, Betty Leggett, Della Faye Bailey, Myrtle Rose Legget, Gretta Ann Leggett, Webb, Freddie Hays, Ray Woodson.

Back: ___, Webb, Tommy Leggett, Mildred Tyler, ___, Evelyn Leggett, ___, ___, Annette Bailey, Louise Woodson

The Leggett Twins
Born 10 Feb 1850

Francis Marion and George Washington Leggett, Twins

The following research includes census records, marriage records, old letters, cemetery records, and some family lore. I have tried to group them together to tell their story as best I can.

By: *Tina Gray, Genealogist*

Lawania Bird – Her mark "x"

According to folklore, Samuel David and Margaret Lavinia (Davis) Byrd Leggett migrated to West Tennessee in a covered wagon from North Carolina in the late 1840's. Samuel David (born 1800, NC) and Margaret (born 1810, NC). They settled in Madison or Gibson County, in or around what is now the Gadsden area that in 1872 became Crockett County. Not long after arriving, Samuel David was killed, leaving Lavinia with twin sons and possibly three children by her first marriage. According to one old letter, there was a daughter (Bird) that married a Lewis. It is unclear at this time where Samuel David or Lavinia are buried or who their parents were, but research is still being done on this couple as this book goes to print.

According to an old letter, Lavinia married first, a gentleman by the name of _____? Bird in North Carolina and then came to Tennessee. He worked on the railroad and was killed there. Not having a given name, I have had no luck finding the full name or any records of Mr. Bird. Most records at that time were kept in the Family Bible and without a given name, I am unable to trace him at this time.

I did find a marriage record of Samuel Leggett and Lavinia Bird in Gibson County who married on 8 Jan. 1849. I also found an 1850 census showing they were living in District 4, Gibson County in the Quincey Community. There were four children by the surname of Bird living with them. They were Dicey Bird, 6 (born 1844, TN); William Bird, 11 (born 1839, TN); D. Bird, 17 (born 1833, TN); and Sarah Bird, 17 (born 1833, TN). It is possible that D. and Sarah Bird were husband and wife and unsure whether this is a son or relative, or possibly even twins. Could this possibly be Dempsey and Sarah Emerson Bird? This is the only census I found of Samuel David or Lavinia. Samuel died around 1850-51 and Lavinia died in 1861.

Since the 1850 census states that these Bird children were all born in Tennessee, it appears that Lavinia and her first husband were in this state by 1833 and not in North Carolina. They could have been in Wilson County before coming to West Tennessee. By all indications, the above census record is the Leggett family. Just when you think you have found someone, you have to change directions. I also note as to why the twin Leggett sons are not listed on the 1850 Gibson County census since they were born in 1850, but some censuses were taken earlier than stated on the records since they had to do all this on horseback.

Sons – The Leggett Twins were born in Gibson or Madison County, TN 10 Feb. 1850. According to the 1900 census, both twins stated they were born in February 1850. They went to school at the old Emerson School. According to an old letter, at this time they were living near the school where Henry and Cordia Arnett used to live. Their mother Lavinia died in 1861. The old letter states that the twins were 11 years old when someone came to Emerson School and told them their mother had died. We do not know where Lavinia was buried. This left 2 eleven-year-old boys and possibly a daughter (Bird) alone after their mother died, and it was the beginning of the Civil War. It is assumed that friends or relatives may have taken them in. So far, I can't find any records of them during this time. There were several Leggett families with the names of Francis Marion and George Leggett, but research found those were not these Leggett twins. It is believed that their father, Samuel David, had relatives (possibly a brother) living in this area, including Dyer and Lauderdale Counties. At this time without other information, it can't be proven. Finally, they both showed up on the 1870 census records. Both twins indicate that their mother was born in North Carolina. Francis Marion states that his father was also born in North Carolina on all his census records; however, when reading the later census records of his brother, George, he indicates that his father was born in England. Even on George's death certificate, the informant indicates that his father was named Sampson Leggett and was from England, and his mother's maiden name was McKerman. I believe these are the twins' paternal grandparents. I also believe these twins were split up after their mother Lavinia's death in 1861 since they both name completely different parents.

The parents of Lavinia (Davis) Bird Leggett are unknown, but old letters state they were from Holland. It is possible that the Isham Davis family that settled in Gibson County near Trenton was her family or part of her family. They were from North Carolina and migrated first to Wilson County and in the early 1820's came to Gibson County. Her parents were very wealthy and didn't approve of her choice of marriage and she was disinherited. Later on after her husband was killed, her brother-in-law rode up and gave her a leather sack of gold for her inheritance from her father. This helped her to find a proper place to live and food for the children.

Francis Marion – First Wife and Family

By 1870, Francis Marion appeared in the census records of Lauderdale County with his first wife. Marriage records indicate he married Miss Nancy Ann Emison on 11 Aug. 1867 in Madison County. Nancy was born 20 Mar. 1842 and was the daughter of John and Margaret (Boals) Emison, who were also from North Carolina and migrated here in the early 1800's.

After their marriage, Francis and Nancy moved to Lauderdale County, District 8 next door to Nancy's sister, Sarah and husband, Dempsey Byrd. In the 1870 census, I found them living next door to one another, and they had their first daughter, Margaret Lavinia (born 23 Jul. 1868) in Lauderdale County, age two. Another daughter, Mary Susan Leggett, was born 12 Jan. 1871, also in Lauderdale County.

Between 1870 and 1880, records are not clear. I do know that Nancy died 1871-1873 after their second daughter, Mary Susan was born. Records online indicate she died in St. Francis, Clay County, Arkansas, and is buried there; however, this is not confirmed. She did have sisters and brothers living in Arkansas and may have traveled there to visit at the time of her death. Her sister Sarah and Dempsey had lived in Arkansas for 10 years, prior to moving back to Lauderdale County. Dempsey died between 1870-1880 and wife Sarah with her children were living in Clay County, AR near her sister, Mary Ann (Emison) Boyd Freeman, in 1880 census.

In the 1880 census records, I find the younger daughter, Mary Susan, living in Crockett County with her mother's sister, Susan Emison, and her husband, Daniel Laman, stating she was their niece. She continued to live with them until she married later on. Susan and Daniel also had a daughter named Susan (born 28 Feb. 1862). That may confuse researchers and would have been easy to get the two Susans mixed up since Susan Leggett sometimes used the Laman surname. Susan Laman (1862) was 10 years older than Mary Susan Leggett (born 1871).

Also, in the 1880 census, Lauderdale County District 12, Francis Marion had married his second wife, Charlonas Emison, daughter of Benjamin Emison. She was the niece to Francis' first wife, Nancy. The census also shows Margaret L., his oldest daughter (age 11) living with them along with their two children, Ella M. (age 4) and Walter C. (age 2).

Margaret, the oldest daughter of Francis and Nancy, later married Tilman R. Poindexter in Russellville, Arkansas. They lived in Arkansas until Margaret died in Gravely, Arkansas, 13 Jul. 1913. They had 13 children: Udella (born and died 1885); Theodore (born 1886); India (born Jun 1888); Thomas M. (born 1890); Liburn (born Dec 1891); Lillie (born Dec 1893); Brice (born Nov 1895); Dewey (born Jun 1898); Maxi (born 1900); Susan (born 1902); Bonnie (born Dec 1903); Tilman (born 1906); and Aubrey (born 1908).

Mary Susan Leggett (born July 1871), the youngest daughter of Francis and Nancy, according to Crockett County marriage records, married Joseph L. Gaba on 2 Aug. 1891. Joseph was born 15 Apr 1861. (The records also show he married first Susan Laman on 29 Nov. 1885 and had a son, Charles L., born 28 Nov. 1886.) Susan Laman (first wife) died 27 Aug. 1889. In the 1900 census record, it shows four children living with them whose names were Charles (born Nov. 1886); William Robert (born May 1894); Jesse G. (born Aug. 1897); and Francis Martin (born Mar. 1898). After this census, she had an only daughter, Pearle (born 1901).

The only record I found of Joseph L. Gaba before he married was in the 1880 census living with Neal A. McMillan and wife Ashly and family as a farm laborer. He was born 15 Apr 1861 in Tennessee and mother and father were Martin and Sarah Hymes Gaba.

Mary Susan died 8 Feb 1904 at age 33 and husband Joseph also died (17 Feb. 1904) that year leaving young children. Researching the family, in the 1910 and 1920 census, I found Pearle (age 9) living with her grandfather Francis Marion Leggett and wife Carlonas (Lony). Jesse went to live with Dorse and Irin Leggett; William R. lived with Cleveland and Viola Rust; Francis Martin lived with William and Ora Lee Vandyke.

You will find these children mentioned in other writings in this book.

George Washington Leggett

It was not until the 1880 census that I finally found Francis Marion's twin brother, George W. Leggett, along with his wife, Amanda E. Griffin (born 1851). They were married in Dyer County, Tennessee, on 26 Apr. 1880. The following year they had one child, Clyde Wilson, who was born 18 Jan 1881, and it is believed that Amanda died during childbirth or right after Clyde was born. I cannot find any more records for her and do not know where she is buried.

On 26 Nov. 1884, he married Ruth J. Milligan in Dyer County and shown living there in District 3 (Bonicord) in the 1900 census. Shown on the census, the children were Clyde (born 1881); Alva Glenn (born 1885); Benton Earl (born 1887); Sarah Viola (born

1889); Mary L.(Jettie) (born 1891); Gus Meadows (born 1894); Elizabeth (born 1896).

On the 1910 census, it shows George a widower with four children still living at home with Guss, Viola, Jettie and Bettie. Ruth died 1909-10 in Dyer County. She is possibly buried in the Palestine Cemetery there without a headstone since George and several of their children are buried there.

On the 1920 census, Bettie was still living at home. George was 67 years of age then. This is the last record I could find of George. He died 24 Feb. 1921 and is buried in the Palestine Cemetery near Friendship. His death certificate is shown in this book.

Information on George's children below:

1. Clyde Wilson, born 18 Jan 1881 and died 4 Apr. 1962 - married Josie Gibson on 28 Dec. 1903. They are both buried in the Pisgah Cemetery in Dyer County. Records show he registered for WWI showing his address as Route 1, Dyersburg, Tennessee. They had 7 children. (Listed on descendent chart)

2. Alvin Glenn, born 7 Apr. 1885 and died 1965 - Married Cready M. Esprey on 8 Sep. 1907. I do not know where they are buried but they did live in Dyer County. Records show he registered for WWI showing his address as Route 1, Dyersburg, Tennessee. They had 5 children. (Listed on descendent chart)

3. Benton Earl born 5 Jan. 1887 and died 31 Oct. 1918. I do not show a marriage for him. He is buried in the Palestine Cemetery in Dyer County.

4. Sarah Viola, born Apr. 1889 (no death date) Married Rufus King. No other information.

5. Mary L., (Jettie) born 22 Sep. 1891 and died 24 Feb. 1932. Married William T. Nash, Jr. on 6 Apr. 1921 in Dyer County. They are buried in the Zion Hill Cemetery across from Zion Baptist Church on the Dyer County, Crockett County line.

6. Gus Meadows, born 14 Feb. 1894 and died 31 Mar 1922. Married Hattie L. Conder on 25 Sep 1917 in Dyer County. They are buried in the Palestine Cemetery. Records show he registered for WWI Draft, showing his address as Route 2, Friendship.

7. Elizabeth (Bettie) born Apr. 1898. (No death date) Married Carlie Hammonds on 24 Mar 1920 in Dyer County. No other information.

Florence Leggett Culp - The Leggetts

The following compiled by Florence Leggett Culp in a signed letter to Myrtle Rose Leggett Emerson:

My mother, Charlonas Ann Emison, was born in Crockett County in 1856. My father, Francis Marion Leggett, was also born in Crockett County in Tennessee. His birthday was in 1850. Their wedding date was Dec 23, 1874. They were both Methodists. Dad was a farmer and carpenter and he died May 1, 1932, and is buried in the Cypress Cemetery in Crockett County. My mother died July 7, 1933, and is also buried there.

My mother was a good cook and seamstress, fun-loving but very serious about some things. Dad was a Bible reading, God-fearing man; he liked to hunt some. Both my parents wore glasses. Mother was a very small woman and Dad was over six foot tall. She was dark and he was fair with sandy-colored hair. They lost one child that caught his clothes on fire while helping burn off a corn field and burned to death.

Dad loved religious songs and we had daily devotions. With nine children they endured many hardships. I am next to the youngest so can't remember seeing it all.

We had the usual animals at our house. Four or five horses and three cows and enough chickens to use the eggs and eat. We had one buggy and one wagon.

Our house had the usual beds, dressers, chairs, sewing machine, etc. We had two fireplaces and an upstairs and back porch. First we had a log house, then the Gaba place, which was a large frame house, nice for the times. There were cabins that were used for slaves at this home.

We did not go to town often. My dad was superintendent of Sunday School at Cypress for many years and was a delegate to conference at different times and to Lake Junaluska retreat once.

I remember there never was a stranger turned away so we were always poor, but had a good life.

Note:

Aunt Florence was in her eighties when she wrote this for me. She could not remember some of the questions I asked her, but she did great for her age. She was a very gentle person and ever so polite and lovely woman. She was my granddaddy's sister and they had the same easy agreeable ways and I loved them both. I am speaking actually of my Uncle Walter that I always knew as Granddaddy. He was my real granddaddy's brother. No one bothered to tell me this fact until I was grown. People, talk to your children and let them know who you are so they can grow up knowing who they are. All of us put together make up what the next generation will be. *(Myrtle Rose Leggett Emerson)*

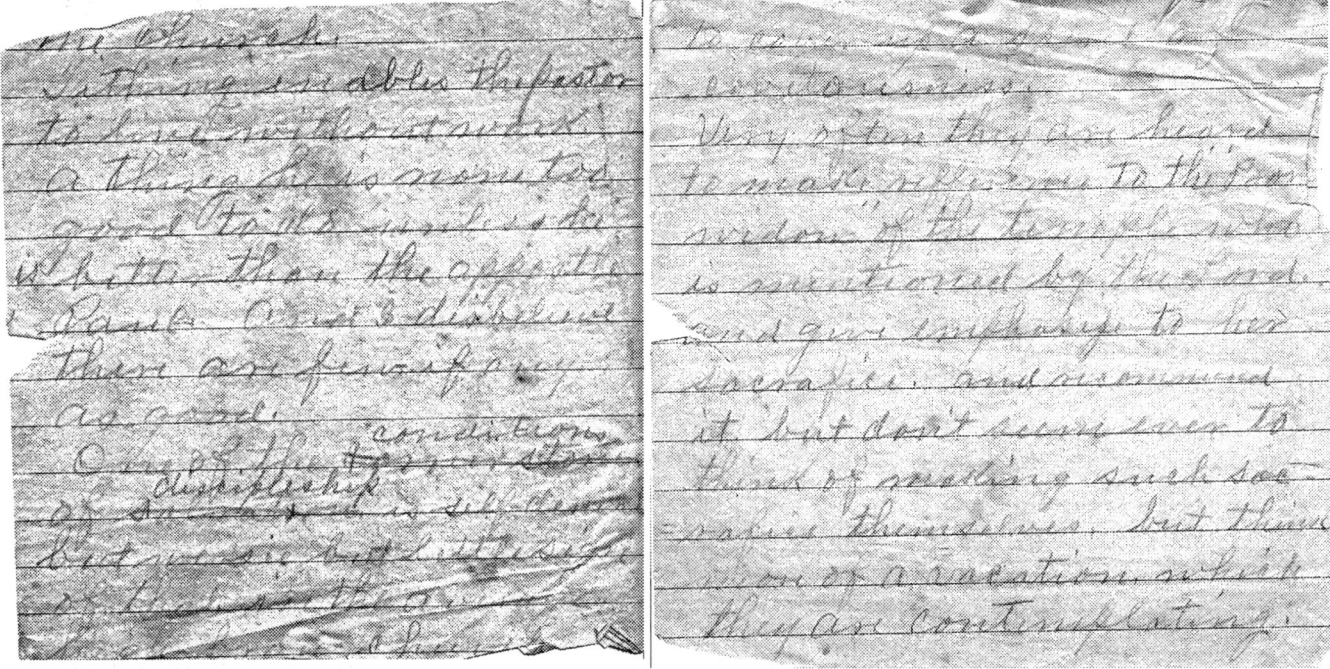

Original writing from Francis Marion Leggett

Tablet covers Francis Legget Used to Write In

Uncle Remus Series

Canary Bird Series

Happy Days

Plough's Black and White Pencil Tablet

The Men in the Leggett Family

Uncle Walter, whom I knew as granddaddy, seemed to have set the stage for the Leggett men personalities. I do not know how far these traits went back but do know that my great-grandfather, Francis Marion, was also one of the kind, loving and sensitive men. This goes on to my father, Jody, (my son) and my grandsons, Silas and John Fenner, Jr. I am really a little biased here, but anyone who knows these Leggett males know they are a wonderful breed. I could see all this in my dad and his brothers. Daddy had no ambition but to care for and love his family. I see this as good in these times where power and money seem to be the main goal in life. My dad had no enemies and had everyone's respect. My Uncle Doode was so like him; Uncle Raymond was the same. We still have Uncle Tommy and there is no sweeter, kinder man on earth. He is so calm, and the love he has for us all surrounds us when we are with him.

I have already recorded the female Leggetts, who added the spice to the life of the clan, keeping us all entertained and creative.

We have artists, great cooks, lawyers, doctors, teachers, and pharmacists, to name a few of our fellow Leggetts. Move over world! The Leggetts have arrived!

Tommy Leggett
As a Teenager

When Tommy was a teenager, he came to our house every night sometime before and sometime after supper. He came because we had a radio and Granddaddy Walter didn't have one and being at his age, he liked to be entertained. Can you imagine our teens being content with listening to the radio? This goes to prove that you do not miss what you have never had. The radio was the height of entertainment for the times.

Sometimes he would spend the night with Mama and Daddy when they were living in the little house behind Ira Webb. He had always stayed close to my father. The house was tiny and with only one place to sleep, so Tommy just crawled in the bed between the couple and had himself a good warm place for the night.

He had a "certain" rocking chair that was "his." There was a hill between our house and his, and we could see him coming over the hill. First, we would see his head and then his body would materialize as he walked at the same pace every late afternoon and could set our clock by his appearance. When we saw him coming, whoever was in the chair would move to another; and when he came in, his chair was always empty.

This same rocker was a haven to me when we had a bad cloud or storm. When the thunder and lightning started, I would crawl under this chair and stay there until it was "safe" and the weather was calm again.

Aunt Tint was living in Texas, and she and her family decided to come to Tennessee and visit all the kinfolks here. They came all the way in an old Model T car. Tommy was not used to riding in a car and he was still a young boy. Aunt Tint decided they would take Tommy riding to Bells and show him how the old car rode. Tommy said the old car could barely make it up a little hill; and when they came to a big one, he just knew he would either have to walk home or push the car up the hill. He said he did not know how they ever made it all the way to Tennessee from Texas. It was a miracle!

Tommy had finally gotten some new shoes. This was a very special thing in those days when people in the country had to wear their shoes until they fell off their feet. Tommy was elated over his new black patent shoes and they were just right. He went to his sister Jewell's house to visit and left them on the porch and the dogs chewed them up. Horrors...! May sound trivial now, but to him it was a disaster.

Tommy had a dog he called Bob and was his companion growing up, and we all know what the phrase "a boy and his dog" means for a country boy and the baby of a large family, Bob was certainly cared for and a loved dog.

Uncle Tommy Leggett

Joe and Sudie Leggett

Joe and Sudie Leggett lived past Grandpa Archie's house down in a grove of trees in a log house with a dogtrot and a lean to kitchen. They both died young and left 5 or 6 small children and they were all separated and sent to different homes. At the time this happened it was hard enough to raise your own children and keep them clothed and fed, not to mention taking children that were not your own, but the times demanded a lot of this practice because of people dying young with diseases that today are cured by a mere shot or bottle of antibiotic. Sometimes there were no relatives that could take on more family than they had, and many of these orphans had to go to people that were no kin to them or even someone they had never seen before. The children were Charlie, Jessie, Robert, Annie, Pearl and possibly one more. Mr. Francis Marion Leggett moved from Mr. Will Evans' house into Gaba's house and kept Annie and Pearl. A dinner bell fell on Pearl and damaged her brain. She almost died, as you can imagine this iron bell falling on anyone's head. Reams took Jessie and he ran away twice to Mr. Leggett and Charlie in Jackson. Erin and Doss had been married only a year and they took Jesse. At the time they resided where Neal Webb lives (Neal's grandson lives there now.)

Grandmothers Are Friends

How fortunate can you get but to have two grandmothers that were good friends when they were young? Mine were together a lot and I am so proud to have a picture of them when they were teens together. They had picked strawberries all morning and went home and dressed up and then went to Gadsden to a fair and had their picture made. They are both so lovely and young and I am so glad to have known Granny Bailey for most of my life before she died. I did not know my Granny Leggett, for she died the year before I was born. I have been told so many good things about her that I really feel she is a part of me too.

The most personal thing about these two ladies is that I was named after the two of them. Their full names were Rosa Belle (Webb) Leggett and Lou Myrtle (Forsythe) Bailey. My parents took the two names and came up with Myrtle Rose. I have to admit that when I was growing up I was none too pleased with this name, for I thought it to be so old-fashioned and I wondered how my parents could do that to me. As I grew older and my feelings for Granny Bailey grew, (and I did learn about the great lady that was my Granny Leggett) I slowly became proud of my name and now I would not want to be anyone but Myrtle Rose. I feel very honored and thank my parents for their insight in recognizing the importance of my name.

I have included this picture made after the strawberry-picking morning in this paper and hope you like it as well as I do.

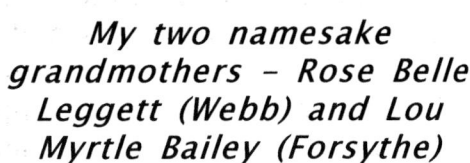

My two namesake grandmothers - Rose Belle Leggett (Webb) and Lou Myrtle Bailey (Forsythe)

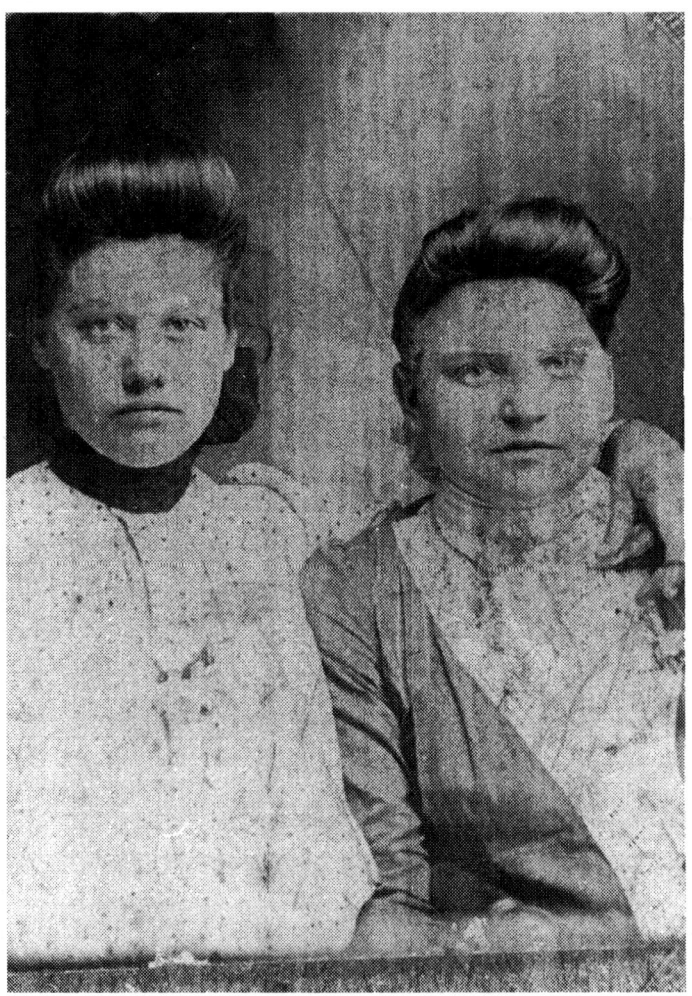

My Daddy, Buster
Cyrus Liburn Leggett

I never knew the real name of my dad until I was in my teens. I had always heard him called Buster and Buster Leggett all my life; and when I learned his given name, I was amazed that he had such a dignified and beautiful name. Cyrus Liburn Leggett has a ring to it.

Daddy was a handsome man with beautiful brown hair that waved around his face. This wave did not show up in either my hair or my sister's straight locks either. It did show up in the boys of the family in later years when they were young. He always wore overalls until they just appeared to melt away. He was always clean and clean-shaven. He always had one good pair of overalls for Sunday. He wore these to church, and Mama never missed having them washed and ironed with creases in the legs. He was a gentle man and I never saw him mad. (Well, maybe a few times when I got creative.) I never saw Mama and him fuss or fight over anything. I know they had their disagreements, but they always did it in private and we never witnessed any of this discord. He had almost no ambition for himself, other than to provide for his family and love us unconditionally. What a man! He was my idol and when he died, I thought my world had come to an end.

When he got so sick, they took him to the Baptist Hospital in Memphis. His diabetes was getting worse and he was jaundice and when added together, he was not able to fight it. He was a dark yellow color before he died.

Dr. Mayfield was interning in Memphis when this was going on, and Miss Carrie would come and get Mama's clothes and wash them for her and then bring them back. She also washed for Daddy and was kind to them. Mama was often hungry when sitting in the hospital, and Miss Carrie would bring her apples and oranges and other things to eat. It was amazing because neither Dr. Mayfield nor Miss Carrie knew Mama or Daddy, but only knew they were home folks from Bells. Mama never forgot this kindness as long as she lived. She made special things for them and baked things as gifts and sewed handmade pillows for them as long as she was able. They loved Mama's quilts and purchased some of them and so did their boys. Mama got Christmas cards from Miss Carrie every year and from one of the boys as well. They had a special relationship.

Mama never left the hospital for a full six weeks that Daddy was there. She stayed in the room with him night and day. She left home with him to enter there and returned with his body when he died. She was thirty-six and he was forty. She remained faithful to his memory until she died at eighty-eight.

When they brought Daddy home, he lay in state in the dining room in front of the double windows there. All the furniture was removed except chairs for the steady stream of mourners coming in at all hours with flowers and food. I was devastated and just wanted to be by myself and went into the back room and shut the door. *This could not be happening to me.*

At the funeral, there was not enough room in the church for all the mourners. The yard was full of people that could not get inside. When we came out of the church, my Joe was standing on the walk and I was so glad to see him. Being not thirteen yet and so very upset, I walked up to him and said, "What are you doing here?" I knew when I spoke, it came out wrong, but even then he understood and my fate was sealed.

While Mama and Daddy were still at the hospital, Betty and Russell were staying at the house with me. Betty was carrying her first child, and Russell was working at the Alamo Construction Company in Alamo.

We had several storms that ripped through the community at this time. I had always heard that lightning would not strike twice in the same place, but believe me when I personally know that this is not true. We had one of those heavy, old wall phones with the receiver that hung on the side; the speaker protruded like a cone in front of the phone box. The lightning struck the house right where the phone was hung flinging the whole apparatus across the floor. It was like dynamite going off inside the house, scaring us all. *I wanted my mama!* A few days passed and yet another storm came roaring through, and "low and behold," it threw the phone we had just repaired across the room and this time set fire to the wall. Was this some sign of something to come, or was it purely an accident that it happened yet again in the same place? I REALLY WANTED MY MAMA!

When Daddy was in the hospital and Mama was with him, there was only Betty, Russell and I at home, and the fields were running away with grass and weeds. I got up each morning and fixed Russell's breakfast, and then Mike (the hired hand) and I went to the fields and were overcome with the job to do because we both realized that it was impossible for two people to work it out. Then a miracle happened in the form of friends, neighbors and family. About eight o'clock, trucks and teams of horses, and many people came down the road with hoes, plows, food, water and lots of energy. They cleaned out all the weeds and grass and plowed up the middles, and I have never felt such relief. It was such a wonderful thing and you would have to see it to believe it. I have never felt so relieved and loved in all my life. It was a heartbreaker! I have seen things like that in movies since then, but they can't reproduce the real thing. These feelings are too intense and real to act out.

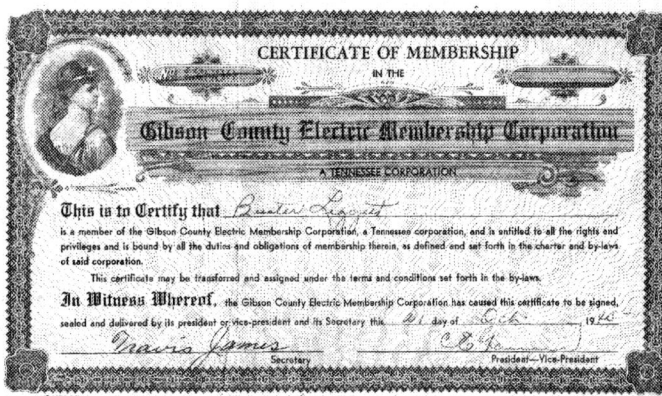

Gibson County Electric Membership Corporation – Buster Leggett (original)

Receipt for Buster Leggett

Clarence Hollis (Doode) Leggett
By: Gretta Ann (Leggett) Hughes, daughter

My daddy was Clarence Hollis "Doode" Leggett, born to Walter and Rosa Belle (Webb) Leggett at the Leggett farm just north of where Cypress Methodist Church still stands. He got his nickname one day when Grandmother was getting ready to do the week's washing. The family was standing around the washpot fire out back of the house when Daddy, a little boy of five or six, came out of the house wearing one of Granddaddy Leggett's ties over his overalls, no shirt and barefoot. They all began to laugh and one of the other children called out, "Look at that little dude!" Needless to say, the name stuck.

It always seemed to me that the Leggetts were a fun-loving bunch. My mother, Virginia Spraggins Leggett, told me when she was a young girl, her family worked the ground across the road from the Leggett farm. While Mother and family were still working in the field, the Leggetts would be on their front porch singing, laughing and talking. My daddy always had a smile for everyone as long as he lived. All the Leggetts were that way: Uncle Raymond, Uncle Cyrus (Buster), Aunt Jewell, Aunt Louise, Daddy, Aunt Evelyn, Aunt Litt, and Uncle Tommy. The whole bunch always enjoyed one another's company.

Mother and Daddy married on January 3, 1937. Their lives were hard, but they never forgot how to enjoy the small things like Homecoming at Cypress Church, the 4th of July on the river, the big meeting in August, and Christmas, which was always a time for fun. I, Gretta Ann Leggett, was born October 11, 1937, on the Leggett homeplace. In the early years of my childhood, it was not unusual for the Leggetts to celebrate Christmas by visiting from house to house, eating and playing for days at a time. I remember the Leggetts' love of singing. Daddy and Uncle Buster had fine voices and enjoyed singing old church hymns on cold, winter nights.

My memories of our early life included frequent moves from farm to farm. Despite the changes, each place felt like home. A younger sister, Brenda Kay, was added to our family on June 3, 1942. Daddy and Mother were sharecroppers, and it took several moves to finally settle on land owned by Eugene Permenter in the Cypress community. This remained their home until they built their own house in 1965. Mother lives there to this day.

Mother and Daddy were a true team. Neither one would sit down until all the work was done. If Mother was washing dishes, he was drying. If she was canning vegetables from the garden, he was there to tighten the lids. If he was planting cotton, she was there to fill the hopper. Mother was a great cook and she could take anything and make a great meal. Our meals centered around home-grown vegetables and her wonderful biscuits and cornbread. In the spring, we would have chickens we raised. We could hardly wait for the chickens to get big enough to kill. Daddy would ring off the head, pluck off the feathers and roll up newspapers to singe off the fuzz. Then Mother would take over and make her famous fried chicken. In winter, the family would kill two hogs and we would have salt pork as long as it lasted. Hog killing time was a great time. We were ready for some fresh meat and Uncle Buster and Aunt Pig, or Ma-mama and granddaddy Spraggins would come and help. It was an all-day job killing, scalding, and cutting the meat into sections. Some to be salted like bacon and hams, and other to be ground into sausage and then put into homemade sacks. Mother would make a stew with the livers, the lights, feet and head, which some enjoyed. Nothing was wasted.

Daddy taught us to love the different seasons of the year. He loved them all. He would point out birds that were migrating north or south. He knew the names of all the trees and wildflowers. He showed us how to fish for doodlebugs with broom straws and build frog houses. He loved all of nature and would pick up snakes and tell us not to kill one unless it was stealing the chicken eggs. He taught us to love rain and even thunderstorms. Snow falling was a thing of joy even though it meant he would have to bring in more coal to keep the fire going. In those cold winters, we enjoyed skating as a family on the farm's pond. We had a good life with Mother and Daddy down the lane in the Cypress community. Our family, the Leggetts and Spraggins, Cypress Methodist Church, our friends in the community were the center of our life.

Leggett Home Life in the 30's and 40's
By: Uncle Tommy Howard Leggett in New Orleans, Louisiana

Louise, Doode, Evelyn, Litt and I lived with Mama and Daddy in the 1930's. I was born Sept. 8, 1926 so I was too young to work in the fields, but the others (except Litt) worked with Mama and Daddy. What I remember is that my mother was a rather tall woman. I don't remember much about her because I was ten when she died from an infection caused from her teeth. She dipped snuff. (Garret snuff that came in a small tin can.) Women visiting each other sat around dipping snuff. To dip they used a small brush made from a gum tree branch shredded on one end. They spit into a can near them. I think Grandma lived with us for a short time. She may be the woman you are referring to who spit in a can and never missed.

Our house was made of rustic boards with tongue and groove (weathered). On the inside, the floors were made of rough boards. The house had no windows in the front with a front porch across the house and two doors to go inside. The door on the right went into the living room. The door on the left went into one big bedroom. In the living room was an iron bed and chairs. The room next to the living room was the dining room with large table, bench and chairs, washstand (with pan and bucket for washing hands). There was also a bed in the dining room; a door lead out to the porch; the door was next to the washstand; this was the only door in the back of the house. In front of the washstand was a swinging door leading to the kitchen. The kitchen had a table with chairs and a large wood-burning stove. In front of the stove was a counter with a flour barrel on the end of counter. There were two windows in the kitchen; one window in the dining room, and one in the living room on the north side, and two windows in the bedroom on the southwest side. In the front yard was a large cedar tree next to the road.

In the back, outside of the house, was a barn with four stables, corn crib and hayloft, with a drive-through shed in the back of the barn. Close to the back of the house was a chicken house, and behind that, an outhouse. To the left of the back of the house was a smoke house.

On the south side of the house was a vegetable garden. Past the garden was a huge sweet gum tree, and in front of it was a horse pond. We raised hogs so the hog pen was near the gum tree and pond. It ran down to the corner where the roads fork near the church. We had two mules, Halley and Jack, and a wagon. One of the mules died and we replaced her with a gray mare, Maude, a Texas bronco we got from

Buster. These were the last animals we had on the farm.

We had lots of quilts because it was very cold in the house. Women got together at each other's house and had quilting bees. It was so cold that a bucket of water would freeze in the living room. The only heat we had was a wood stove and a coal stove we burned the last few years. In the summer, we woke up at daylight, but in winter, we woke up much later.

When I was real young, I went to Emerson School (walked there). Later, I went to Fruitvale when Emerson School closed. Litt and I went to Gadsden School for a short time, and I did not like it there so I caught the bus at Jewell's for Bells School, where I graduated.

We had a cat (can't remember its name) and I had a Terrier dog named Bobby.

Aunt Irene, Aunt Florence, Aunt Tint from Texas, Uncle Brad and Aunt Gertie came to visit us frequently. When Uncle Brad and Aunt Gertie lived near us, we would walk there to visit. When they moved a distance away, we would visit and stay overnight. At Uncle Brad's, we kids would have fun pulling buggies and riding each other in it. I don't know if it was our buggy or Uncle Brad's, probably his. Occasionally we ate goat that Uncle Brad raised. When Aunt Tint visited us, we rode to town in her Model T car (two seats). We bought our clothes at Rust's department store, and we did not buy many since we couldn't afford much. I had one long sleeve shirt, one pair of pants and a coat. We wore long underwear from October until spring. We bought our groceries from J.O. Boyd because we could charge and wait to pay when we got money from our crops. After Evelyn and Litt left, Daddy and I walked every night to Buster's to listen to the radio.

Most of our Christmas shopping was done on Christmas Eve. One Christmas Eve, the weather was so bad we had to put a tarp over the wagon to keep from freezing. As gifts, we got firecrackers, candy, nuts and fruit in brown paper bags. Daddy put these in a box under the bed and no one was to touch this box. We would sit around the fire and he would bring the box out and we'd eat candy, nuts, orange slices and candy corn. We really enjoyed Christmas so much. One year, my Christmas gift was a tin toy (Jumping Jack). Another Christmas I wanted a BB gun but Daddy couldn't afford to get me one. On Christmas morning I woke up, hoping to see my BB gun but was very disappointed when I had none under the tree. Daddy told me to go see Buster, that he had one for me. Our Christmas tree was a cedar we cut and decorated with strings of popcorn, colored rope, painted sweet gum balls, or whatever we could find. Christmas dinner was a big one with all the family there. We had chicken, roast, cornbread dressing, and all kinds of vegetables. The cakes were coconut, chocolate, banana, and jam and pies were apple, chess and cobbler, etc.

When weather permitted, we went to church. If there was preaching for a week, we went every night. I slept with Daddy after Mama died until I was drafted into the service, after graduation in 1945. I got out in 1946 and made a crop with Arthur. Daddy had sold the farm to Neil Webb and was living in Bells. I was very upset that Daddy had sold the farm to Neil. Doode wanted to buy the farm but Daddy would not let him since he did not think it was a good buy.

Uncle Tommy Leggett

The Rust Grocery Store and Joe Lewis Fights

Some of my earliest memories are of going to the grocery store that Ewell and James Rust had years ago. They had a "shotgun" structure that went straight back and narrow that sat on a small hill on Cypress Church Road. Sylvia Studdard lived across the road. It was about halfway to Bells and saved us a lot of traveling not having to drive all the way to town in the wagon with the mules. The main attraction for the men was the radio the brothers had in this primitive store. It had better reception than any radio in the community, although it had much static still. The nights Joe Lewis was fighting (it was broadcast on the radio), most of the community would congregate there to hear the fights. Now this was a very entertaining thing for the men and remember, there was not much back then in the way of fun or enjoyment.

The male population was very strict on us children on this special night. We had to stay outside and play so as not to interrupt the show. The women sat on the porch or in the yard and gossiped and swapped stories. We children loved to play in the dark and had many scary things we played on each other. Pretend monsters was a favorite and hide-and-seek could end up with the boys turning into ghosts or living dead people jumping out from behind the building or trees and scaring the girls into screaming fits. I often wonder now how much of this was actually terrifying or was it a pretend thing. Nevertheless, it produced much fun and frolicking. Sometimes we would walk all the way from our house and sometimes taking the wagon and picking up neighbors on the way. It was a wonderful way of keeping us all together and being close and taking care of each other and bonding as a community.

Daddy's Water Jug

On the trip to Louisiana, there were very few service stations to get something to eat or drink, so Mama and Aunt Louise would make sandwiches, etc. For water, Daddy had this unique water pouch; it was not glass nor plastic, but cloth. It was a special weave cloth that looked like a square of canvas but was very thick and waterproof. It had a spout to drink out of and a plug to stop this up. We hung it onto the front of Uncle Dutch's car and had water all the way, stopping to refill it when we saw a place to do so. We also used this in the fields. It hung on a tree limb or on the front of one of the cultivators.

Myrtle Leggett When Young

I have the most unusual nickname and I hesitate to write about it but was like a second skin when I was home growing up. Betty, my sister was older than me and she could not say "Myrtle" and skipped the Myr and started with the *T* and then just added sounds and called me "Turt." This was not so good as I got older but was impossible to change it at school when young, and with the family and friends at home, so "Turt" I was! My nephews called me, "Aunt Turt" and one still does and I kind of feel young when he calls me this now. Guess that name calling kind of comes and goes around like everything else. I know I always thought, How could my parents have named me Myrtle Rose? I really didn't like it much at all. It sounded so old-fashioned. But you see,

I was named after my two grandmothers, and now it is an honor to be called Myrtle Rose. The grandmothers' names were Lou Myrtle Forsythe Bailey and Rosa Belle Webb Leggett. Are they not noble-sounding names or what?

I know that this one will knock the socks off the youngsters in the family, but Saturday night was bath night at the Buster Leggett house. I don't mean that we did not bathe but one night a week, but this is the big night when we brought the old tin washtub in from the porch, piled up the wood in the old stove and heated dishpans full of hot water and actually "got in" the water and took a good scrubbing. The bad part was the number you got to actually get in the tub...I had # 1. Was I lucky or what? This was not because I was the best, prettiest or the smartest. Far from it! I was the first to take a bath because I was simply the youngest and smallest. (At the time that is.) Betty, then Mama, then Daddy were last. In between one Saturday to the next, we had a pan of warm water, soap and washcloth and did the best we could. In the winter Mama would not let us wash our hair often, saying it would make us sick to get our hair wet and then get cold too soon.

If you did get sick, and I mean anything in the whole world that could bring you down, you got a big dose of "castor oil" and that stuff was MEAN! It would make you so sick and feel so slick going down and have this icky feeling for a while after taking it. Believe you me, we tried our best to stay well in that house! If you had a cold, you got the usual dose of poison and your chest rubbed in Vicks salve with a bit of it put up your nose and in your ear. This was really made potent by placing a towel or rag on the stove to get it hot, and then place it on your greasy chest. Lesson for the day...Stay well!

Frank Moore and I grew up together and he was (I'll have to admit) a lot younger than I. I pretty much ruled the twosome unless his mother was around and she doted on that boy. We "swapped out" work with his family so we would have someone in the fields with us. We were chopping cotton right by the house one day when Frank was about half as high as his hoe, and the cotton was very grassy and his dad was bent over just working so hard cutting the grass out of the cotton stalks so careful as not to damage the stalks. He was going right on down that row slowly and concentrating on his job and not watching Frank. Well, old Frank did not take much liking to the grass because it was so thick, so he just came behind his dad with his hoe and chopped the cotton stalks down, and I mean every one of them! I was sure glad that I was three rows over helping Mama. I guess you could call this deed the "Real Chopping Cotton Event."

Mary Ann Mayhall and I were the same age and our mothers were double-first cousins. She was also a very dear friend to me. When we were in school, she would sometime come and stay a week or so with us because her school had different schedules because of our cotton-picking turnout that they didn't have. When we were about 5 years old, we were in the field with my parents and playing at the wagon and discovered axle grease on the wagon wheels. We smeared our faces and arms and any uncovered parts of our bodies with it. When Mama came up to us, she got so mad! I had never seen my mom that mad. You see, axle grease is one of the hardest things to get off your skin and maybe never out of your clothes.

Frank and I had this little game we played where we would dig holes in the bank by the road close to snake holes because the dirt was already turned enough, you could make a really big hole in a hurry. Well, one day we really dug a major hole and dug up these little speckled eggs and were just delighted. They could be dinosaur eggs, alien eggs or anything! We took them to my mom and she announced that we had some genuine snake eggs. We were still delighted and she suggested we bury them in the garden and see what happened. I still do not know if she thought they would actually hatch but actually hatch is what they did! Little, green, slimy things that I thought were awful but old Frank, he sort of liked them all.

To each his own!

Old Frank Moore

Mama Pig...Daddy Buster

Everything seems to be about Mama. This is because my daddy died so young at 40 years old. He never saw any of his grandchildren. Betty was expecting Steve, but by the time Mama told him this, it was probably too late. We hope he understood her but can't be sure. He was a very nice-looking man. He always wore overalls and a hat. (Not a cap.) An everyday hat that was shaped like a dress hat, but either straw or khaki. He also had a round hard hat that looked like a turtle. Mama always had him a clean, starched and ironed pair of overalls for church. He always looked clean and neat. Everyone says Jody looks like Joe and he does, but I can see my daddy in him in looks and gentle ways. He liked to fish as much as Mama and Daddy Jim. We would go to a place on the Mississippi River called Dee Webbs. The dirt was black as tar and when wet, it would stick to your shoes in huge clumps. Sometime suction would cause the mud to suck your shoes right off your feet! There were huge cypress trees lined up on both sides of the slough with knees high and low and so close together you would have to pick your way through them to get to the water. Daddy hung this huge catfish but the big fish got hung up in the knees and Daddy jumped in the water and brought this oversized fish up with his bare hands! He was overjoyed! We have a picture of him in his overalls, cigarette in his mouth with his hat and this unbelievable, joyous expression on his face. Now what do you think this picture is worth? Millions would not buy this one! The whole family and sometimes community would travel to this backward, muddy hole and have a day of fishing, picnicking and loving every minute of it all. What is this place? Not much—but put the love and friendship of people and you have a vacation spot of all vacation spots. I've seen proof of this and it still lives in me sixty years later.

Cyrus Liburn Leggett

Cyrus Liburn Leggett (Buster), Mamie Elizabeth Bailey Leggett (Pig), Betty Ann Leggett, and Myrtle Rose Leggett – 1940

25 Acres Is All It Took

We always had a hard time making ends meet when I was growing up. I always heard my parents talking about this but never really grasped its meaning or realized how this affected me. I just knew that we were always taken care of somehow.

When Mama and her sisters married, they were given 25 acres as a dowery from Daddy Jim and Granny Bailey. This practice of the dowery had just about phased out by this time, but it really was a life saver for our family because we lived off this land for years.

When Mother and Dad first married, they moved into a small rundown house behind Ira Webb near the levee. I say they moved, but they didn't have any furniture and slept on a pallet on the floor. My sister Betty was born there. Once when Daddy Jim and Granny visited them, he said, "Sally, we might ought to buy them some pillows!" I am sure this would have been a great improvement on their lifestyle then. It hurts me to think of my lovely parents living under such conditions. I know now it was not an uncommon situation for the times, but nonetheless, it sounds like a nightmare, but it wasn't to them. I know for a fact they loved each other with all their hearts and didn't realize half the things they were distained to endure but were still always happy together.

Some years we managed to pay most of the bills; the grocer, druggist and banker never called in our loans, but gave Daddy some slack, for they knew he would pay them as soon as he could. There was never a contract or anything put up for collateral, nor any signed papers. Just a handshake was all they needed to seal the deal. We could not get any insurance because of my dad's diabetes; then our banker stepped in and found a company to insure him. In just a few months, he entered the hospital, never to come home alive again. The money from the insurance paid off all debts and the hospital, and it was a lifesaver for my mom. The town of Bells and the Cypress Community took care of their own and had more than "A Few Good Men." Try to borrow money now on a handshake and you would probably be laughed out of town.

A Peek at the Leggetts in the Forties

Daddy smoked a lot and I believe that is one thing that killed him so young. He was only forty years old. I know that people back then did not have the longevity that we have now, but forty is still young by anyone's standard. He rolled his own cigarettes. He would take out the thin, oblong tissue papers and open a can of Prince Albert tobacco and roll a pinch of it in the paper, then lick the length with his tongue to "seal it up." He was ready to go with a brand new cigarette. Even at a young age, I knew that this was not good. This was before any surgeon general warned against them. He had this hacking cough that was not normal. I have his last can of Prince Albert and it surely brings back memories of my dad.

And with this habit, he had diabetes. This was a very bad thing to have in those days. He had to take three shots of insulin a day, sometimes having to give them to himself if Mama was not close by. Mama had to test his urine every night to see if he was getting enough or too much medicine. Back then, the insulin was not perfected and not as effective as it is now. The way she tested his urine was to take a sample in a test tube and burn this pill that looked like what we called a horse pill, set the pill on fire, then get the urine hot; and if it turned yellow, he needed to have his insulin in a bigger dose; and if it turned green, he needed to have less. This made for a primitive way, for him to stay healthy. A jam and biscuit usually took care of too much medicine.

It was my job to go to the field with Daddy and keep check on him. I rode the cultivator, planter, harrow or whatever he was pulling behind the mules. If he got sick, he sent me running to the house for his medicine or a jam and biscuit, whichever he needed. I was so frightened! I had been drilled and drilled on how important this job was. Sometimes we were on the other side of the levee in the bottom and I had to cross the creek that sometimes had lots of water, and somehow I would find a high place to wade through. I did a lot of jumping over that old creek. That trip seemed like miles to me, running as fast as I could and then some.

I loved the outdoors even back then. The trees, flowers, the garden and yard...but I never did get any good at milking the cow. I did not like to drink milk then, and I think it was the smell of the hot milk and the barn odors that did it.

We had this old bird dog that Daddy had trained to hunt quail, rabbits and squirrels. His name was "Old Dan." He was very big for a dog and maybe he looked so big to me because I was so young. He was white with caramel spots. He slept in the room where the "pot-bellied stove" was because he was so old and stayed cold all the time. I would try to ride him like a horse and he just took it and was so gentle. Daddy did lots of hunting to put meat on the table. The game meat gave us a change from the pork, which was our staple meat. We had beef only on holidays and special occasions. Mama cooked the rabbits, quail, and squirrel and made this yummy Brunswick stew. She would take the leftovers and can them for a later meal.

CERTIFICATE OF MEMBERSHIP
IN THE

Gibson County Electric Membership Corporation

A TENNESSEE CORPORATION

This is to Certify that *Buster Leggett*

is a member of the Gibson County Electric Membership Corporation, a Tennessee corporation, and is entitled to all the rights and privileges and is bound by all the duties and obligations of membership therein, as defined and set forth in the charter and by-laws of said corporation.

This certificate may be transferred and assigned under the terms and conditions set forth in the by-laws.

In Witness Whereof, the Gibson County Electric Membership Corporation has caused this certificate to be signed, sealed and delivered by its president or vice-president and its Secretary this 21 day of Oct. 1945

Travis James
Secretary

President—Vice-President

Gibson County Electric Membership – Buster Leggett, 1945

Leggetts Continue New Year's Tradition

The Leggett and Bailey families gathered at the home of Mrs. Elizabeth Leggett for their annual New Year's Day dinner.

The family regretted the absence of Mrs. Edith Smith who suffered a broken shoulder in a fall. Those joining Mrs. Leggett for blackeyed peas and hog jowl were: Mr. and Mrs. Joe Emerson, Mr. and Mrs. Jody Emerson, Mrs. John Hart, Mr. and Mrs. Russell Cooke, Mr. and Mrs. Steve Cooke, Jennifer and Sara, Mr. and Mrs. Richard Cooke, Mr. Barry Cooke, Mr. and Mrs. Arthur Bailey, Mr. and Mrs. Jimmy Wheeler, Mr. and Mrs. Arthur Wheeler, Mr. Bob Cozart and Robert, Mrs. Louise Woodson, Dr. and Mrs. Ray Woodson, Woody, Beth and Meg, Mrs. Virginia Leggett, Mrs. Roe Nell Hughes, Mrs. Hallam Lowery, Mrs. Olive Spraggins, Mrs. James Buford, Mrs. Jo Goodwin, Mr. and Mrs. Milton Wiley and Brittany, Mrs. Sybil Holt, Mr. Ronald Holt, Miss Bennie Faye Leggett, Mr. and Mrs. Merlin Leggett, Mr. and Mrs. Malcolm Emerson, Mrs. Locart, and Mrs. G.H. Hart.

Description of one of mama's community dinners

Buster's dog, Old Dan

Leggett Neighbors and Kinfolk

Mrs. Etta Evans and Miss Pearl were close neighbors of ours. Their house was right across the road from the Edwards by Cypress Church. These two ladies would have possum suppers for the neighborhood. Now the women of the community did not take to possum cooking (or eating as a matter of fact). It seemed this delicacy was for men only. These two ladies would cook up a huge pot of possum stew and won the hearts of the men folk. I remember coming home across the field from one of these "social affairs" and getting very sleepy. It was snowing lightly and very cold. My daddy picked me up and was carrying me and Mama said, "Buster, you know she is too heavy for you to be carrying around." and he replied, "I don't care." Now that is love! See why he was one of my favorite people in the whole world!

Mr. and Mrs. Cook lived in the house where Greg Spraggins lives now. They were well off compared to the rest of the community, and Mama made a little money making pies and cakes for them and giving Mrs. Cook home permanents. Do you remember the Tony perm? Am I telling my age here?

My Uncle Walter, I knew as my Granddaddy Leggett, lived in the old house that stood where Neal and Elizabeth Webb's house is now. Their grandson lives there now. I remember three houses being on the same spot of land. Granddaddy's, Neal's and now Vince McGee had rebuilt it into a wonderful modern home.

The original house had two main rooms and a lean-to back behind the kitchen and a long front porch along the front. I remember one of the older women in the family sitting on that porch in a rocking chair with her snuff under her tongue; she would go back and forth in the rocker, spit in a tin can on the edge of the porch and never get a drop anywhere but in that can. If this were a sport, she would get a "Gold Medal" for sure. I really thought she was something. Wish I could remember her name.

Pearl Acosta Leggett, wife of Uncle Tommy, is a very talented artist. She painted on Jackson Square some and did streetcar scenes to sell. They live in New Orleans. Aunt Pearl painted a picture of the old Leggett homeplace for me that is so beautiful. She had a photo to paint from, but she also remembered the home and made it come alive with memories. My Uncle Tommy's memories of this homeplace is included in these writings.

Neal and Elizabeth Webb lived across the road on the north side of the church in a square house with all four sides meeting in a point in the center. They lived here before moving to the Leggett Homeplace. There was a porch all across the front.

Joe Emerson, Bill Williams, Louise Woodson, Tommy Leggett, Pearl Leggett, and Lydia Williams - Lydia, Louise and Tommy are my dad's brother and sisters

Women in the Leggett Family...Their Little Indiscretion

The women in the Leggett family were a lively and clannish bunch. They really had fun together and were a lot like a bunch of teenagers when they were at each other's house. They hardly had just one or two over but whole families and all of them that could get to the hostess' gathering. The men would go to the porch after dinner (lunch now) and talk farming, fishing, and sports while the women washed the dishes and discussed menus, recipes or sewing, etc. After the kitchen was clean again, they would go into the living room and settle down and have a "coke." Children are usually not fooled by adults like they think, and we saw the little something being poured into the glasses with the Coca Cola and ice. We could drink from the bottle, but never from the glass.— Fishy, huh? I thought so, too. Things would get a little lively after that. Now I'm not saying they all did this because I know they didn't. I can only let you guess on this one. This is my little game to add to a rather dull paper. Putting two and two together, and I came up with an answer that may or may not be correct. Anyway, it was a fun thing at the time.

The Leggett Girls - Elizabeth, Louise, Virginia, Eunice, Evelyn, and Jewell

A New House for Daddy Buster and Mama Pig

I don't remember building the new house. I was still a toddler when it was completed. The old gray- boarded house we were living in was only two rooms. No closets or anything obstructing the four walls but a door and two windows. One room was used for the living, bedroom and for bathing. The other room was for the kitchen, the pot-bellied stove and the cookstove with a big wood box. There was no running water nor bathroom or any luxury at all, so we were in dire need of a new house.

All the lumber for this house was milled at Daddy Jim's sawmill and brought there on wagons with mules or horses down the dirt road. A neighbor and friend helped Daddy build this house. His name was Mr. Clinton Moore, who had some experience with building, but Daddy had none. They built the house themselves and took great pride in their finished product and, indeed, it was a "looker" for the days and being so clean and convenient for my parents, my sister and me.

The kitchen had actual cabinets for Mom's dishes, pots and pans, not to mention shelving for her many, many cans of home processed vegetables, and yes, even meats. Her stove was cast iron but did not have the pretty porcelain extras but was, nonetheless, effective in putting out the most succulent foods. There was room for a kitchen table and chairs that Mom found second hand somewhere and it was a beauty.

We had two bedrooms, a living room, dining room, and a back and side porch. No bathroom until two years after I married, and no electricity until I was 8 or 9 years old; however, we did not miss this because we had never had it. You know the old saying:

"you never miss the water until the well runs dry." This is also true in reverse, which you never miss what you have never had.

We had the usual pot-bellied stove in the big bedroom and Mama's one try at beautiful was a built-in china cabinet in the dining room that was her pride and joy as far as decorating goes. That was about it when it came to something just for pleasure and beauty that she had.

The floors were wood and covered in the usual vinyl rugs that we bought at U-Tote-Em store in Bells. The back porch was screened in, and we had an old table to eat on in the summer to get away from the heat of the wood cookstove. The icebox was on the porch with a hole bored in the floor under the icebox. A tube was placed in the hole, and the water drained under the house where the pets drank in the summer from the melted ice. The icebox was wooden with a zinc lining to better keep the ice from melting so fast. The iceman came once a week and brought enough ice to last the week if we were careful how we used it. We had an ice card that hung by the screen door with an arrow pointing to the number of pounds of ice we wanted. This metal arrow was on a heavy cardboard that had numbers around the edge much like a clock that pointed to the desired size of ice; this was a luxury to us. The iceman also sold packets of kool-aid. Yes, almost like the ones your kids buy now. It sometimes could be a worry because Betty and I very seldom wanted the same flavor, so Mama would have to give us alternating weeks to choose the flavor we wanted.

As my sister and I grew, the house got smaller; and Daddy closed in the porch on the side of the house, making another bedroom and later boxed off the attic into two small bedrooms for us girls with a huge closet in between.

Sometime later after we had been in the house for a few years, we got running water and electricity. The hot water came even later after I was married when the small back bedroom became, wonder of all wonders, "a bathroom with hot and cold water."

Progress came slow in the country, but usually came nonetheless, and a few years of roughing it never hurt anyone. My dad always said it built character and he ought to know, he had plenty of that!

Looking back, the old house we had when I was a toddler was a boarded house that had never been painted—You might say when we built the new home that we now live in "A Painted House."

An original ice card

World War II – Happenings

I can barely remember a few things about World War II. We were involved directly with this because my dad's brother, Uncle Raymond, was fighting for our country then. I do recall bits and pieces of things that were going on in our household at that time, although I was small.

Uncle Raymond was in the thick of things in Europe and knew he would be gone for quite a while, and he and his wife were living in Louisiana and he thought she would be better off with us. She came to live with us during his tour of duty, which was about three years.

The old tall radio stood by the bed in the den and the coal stove was in the bedroom. Each night we turned it on to the nightly news. Gabriel Heater would come on and say his famous greeting, "Well, there's good news and bad news tonight!" Aunt Eunice promptly started to cry, and I usually put my head under the covers to try and shut out the grave scene going on around me. I would worry about my uncle and could not for the life of me figure out why men would shoot and kill each other when they did not even know who they were or even speak the same language!

Aunt Eunice was Cajun, Louisiana stock, and a very beautiful woman that we all loved from the day Uncle Raymond married her. He knew this and I am sure is one reason he wanted her with us while he was gone. Aunt Eunice talked with a brogue that I thought was worldly and grand because I had never heard anyone talk any way but our long, drawn-out southern drawl.

Aunt Eunice did not help in the fields but contributed her part of the workload in the house. She was a great cook, introducing new dishes and flavors to our diet that we loved. She washed and ironed, made beds and cleaned house for Mama and really helped to keep the house going while we were in the fields. We have a picture of her outside the back door under the old willow tree with the washtubs and her hair all tied up with a head scarf working away. She has her hands in the tub with the old washboard and Ivory soap.

There were no women like her in my world and I watched her very closely. Being so beautiful, she worked very hard on her looks and appearance. She would wash her face in hot water and soap and then put ice slivers on it to "close the pores." A procedure that was alien to me because we "country people" at that time had never heard of opening and closing pores.

When Uncle Raymond came home from the war, he brought three of his buddies from New York to our house for a few days. This really was an eye-opener for us to meet someone all the way from New York. It was like having company from the "moon" to us then. These boys were on their way home and we were a rest stop for them on the trip.

It was in the summertime and we always ate at a table on the back porch to get away from the heat of the cookstove in the kitchen. Now these three boys had very different ways from us. They did not pass or ask for anything on the table. If they wanted something, they got out of their chairs and walked around the table to get it. This habit did not sit well with Mom. They also said they had never seen anyone eat lard and flour and water before. This meant thickened gravy after frying the chicken and it may have been alien to them, but they could sure put away those biscuits with that "strange stuff" ladled on top.

*Aunt Eunice Leggett
"Washing up" the clothes*

Sour Kraut and Willow Limbs

I will have to admit that my mom did most of the discipline in our family. My dad did a lot of talking to us girls but not a lot of putting pressure where pressure hurt. But there are always times when things do not follow a given path; one of those times was when I was about eight years old. I had come home from school and gotten off the bus and must have had a bad day because Daddy told me to go down the lane in front of the house to the neighbor's house. Mama was helping to make sour kraut with the cabbage before it ruined. I just simply stated that I was not going down there because they had some boys there that I was afraid of. Daddy just turned around and went to the old willow tree in the backyard, cut a limb and popped that willow branch right where it hurt the most. It shocked me more than it hurt, and the hurt was more from the shock because my daddy simply had never done such a thing to me before. It didn't take me long to go running down that lane and I never said "NO" to my dad again.

I now have willow trees from this infamous plant. When Joe and I married, I took a cutting from it and planted it in my backyard and it grew to great proportions. It was a beautiful thing to see, but a storm came through and knocked it over by the roots. I took cuttings from it and set some out again and they grew and grew. When we built the new house, I brought cuttings from this grandchild of the first tree and set them out here and had a huge one in my back yard, BUT the poison the farmers put on the cotton drifted over and made the willow sick so I immediately cut trimmings and put in water that soon rooted. Now Jody has set some of these in his tree farm land and they are doing nicely. I have one left in the yard that is not doing as well, so this next spring, I will cut some of the third generation of the species and have a fourth one as the baby. We set some out in Mississippi for Shane near the lake, close to the water, and they were a sight to behold until the eager beavers got hungry and cut them down. I simply must get some more twigs down there soon! Get those "seeds still growing" down there!

Bitter Weeds and Other Weeds

This looks like such a trivial subject but, believe me, back when I was growing up, it was a big problem with these *Bitter Weeds*. We depended so much on the cow because we could not get to town for milk and couldn't afford to pay the price for it. We needed the milk to drink not only for our health but for cooking. When you look at recipes, you can see the importance of this one ingredient.

The pasture where the cow and the horses stayed was not a big affair but very essential to our well-being. The horses were our salvation in the fields for cultivation, the wagon for transportation, and the cow for food, so keeping the pasture was a big deal. Keeping out the *Bitter Weed* was not an easy task. We had no sprays that killed unwanted weeds and grasses like we have today. The *Bitter Weeds* had to be either pulled up by hand or kept mowed very low to keep them from spreading.

When the cow got into a patch of these troublesome weeds, her milk would be bitter and we could not drink or cook with it. It was a constant battle with the invasion of the weed.

Also, there was the *Johnson Grass* that was very aggressive and hard to eliminate and, of course, the ever present *Crab Grass* that we were constantly chopping out of the cotton and corn fields. Then, too, the old *Cocklebur* was a demon. It seemed you chopped out one and five grew in its place.

Weeds may sound boring and an unnecessary topic for discussion, but in the forties and fifties, they were a big factor in our lives and took up a lot of our days trying to eliminate them.

Daddy Buster
Singing Talent in the Family

Singing runs in my family but, alas, it totally skipped me and I did not get an ounce of talent for singing. My dad, called Buster, sang such a beautiful tenor. He sang in a quartet with Mr. Charlie Porter, Annie Lou Brasfield and Dorothy Porter. Annie Lou played the piano and they sang at church. On Sunday afternoons, especially in the summer months, they would go around to the different churches and sing all afternoon with other quartets, solos and duets. Families from all around would come to hear them. It did not matter what denomination the church was or who you were, everyone was there for entertainment and to see other friends and family. They went as far as Halls and all the little churches all around. Mama, Betty and I would go with him and lots of Sundays had dinner on the ground before the singing began.

I had never heard Shane sing before, and someone told me how well she could sing and I thought they had their wires crossed. Then I heard that in New Orleans she had been on the stage to sing Patsy Cline's *"Walking After Midnight"* and did a believable impression of her. (And we think we know all about our children.) Then Jody sings at church and I have been told is very much like hearing his Grandfather Buster. He loves his church songs. Then Kayley got up in church when very small and sang (I was told) beautifully and have seen Rebecca singing. Her voice is very high soprano, especially for her to be so young. No one plays the piano yet, but Rebecca shows signs of maybe playing when she gets a little older.

When I was about 5 years old until my dad died, we had cousins from Haywood County that had a band and would come on Saturday night and play for family and neighbors. Homer Castleman and his family played guitar, keyboard, fiddle and more instruments; they were very good. There would be so many people in our house that you had to sit on the floor or stand up because the older people used the sitting space. The floor would be so trashed that you could not walk without your shoes. Popcorn, peanut hulls and this all stuck together with cake or candy or anything else that the women brought in. Mama would cook for days if she knew they were coming. After Daddy died, I lost contact with all of them and think of them with affection when I do. It's strange that you are so close to someone and when the connection that puts you together is gone, they seem to fade in the past.

Then there were the possum suppers that Miss Etta Evans and Pearl had for the community. Actually, this supper was mostly for the men because not many of the women would eat it. Have you ever seen a bunch of possums simmering on the stove in a big pot of boiling water and whatever? It is not a pretty sight! (Nor a pretty smell or thought) But—this was another way for the people to get together and talk and laugh and give each other encouragement in a hard way of life on the farm at the time. Remember there was no TV's, telephones, email, and few could afford to go to the movies; and if you did, you rode in a wagon, usually full of cotton. Older people could not endure these bumpy uncomfortable rides, even if the children loved it.

Cyrus Liburn Leggett (Buster) and Mamie Elizabeth Leggett (Pig)

The Leggett Boys – Dutch, Tommy, Raymond, Walter and Buster

The Buster Leggett Family – Betty Ann, Mamie Elizabeth, Cyrus Liburn and Myrtle Rose

Check signed by Buster Leggett

The Christmas Duck
By: Allyson Webb Wimberly

I was asked to write a term paper on the best Christmas present ever in English Comp 101. Oh, please, I thought. I hate pressured writing assignments. It had to be completed before I left my college classroom that day. I quickly remembered something more incredible than that box filled with my favorite blue sweater from Aunt Amy or a beautiful hand-sewn Christmas stocking that Aunt Sarah made just for me. My mind was filled with wonderful family memories. Times seemed so much simpler then. Everything seemed bigger also. The hills in the country, the trees that we climbed and got stuck in seem to have shrunk in some sci-fi kind of way. I guess it always seems that way when looking back to more youthful days. I remember a special Christmas, one that none of us will ever forget. It was much too incredible.

The year was 1975 on Christmas Eve. The place - Maw and Paw's farm. All together, there were more than 20 of us! Oh, the anticipation....the tasty turkey and dressing, the brightly wrapped presents, and the fact that Santa was coming soon made Christmas Eve the event of the year. It was tradition in our family for Uncle Gene to "guesstimate" how many more miles that Santa had to travel to reach us there in Cypress. "399 miles away!!!" he replied. Oh, my, I thought, we have got to hurry with the rest of the festivities. I began to gather all of the children around with great excitement because I knew that in order to get home and to bed pretty fast, we had to shoot all the fireworks! This was a Webb tradition. No Christmas was complete without the fireworks! "Bundle up in a big coat, put your toboggan on your head," the moms yelled to all of the children. And out the door we went. Uncle Trent manned the fire as we proceeded with the beautiful display of Roman candles firing. They were booming into the winter sky when suddenly a duck descended from the sky and fell right in front of us! (We thought that she might have come straight from Heaven.) Just a regular 'ole brown duck. She was just sitting there. (Slightly dazed.) We were looking at her and she was looking at us. Of course, we ARE Southerners (by the grace of God) and thought she might be hurt or something. We showed the little duck some hospitality. Brad, my uncle, took her into the house and fed the poor little creature. No tellin' how long she'd been flying. We fed her anything and everything we had to spare. She warmed herself by the fire. As if to repay us for our kindness, she danced a little jig about the floor and flapped her wings with excitement. I think she even smiled.....I know I did. We returned the Christmas duck to the midnight sky. With one gentle lift from Uncle Trent, the sweet creature left as swiftly as she came. Every adult and child had a bright glow about them that Christmas Eve. I even remember Paw's face was especially beautiful that night. Paw wasn't one to show his emotions too often. He was from the old school - no emotions. He was a farmer and a sharecropper in his early life. A simple man. He wore overalls and chewed Bull's Eye tobacco. Every Christmas, he dressed in a red suit and gave candy to children in our local town. I thought that bearded man looked familiar. It was his eyes. They twinkled and were a mirror to my soul. I have those same eyes.

That Christmas duck commemorated Paw's last Christmas with us, and memories of that year are etched in my mind and heart forever. They have been a source of comfort as the years have passed. Through divorces, deaths, family feuds, and all the other things that occur in families with the passage of time, this memory sustains me. It tells me of good times and the way things should be. It gives me hope for the future as I pass along this very story to children of my own. Because I am the oldest grandchild and the self-proclaimed historian of the family, it is my job to pass the love along. When we gather around the Christmas tree every Christmas Eve, someone always remembers to tell the story of the special little visitor and the memories we hold dear of our Paw. This, too, has become a family tradition.

Appreciation of Santa
By: Myrtle Rose Leggett Emerson

Allyson Webb Wimberly is a cousin of mine on my dad's mother's side. Rosa Belle Webb Leggett and Brad Webb were brother and sister. In other words, Allison's great-grandfather and my grandmother were brother and sister.

The story she wrote is about her grandfather, Nelson Webb, that played Santa at Cypress Church for years about the time that my children were growing up. He was, indeed, the perfect Santa with his booming voice roaring into the church where the children were all stretching their little necks for a first look at Santa and their young faces bright with expectation. They were not disappointed when the jolly figure leapt into the room, waving and smiling and Ho-Ho-Ho! He knew just the right moves and expressions that the role called for. The children lined up for their turn to sit on Santa's lap and divulge all the toys and wishes to the jolly old man without a doubt that these goodies would appear under the tree on Christmas morning. It was a talent that Nelson Webb had and though many did not know his real name, they nonetheless remember the Santa that came to every Christmas program at the Cypress Methodist Church. Thank you, Mr. Nelson Webb. We love you.

One of Myrtle Rose's Santas

CHAPTER 5

The Early Bailey Family

The first Old Bailey Homeplace - Nathaniel, Sarah Dilafate, John, Jim Crow, Don in wheel chair, and Marie. Aunt Bettie Bailey is on porch pregnant and was not considered "right" for her to be forward in the picture.

Nathaniel Columbus Bailey

Nathaniel Columbus Bailey "Old Nate"

Daddy Jim's father was named Nathaniel Columbus and was called "Old Nate." Old Nate owned the first cotton gin around and at this day in time, I am sure it was very primitive. It was situated by the old Liberty Hall Schoolhouse near the curve going to the Bailey homeplace. At times Old Nate would be short of hands to run the gin. On one such day, Old Nate told Delifate (his wife) that he would have to take Ira McKinley (their fourteen-year-old son) to help with the ginning that day, and the husband and wife had words because the boy's mother thought he was too young to be around the heavy machinery and expressed her feelings to her husband. The boy's father sent him on to do a man's work that day, and while working on one of the machines, his sleeve got caught in a big belt and pulled him into the gin and killed him. Grandma never got over this tragedy and never really forgave Grandpa as long as they lived. Grandpa then shut down the gin and never started it again. Deliphate never forgave her husband for this accident and grieved for the rest of her life. This was natural, but also you have to think of Old Nate living with his grief over the loss and the guilt of being the instigator of the catastrophe.

The Liberty Hall Schoolhouse that sat next to the gin was used for schooling but also as a Community Center and family gatherings and picnics. Nathaniel donated this land for the school and said, "It would belong to the community as long as the school stood and was used for the good of the people and then would revert back to the Bailey family." He donated this land in the late 1800's to the school and it stood until just a few years ago. I went to all the meetings, reunions and dances they had there when I was very young, and my dad was still alive at the time.

Old Nate was a hustler. He went to Jackson for parts for the cotton gin and came back with a dozen milk cows. He said the cows were starving to death and they would have plenty of milk for everything. Turns out,

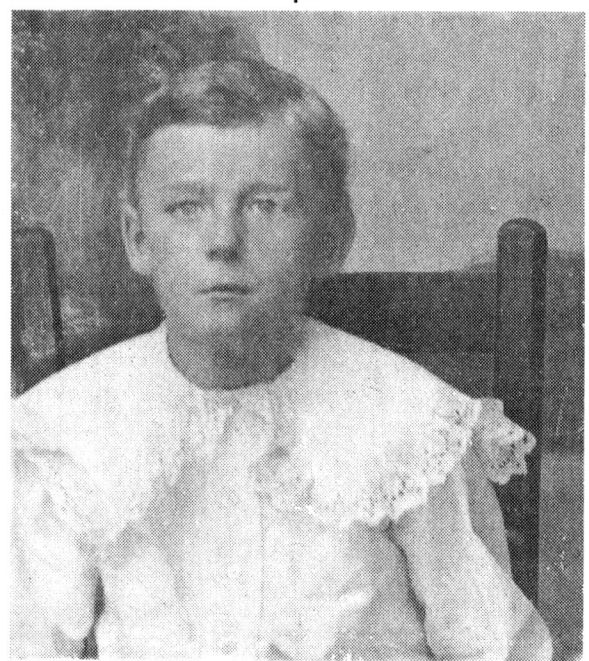

Ina McKinley – Killed in cotton gin at 13 or 14 years old

the cows were all dry as Delifate found out when she took the milk pail to the barn and tried in vain to get milk for their dinner.

Delifate worked all day and went to the pond behind the house at night by moonlight to wash the clothes in the pond water. Can you imagine how white the clothes were that were washed in the pond? And we complain about having to turn on our automatics! There was no electricity so they had no refrigeration. She took care of this by digging a hole under the house (the coolest place around) to keep her milk, eggs and butter cool.

Daddy Jim went to Nebraska to work the wheat belt. While working there, a snake bit him on the foot and blood poison set up. Catholic nuns nursed him and he was going to church with them. They said he could go a few miles down the road and there was a Methodist church. I guess they were giving him choices; even with this good care he almost died from this bite.

Grandpa N. C. Bailey wore a large belt around his waist and carried all his money on this belt. He did not trust banks. Was he smart or what? But can you imagine doing this every day? It is a wonder that someone didn't kill him, for I'm sure that many people knew he had this habit.

Nathaniel Bailey was a magistrate and his brother John put on his black suit and got his horse and two guns and rode into the Liberty Hall Schoolhouse and got onto a table at a meeting about someone running against Nathaniel.

Ike Bailey and his son, Jebeda, had a whiskey still on the Kentucky and Tennessee border. They ran a bootleg business somewhere in the woods there. They had a colored lady that helped them with the vats, and they had a disagreement with her and the boys killed her. Now, this was a really bad situation, so they "headed for the hills" in a different state and waited a few years, then came back and took up right where they left off. Where was the sheriff and his deputies and the posse that we saw so much in the movies? Guess they rode off into the sunset before their cue came in.

John Bailey, Aunt Bettie's husband, went to the *World's Fair in St. Louis* in 1904. He kept his money in his boot and bragged about it to a crowd of people. He got drunk, and somehow someone stole his money out of his boot. The next day, the *St. Louis newspaper* ran a cartoon of a drunk man with one boot on and one boot off, walking off with guns held up in the air. Newspaper headlines ran *The Man From Tennessee...Someone Stole His Money!*

Thomas Jefferson Bailey ran a bar around Little Rock, Arkansas. He left and went to Texas to live and came back to Tennessee in a covered wagon when Uncle Arthur was a small child. Uncle Conrad was teaching school at Cairo, and Uncle Thomas put on his cowboy boots, ten gallon hat, and guns in a holster. All his costume was authentic, coming with him from Texas. He went into the schoolhouse, raising his unloaded guns and told Uncle Conrad, "I've come after you!" Uncle Conrad was so scared he couldn't talk. You see, he didn't know who this person was because he had never seen him before and didn't realize that it was just a joke. It took awhile for him to know just what was going on!

Nathaniel Columbus Bailey had lots of money and his sons, John and Jim, had money, too. Lou Myrtle and Bettie Elizabeth Forsythe were poor and married Bailey Boys with money. John took bales of cotton to Fruitvale and sold it to get drunk.

John Bailey was asleep and woke up and called (Elizabeth) "Susan, Susan, Susan, why do you put up with me?" She replied, "Because you are my husband!"

Uncle John Bailey was reported to have been run over by a train not far up the tracks toward Gadsden from Fruitvale, but the story goes that someone had killed him before the train ran over him. This was not uncommon in those days for people to settle their own disputes in this way. There was not enough room in the small town jails and not many penitentiaries for the guilty. At times, men took things into their own hands while the law and others just looked the other way. I have heard several instances of this happening in and around Fruitvale many years ago. Nothing is ever proven, so nothing is ever done.

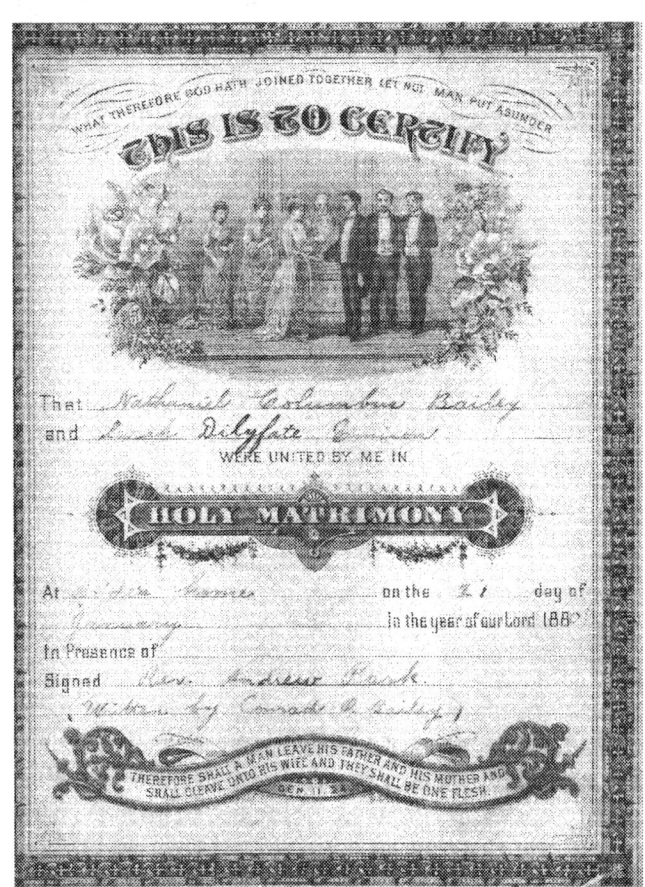

Bible page - Nathaniel Columbus Bailey and Sarah Dilafate Emison, married 01-21-1880

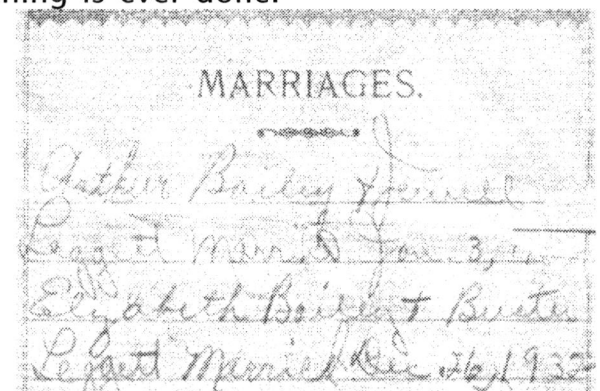

Marriages in Bailey Bible - Arthur and Jewell Bailey, 01-03-1919 Buster and Elizabeth Leggett, 12-26-1932

Bible page – James Arthur Bailey and Lou Myrtle Forsythe, married 12-25-1907

Bailey Bible Births – Arthur, Buhrl, Olive, Mamie, James, Lawerence, Edith and Dorothy

State and county tax for 1919 – Old Nate and Sarah Dilafate Bailey

Bettie Bailey's share in Old Nate's estate from J.A. Bailey

may 24 - 1919
Received of J.A. Bailey admr
one thousand and fifty five
dollars (1055.00)
also one hundred dollars worth of
war saving stamps
Bettie E. Bailey
Gardian for
Prudence & Marie Bailey
May 24. 1919

Payment to Bettie E. Bailey made in money and war bands for daughters, Pruedence and Marie

Application of Mrs. S. D. Bailey to have Commissioners to set aside Years Support to her as the widow of N.C.Bailey, deceased.

Let genner, Humboldt #9
Bud Boals   "
Arch ginzer.

Sarah Dilafate Bailey for support as a widow

RECEIPT FOR DIRECT INHERITANCE TAX COLLECTIONS.

State of Tennessee   County of Crockett

Received of J.A. Bailey N.C. Bailey adm

One Hundred Eighteen 40/100 Dollars,

being the Inheritance Tax on $ 118.40 ..., bequeathed by

N. C. Bailey

who died on

Feby 3   1919, leaving Land & Personal

to Wife & Children

$118.40

Jno. H. Perry

COUNTY COURT CLERK.

J.A. Bailey paid inheritance tax for Nathaniel Bailey's estate - 1919

$50.00   Alamo, Tenn. Oct. 16th.1921

Received of J.A.Bailey,administrator of the estate of N.C.Bailey, deceased, Fifty dollars in full for legal advice and services rendered in wining up said estate.

Legal services - J.A. Bailey for Nathaniel Bailey

Nathanial (Old Nate) Columbus Bailey and Sarah Dilafate Emison Bailey

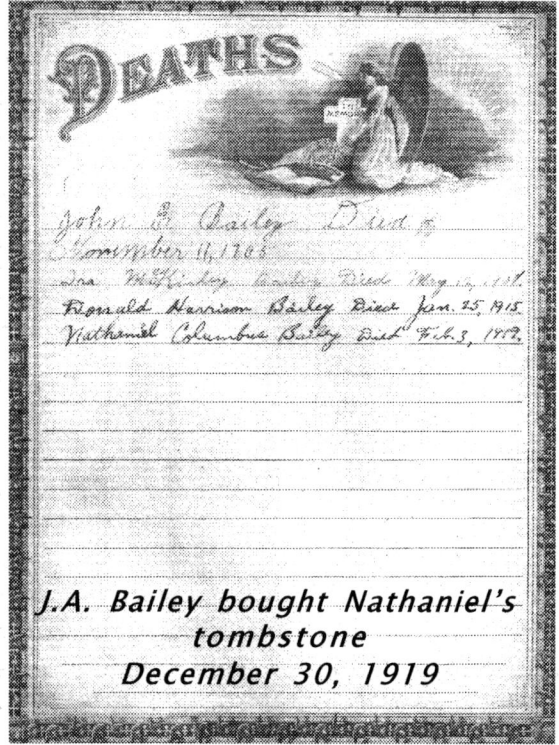

DEATHS

John E. Bailey Died
November 11, 1905
Ira McKinley Bailey Died May 12, 1911
Ronald Harrison Bailey Died Jan. 25, 1915
Nathaniel Columbus Bailey Died Feb. 3, 1919.

J.A. Bailey bought Nathaniel's tombstone
December 30, 1919

$ 9.98   MAR. 12   1930

On or before the   1st   day of   June   1930, I, we, or either of us, jointly and severally, promise to pay to the order of J. O. BOYD, FRUITVALE, TENNESSEE, the sum of

Nine & 98/100   DOLLARS

with interest thereon at the rate of six (6) per annum from June 1st of the year this Note bears date until paid; payable at the office of J. O. BOYD, in Fruitvale, Tenn. for value received in Fertilizers furnished by said J. O. BOYD for use on the farm of J.A. Bailey   in the County of Crockett State of Tenn.

The consideration of this Note is Fertilizers furnished by said J. O. Boyd as follows:

3 Sacks 10-5-10.   Sacks   Sacks.

Sacks Nitrate of Soda   Sacks

To be used under 4000 Cabbage plants on said farm

Due   June 1   1930
P. O. Address   Gadsden, R1

Fertilizer bought by J.D. Boyd from J.O. Boyd
March 12, 1930

*Liberty Hall School about 1933
Liberty Hall School was near
Bailey's Sawmill not far from
Gadsden
First row: Effie Mae Williams,
Evangeline Williams, Jim
Williams, Martha Ann
Spraggins, Genrose Spraggins
Second row: Catherine Davis,
Teacher, Hiawatha Williams,
James Alvin Williams, Frank
Williams, Jr., Larry Williams
Third row: Susie Daniel, Mary
Evelyn Ferguson, Clarence
Ferguson, Dorothy Bailey, ____,
Mary Daniel
Fourth row: Edith Bailey, Allene
Williams, Hershel Follis*

The Family
Aunt Cynthia (Crissy), the Sorcerer

We have all been in awe of the tales of magicians, witches and fortunetellers. We have always been led to believe that these people were just living in a dream world or trying to "pull one over on us." This has always been my belief that the tales were just that...tales. Then I began to hear these stories about one of my ancestors named "Aunt Crissy." I'm not sure of her last name. She was three generations before me, and I never saw her except in a picture and she is more vivid in my imagination with that image in my mind. I was told that this well-known older woman was a sorcerer or fortuneteller. She never had a crystal ball or sat in booths at a fair and read palms, but she predicted things flying in the air and going to different planets, when and how much it would rain, whether a woman was having a baby boy or girl and on what day. She was predicting these things with great accuracy and in detail. She always wore long, black dresses and bonnets and looked much older than she really was. She is in one of the old pictures of a Bailey Reunion at Liberty Hall School that was made in about 1903.

Bailey Reunion at Liberty Hall School House Front row: Evelyn Kenner, Louise Kenner, Effie Kenner, ____, Fredda Kenner, Addie Jo Kenner Second row: Jim's brother and wife (seated first couple), Dilafate, Baby Arthur, Old Nate, Sarah Winn, Emily Cynthia Kenner. Next row: Tom Bailey (behind Jim's brother and wife), Newton Bailey; Corner back: Jim, Myrtle Burhl (baby), John Bailey, Bettie Bailey, Granny

Row 1 seated: Evelyn Kenner, Louise Kenner, A. Jo Kenner, Effie Kenner, Freda Kenner, Alta Thomas, Marshall Kincade, John Kincade, Ewell Thomas ,Arthur Bailey (by last watermelon),

Row 2 seated:
Unknown, Naomi Kenner, Harlin Thomas, Counsil Forsythe, Marie Bailey
Row 3 seated:
Unknown, Effie Kenner Patterson, Unknown, Della Fay (Sarah Dilafate) Bailey, Sarah Winn, Emily Cynthia Kenner – rest of the row is unknown.
Row 4 standing:
Owen Winn, Grace Bledsoe, Ellen Bailey, Dera Bailey, Tom Bailey, Newton Bailey, Nathanial Bailey, Dan Kenner, _____ Kenner – rest of row is unknown
Row 5 standing:
Alma Kenner, Winn's son, Conrad Bailey, Bernard Thomas, Lula Bailey, Oliver Kenner, Alice Kenner, Dan Kenner, Mamie Bailey, Leslie Thomas, Jim Thomas

Dizzy Washington (Craig) Bledsoe Bailey

When it comes to the early Baileys, I am short on information that I can use. Tina Gray has done extensive research for me and has helped so much with this. The earliest story of an ancestor or ancestress is of Dizzy Washington Craig Bledsoe Bailey. This alone should have enough clues to help find this energetic lady. She is the basis for beginning stories of our family on this line. We found her parents to be Joseph and Cynthia Craig living in North Carolina. They had a large family with six or seven children, the oldest one being the said Dizzy. They migrated from North Carolina in the late 1830's across the Smoky Mountains into eastern Tennessee. This was accomplished by riding horseback and was bound to be a perilous journey with nothing but trails to follow, and then I am sure that there were places that even the trails did not exist. Census records show that the family was in Gibson County in the 1850 records. On this record Joseph was not recorded, so it was assumed that he either had died or left his family at some point. We know that Dizzy's mother Cynthia moved to Madison County, for there are records that show this move. How long they were in this space of time is not known, but Cynthia did bequeath a will, leaving land there to her children in 1867. We then come to Dizzy and her story. She was only 15 years of age when she married a Mr. Bledsoe. She was born in 1826, just a few years before the Civil War. She had two sons by this Mr. Bledsoe, making them young men at the time of this war, Joseph being born in 1842 and William Jefferson in 1844. Both of these boys fought in the war for the Union army. One, named Joseph, survived, but the brother William was wounded and sent to a hospital in Union City, Tennessee. He was serving in the 13th Calvary of the Union army when his wound brought on his death. I have included his death notice in the back of this book. Mr. Bledsoe died shortly after William was born, leaving Dizzy with the death of one son and one surviving.

The situation by this time did not look good for Dizzy Washington Craig Bledsoe, and it looked like she had a name to live up to! She was only in her teens still and had raised two boys on her own, so to speak, and after the war things were not so good for most of the people in the South, let alone a widow with boys to raise.

This is where Martin Luther Bailey appears on the scene. Not much is known about this ancestor before or after he married Dizzy, but we do know by records that they had a large family. The couple married on March 15, 1846. They had seven children: Emily Cynthia, Sarah Ann, Nathaniel Columbus [my direct ancestor being my great-great-grandfather] Mary Elizabeth, Samantha Adeline, Newton Warren and Thomas Jefferson. Several of my cousins' names have been chosen out of this group of ancestors. We have a Sarah, several Elizabeth's, and a Jefferson, to name a few.

We have one story with two versions of Martin Luther, one having been passed down to me by my grandmother and mother. This one will be called the family lore, but I have seen this story recorded this way by distant relatives but have not seen the old record of the other version until last week so I am recording both versions for you to see.

The lore version goes like this: Thomas Jefferson was a Union soldier. At the time he was killed, he had come home for a "furlough" to tend to business and see to his large family. While there, he hitched the horse to the plow and was getting the ground ready to plant and knew that being in Tennessee he would find many enemies close by, so to get the job done he thought he was playing it safe and dressed like a woman in a dress and bonnet. Southern bushwhackers saw him behind the horse and plow and came to the conclusion that he was indeed a man and shot him on the spot. It was Dizzy, who discovered him lying on the plowed ground behind the plow and dead with his bonnet beside him. At this time, all able-bodied men in Tennessee were expected to fight for the South in the war, thus making this a complex situation from the start.

Martin belonged to the Methodist church and owned a large farm in Madison County that later became Crockett County, this being the same farm that Dizzy and her two young sons moved to when she married Martin. The two boys were two and six at this time.

So that is the way the family has told the story over and over for the last one hundred fifty years or so. The other story is in the back of this book in document form. Totally different stories but the document is not official information. Judge for yourself what happened to Thomas Jefferson Bailey. Every family has a mystery. I cannot say that something told to me by my family is exactly what happened, but I do think that it has some merit somewhere in it.

It would be like the game, Gossip, where one starts out with a simple fact and it is whispered on down the line and the last one to "get the message" doesn't have a clue as to what originally started the trip from one to another until he got his version of the said fact.

After Thomas's death, a fact that I am sure of for its documentation, Dizzy was widowed at 37 with seven children and, let me tell you, she was "up a stump." After the war things were not really like we envision them. We see the movies where the plantation is a slum [*Gone with the Wind* and how we loved it all] and people wearing long dresses and lawn attire with umbrellas and white gloves. Not so for Dizzy. She has the farm and starts raising strawberries for the market and keeps the wolves at bay doing this, but, let me tell you right here, Dizzy Washington Craig Bledsoe Bailey by this time knows a lot about life and lived up to her abilities and was kind of a hero to me to have endured so much in such a short time. She lived up to her extremely prominent name and became the first woman in the family we really had a lot of information on and is not a disappointment to any of us, even though she could not sign her name but signed her will and all the documents we have on her with her "X," and I cannot for the life of me look in her life's story and see even a minute she may have had to go to school. Gumption and determination would cover her pretty well, in my opinion. She died in 1877 and her will, which follows this story, was probated in November of that year. She was 51 years old.

Last Will & Testament of Dizzy W. Bailey
Probated November Term 1877
Crockett County, Tennessee

Recorded: Will Book A, Pages 60-61

In the name of God amen, I Dizzy W. Bailey of the County of Crockett and State of Tennessee, being of sound mind and memory, and considering the uncertainty of this frail and transitory life, do therefore make ordain publish and declare this to be my last will and testament, that is to say,
First, after all my lawful debts are paid and discharged, I give and bequeath to my son Joseph M. Bledsoe, one half of a fifteen acre tract of land purchased paid for by me and deeded to me by W. I. McFarland, and bounded as follows (to Witt) on the north by the land known as the Elisha Raine's heirs, on the west by the land of T. H. Follis, on the south by the land of Allen William, and on the east by the land of Elijah Raines, and situated in the County of Crockett and State of Tennessee.
Secondly, I give and bequeath also to my said son, Joseph M. Bledsoe an equal share with the rest of my children in all my personal property.
Thirdly, I give and bequeath to my daughter, Emily C. Kenner, fifty dollars in cash over and above the rest of my children to be paid her by my Executor on account of her not receiving as much by that amount in the payment for a horse as the rest of my children to whom I have given horses.
Fourthly, I give and bequeath to my daughter Samantha, a gray horse she now claims, in addition to her distributive share with the rest of my children to make her equal with the others.
Fifthly, I give and bequeath to my son Newton W., the bay filly now claimed by him to make him equal with my other children in a distributive share of my property.
Sixthly, I give and bequeath to my son Thomas J., the Roan horse colt claimed by him to make him equal also with the rest of my children in the distributive share of my estate.
Seventhly, This will is made by me for the purpose of making all my children share and

share alike in my whole Estate.

Eighthly, It is my desire that my children not named above (to Witt) Sarah A., Nathaniel C., and Mary B., together with the rest above named shall share equally with them in the remainder of my Estate not mentioned above.

Att N.I. Hess	Her Mark
T. J. Hicks	Dizey X W. Bailey (Seal)

The above written instrument was subscribed by the said Dizzy W. Bailey in our presence and acknowledged by her to each of us and she at the same time published and declared the above instrument so subscribed to be her last will and testament, and we at the testators request, and in her presence, have signed our names as witnesses hereto and written opposite our names our respective places of residence.

Gadsden, Tenn .	Nelson I. Hess
Gadsden, Tenn.	T. J. Hicks

Court Minute Book B
1876–1879 – Page 299

Crockett County, Tennessee

J. W. Bailey
Administrator of
Bailey Dizzy Bailey

A paper writing purporting to be the last will and testament of Dizzy dec'd was this day produced in open court and the execution thereof was duly proved by the oath of N.J. Hess and R.J. Hicks, said will was ordered recorded. J.M. Bledsoe Executor named in said will failing to qualify, J.W. Bailey, on motion was appointed administrator of Dizzy Bailey, dec'd with the will annexed. Thereupon the said J. W. Bailey came into Court and entered into bond in the sum of one thousand dollars with T.J. Hicks and N.C. Bailey as his securities ————— Monday   3rd,   November   1877.

Gibson County Tennessee
Deed Book G

Joseph Craig
To Deed 100 ac
Daniel Cherry

Registered April the 19th 1841

This Indenture made and entered into this Twelfth day of March, One Thousand Eight Hundred Forty One between Joseph Craig of the County of Gibson and State of Tennessee of the one part and Daniel Cherry of the County of Haywood and State aforesaid of the other part. Witnessed that the said Joseph Craig for and in consideration of the Sum of Three Hundred dollars to him in hand paid by said Daniel Cherry before the signing sealing and delivery of the presents the Receipt whereof is hereby acknowledged that given, granted, bargained, and sold and by these present doth give, grant, bargain, and sell alien and convey unto the said Daniel Cherry his Heirs and assigns forever a certain tract or parcel of land lying and being in Gibson

County and State aforesaid containing 100 acres being the same whereon I now live and being the same that I purchased of one William B. Jones, agent for Henry A. Rutledge which is bounded on the south by a tract of land belonging to Margaret Boyd for fifty four acres of land and on the north by tract of land whereon Jonathan Williams now lives, which said Williams purchased of one Nathan Ingram and bounded on the east by a tract of land whereon J. Wesley Scott now lives and the tract of land called the Bledsoe tract for one hundred acres and bounded on the west by a five hundred acre tract called the Rhea or Brown tract of land. To have and to hold with all and singular the aforesaid described tract of land and bargained premises the rights, profits, hereditaments, and appurtenances of and unto the same belonging or in any wise appertaining to the same to the same to the only proper use and be hoof of him the said Daniel Cherry, his heirs executors administrators or assigns against the right title claim or claims of all and every person or persons whatsoever. In testimony whereof I have here unto my hand and affixed my seal the day and date written this 12ᵗʰ March 1841.

Attest   Joseph Craig (Seal)
Edward J. Reid
Benjamin F. Jones
Calvin W. Cherry
Benjamin C. Manning

State of Tennessee
Haywood County   Personally appeared before me Litttleton Joyner Clerk of the County Court of said county Benjamin F. Jones and Calvin W. Cherry Subscribing witnesses to the within and foregoing deed who being first sworn depose and say that they are acquainted with Joseph Craig the bargainer and that he acknowledged the same in their presence to be his act and deed—

Molasses

Daddy Jim and Grandpa (Nathaniel Columbus Bailey) put four horses on one wagon with kegs of molasses they had made and went to Eloise and Halls on the Mississippi River to sell. This took them at least two days, stopping for the night and feeding the horses and getting a little sleep themselves. They sold the syrup on the river banks where the boats would land and then to the people along the way and in the little towns jotted on the road. They sold it at home too and to the neighbors, friends and family. I don't have a record of their making it at a certain place or even the kind of molasses it was, but in all probability, it was sorghum. That was a favorite of everyone back then and still is for me and my family. I tease my grandson, Silas Austin, about it. He loves biscuits and this syrup on them. He will ask for some molasses and I will say, "Son, you can't have mo-lasses until you have had lasses!" This both entertains and frets him at the same time. Joe's Grandpa, Archie Goldsmith, made sorghum too. I saw him making this right after Joe and I married. He also made handmade brooms out of sagebrush and hand whittled handles on them. How I wish I had one of those brooms now.

Interview with Olive Guindeline Bailey Spraggins
By: Mary Annette Wheeler

Olive talked to me about not ever going anywhere when they were growing up. Before they got a car, she said they didn't go to church hardly at all until after (Daddy) Arthur married.

She said she was sickly...(asthma)...Graney and Daddy Jim didn't really spend time worrying about her. When she would visit the Lewis family, they would tell her to go outside if they were going to dust. Her teacher would send her in or tell her to soak her feet in warm water when she got home. These people realized she was not well. She didn't feel like eating a lot so she was skinny. She stated what she did like was white Karo syrup, so she would slip into the kitchen and get a spoonful.

Rosie Irene Jackson Lewis (Anna Cates' grandmother) died at 42 years of age. She is the lady that helped Olive when she was young and sick.

When she was growing up, if she wanted to go somewhere, she would ask Graney and she would tell her to ask Jim, *she wouldn't!* She said she was as scared of him as she was of a bear.

Olive said she made herself a purple dress before she started 9th grade, and it was the only dress she had to wear to school. She wore it until she graduated. She said it showed every place she had let the hem out as she grew.

When she graduated, Graney carried her to Memphis and bought her a suit and a prom dress for eight dollars.

Interview with Mamie Elizabeth Bailey (Mama Pig)
Interviewed by: Annette Wheeler

This paper was written by my double first cousin, *Annette Wheeler,* several years ago after she "interviewed" my mother and Aunt Olive. These are the exact words that Annette recorded:

The only time her father ever kissed her was when she went home for the first time after she married. She spent her wedding night in a house full of kids.

She and Buster borrowed a car to get married and Olive and Theron went with them December 26.

When she was in the 8th, 9th, and 10th grade, during the winter she and Olive would spend 3 or 4 nights a week with an aunt in town who was a sister to their grandmother Deliphate, who was Theo Emison's grandmother.

Pig played on the basketball team 8, 9, and 10th grade. They re-zoned for a new school in the county and she had to finish at Gadsden. They had a new high school. (She had gone to Alamo.) She couldn't play her junior year, because of NWA rules, so they let her be a cheerleader and manager. She got to play her senior year and they went all the way and played in the State Tournament. Graney and Daddy Jim never saw her play (her mother and father).

Pig, even with all the moving around, was second in her class. On graduation day, she went to school, came home, fixed supper, and got ready. Daddy Jim was late coming in and when they got to the graduation, it was half over and she wouldn't go up and sit with the rest of the class. The principal came out and got her to go up and give her Salutatorian Address.

Pig said Graney and Daddy Jim were partial to the boys. The only thing the men thought women were good for was to have babies.

She said Daddy Jim was always bringing men (2 or 3) home and boarding them upstairs. She said she and Olive had to wash, iron, and tend to them but weren't paid anything.

Pig talking about her brother James; she said he was two messes. When people wanted to make money for a project at school, they would donate chickens or eggs, things that could be traded or sold for money. Her class was trying to make money for some project and she carried (walking) a hen to school. When it came her turn to tell what she had brought, James stood up too. He said his mother said it was part his too. They had an argument about it there at school.

Mamie Elizabeth Bailey
(Notes that my mother wrote and I am copying word for word)

I, Mama Pig, was born Mamie Elizabeth Bailey and married Cyrus Lyburn Leggett Dec. 26, 1932. He was nicknamed Buster. We had only eighteen years of married life when he passed away. I, at time of writing am 76 years old and still remain a widow, so I still enjoy my grandchildren, one which is the builder of this house. He has asked that I write something about my ancestors. So Richard Lynn Cooke on his grandmother's (Mama Pig) side of the family was his great-great-great- grandfather named Martin Luther Bailey, and his great-great grandfather was Columbus Nathaniel Bailey who built and ran the first Cotton Gin in Crockett County and lost one of his 14 year old sons, which was caught in a belt, and then his great-grandfather had a steam engine saw mill, which was the first one in Crockett County. N.C. Bailey was born Jan 7, 1851 died Feb 3, 1919; his wife Sarah Dilafate Emison was born June, 28 1859 and died Dec 3, 1943; his great-granddaddy, James Arthur Bailey was born March 20, 1881 and died Dec19, 1968; Lou Myrtle Forsythe was born Nov.25, 1889 and died Feb. 1,1980.

First pies to come off in stores were individual pies called pecan pies in a thin paper cup so one man ate one of the 1st ones and said it sure was a good lasting pie but the crust was the dammed toughest one he ever tried to eat! (this after eating the paper cup and all)

It was so many of us in our family plus 3 hired hands. Papa kept to work at the saw mill, when in the fall we had sweet potatoes galore. When we made sweet potato pies, we cooked them in tin pie pans and took them out and stacked them 4 to 6 pies high and cut down through them all at one time.

Ice cream suppers were held in the church yard and also in woods lots. Homemade ice cream was sold for 5 cents a cone to make money for someone's family in need. Mr. Lillard came by in a horse and cart every two weeks with stick candy and O'boy Chewing Gum, that Mama would let us exchange for eggs. He also had other things for people to buy.

In the old school house, (two rooms with an organ) we had Sunday School every Sunday morning.(no preacher). A neighbor or two was elected to be president and secretary and treasurer. Sometimes we had different denominations to come and set up tents out in the woodlot and everyone would go after work at night with lanterns and candles for light. They had wooden benches and no backs to them! Kinda hard for us after working all day.

As you can see, Mama had a few things mixed up by then. One is the houses she lived in was built by my dad and Clinton Moore.

Early Forsyth/Forsythe

Motto "Let Us Rise from the Ruins"

James E. Forsyth first appeared in North Carolina record of Granville County in 1778 when he took the Oath of Allegiance there. He is the first proven ancestor of the Forsyth family of that county and West Tennessee. He was the only Forsyth, who remained in Granville County to rear his family and die there.

James E. Forsyth was born in 1759 and died 1831 in Granville County, North Carolina. He married Pharah (surname unknown) in 1783. She was born 1760-5 and died 1849-50 in Granville County. They had seven children who were William (1784); James (1786); Samuel (1788); Nancy (1790); John (1792); Thomas (1794); and Philip (1796). They reared their family in the Knap of Reeds community of Granville County, North Carolina. This is located in the southwest corner of the county.

His son, John, was an alcoholic and could not support his family and knowing that John might squander any inheritance, James willed the homeplace to John's youngest son Philip, to assure the children a home and a place they could live together until they became of age.

John Forsyth was born in Granville County, North Carolina, in 1792 and died there in 1850-7.
He was married twice; his fist wife's name is unknown and believe she died during childbirth of her last child, Phoebe, in 1822. He and first wife had five children: Pharaba (1814); Smith (1816); James (1818); Lucy (1820); Phoebe (1822).

He married again to Lucretia Christian (Crissy) Parrish, who was born 1780 and died 1860-70 in Granville County, North Carolina. They had three children who were Philip (1825); Simpson (1731); John, Jr. (1832).

James Epperson Forsyth was born in 1818 in Granville County, North Carolina, and died 1880-90 in Crockett County, Tennessee. He is buried in the Cypress Church Cemetery. In 1847 he married Elizabeth Lowery in Haywood County, Tennessee. She was born in December 1832 and died in Crockett County in 1903-4 and is buried in the Robertson Cemetery near Johnson's Grove. She died during the winter months, and the ground was so frozen they could not get to the Cypress Cemetery to be buried next to her husband. They had ten children who were Nancy J; Thomas Jefferson; Lucretia; George Washington; Sarah Frances; William M.; Jesse Lee; Mary E.; John Wesley, and Robert.

His grandfather, James, died in 1831 and this loss of his security and loving care must have had a bewildering effect on the 13-year-old boy.

According to family legend, relatives were leaving North Carolina en route to Tennessee. James, knowing this route, slipped away from home and waited to join the wagon train when they came by.

His cousin Redmond moved his family to West Tennessee by 1848, and they were probably the relatives with whom he traveled.

Family legend says that James Epperson Forsyth lived with the McDonald family at Bells, Tennessee, and that he hired out to a Mr. Duffy. His brother Simpson, having first moved with his
in-laws to Mississippi, then to the Gadsden community in 1848-49 (then Mason Grove) in Madison County, Tennessee. He hired out to Mr. Deloach, and one day the family brothers were each unloading produce from their wagons in Bells and unexpectedly came face to face for the first time since James had left North Carolina several years earlier. This was a joyful meeting, as they clasped one another in an emotional embrace.

James Epperson is listed as a Private in Captain Baylor Palmer's Tennessee Light Artillery Company "Renaw Battery" of the Confederate Army. It was organized 1 June 1863.

James lost one of his arms in a hunting accident. He rode horseback and tied his horse to a rail fence while hunting. When he returned, he tied his squirrels to his saddle, then mounted his horse. He reached for his gun, which was standing against the rail fence, and shooting him in the arm. He rode home and someone rode horseback to bring Dr Hess, who amputated his arm.

Thomas Jefferson Forsythe
James Epperson Forsythe's son

The Forsythe Clan

I really never knew much about the Forsythe side of my family. I had asked my grandmother about her family and she could not remember her grandmother's name and, to tell the truth, she was not interested in family trees. I then went to my great Aunt Bettie and she was very much interested, but she was blind and talked in low tones and held her head low; I was deaf and could not see her face, so you can see this interview did not go well either.

One Saturday night before Homecoming at church the next day, there was a Forsythe cousin that was at this supper and had with him a two volume set of the said family for sale. I was not there and Pat bought only one set and told me about it, and I called immediately and bought me and my children copies. After some time had passed, I got a call from another Forsythe cousin who said the man that had the books had died and his wife wanted to sell the ones left. Joe and I met him in Paris, Tennessee, and bought the lot. I mailed these copies to different branches of my family for Christmas. There are several copies of the Forsythe family back to the Revolutionary War on through the Civil War and on to present time.

Graney Bailey's (Lou Myrtle Forsythe Bailey) grandfather, Thomas Jefferson Forsythe and her mother Syble Lewis (Kink was her brother) lived close to Maury City and Johnson's Grove. She remembered a few things about her grandmother (but not her name) and nothing about her grandfather. Her father was killed when she was two years old. He was coming from town with a barrel of flour, and the horses got scared and ran over a rut and threw him out and killed him. This happened on the road between Alamo and Bells. He had been to Bells to get the much-needed flour since it was very basic to their diet and cooking; they bought it by the barrel.

Aunt Olive (my mother's sister) was six months old when Graney's mother died. She had pneumonia and kidney trouble and took sick and died within a few days time. Graney was born near Bells around 1869. She went to school in an old schoolhouse by Sunnyhill out of Alamo going toward Cypress. She met Jim Bailey at school there. (One room and the teacher was not there.) Jim taught some there. She had a slate and she drew on one side and wanted Jim to draw on the other.

Picture made in 1947 at Prudence Bailey Teal's house

Back row: Jim Walker (From Bells, M and Martha Jo's husband) Marshall Kincaid (Counsil and Vandon's half brother).

Second and third rows: Prudence Bailey Teal (Betty Forsythe Bailey's daughter) Council Mayo "Scotty" Forsythe, Betty Forsythe Bailey (Betty was married to John Bailey)

In addition to Prudence and Marie, Betty Bailey raised Counsil and Vandon Forsythe after their parents died in 1906 and 1908

Perry Forsythe, Floy Kincaid (Marshall Kincaid's wife and Martha Jo's mother) Ann Forsythe (Counsil Forsythe wife) Martha Jo Kincaid Walker (Marshall's daughter) Marie Bailey Mayhall (Betty Forsythe Bailey's daughter) Sandra Forsythe (Counsil Forsythe's daughter) Mary Ann Mayhall (Marie's daughter) Jo Mayhall (Marie's daughter) "Edwin Forsythe was present but in the photo, it seems he got very dirty playing and his mother wouldn't permit him to be in the photo.

Picture made in Cypress Cemetery in the 1940's - Arthur Bailey, John Forsythe, Bettie Bailey, Lou Myrtle Bailey, Perry Forsythe, Jim Bailey and Prudence Forsythe Teal

Bettie Elizabeth Forsythe

Forsythe Family
Front Row: Marie Bailey, Pruedence Bailey, Lily and Homer's girl and boy, Council and Vandle Forsythe

Second Row: Jim and Myrtle Bailey and baby Arthur
Third Row: John and Bettie Bailey, Florence Forsythe (Uncle Will's wife), Cybil Forsythe, Perry and Edna Forsythe

Aunt Bettie Forsythe Bailey and Lou Myrtle "Granny" Bailey

136

John Bailey and Bettie Forsythe Bailey with children, Prudence and Marie

James Epperson Forsythe Family Photo – 1899 or 1900

Back: John, Perry, Jim and Will

Front: Betty, Myrtle, Sybal, Thomas Jefferson's picture

Edith Carmen Smith, Buhrl Bailey, Mamie Elizabeth Leggett, Arthur Bailey, and Dorothy Faye Lowery

The Kenner Family

The Kenner family has been a big part of the Bailey family for generations, having some of the same ancestors. When my mother was growing up, the Kenner sisters visited often and at one time, one or two of them lived with Graney and Daddy Jim Bailey. I don't remember the circumstances behind this, but back then there were so many deaths separating families permanently, or for just a while as was the case here. With medicines as scarce as they were, even a bad cold could lead to pneumonia and death.

The girls in the Kenner family were close to our family back then. Naomi and Freda were connected to the school. Naomi had a job in the county with the running of the schools, and Freda was drama teacher there after many years in Memphis schools. This was long after I graduated. The others were visitors at reunions, etc.

If you will notice in the photo in this book of early Baileys' family reunions, the Kenner girls are lined up in front with all the watermelons. They were about the same age, or a little older than my mother's siblings.

Family connections is what this is all about. Our tree has many branches, and one book could not make a dent in the number of branches growing from our tree.

The Kenner family line includes Thomas Wilson Kenner, who married Cynthia Bailey; their son, Joseph Rhodam Kenner married Alice Kincade and had the following children: Alma, Naomi, Freda, Effie, and Addie Jo.

CHAPTER 6

Bailey Grandparents

Granny and Daddy Jim's 50th Anniversary - December 29, 1957

Granny and Daddy Jim's children - December 29, 1957
Elizabeth, Pritchette, Dot, Olive, Arthur, Burhl, Lawerence. (Uncle Frog could not be there)

Daddy Jim and Granny

I remember that the homeplace always had a fire in the fireplace from fall and into the spring. The hearth never got cold. The main heat in this big old house came from this one source. Granny could not put the "back stick" on because they were so heavy and big. She could manage the smaller ones that went in front. Uncle Arthur came up every morning and put the huge log in the back of the fireplace, and it lasted with the smaller fire in front of it all day long.

The homeplace had a big back porch; that was where Granny and the girls did the weekly washing in tubs and lots of water for the family of ten. One summer day Granny was on this porch and a huge black snake fell out of the rafters and almost on her; she was so terrified that she never forgot it and was wary of that porch the rest of her life.

Like all houses of the day, the Bailey house had a chicken house directly behind the back porch. The chickens laid their eggs in nests and hatched their baby chicks here too. One day Aunt Pritchette (Edith) was burning trash from the house outside the door between these houses, and the fire got out and burned the chicken house to the ground and the main house was so close to it they thought for a while it would burn down too.

The roof on the front porch was used to lay vegetables and fruits on to dry them out. It was on the south side of the house and got lots of sun. This was one reason for using it to dry food and then it was to keep tramps and wanderers from stealing it while it dried. Apparently there was a lot of this going on at the time. Later we granddaughters used the roof for sunbathing, and all the grandchildren loved to play "jump off the house." This didn't last long, just long enough for the adults to find out and put a stop to it. It did stop it for that day!

When I was in the eighth grade, I went outside the state of Tennessee for the very first time. I went to Florida with my grandparents and Dr. Bailey (Jim's brother) and his wife Thelma. It was quite an experience for me. I had never stayed in a motel or eaten in a restaurant. I had eaten in dime stores, etc. but never in a place where there were waitresses and menus. I had only eaten home cooked meals and that seems to be a novelty to a lot of children these days. We did the regular tourist things. The thing that amazed me the most was seeing the ocean for the first time and could not bear to leave it so soon after discovering it. We saw the water shows and St. Augustine and the Everglades. On our way home we stopped to see Uncle Frog (Mom's brother James) and his family. That was a treat because he was a doctor in the army and we didn't see them very often.

Aunt Dot slept with Granny until she married and I kind of took her place in Granny's bed then. We slept on the wall next to Daddy Jim's bed in the next room and, believe it or not, it was a half-bed, but we somehow accomplished this and loved it. Something like "two peas in a pod."

Daddy Jim Grocery Shopping

This has got to be the most falsified heading for any of the chapters so far. But it is close to being the truth. You see, my Granny didn't drive and Daddy Jim had no alternative but to do a little help in the food category. He loved a good glass of cold milk all through the day, and a good glass of milk to this big guy was almost a quart at the time. Therefore, they went through many gallons
of the white stuff.

The way he had it all figured out (and this plan worked without a hitch like most of his planning did) was to get to the little store in Alamo called Pappa Wade's Grocery and drive up as close as he could to the door and blow the horn as many times as he could get it done before someone came out and brought him two gallons of milk. Never did his foot enter there and never did he go home without his two gallons. The cashiers in that little store knew that the faster they got the milk to his car, the faster he would lay off the horn. Guess everyone in Alamo knew when Jim Bailey was out of milk.

Daddy Jim's Sawmill Business

Daddy Jim's sawmill business was very extensive. He had a big operation that he loved. He was very much the outdoorsman and trees were his pride. His favorite place was a wooded acreage called "Black Bottom." Don't ask me where this name came from! The only thing I can figure out is the trees were so big and close together that when you were there, no sunlight could find a very big place to shine and visibility was not good. It was dark and dark is black so I'm assuming that this is where the name was derived.

This forest was close to Brazil. He cut big trees there that were sawed into lumber of all kinds. I remember the huge logging trucks, caterpillars and several men working in this mill.

They used mules to pull the big logs through the mud where they could not get any trucks through. They had temporary roads they made themselves that were very primitive and when wet almost impassable, except by mule or horse.

Cypress was a specialty lumber he cut and was also his "baby." Most all houses in the area had some or all lumber cut by my grandfather.

There was one big cypress tree in Black Bottom that was at one time considered to be unequal in size anywhere in the country. People would drive there from afar and many miles just to see this tree. It is sort of a family heirloom if that is possible for a tree to be one.

All members of the family loved this wooded acreage. They shared Daddy Jim's passion for this land and its beautiful trees. They were so large and impressive because of the rich bottom land and plentiful water and some of them lasted for centuries. Also cypress trees are known for their durability and their endurance against rot and decay. The big tree was so big that it took several men joining hands to reach around it. It is one big tree and overwhelms those that look upon it.

There was so much appeal to this land that everyone in the family wanted a piece of it. It also caused some dissension in the family when Daddy Jim's will was read.

I think the appeal was the unusual intensity of the trees and the unsettled, almost *eerie,* feeling you got when you entered this forest.

There are not many places left in our country to experience this unless you go far off to the National Parks, etc. It is one place that has not been altered much by "the white man" since the Indians inhabited this part of our world.

Jim Crow and his sawmill

Daddy Jim's Room and Habits

Daddy Jim's room was a small space that was originally a side porch going into the dining room. It was closed in and a door added to the outside. When they put his bed and a small table and one chair in the room, it was full with only a space left to walk in and out. The grandchildren were not allowed to go into this room for any reason unless asked to come in. We sometimes joked around about it (when our grandfather was absent). We very silently walked to the door on tiptoe and put our foot just inside the door as if to say "I can too!" When we were there and he was "in," the door mostly stayed shut.

When the family was all there for a meal (this was many since there were eight children and many grandchildren), the women put the food on a large banquet-size dining room table. All the women had brought a lot of food. Granny would have been cooking for days; therefore, a fully laden table was the usual score. All ready to eat and Granny would knock on Daddy Jim's door and say, "Dinner is ready." He came out and went to the head of the table and sat and ate his meal and dessert, then got up, and went to his room and shut the door. Then the men ate and talked a bit; then they got up and left also.

The women and children were then free to eat whatever they wanted, and there was still plenty of food but it was picked over and cold by this time. The upside of this was by this time we were so hungry that we hardly noticed the temperature of the food.

I also remember when at my parents' house and we had company, especially when the preacher came, the men always ate first and then women and children, but no one ate by themselves. Times change and sometimes run full circle. Now the children always get the first round of things.

James Arthur Bailey
"Jim Crow Hooker Bailey" (Daddy Jim)

Dancing

Granny and Daddy Jim loved to dance. I remember seeing them dance at Liberty Hall at a "social" they had. In those days they used the old school for picnics, dances, ice cream suppers and anything they could think of to just get together and mingle. This was the prime time of their entertainment. At the mentioned dance, my grandparents danced and they were a pair. He, being so tall and big, and she, so short and big, you would never think that they could get around, much less dance. But dance they did and just glided over the floor smooth as you please, and no one there could come close to the grace and movements that they had.

On weekends they would go to Memphis and dance on the riverboats there. They would leave the smaller children with the older ones in charge and take off. They were opposites in size and temperament and opposites in almost every way but were a couple that loved each other and enjoyed their dancing and time spent moving to the music, be it fast or slow at any tempo.

Daddy Jim had a big body and his feet were surely large enough to support him. He wore a size 14 wide shoe and could not find them big enough in the stores and had to order them specially made. You should have seen his boots. You could take one (o) out of boots and put in an (a) and have exactly what his shoes looked like, a couple of twin boats.

As I have mentioned in another page, Mama wanted to be a nurse. She did not get to go to nursing school, but she had plenty of practice on this line and became a self-made medic anyway. She had such a gentle touch and caring personality that people from all over would call her to come and help care for themselves or a loved one. She was always "on call" for anyone that needed her. Then she got plenty of practice with

Daddy having diabetes and sick so much with the medications being so primitive for this disease.

One such occasion was when John Forsythe got really sick and his sister, Louise, called Mama and said she needed her because she was afraid John was going to die. Mama helped to nurse him, but this case was too far gone for her to help him. The family all got together and decided that he would need more help than an ordinary person could give, so they contacted a faith healer in Oklahoma to try to help, but to no avail.

As I have mentioned, Aunt Bettie was a big worker in the Cypress Church helping to keep it going and before she lost her sight, she used to walk across the bottom from Granny's and go to church with Mama. It was a long walk over a narrow dirt road that she had to cross over farm fields and cross a creek on a foot log. It was over an hour's walk just one way. I know about this walk because it is the same walk that my sister and I took to go to take music lessons from Mrs. Henderson.

You know it's funny, but we were allowed to walk this far, through the hills and vales (so to speak) and over a foot log, yet when I had the grandchildren, my mom would worry about them when they even stepped out the door. The same with Joe's mom, and yet Joe and Bill would play in the creek and walk almost to Cypress in it and threw corn cobs at each other and all kinds of things. I guess that grandchildren are so special when we get older we appreciate life more and I know the feeling now with all my grandbabies.

Daddy Jim (Jim Crow)

To describe my Daddy Jim is quite an undertaking. He was a very tall and large man. Not fat but just big and strong-looking. His facial features were very distinct. You would never meet any other man and mistake him for Jim Bailey. He had high cheek bones and large forehead, very broad shoulders and long legs. His features were carried through two of his boys very strongly. Several of the grandsons look like him today. He very seldom laughed; but when he did, he chuckled and vibrated all over. He was very observant of his surroundings. He was a very determined man, and I suppose you would call him the last of the "old school" men, where he ruled his household with an iron hand. Never striking anyone but they all knew to do as told when directed by him. He never asked anyone to do anything. He told them what to do! No questions asked nor any excuses accepted... This does not mean that the children did not get into things, but they knew to do it when their father was not around or not to leave any evidence of mischief behind.

Daddy Jim had an old Ford car he drove until it looked like an inch of mud had been baked like a crust all over it with just a spot or two in the windows to peep out. He took it to the logging sites and through the muddy fields, and it had never been washed in all this time. He decided that it looked so bad he need to buy him a new one. So he took it to town to have it cleaned up to trade in, and it looked so good washed and cleaned up that he just kept and drove it another year or two.

He was "THE" Great Fisherman! He fished every week or day he could. When he got old, he had to take two people with him to get him in the boat and bend his legs to get him out again. One person could not do this. They also had to bait his hooks and keep them coming. He did not like to wait on them to get one baited, so they had to work and keep one on hold so he would not miss even one minute dangling his pole for the big one! Their job also was to string the fish and hand him something to drink if he got thirsty and something to eat if he got hungry. You know women have maids and men have hired help, but I do not know what you would call these two people that bent legs and hooked worms!

Dominos was the great game at the Bailey house at night and in the winter time in front of the ever-burning fire in the fireplace, the game could be going on at any given time. He would pick who could play with him each game; and when he made a five or ten or twenty for you to put on the score card, you had better wait until he was watching you put it down because if he did not witness the marking, well, you had to put it down again. He won lots of games this way and you had better be quiet about it!

Daddy Jim raised his family to think they were poor. The pictures of the children when they were growing up show that they had few things and their clothes were very worn-looking. There are many, many pictures of the children lined up in front of a house that needed much repair. The boys were evidently kept a notch above the girls. The girls were expected to wait on the boys and do everything around the house. There were boarders at one time that stayed in one room upstairs. They were men that were helping in the mill and had no place to stay. The girls had to do the washing and cleaning for them, along with cleaning the room and cooking for them too. The girls had to sleep on pallets on the floor to make room for the boarders.

After Daddy Jim died, there were bank drafts that showed he had $25,000 dollars in the bank in a checking account. This was when the children were living like they did, sometimes without shoes. Later on in years, the house was repaired; and when my grandparents died, it looked very nice and was a tribute to the family.

There was a small pond behind the house where my grandfather would put his leftover bait, which was usually goldfish. These fish grew to be enormous and so very pretty. We would go to the pond and watch them in the water, and they were not scared because we were not allowed to fish for them but could go and feed them, and we really enjoyed this task and will always remember them. I have seen these fish that big in fancy gardens, etc., but it is not the same as walking down a tree-lined lane behind the house and sitting on the bank with them right in front of you on a hot summer day with nature all around you!

Once when I was about twelve years old, I was in Bells and saw Daddy Jim come out of the barber shop and I was not used to seeing him anywhere but at his house and I ran up to him and hugged him and he looked down at me and said, "I don't believe I know who you are." This was devastating to me. Jim Crow Hoker Bailey (as he was called) was a tough, hard-working and intelligent man; he was a very complex man. He was sometimes beyond my comprehension. Still, I had to admire his sheer determination and his will to accomplish, and strength and his stability. He was a rock! Perhaps he had to be this way with eight children and a depression just ending. Despite all this or because of all this, I loved him.

James Arthur Bailey
"Jim Crow Hooker Bailey"

Lawerence, Pig, Dot, Prudence, Olive, Burhl, Arthur, Jim and Bettie on porch

Jim Bailey and his mother Sarah Dilafate Emison – Made in Memphis

Jim Bailey at homeplace with new car

Mama and Her Siblings at Home in the Bailey Household

Mama and Aunt Olive were the two oldest girls out of the four girls and four boys that Granny Bailey had. This amounted to a family of ten and can you imagine the dirty clothes and dishes that it took in a day's time. Therefore, Mama and Aunt Olive were kept home one day each week from school to help with these chores. Mama never went to school on Thursdays. She stayed home and washed clothes. There was no running water, nor soap (only lye soap that was made from lye and ash there at home.) no wringers to wring the water out of the said clothes. It took many buckets of water to wash them and many more to rinse them. They had to wring them out by hand, hung on the line and after that brought in and folded. If the water was needed to be heated, well, you simply put the wood in the stove and the water in a pail and waited for it to heat up. By then the kitchen was sweltering hot and no air conditioner to cool it down. You get the picture of my mom's Thursdays. Then came Friday and it was Aunt Olive's turn to miss school and iron, sort all the clothes out and put them away. The irons were the cast iron type that you had to heat up the wood stove to heat the irons and press the clothes. You had to be careful and not let the iron stay there too long because it would scorch the clothing. In other words, you had to have a built-in thermostat to regulate the irons. This kept you going and going and I might add— going!

One thing my mother told me that stands out in my mind is one of her jobs she had when growing up. I had never heard of this one before. She had to go down to the sawmill each day before getting her lessons or helping cook supper. This job came first so Jim Crow would not get behind with his work. She had to go to the mill and actually pick up so many bundles of sticks about two by two and three or so yards long. These were made for some manufacturing plant and were made from the scraps sawed off the logs, then to planks, and then the small sizing cut off the edges were sawed into these "sticks." She told me one day how many had to be in each bundle, but I have forgotten long ago how many, but each bundle had to have so many, and then tied together so they could know how many was on the outgoing truck and could be handled so much better too. Every minute of the children in the family was put to use. What would our children do today if we told them to do this? In the first place, we would never expect this of them, and in the second place they would not do it; and if we had those sticks today, they would probably rot in a pile. But...think again about them. Would not our children be better off with bundling "some kind of sticks"? Too many sticks are bad, but no worse than no sticks at all. Everything is better in moderation.

Uncle James (Frog) liked to wear white pants to school and Mama would wash them and Aunt Olive would iron them for him. Could this have been some sort of sign that he would become a doctor? Sure followed a thought there.

This said brother kept the family on their toes. He was lively and had a very active brain and sense of humor. One stunt he pulled did not sit well with my mother. The school children had to have money brought to school if they were to have clubs and class projects. Mama and Uncle Frog were in high school and were to bring either money or something that could be sold to raise their projected goal. This in actuality amounted to the children bringing something that could be salvaged from home and sold. Granny gave Mama a chicken one morning just for this purpose. She walked all the way to Gadsden School from home with the chicken squawking and wiggling all the way. In homeroom she stood with the chicken and said this was her contribution, and at that moment Uncle Frog stood (from the back of the room) and announced that half the chicken was his contribution to the cause.

Mama played basketball and they had this amazing team with lots of talent. She was a senior and the little team from Gadsden went all the way to the State Tournament. This was her senior year and delighted her to no end having had so little in the way of fun or entertainment. (Yes, they did have a State Tournament way back when.)

Also that year she was to give a speech at graduation. She went to school and came home, fixed supper and got ready to go to her graduation. She had to wait for Daddy Jim to get home before she could go to the school. He was very late getting home, making them very late for her graduation. When she finally got there, the exercise was already half over, and Mama would not go up to the stage to give her speech. She was embarrassed and so very shy. One of the teachers came to the back and took Mama by the hand and led her to the stage, where she presented her speech. (How I wish I knew who this angel was that helped my mother. Bless her please, God!) I am very proud of my mother. She was an intelligent woman and a very loving mother that did all she could for her two daughters and was such a good wife to a man she loved with all her heart, even though he was sick for most of their short life together. Her dream as a young girl at home was to be a nurse, but her parents would not allow this. If she became a nurse, she would see naked men and that would not be allowed. All this to me is the reason she encouraged us to be all we could be, and she was happy in our happiness after she lost my dad.

Right after Mom and Dad were married, he bought her a ruby ring. (In this case ruby just meant red.) Mama loved this ring because she had never really had anything so pretty in all her life. It was set in a silver filigree mount that was the rage of the day back then. She lost this ring and became very upset over it and could not put the depression aside. One night in the middle of the night, she dreamed that the red ring was in the wood-box. She jumped up out of the bed and began to remove the wood from the box and, sure enough, under all the wood and splinters, there was her ring! Her prayers were answered and I believe the Good Lord whispered in her ear before the ring was thrown out.

When I was in the eighth grade, we always had an eighth grade graduation, and my mother had no money to buy gifts with. She had the red set put in a plain setting that was the "new" way to think rings, not the old filigree from days gone by. She gave me this ring for graduation. I knew it was a love gift for I had heard her story about the jewel many times, but I longed for the beautiful silver original settings. After Mama was gone, my sister came to me and gave me the original setting. This was the second love gift that the ring has given to me. I do not wear much jewelry but that ring is there and it gives me much joy.

Mamie Elizabeth Legget – third player from coach, this is their state tournament

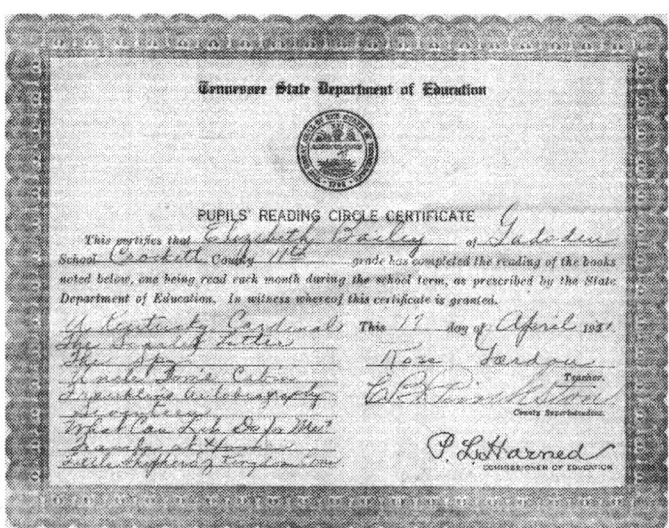

Reading Certificate – Elizabeth Bailey

Uncle Frog's Pickles

My Uncle Frog (James) loved pickles. You name it and if it was a pickle, he would eat it and not just it but a lot of "its." He was a doctor in the army. My mother was his sister and a farm girl and, boy, could she make a mean pickle. She made churns and churns of sweet pickles, jars and jars of huge dill, and churns and churns of brine pickles. I have not had a good brine pickle in years and years. She would put a layer of salt in the bottom of the churn and then a layer of whole pickles (the big ones). Now these pickles could not touch each other or they would spoil. After this layer of cucumbers, she laid another layer of salt and this layering went on until the whole churn was full. Then she put a rag over the top and then the churn top. She then set them aside and those things spewed and the salt melted until the churn was filled with liquid salt and fermentating cucumbers that were salty as.............! They were just great with peas or butterbeans and added lots of interest to any meal.

Uncle Frog (James) and his empty pickle jar

Now Uncle Frog was partial to those salty jokers, and Mama gave them to him by the gallon; and when he ate those, he would send her a picture of him holding the empty jug upside down to let her know that he needed another gallon of brines. I still have a picture of him and his empty jug and holding the last pickle.

Uncle Lawerence Bailey and his sisters - KKK

Uncle Lawerence was headed to school in Gadsden one day, leading an old horse with two of his sisters riding horseback. One of the girls was very unlucky that day because she had no shoes to wear to school. The others had shoes somewhat. Daddy Jim (their dad) came by in an old flatbed truck and stopped them, and Uncle Lawerence told him that his sister needed some new shoes. His dad's reply was "If anyone gets new shoes, it will be you." Uncle Lawerence told him that his old ones would do and he could clean and polish them up. Jim then informed him that he was getting the new shoes and that was that—and so he did!

Daddy Jim had to have lots of help to run the sawmill. To get the job done, he sometimes hired black men. This was back in the depression and did not sit well with some of the white men in the community. They had no jobs nor prospects of one when they were doing good to just put food on their tables for their families. Turn the card over and Jim was in a spot too having to pay out wages with eight children and was trying to get the labor as cheap as he could to turn a profit. One night there was a big glow in the front yard, and the Baileys all ran outside and there were the KKK Klansmen gathered in the yard with the dreaded cross burning brightly in the dark night. This was a warning and I have not been told any more than this. I do not know how my grandfather handled this, but there were no more tales of burning crosses in the middle of the night that I know of. Although I am sure this is not all of this story nor was it solved in just that one night. I wish I knew the full details of the event.

My grandfather was not a sympathizer to the plot of the black man in his time. As you have read, he was a very stern man and not given to understanding others. But I will say this, when he got older and was confined to his bed, he had a colored lady that took care of him. She was very kind and gentle with him, and he forgot her color and loved her and was kind in return. Ain't that grand?

I knew him then too and he knew my children and their names; and if I didn't take them to see him at least once a week, he had "Sally" call me and tell me he wanted to see the babies. He talked and laughed with them and they knew a gentle and loving great-grandfather. I am so grateful for that and know that he was on the right track at the end. That too is wonderful and something good to live within my memory now. Our family that has gone on before us are not just a memory. They live in my heart and will always be with me—Dad, daughter, Mother, grandparents and many friends and fellow church goers, "to name a few."

Trip to Jackson

There was a time when things we needed here at home were not always available to us. This called for a trip to the big town of Jackson, Tennessee. It was a long trip back when my grandparents were raising their family. There was no four lane Highway 412 going from Bells straight to town then. There was a narrow two-lane road with many curves and hills along the way with cars that just chugged along instead of "cruising on down the road." Granny had some things that she really needed, so Daddy Jim gave in and took her to Jackson to Woolworth's five and ten store. When she finished shopping, she waited and waited for Jim and he just didn't appear. Come to find out, he was home and had forgotten that he had taken her over to Madison county. her half-day shopping turned out to an all-day waiting, and I'm not sure what she said when rescued.

Granny Bailey and Daddy Jim's houses

Granny and Daddy Jim first lived in a small house across the road from the last house they lived in. They then moved into the old Bailey homeplace where Nathaniel and Dilafate lived in a log house. This house had a dirt floor. After a while in this house (I do not know how long they lived in this house), they added a two-story addition that had a wooden floor and long narrow windows with small panes. The old part had a front porch that had a wooden shelf, where they kept a white bowl and pitcher to "wash up" before coming into the house. They had a big, long mirror that hung over the window to comb their hair and groom themselves, too.

There is an old picture of this house with the addition, and Aunt Bettie Bailey is sitting on the porch in a straight chair for the picture. It is a family picture and the rest of the members are in the
front yard posing for the photograph. You see, the reason that Aunt Bettie is in the background is because she is pregnant, and back then you were not considered as

presentable if you were "in the family way." In the foreground is Nathaniel Columbus, Dilafate, Jim, Donald, John and cousin Marie (Aunt Bettie's oldest child). Donald is in a wheelchair because he had TB and was sickly. I suppose this house was originally "Old Nate's" and Dilifate's house while they were still living.

The third Bailey house originally had only three rooms. More were added through the years as Granny and Daddy Jim (that is what we all called our grandparents) had more children and the younger ones got older and more space needed all around. There was always lots of construction going on, more and more children born, and later Aunt Bettie lived with them. At one time some of the Kenner girls that were cousins and several more sets also.

There was a porch on the west side and one on the north side that were eventually closed in to make a room for Daddy Jim and one for Aunt Bettie. And later a much-needed bathroom was here too. Granny slept on a half-bed on the wall that separated her and Daddy Jim. This was not just a coincidence; he wanted her there so if he got thirsty or couldn't sleep, he would take an old judge's gavel and knock on the wall very loudly and yell, "Ho! Sally! Bring me a glass of water!" (He called her Sally—Why? No one really knows or if they do, I have not found out.)

As I knew about this old house, it had nine rooms. It was a typical old house with a long front porch, one in the back and huge dining room that was always full of family. On the front porch that reached the full length of the house, there were two swings that seated two, but three if they were children. All of us cousins would divide into two sets, and no matter how many of us there was, we got into those two swings and would get them going as high as they would go and someone would holler "go" and we would all hit the floor, running to get into the opposite swing as fast as we could. The last one in was, of course, the "rotten egg" and their team lost the bout. Then the whole thing would be repeated over and over again. It is a miracle that some of us did not get hurt badly, but I do not remember anything worse than a skinned knee or elbow.

The house sat on a big hill that went all the way to the road. The said cousins would line up and lie down in the grass and someone would yell "go," and we would all roll as fast as we could to the bottom of the hill and this too produced lots of "rotten eggs."Sometime after a rain there would be water in the ditch between the hill and the road and one or two of us always over, or under, estimated the speed with the distance and ended up in the ditch of water and would always be followed by lots of laughing and teasing. There was always someone to do it on purpose if things were going slow that day!

The "New" Bailey Homeplace - 1975

Granny's Cooking

Granny always had pinto beans on the stove and boiled prunes plus homemade yeast rolls. Sometimes these rolls were cold but still so good and never wasted at the Bailey house. You went to their house knowing that you would not get fancy food but the plain cooking of a woman with many years of experience under her cap and knew that the food would be wonderful and filling and always there for you and your friends or cousins. These three things mentioned were always among the many choices you would have. She cooked fried okra whole, and she put it on the stove early in the morning and let it simmer until lunch time. I never could cook it like she did. I did learn how to make those yeast rolls though when I was about ten years old. I still make them the way she told me, and it does not take anything but yeast, flour, a little oil and small amounts of sugar along with the warm water.

Granny's Yeast Rolls: *Take 1 and 3/4 cups warm water and dissolve 1 cube of yeast or 1 pkg. of dry yeast; add 2 heaping cups of plain flour and beat well (not firm) and let rise in glass bowl 1 and 1/2 hours or until bubbles start to appear and burst. Whip down and beat some more and add 2 T. sugar and 4 T. oil and whip some more. Add enough flour to just be able to handle it and roll out on a heavily floured board and cut into biscuit size circles. Then put in a buttered baking dish and bake at 350 degrees until they start to get done, and then turn up oven to 400 degrees until lightly browned. Never get the dough too thick and heavy. The rolls will be heavy when cooked. You can pour a little melted butter over them before baking and they will have more flavor.* Yum! Yum!

When she had watermelon, Daddy Jim would not touch the "seed" of the melon. He just ate the whole heart out and let us have the rest. He also did a job on cakes. He loved the frosting and never the layer so, you guessed it, he took his finger and swiped the icing right off that cake and it was a pitiful sight to behold. We called it our naked cakes. Sometimes Granny would make extra icing and hide it and re-ice the cakes before putting them on the table. The naked cakes got a new coat to wear.

If there ever was a flower lover, my Granny was the one. She always had hollyhocks, and larkspur in her flower beds that came up every year. I have seedlings from the larkspur that come up every year in my yard and mailed out seeds to cousins far and near and have been told by many that they too have them in their flower beds. Kind of like generations and generations of Granny on hand. I have a willow tree that came from a cutting of the tree that Betty (my sister) and I played under by our back door at my mother's house. My dad set this tree out when I was very small and by the time I got to be eight or ten, the trunk was almost as big around as a washtub. This is the tree that my dad gave me the switching from that is mentioned on another page. I think that a good willow switch would work wonders on this generation too if it were applied the appropriate way.

My relationship with Granny Bailey proved to me that the young and old can have a loving and meaningful mix. We enjoyed each other's company and we cooked, baked, sat and talked in the swing and walked in the yard and garden. Each spring we went to the greenhouses together two or three times to pick out her many plants for both the yard and vegetable garden. She taught me how to select plants and flowers and to appreciate their beauty and calming effect on one personally that loved them. She had a green thumb and loved her flowers as if they were her babies. When she went to Humboldt to the nursing home, she kept her smile. Always with a bloom or two for her to look at. She kept her smile even there but insisted that one of her daughters stay with her 24 hours a day. Not one could leave until the other got there to relieve them. They did this for her as long as she lived. It was a pact they had, for her to agree to go. She made them promise that she would always have some member of the family there all day and night. When Bailey Lowery would go and see her, she would look at him and say, "Hello, Jim."

Granny's Appearance

Granny Bailey was a very short and stout woman. She had bowlegs and was always a jolly person. She was very neat in her appearance. She never had a haircut in her life. She wore her long hair (that came past her waist and was very thin) in a bun twisted on the back of her head or sometimes on top. When something special was coming up, she had one of the girls, us granddaughters, pin the front section up in "kiss curls" with bobby pins to make it fluff around her face. We would comb it out for her and leave the curls loose, then pin the ends in the bun with the rest of her hair, and it really looked good on her.

All her dresses and night gowns were made from the same pattern. Plain with shirt collars with short sleeves for summer and long for winter. The dresses were buttoned all the way down the front with very large buttons and holes. This made it easier for her to get into and close the dress up. Her nightgowns were made from outing or soft cotton and sewn up the front with more gathers in the yolk to allow her to get it over her head. The dresses for everyday were made from cheap cotton floral or checks, and the Sunday dresses were sewn from crepes and blends. Mrs. Moore (down the road) was a seamstress and made her clothes for her. Mrs. Moore also made my formals for school and the prom. I designed my beauty review dress once for her, then she made it from a picture I had drawn. She was very good with her needle and machine. Her work was very economical and good, and compared to ready-made, worth her fees.

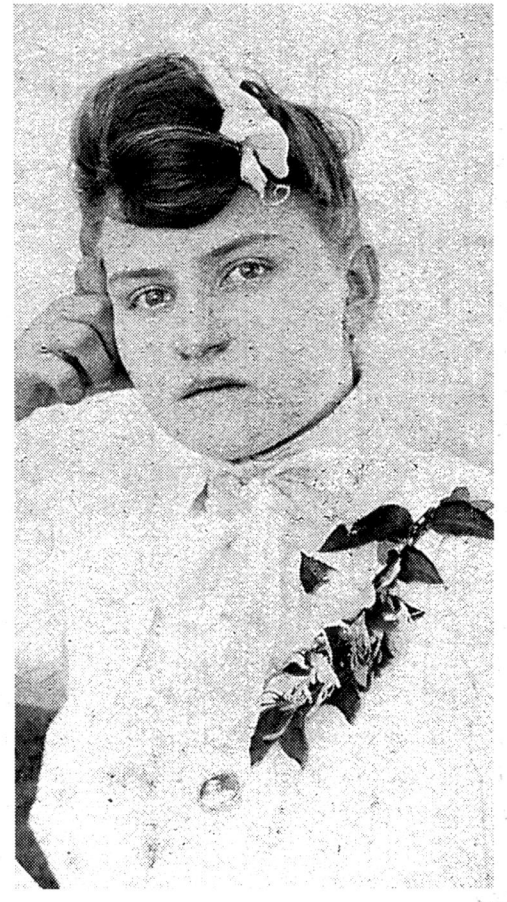

My grandmother
Lou Myrtle Forsythe Bailey

CHAPTER 7

Mamie Elizabeth Bailey – Graduation Picture

My Mama Pig

Mamie Elizabeth Bailey about 1954

I have no knowledge where this nickname came from. My mother was a very slim and energetic person and in no way favored, acted or looked like a pig. This is just a figment of someone's imagination, but it surely "stuck" with her all her life, and there are lots of people that knew her well and really never knew her real name. And such a pretty name she had, Mamie Elizabeth Bailey Leggett. "A lovely name for a lovely lady."

Mama never was one for collecting "things" or anything materialistic. Of course, she never had the means to really be big on this, but when she did buy something it was usually for someone else or something to share or to feed the ever-growing crowds that gathered at our house at any time or season. My dad and a friend built our house that we lived in while I was growing up. The lumber for this house came from my Granddaddy Jim's sawmill. She never had many rules about what we or other children could or could not do in her house. When Richard and Pat were three or four years old, she let Mike (the hired hand) bring in some pans of good old dirt and put this on the kitchen table for the children to make mud pies with. She told them not to get any water until she came back. Of course, when she came back into the kitchen, there sat Richard and Pat at the kitchen table with the floor and chairs all covered in mud along with a few little pats of mud, that did make it into the anticipated "pies." Mama pretended like she didn't know what was going on and put her hands on her hips and said "Who made this big mess?" Pat looked at her with her big eyes shining and said, "I didn't do it!"

As I said, Mama never had any unnecessary "things." There was one exception to this, though. I remember she had two very pretty cut glass bowls that were kept in the built-in china cabinet in the dining room. I don't know what happened to these bowls, but I have a feeling that someone down the road was sick and she probably sent some butterbeans out of the garden to them and forgot about the bowls. To her they were "just bowls." Had she remembered them and not gotten them back, she wouldn't consider this a big loss.

Mama's Cooking; Another Work of Art

In summer when we were home from the fields and hot and tired, we would get an old quilt and lie out on the "pallet" under the apple tree. (Yet another reason that I have a passion and love for the old quilts?) Daddy loved fruit trees and we had lovely fruits in season and jams and preserves made from every flavor. We had apple, peach, damson (these made the best preserves) and cherries. We had wild blackberries and strawberries too.

For cooking we had to bring in small pieces of wood for the stove. They had to be tiny so they would go into the "eye" of the stove to make the fire to heat the stove to cook on. Nothing we did was only one procedure. You blanked, and blanked, and blanked so you could blank to finish the blank like cut the tree, saw in sections, split the wood, bring in the house, make fire in the stove, cook the meal. Pushing a button or turning a knob sure beats all this. And this went on and on. Nothing was fast or easy. Of course, you did not know this at the time until you got electricity and buttons to punch and things to plug up. Mama made everything we ate. I remember the second time I ate in a restaurant. I was ten years old and we went to Memphis to visit our uncle, Dr. Conrad Bailey. He took us downtown to eat at the old B and W Cafeteria down close to the river (another miracle if I ever saw one), no stove to heat up, no food to cook, and wonder of wonders, no dishes to wash in a dishpan.

Mama made all our sweets with saccharin tablets because of Daddy's diabetes. These were great tasting desserts and I will never know how she did this. There were no diabetic cook books, etc. She just experimented over and over until she came up with a winner. This was a time when no one knew it was possible to cook sweets this way. Way to go Mama!

We made our own cheese by putting heated milk in a lard stand and letting it clabber, then cutting the firm milk with a knife into squares and letting the whey come to the top to drain off. Taking the curds and putting them in a large container with a plate on top and a brick on that to press the excess whey off by turning it upside down on the brick and the liquid drained out and left cheese to set so you could cut it. It was delicious.

"Chef, Mama Pig" cooking one of her famous cakes, wearing her button necklace. 1975

Mama's Disgraced Pet Squirrel

I do not remember this, but Daddy loved telling the story about when they first moved into the new house. Mama had found a baby squirrel and had raised it as a pet. He was very active and really made messes, but Mama loved him just the same.

The family went out one day and when we came home, the house was a wreck where the pet had chewed the furniture and gnawed on everything. It was like he went from a pet to a wild thing, showing his true colors all in one day. We did not have much furniture to start with and vases kicked over, and this was just not to be tolerated. Mama was mad and turned him loose in the yard and was heartbroken.

About this time we got a puppy that turned into the greatest hunting and pet dog of all times, and the disgraced squirrel memories were put to rest.

Joe and I had a squirrel that got into our house, and we have lines of half-eaten window sills in the den. They got behind our outside shutters and chewed the corners off them and made big gaps that are still there.

My Mother

My mother was one of the unsung heroes in life. My dad was always sick with diabetes and never had many well days in his life. He worked but was not strong and so Mom had to do so many things that most women did not have to do and did them with no modern machines to help her.

Long after electricity was in most houses, we were still using coal oil lamps, a wood burning cookstove long after most women had electric ones. Mama never complained while doing housework, cooking, yard and garden work, and all this around the backbreaking field chores.

She was gentle, loving and, with all this, a very artistic woman. She never made "just a quilt" or "just a cake" or just anything. She loved for her table to look inviting and her food good, her beds to look pretty and comfortable. I really don't know how she accomplished as much as she did.

She drove the old white car after Dad died until it looked like it was about to fall apart from sheer exhaustion. But, on top of all this, she wanted Betty and I to have what we needed and more than what she had. I do not mean dresses and jewelry or anything fancy. She wanted us to be all we could be and know happiness and how to give of ourselves to others.

You know, she never really talked about most of these things but conveyed this knowledge to us with her gentle ways, sweet personality and being herself and showing how you could be happy with someone you love without all the "extras" in life. I felt loved, needed, protected and, above all, "at home with my mother." Could any person ask more from another? Not when that person is giving you their all. I love you, MOM!

Mama Pig in the Nursing Home

When Mama had to go to the nursing home, she still kept busy with one thing or another. She had many visitors. She always knew what was going on at home. I usually got all the news about family and neighbors from her when I went to see her there. When her mind began to dim, she told us all with regularity that she had to work all the time and help out there or she would lose her room and they would not let her stay there anymore.

One of her projects was this weird plant that I do not know the scientific name for, but the common name (very, very, common name) for it was Pregnant Onion! Talk about an opening for a, "no-where to go but up" conversation...this was it! There was this onion-like plant that actually had a bulb like base like an onion that sat on top of the soil and blade like spirals sticking straight up in the middle. When the "onion" got mature and old enough, little buds would sprout out from the base of the bulb and grow into (sure enough) little onions! As the (babies) got a bit larger, you could just break one off and start your own little family. Does this story ring a bell and sound a little like human life or something? Pretty soon almost everyone that Mama knew had adopted one of her offspring. I'll leave this one for now because it is beginning to sound a little like "I'm my own grandpa."

CHAPTER 8

A Flight in Time with Joe and Myrtle

The Great Romance

Talk about romances, Joe and I had "claimed" each other since grade school. When we got to be seniors in high school, we were very "mature" and decided that we would date other people because we had never been out with anyone else and wanted to prove something. I'm not sure what—but something! He went with a wide range of girls and I dated a few boys. I'd been going with a college freshman that joined a fraternity, and he had asked me to wear his pin. I told Joe this and he said, "You're not wearing anyone's pin," and that settled that. We started to Murray State and had been there almost two months and I knew he didn't like it there. One day we were sitting under a tree on campus and he announced, "Hey, Baby, I'm going home Friday and not coming back! Do you want to go with me?" How could a girl resist a proposal like that?

Mini College Education

Joe and I started to college and went only a few weeks. He was not happy at all away from home and Fruitvale, and I was having trouble hearing the teachers. I did not know anyone in my classes to ask for help and back then there was no one to go with you if you were deaf or hard of hearing.

The last straw was in an English class, and I was on the front row straightening my books when I realized the teacher was talking very loud. When I looked up, she was looking straight at me when she said (and I quote, I will never forget) "Miss Leggett!! What is wrong with you! Are you deaf????" I looked her and said, "Yes, Ma'am, I am," and I walked out and could not bring myself to go back in there.

When Joe asked me to go home with him and stay, it was a solution for him and for me. We knew it was just a matter of time before we were to get married and just took the leap a little sooner than we had planned. Now more and more people are understanding of others with (I do not like to call it this because I do not think of it as this) disabilities. Now they are more compassionate and considerate, especially adults. I do not consider myself unlucky, but the very opposite of that. I am a very fortunate woman with the life that I have had and still enjoy with children and grandchildren and the very best friends a girl could have. And too, a wonderful husband that has been my life for more years than I can count. *Myrtle Rose Leggett Emerson*

Joe and Myrtle's Honeymoon

Joe and I were married in Mississippi. When we left to get married, Joe's brother Bill and his girlfriend June went with us. They were not married at the time. The only "Sunday" dress I had was a black, scratchy suit so that's what "I tied the knot" in. (Don't tell me the black suit was a sign because I have already thought of that one.) After we came back home, we went to Natchez Trace for our honeymoon. We borrowed Paw Paw's car and we got one of the cabins on the lake. It was late when we got there and we had forgotten to bring food. So we got up that first morning and went to the park store that had bare necessities with no eggs, bacon, nor perishable foods, so our first breakfast was a can of Franco American spaghetti. (I know, another sign.) We had no phones in the cabin and this was long before cell phones. Every time we would go in the store we would have a message from either his mom or mine and sometimes both to see if we were all right. This went on for three days and began to pick up pace so we just packed up and went home. Sometimes the ranger would have to come by with messages and he was not too happy with this. What was the problem? I had been eighteen for two months and Joe had been eighteen for almost half a year and we were grown-ups then! Now I understand all this because I have three "grown-ups" over forty.

Doctor assessment of Myrtle Rose's hearing loss - August 11, 1955

Fruitvale, Tennessee
June 13, 1951

Dear Myrtle Rose,

I hope that you are having a wonderful time in camp this Spring. We are expecting to go to some swimming pool right soon now. Wayne and I go swimming most every day now. Right lately we have started turning flips into the water. Sometimes we get a log and try diving under it. Mother caught me the other day and I missed one day. I hope you are felling well lately and look as beautiful as ever. They have got up the frame of the doors and have started laying brick on the new gymnasium. That show last Sunday was a very good one. Comming back we saw June, Bill's girl. Raymond is giving a party Wednesday night and Bill is going. I have been going to school for eight years and haven't learned how to write a letter. I miss you very much.

Love,
Joe

P.S. I am sorry I did not see you when I went to the show Saturday night. When I saw you someone already had the seat next to you. I still like you very, very much. You are still very beautiful as I seen you last Sunday.

Letter to Myrtle from Joe

Joe Silas Emerson and Myrtle Rose Leggett Emerson – March 1956

Joe and Myrtle Rose Emerson – 1955

Joe Silas Emerson and Myrtle Rose Leggett Emerson – March 1956

"Not a bale yet!" Myrtle Rose Leggett Emerson – 1957

Early Marriage of Joe and Myrtle

Joe and I lived with my mother for a year after we were married. We were just eighteen and had no experience in the way of making a living. To tell you the truth, we did not know much of anything about life and, as I remember it, we thought we were at the high end of knowledge. I look at the eighteen-year-olds and think how much they have to learn and then it dawns on me that *There I go at eighteen*. But you know it is a wonderful time in our lives because the pressures of life have not crept up on us yet, and our minds are a sponge, ready to soak up everything life throws us.

Since this great wedding took place in the late fall, we went to Ollie's store and bought us each a cotton sack. Well, I knew all about these things but Joe didn't have a clue. We picked cotton through the fall; and when winter came around, Ollie gave Joe a job feeding cows for $3.50 (no, not an hour) a day!)—*add*

While we were living with my mother in the Cypress Community, we decided we needed an extra income to add to the "cotton sacks" we had bought. Joe said he knew how to raise pigs so we bought us a sow. There was plenty of room in the old barn since Mama had given up raising crops and it was empty. We bought this sow and she finally came due to have her piglets; she did very well except she only had two and one died. Well, we still had one, didn't we? Maybe not! After a day or two, the old sow rolled over on the single piglet and it died. What next? I can tell you what was next; the first cold spell we had—we made sausage.

After living with Mom a year, Ollie fixed up this older house. You could see the chickens from the colored man's house under ours and hear them clucking away. The air coming through those cracks was pretty cold in the winter. One good thing about it, we always had fresh air inside and outside.

After that winter, Ollie had a carpenter come and put in some wood floors and, boy, were they a sight to behold! He

Joe Silas Emerson and first old sow - 1956

also had the men lower the ceilings and I begged and begged for them to stay, but NO NO NO! Down they came! This goes to show that nagging does not always pan out the way you meant for it to. We then bought this huge iron pot-bellied stove and put in the room by the kitchen and with a little coal and very little else, it warmed the whole house. Of course, it was hot by the stove and the further you got from it, the cooler you got. So if you got hot in one room, all you had to do was move into the next. Like the Roman Baths in Italy, you start with scalding water, and then to warm, and then on to cool your body last. We also had a bathroom installed! Heavenly, I had never lived in a house with indoor bath fixtures. What else could anyone possibly want after such an amazing thing as that?

All our children were born while we had this house: Mame' in Ft. Bragg, North

Carolina; Jody and Shane in the then Catholic Hospital in Humboldt; Milly in Jackson at the big hospital. When Shane was born in the Catholic facility, Mama had told me to take off all my jewelry, which meant my wedding ring and I had left it at home. The nun kept watching me and I knew she had something on her mind and finally she asked me, "Are you married?" I wonder what she would have done if I had said no!

We had wanted a new house for years, and I had played with cardboard after cardboard sheets getting everything where I wanted it; I did most of it in the back yard of the old yellow house on a pallet with the children playing all around. I could watch them and "work" too.

We started the "new" house in January of 1969 and moved in on June first of the same year. Kenneth Jones built it for us and he was such a delight to know. He took great pride in his work and knew his business when he had a nail and hammer in his hand. He could not understand why I wanted to paint anything a color. To him everything needed to be white, inside and out. That was our biggest thing the whole time. No arguments, but disagreement after the fact. Mr. Humphreys did most of the finishing work, cabinets, moldings, etc. and Mr. Spitzer did the painting. I stayed with them every day and cleaned up shavings and short boards and soon became one of the crew. I made a buttermilk pie each morning before I went to work and we had this and cool Cokes at ten o'clock sharp every day.

For years after we moved in, I would have this hunger craving at exactly ten in the morning; I could set my watch by it. These men soon became good friends of Joe and mine. It makes everything so special to me to know that someone I loved built my house. I wanted things to move fast so we could move in with the children, and I soon started painting and staining the woodwork and loved the job. Joe was in the fields then farming, and so it was usually dark when he saw what had been done for the day until we got electricity and then we toured the timbers at night.

The bricks on the outside of the house came from the old Presbyterian church that had sat by the old Greyhound Bus Station in Jackson. The architectural pieces came off the same church that held up the Bell Tower there. The bricks on the front steps came out of the old house chimney, where I was born. The bricks on the wall in front of the house with the high steps came from old homeplace chimneys from around the community. Most of them came from an old Crossnoe house. Joe and I cleaned them all, a few at a time.

The logs for the log house out back came from an antique dealer in Selmer, Tennessee. They probably came from one of the Mennonite settlements out from there. We bought it in a pile that had been numbered and with directions on it. One would read: 1-W—this meant the long was the first one to put up and it went on the west side; 7-E—would be the seventh log on the east side. It was simple enough to figure out but very hard to handle the heavy log and get it up exactly straight because if not straight, this would eventually make the house lean to the lower side. Joe and I decided we could do this, but when we got about four logs high, we soon saw that "this was a job for Superman!"

The tall, early flowers in my yard are larkspur from Granny Bailey's flowers she had in her garden. The lilac and hollyhocks came from her too.

The old gas pump by the log house was one that Daddy Jim used to pump gas in his logging trucks and heavy equipment that sat close to their homeplace. When Aunt Dot inherited the homeplace, this relic went with the house. I had always loved the looks of the old thing and loved what it meant to the Bailey family, so when Aunt Dot died,

Pat and Bailey sold it to me and we moved it here.

This gas pump was a basic asset to the Bailey Sawmill business. There were so many huge hauling trucks, bulldozers and other trucks to fill with gas that made it a necessity. It was also a kind of landmark for the community, and we didn't want it sold out of the family. If this old gas tank could talk, we would hear some very interesting tales from the past for sure.

The small log house on the other side of the main house came from behind one of our rental houses on the highway. I had not noticed this house because it was completely covered in vines behind some trees. I accidentally saw one of the corner logs protruding out one winter when the leaves were gone. This did not sit well with Joe because he knew we would soon be trying to put up yet another old house. This one was very small and was, in fact, "the chicken house" that went with the rental. It makes for a very good storage; and when we had big gardens, we put the potatoes on the floor and hung the onions from the rafters.

Milly was two years old when we moved into our present house. I had been so careful with all the steps and had put gates in every place that I could. Wouldn't you know that we had been there only two weeks when she fell in the shower and burst her chin really bad. She still has a scar from all the stitches. It goes to show you that you cannot predict what will happen.

I have the old curtain, screen or canvas that was hanging in the old Fruitvale Schoolhouse even when Joe went to his first four years of that school. It is a huge canvas painted in the center with what looks like Reelfoot Lake and is surrounded with square advertisements of most of the merchants in Bells, Alamo and Fruitvale. The school sold ads for it and hired a painter to paint the scene surrounded by the ads and it made a front for the stage. It covered the entire stage area and all the way to the ceiling. Some of the ads are very special to Joe and me. Our grandfathers, uncles, and friends have an advertisement on it. It is a special thing and priceless to us. I had wanted this article for years. The school had closed when Joe passed to the fifth grade, and the old building was then used for the Fruitvale Club meetings and for families in the community to have reunions and picnics. I had not asked about it because I hated to ask. One day, I had a knock at my back door, and three ladies from the Fruitvale Club asked me if I would be interested in buying it and I said a little too loudly, "YES!" They said, "Aren't you going to ask how much it is?" and I told them I wanted it pretty bad and would probably buy it at their price. They explained that they did not have the money to order coal for the stove that winter; and if I would pay for the coal, I could have it and they could continue their meetings. Needless to say, I bought the coal and thought I got a good deal, and so did they. (A case of, if you are happy, so am I!)

One of our favorite advertisement drawn on the old curtain is for the corner drugstore that the Tooms owned. Joe and I would go there after the movies and have a Cherry Coke with peanuts in it. Some others included are The Tri-County, where Mama got her flour and chicken feed, Ollie's Store, Leggetts Grocery and Filling Station, Daddy Jim's Sawmill, etc.

This painted canvas is shown on the back cover of this book.

*In Joe and Myrtle's back yard, Log house
with Daddy Jim's gas tank*

"The Hen House" at Joe and Myrtle's house

El Paso, Texas

We had been to Natchez Trace for a week with Joe's family and some close friends and came home by the Fruitvale Post Office to get our mail. In it was a notice from the US Army that Joe had been drafted. He went to Ft. Benning, Georgia, for basic training. His parents took me down once for a weekend there; then he was moved to Ft. Bliss, Texas. He had to go with his unit and I was to come later by Greyhound bus. I had never been anywhere by myself and took the bus to El Paso, Texas, with a four hour layover in Dallas; I learned a lot there! When I got to El Paso, Joe and I took a taxi to the base guesthouse. We rode and rode and barely had enough money to pay our fare.

The next morning, one of Joe's buddies took us around, and about five minutes out we passed the bus station. We had been had! We found an apartment on the Mexican Border; a fence in our backyard was the line between Texas and Mexico.

We were about three blocks from the store and had no car, so we walked there for some bread. We noticed the wind was picking up, and before we got home we were in a terrible sand storm. We could not see where we were going; sand was stinging our faces and eyes. When we got to the apartment, we could hardly open and shut the door. Even with the doors and windows closed, there was sand in everything: the bathtub and kitchen, and even in the bed and in our clothes. I had to wash his heavy fatigues in the bathtub and hang them out on the line right outside our back door. The air was so dry; they would dry by the time I got inside good. Ever try to wash Army fatigues in a bathtub and wring them out by hand, then iron them? I didn't think so!!

We went to Ft. Bragg, North Carolina, and lived in a cottage behind a colonel's house where his wife and aging aunt lived. The aunt's name was Frannie. We soon were living in the "big house" with them, and I took care of Aunt Frannie and gave her Digitalis. Tiny little things, they were. She hated those little critters. One day, I gave her the small pill and she threw it on the floor as far as she could. The floor just happened to be covered with an antique oriental carpet. I was eight months pregnant with my first child and had to get down and crawl across the floor looking for the pill. Aunt Frannie said, "Honey, if you find it, I will take it and not throw it again!" I must have looked more pitiful than I felt and that would have been bad!

Mama came when it was time for the baby to be born. Twin beds were all we had, so we pushed the beds together and I slept between Joe and Mama. There was this big crack right under me and I was neither "here nor there."

When we got to the hospital, I had never seen the doctor that was to deliver my baby. He looked about fifteen and I asked him if he was sure he was a doctor. I never saw him again! Joe and Mama walked the halls to get a look at him but they never found him. I told them it was not my imagination because I had a baby to prove it.

When Mame' was five weeks old, Joe was ordered to Germany during the Berlin Wall crisis. He was there ten months; and when he came home, Mame' was scared of him.

In 2008 we went to Eastern Europe and saw a fragment of this wall Joe went to protect. He never saw it while he was there.

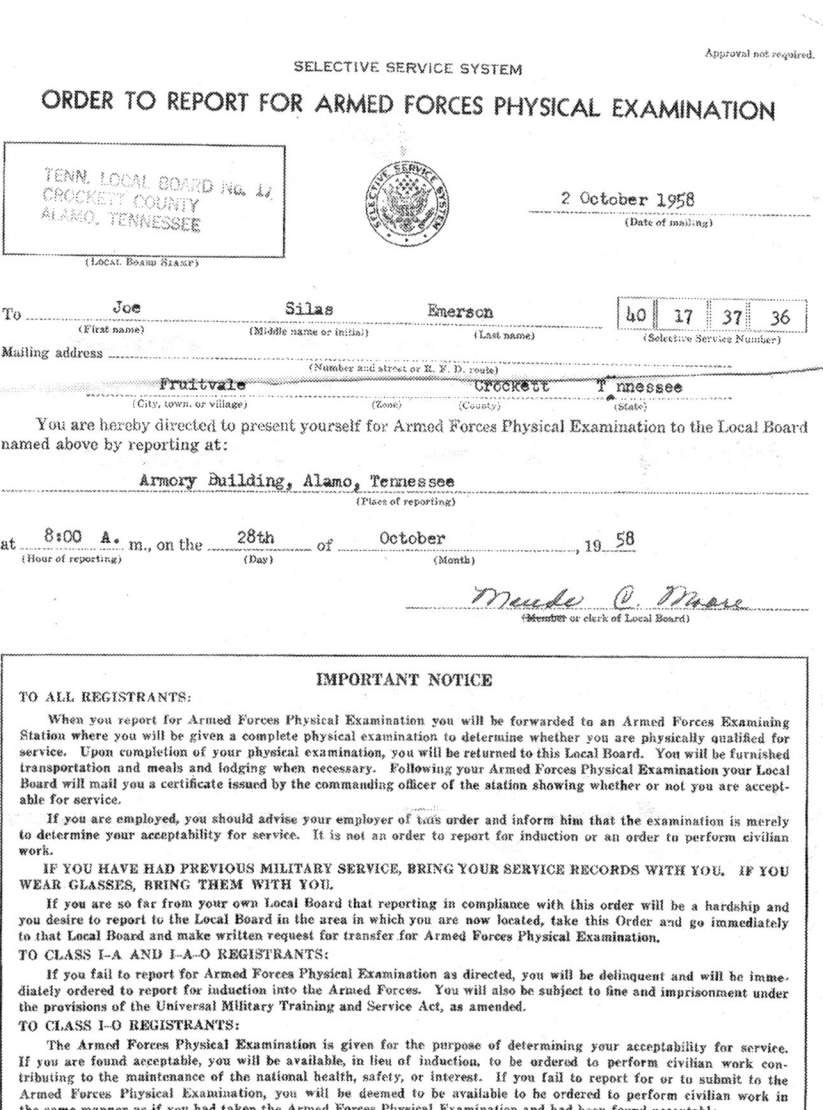

Draft notice for Joe Emerson

Coming Home from Ft. Bliss

When the time finally came to come home from Ft. Bliss, we were going to have to take the bus back and not pleased with how long it was going to take. One of the boys from post offered a ride in his car with him and his wife whom we knew, so we decided that was the way to go. What we did not know until time to leave was that two more people were also riding. We were to share the cost of the gas with the added couple, so the owner of the car would not have any expenses. This was still ok with us, we thought. Here we were: three couples, one small car and all the belongings that we had, including some household things. Needless to say, the back was packed to capacity, leaving the floorboard under my feet as the only place for my suitcase. We drove non-stop from El Paso, Texas, except to get gas. If you were hungry or thirsty, you had better jump out and get your candy bar and coke in a hurry because the car left as soon as the gas was pumped. There were no sandwiches and fast food back then, only packaged junk. No one was allowed to drive but the owner of the car; and if you had a bathroom stop—too bad, next gas station coming up! My legs were so cramped and there were three of us in the backseat, so no place to move to stretch your legs. You were already packed so close to the next person, you could feel their heartbeat. Coming into Memphis, we ran over a deer on the levee in the bottom with water, sloughs and trees on both sides. We almost went into the water. When we got into Memphis, Joe got us out of the car and called some classmates of ours that lived there to come get us. They picked us up and we stayed that night with them; some of the family came after us the next day. I could do a horror movie with just this ride of misery and danger!

Ft. Bragg Experiences

We learned a lot about life at Ft. Bragg. Our landlady was well-traveled and educated. She talked and taught us a lot after she got used to us being there. She taught me a lot of do's and don'ts about manners and thinking. I admired her very much and learned to love her in the months we were there and kept up with her until she died.

We did not make much money in the army, but the cost of living there was amazing. We bought everything at the commissary. Hamburger meat was 29 cents a pound and everything else in the grocery department was in line with this. The movie on base was a quarter, and the popcorn and a coke was a nickel each. (You think I am makin' this up, don't you?) I have some receipts that prove this.

Joe's Tour of Duty - Germany

Joe's father would not let me go to the bus station to see Joe off for his tour of duty in Germany. He told us that it would be worse saying goodbye there than at home. So off he went to ride the Greyhound away from us.

We had been married for five years when Mame' was born and had waited for her all this time only to be separated so early in her life.

I understood the circumstances of Joe's going with his unit (a chemical company with the Army) but not until we saw this famous wall did I comprehend the significance of his tour of duty. I saw the "why" of all this separation.

On an upside of all this was that Joe had time to tour Germany and go to Salzburg to see the salt mines there, and Austria was awesome to him. After he got home, he wished he had taken more time to see more than he did. Since seeing so much while over there, he has wanted to travel more and we have been lucky to do so. The times we have traveled abroad, each time we learned so much more of our world and its people while staying in B&B homes and talking to the people of all nationalities and works of life. We have stayed with a policeman's family, sheep farmers, in manor houses, landowner's 16th century house with all the original furnishings, half-timbered, and in the same original family that we have been so many times.

Joe and Myrtle – Boot camp, Fort Benning, GA, September 1960

Joe Silas Emerson Germany 1961

Joe's Return from the Army

On Joe's return from the Army, it was a joyous reunion for the two of us, now that we were all three together again and finally finished with military life. It was not as bad as I probably insinuated, but for us being raised on the farm and loving country life, it was a bit too different. We did do some interesting things through this experience and learned even more of our country and its different people and would not take anything for the opportunity we had, but let's just say that we do not want to do it again.

As I said, we were happy to be back together except Mame'. She and I had lived with Mama during this whole time and moved there when she was five weeks old and moved back home with Joe when she was over eleven months, walking, attempting to talk and getting what she wanted. What she wanted and never had was long-term male company. She had had a very bad reaction from a shot of penicillin for a bad chest cold and was sicker from the shot than from the cold. When Joe walked back into her life, she did not want him to hold, feed or get close to her. This was very disturbing for him, for he had long been dreaming of having her in his arms again. His gentle ways and loving her so much finally broke down the barrier, and he soon became her favorite but it was a heartbreaking road to get there.

Right after Joe left for Germany, Mame' got really sick with high fever and we took her to young Dr. Mayfield. She was only about two months old at the time. The doctor gave her a penicillin shot and we came home; then she began to break out in big red welts all over her body. Mama and I were about to carry her back to Bells when Dr. Mayfield knocked on our door to check on her and began treating her for reaction to the medicine. She was sick a long time. She was not a healthy baby and was tiny but soon began to grow at a fast pace. By the time Joe got home from Germany, she was beginning to pull up.

Mr. and Mrs. Joe Emerson, stationed at present at Ft. Bragg, N.C. are announcing the birth of a daughter, Mamie Lou

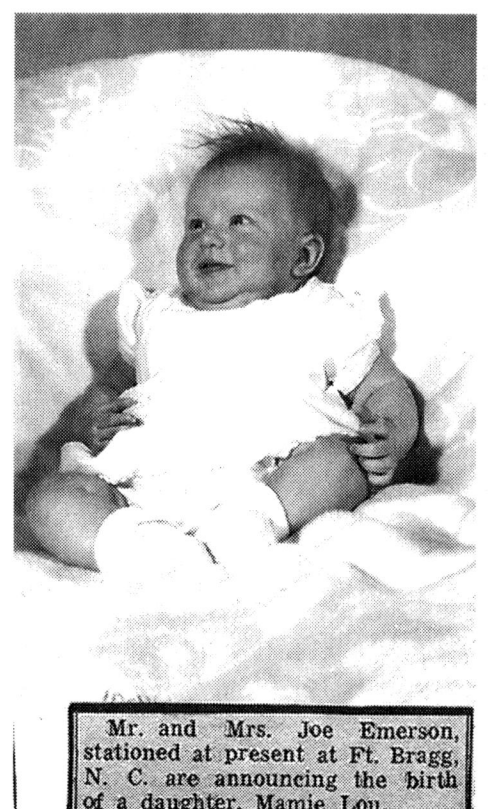

Mr. and Mrs. Joe Emerson, stationed at present at Ft. Bragg, N. C. are announcing the birth of a daughter, Mamie Lou.

English Friends

In our travels through the years, we have found one especially wonderful place that we loved to visit. In England there is this B&B, where we stayed the very first time we went to that country. It is in such a place that we literally fell into it when completely lost one day down a two-way dirt road that was only wide enough for one car. If you met someone coming toward you, one car had to back up until they found an indenture in the hedge row so the other could go forward. The road was about five or six feet below the pastures and hedge rows on either side, and it was kind of like driving down a cave without a top. We saw the house and were amazed. It was a country house on the side of the moors. We found out it was built in the 16th century by the present owner's ancestor and had been in the same family since it was new. It is a half-timber house in the Jacobean style with the barn attached to the house. There is a small chapel on the grounds that looked like a small cathedral and was surrounded with old relics, gold statues and frescos. Like a dream!

We went inside and the couple who owned it were so nice and friendly that we stayed extra time there, and every time we went from then on, we set aside a few days to stay with Jeanette and John, the owners. We loved talking to them and sitting by the fire and hearing their story. They had no children and John's brother had never married and died soon after we met him. They were leaving everything to a distant cousin in Canada that they had never met and talking to the cousin had come to the conclusion they would probably sell the house and contents by auction never coming to investigate their inheritance. This was so very sad.

The house had all the original floors and beams, the original grandfather clock, ancestor portraits in oils in the original frames and Jacobean furniture original to the house and many pieces of needlework made by ancestors from the beginning. It was such a delight to see all these wonders in one place that had always belonged to the same family. I wanted to just move in with them and they realized that I felt that way. Joe and John were soon fast friends.

Each time we went over to England, I was looking for one particular thing for our house. One time, antique samplers; another, old candlesticks, etc. On our last visit, we were sitting in the living room by the fire when Jeanette asked me what I was looking for this trip and I told her we were expecting a new grandchild and I was looking for an antique christening gown. She looked over at John and he said, "Go and get it!" They gave Joe and me the gown that had been in their family for centuries and a day gown from the fifteenth century. I told her I could not take them, and she said there was no chance that they would use these gowns.

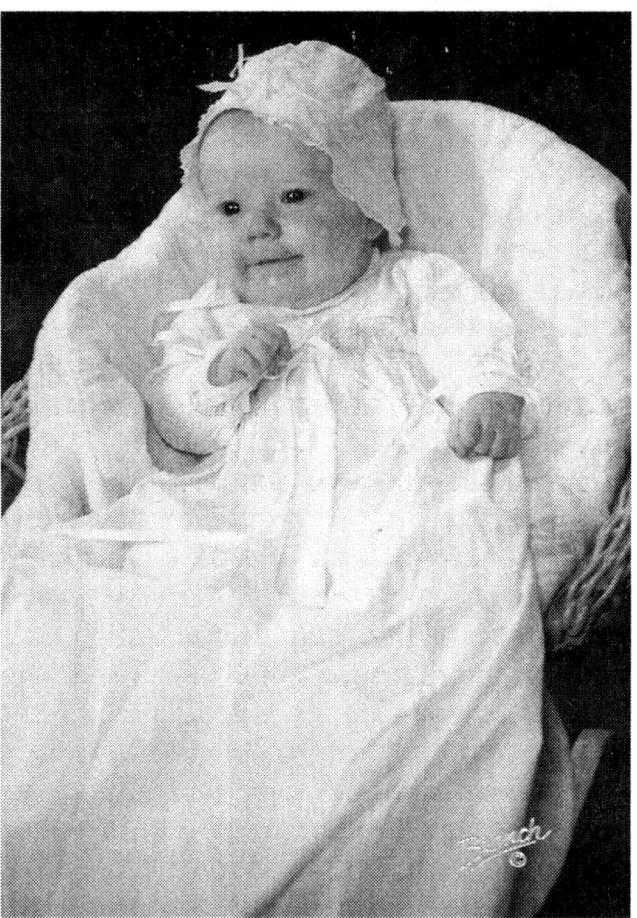

Oliva-Rose Hart in antique christening gown and Granny Bailey's wicker chair

She said they would love to know that someone they knew loved them and would take care of their heirlooms. I was bowled over and sent her pictures of the christening. We exchange Christmas cards yet and letters once in awhile. I hope someday they come to visit us, and I can show them the hospitality they showed Joe and me.

Acquiring the First Farm

Joe has always loved farming. The Morris Farm, not far from the store, was rumored to be going up for sale in the future when Joe went into the army. It was indeed offered for sale and we were in Ft. Bragg, North Carolina, at the time and didn't know about it. Joe's dad knew we wanted to buy it. He went to the bank and asked the banker the amount of money we had in the bank and was told we had five thousand dollars. His dad told the banker he wanted to take out our savings and borrow the rest in our name to have enough to pay for the land in full. The men agreed on this; his dad signed Joe's name to the loan and shook the banker's hand and walked out of the bank with a deed to the farm. Paw Paw (as we called him) called us at the army base and told us we now owned a farm. Of course, we were overjoyed over this transaction on our behalf. Could you do this today??? I don't think so!!!

Journey's

When we were first married and had not established a good farming system, I started to work at the corset factory in Alamo to help supplement our income; this was before we had any children. Everyone should work in a factory a year and in the school system one year, and believe you me, there would be a lot of better understanding among folks in this world.

I sewed on a one-needle machine on corsets of all shapes, sizes, and lengths. If one little stitch was not in line with the others (kind of like the little French orphan, Madeline, and her inmates), you had to rip it all out and start over. This took time and time was one thing you didn't have. You had so many minutes to sew each garment or you didn't get paid as much. If you got too slow, you were replaced with someone who could go faster. You had 15 minutes for a break and 30 minutes to eat lunch. Music blared at top volume all day and a certain pace to keep you working at this pace. It really, really got bad at times. Bathroom breaks were non-existent.

Shaw Emerson cut hair as long as I could remember and always cut Joe's hair. When we married, we thought if I learned to do this, we could save a bundle, especially after Jody was born. So I practiced on Joe's hair. He had some dilly of nicks and holes and just plain messes on his head for a while. Jody was six and had never been to a barber, so when he was asked to be in a wedding, we decided it was time for him to go and get a proper cut. He was scared to death of that barber chair.

Then there was the job at Bells Elementary School way back when. I had all four of our children with me when I started as an aide in school there; it was a good little school. Jody was in second grade and his teacher taught him how to type. The little library was well-stocked. I sometimes worked in the library and loved working with the little ones and the books. Our principal was a man of color and he was tall and impressive. A very good man that was also a preacher and he lived what he taught with great patience and principles. We became friends.

One of my jobs was to create interesting things for the bulletin boards. In the hall, I worked on one to demonstrate the earth, sky, water, and living things. The part under the earth, I drew tunnels with ants in them. One ant particularly was big and solid black. The principal looked at the board and started laughing and pointed to the big black ant and said, "Miss Myrtle, is that big black ant me?" And I told him "the spitting image!" and we had a secret joke between us. When our daughter was killed, he sent us a very wonderful memorial; and when he died, I had lost a very good friend.

I had so many experiences with the dreaded snake through the years and some of them have been mentioned in these pages before but wanted to make a "list" of some of the most memorable ones. One was the huge black chicken snake in the corncrib at home that Daddy protected all his life; one in the cotton field when I was chopping by myself and I was barefoot and walking across one row and cutting grass out of the cotton on the other and walked right over the snake and it turned out to be a copperhead. The hoe in my hand took care of him. Another was when I was still at home before I married and was picking strawberries for Uncle Doode. I ran my hand through the berry leaves looking for the red ones and ran my hand over the back of a big one. I did not stay to see what kind. I had a similar experience in the butterbean row in the garden after I married. He was another chicken snake and also big. When we moved into the house we are in now, I was outside early one morning looking at the flower bed to see what was coming up. I was once more barefoot and stepped on a tiny green grass snake that might as well have been a six-footer because he scared me to death. The feeling was mutual because he wasted no time getting out of there. I've run over a multitude of them on the mower. Maggie pulled one out of the hole in a tree with a hoe and he did not get away. The most frightening one was the one I found in the middle of the night.

Then there were our bouts with the pets. At the old yellow house, we woke up one night to the loudest thumps under the house one right after the other. The floor shook and we jumped up and the children were up screaming and that's when the odor overtook us. And what an odor!!! We all were running out of the house and out from under the house ran this very agitated skunk and then came our very disturbed dog. He had caught the skunk under the house and could not get out and had some battles to fight before he could get free. We had to stay with Joe's parents for days, trying to get the house aired out. I had to wash every rag in the house and air all the curtains and wash everything.

So we had this stray black dog of no certain breed that the children fed and became like maybe the most important member of the family to them. They named this dog "Little Monkey" and I never could figure the exact reason for this bestowed name. Little Monkey was having puppies by an unknown dog of probably an unknown breed and came time to deliver, she decided that under the house would serve as a good delivery room. We were in the new house at this time. She had five little ones, and my four little ones took up residence with them until they got hungry. They would come in to eat covered in dirt and dog hair, and I would make them clean up and promptly they went back to the new family.

The Pea Cooker

In the old yellow house, there was a lot of things going on and not all good. Jody was a baby and I had him in the kitchen with me in the little roller bed that I used. I kept the babies with me because I could not hear them in the other room. I was canning black-eyed peas that day in the pressure cooker that I always used just like Mama had taught me—I thought. I was standing right in front of it and the cotton-picking thing blew up, and peas and glass went right over me and landed everywhere but on the baby and me. There was an opening between the kitchen and the dining room, and peas went all through this opening and all over the dining room floor. We have not one cut or bruise or burn. And you don't believe in miracles?

Bullfrogs and the Frying Pan (1956–1960)

Of course, when Joe and I were first married, you could say we were quite immature, but you would never hear us admit to this calculation. One of our favorite outings was to go to Henderson's Lake and shoot bullfrogs. I loved the sport but I really, really hated those critters with a passion. After the hunt, we would bring them home, and Joe would skin the legs and have me "fry them up." Well, frying up frog legs is a sport within itself. Those jokers would hop and skip and jump all over the frying pan and just wouldn't give it up. Of course, I did not admit my distaste for them at the time. I actually had pretty good judgment at this time as to when to express my displeasure and when not to. The interpretation of this sentence could read that I was young and shy?? Not exactly shy, but something like that. I just loved every little thing that presented itself in those days. Even cooking those nervous quivering legs, skinning the quail, stewing up the squirrels and rabbits. Thank goodness, some things pass away and go into oblivion!

Florida Trip (Children Small)

When Mame' was eight, Jody, six; Shane, four; and Milly, two, we decided to go to Florida. Well, Milly was in diapers, Shane, not trained, and the two of them, plus Jody, still had pacifiers. I know, too big! Bad Mama! Anyway, that is the way it was. The babies were so picky about these pacifiers and only wanted the natural-colored ones that when lost, just blended in with whatever they happened to hit. It seemed like we spent half our lives looking for these habit-formers, but to stay in the car or room with the little ones, you had better have one handy.

We were in the old station wagon and two hours out; the kids were tired and we started hearing those famous words, "Are we there yet?" We never had made a long trip before with the children, and they were not used to it and didn't know what to expect. They were over the seats and back again, in the floor, on top of the back seat, then fighting, then hungry every thirty minutes and I said, "Never again will I do this," and we did not until the next year, but this first one is never to be forgotten—or forgiven!

Our Second Florida Trip

We had this amazing trip to Florida when Jody was about nine or ten years old. We went with friends that had children the ages of ours and in the bunch, there were six boys the age of Jody, if you can imagine that many boys together thinking of things they could do.

We stayed in a condo and had never seen a one before in our lives and were thrilled out of our minds. There were three swimming pools, tennis courts, workout rooms, golf course and fishing holes all over the place with small alligators all around. This may not sound like much these days with all the fancy places to go, but to us back then it was "heaven on earth."

Jody and the boys wanted to have a fish fry with their catch since they were getting ready to go have a try in the ponds. We made a deal with the boys and told them if they could catch enough fish to feed the three families, that totaled about fifteen, then we would dress the fish and fry them for supper. Wouldn't you believe that about four in the afternoon, here came the army of boys with a big cooler they could hardly carry and opened it up, and it was completely full of fish. It took the rest of the day and early night to get them all ready to fry; and when they came out of the skillet, those boys ate them as fast as we could cook them. I really believe they would have eaten anything that bit the hook that day.

We went to Disney World and Bush Gardens and were to go home in two days when the adults decided to go on a deep sea fishing trip. Joe and two others got seasick and

Joe was so sick, he literally turned green and had to go to the doctor. He was unable to drive home for three more days, and the kids celebrated his sickness until we reminded them of the reason they could stay longer, but it barely made a dent in their enthusiasm. Joe will not go deep sea fishing to this day and that was forty-five years ago.

Lesson: Never underestimate the power of a pack of boys!

POO-DOO, a Dog - POO-DOO Was a Dog?

Our very favorite pet of all times was a basset hound named POO-DOO for obvious reasons. He was the laziest dog under the sun. I never knew laziness as an endearing trait, but it sure worked for this hound.

He was a registered puppy and his mom and dad were both champions at dog shows. My Uncle Raymond (Dad's brother) and his wife raised bassets for show and bred them to sell. They were living in Louisiana when we got the puppy.

Poodoo

He was very hard to train with four small children playing and petting him around the clock. I tried to keep him outside and the children tried to keep him inside. It was a battle from day one. The whole family fell in love with Poo-Doo.

He had a bed in the den by the fireplace, but his most favorite place in the whole house was right on the living room couch. He would be on the couch and hear me coming in the house, and he would run so fast down the hall that he wound up sliding more than running, and so fast to get to his bed. He tried to fool me, making me think he had been there all the while and would jump right over the bed in his enthusiasm to fake his way into my good graces. When we had one of the weddings outside, he was dressed to the nines with his white collar and boutonniere. He was very handsome and he knew it. He went from one chair to another; and if someone had rested their punch on the ground, he would take a sip and move on to someone who had set their plate down in his reaching distance and take a bite or two there, then move on to something more to his liking. After the reception, we were all in the kitchen trying to tie things up and someone said, "Where is the wedding cake?" Sure enough, POO DOO had gotten to it and was really into eating all he could! So much for leftover cake!

This dog was stolen from us. A neighbor saw a truck stop and pick him up. We were all so heart-broken. I never wanted another dog, but of course, we had several bassets after that one, but they were not the same. We did have one that had a litter of 12 puppies, and the kids were going to sell them and make "lots of money" because we had papers on them. But cousins and friends kept wanting one and before we knew it, all the free ones were gone and the pricey ones were non-existent!

Lesson...Never invite Poo Doo to one of your weddings!

Talents of My Children

My children were always sympathetic with my deafness, but sometimes they used this to their advantage or sometimes just for sheer pleasure of "pulling one over on me." They always knew just how loud or low to keep their voices when talking about me to keep me from hearing them or something they did not want me to know. I learned to "read" their faces and expressions, plus their movements too, to tell when these secrets were being told right in front of me. They could have talked somewhere away from me, but the thrill came from doing this while I was so close at hand. It was not possible for them to keep a straight face or fail to cast their eyes a little downwards or maybe a little red show up in their cheeks. I could usually figure out what the culprit had done or was planning to do by just studying their giveaway clues. That's what Mom's do—even deaf ones!

Animals; Some Were Pets, But Some Were Pests

There have been so many animals in our lives they could not possibly all be mentioned. The ones that have had the most impact were mostly pets, but some were more like unwelcomed pests.

When the children were about ten, eight, six and four, we really had a show with a fluffy, furry bunch of little critters. We came home one night and pulled in the drive and there by the bank on the side of the drive, I saw something run and just disappear into thin air. I told Joe to stop the car and see if he could see anything with the lights toward the bank. He backed up and there on the bank sat a little baby rabbit. The children just squealed, laughed and pointed and scared the poor thing. Lo and behold, he vanished too. Joe got out of the car and looked closer; there was a hole in the bank where the rabbit had gone through and out of sight. He pushed his arm into the bank up to his elbow, and I was so afraid of what else may be in there. I started to yell for him to get his hand back and he did but not with just his hand, he came up with a baby rabbit and said, "I could feel another one!" He proceeded to pull these wonderful little creatures out of the hole until there were at least six or seven of them. The children were jumping, yelling, and darting out of the car, and you would have thought it was New Year's Eve on Times Square in New York City. We had a hard time convincing them that the babies needed to stay in their nest a few more days so they would be healthy and older. The days after that passed by slowly with them watching the hole like it would go away if they turned their heads.

When the rabbits got bigger, we let them bring them into the backyard. Joe made a box with wire and put it on legs so the dogs could not get them and we raised most of them; some even had babies of their own. The whole family loved this experience.

Joe's Nickname

Joe and I have always been together, it seems. We have had a good life together but not without our little (did I say little?) ins and outs. When we were younger, the outs were a little closer together and I have always been a little (did I say a little?) outspoken. On occasion I would call him a Jack...the title just seemed to stick and now he is Jack to me all the time. Not in the original sense, you know.

We are a family of nicknames, and some are evident in their origin and some make no sense at all. My mother's brothers and sisters were Skinny (Uncle Lawerence), Pritchette (Aunt Edith Carmen) and that is such a pretty name and never heard it until I read it in some family things, Aunt Dot (Dorothy Fay), Frog (Uncle James). My parents' nicknames were Buster and Pig. Where they got Pig, I'll never know. She was a tall and very slender woman. Dad's sister was Aunt Lydia Belle and called Litt. Dad's brother was known as Doode, but his name was Clarence Hollis. There are more but this is the knack of it all. I think having a special name is great but sometimes a little outside the box and can be embarrassing if you are out somewhere and had rather be called Myrtle than Turt. Sometimes the last syllable is a little blurred and the imagination takes hold. I know there are times where the imagined name is a little more appropriate than the real one. Lesson: Change what you can and live with what you can't!

Smokey Mountain Vacation

At twelve, ten, eight and six, we decided to take the children on a vacation to the Smokey Mountains. After staying a day or two in Gatlinburg, we went up on top to Clingman's Dome for the great view. After getting this far, it seemed only logical for us to go down the other side to see what we could see there. By this time we were pretty off-course and our original plans were already down the tube.

The children were looking at the map and Mame' saw Fayetteville, North Carolina, on the map and knew this was where she was born and started begging to go there because she felt it only her right to see where she was born. Well, this seemed logical too, so we proceeded to go to Ft. Bragg once again. She was delighted and made the extra mile well-worth it.

We were all set to go back toward Tennessee when the children then realized we were so close to the ocean and they had never seen that either. Off we went to Myrtle Beach, and I think the little ones thought it was named after me and that was a pleasant thought too. After much splashing in the ocean, we headed home a tired but happy bunch. On the way home we stopped a little way out of Knoxville for lunch and again headed home. We got 75 miles down the road, and Shane discovered that she had left her "purse." I don't recall exactly what an 8 year old would have in her purse that was so important, but important it was and she proceeded to cry and cry and cry, until her dad decided the best way to get home in peace was to turn around and get the purse. We tried to convince her that someone had already picked it up and in no way was it still sitting on the chair where she left it. But miracle of miracles, the purse was behind the counter waiting for her. Someone had turned it in and the workers had saved it for her. Once again we headed home after a "short vacation in Gatlinburg!"

The Wizards and the Lizards

Some of the Emerson forefathers are buried in the Young Cemetery between here and

Gadsden, close to Henderson's lake. Joe's dad used to take our children and Bill's to the cemetery cleaning each August. The kin of the people buried there kept it clean and would go to clear out the overgrowth each year. This gave way for a noon picnic and much visiting and catching up on family news and gossip. Some new family members came each year and we made new friendships and families grew closer together. Sounds good? You bet! But there was an undercurrent here for my particular branch of the family. Unknown to me, my children took fruit jars and lids with them and punched holes in the tops and collected creepy things, mostly lizards, and brought them home and turned them loose in the yard. They were so discreet that for years I did not— catch on—to what was—going on. I repeatedly saw lizards in the yard, on the porch, up on the bricks of the house, on the walks, and an occasional one in the house. I asked Joe, "What is going on here? We are being besieged by those creatures!" His reply was, "Stop the children from bringing them in from the graveyard." He had been in on this from the beginning. Of course, it was too late by then, and I am still being entertained by running, crawling, creepy things that are the children and grandchildren of the original creatures. I guess this is their gathering place to see their forefathers and have a few characteristics like ours. Maybe a homecoming of sorts, but I just wish they would go back to their old homeplace! Lesson: Always, Always inspect jars going and coming out of your house!

He is Just a Farmer!

My children and I went into a shoe store to get some tennis shoes for one of them. The sales lady there rang up the amount for them and I wrote her a check. (This was before everyone and their pets had a credit card.) She said she would have to have it approved by the manager, and I told her it was just fine with me. The manager was in back of the store and she called out about it. He wanted to know what my husband did for a living, and I told her that he was a farmer. She then shouted back to him, "He is JUST A FARMER!" I looked at her and said plainly, "My husband is not JUST A FARMER, HE IS A FARMER!" I then laid the shoes back on the counter, took my check from her and left the store.

The Big Stick of Bologna

Well, there are friends, and there are friends! We have had lots of friends through the years but one of the best back when and now too is 'ol Ralph Wilkerson. He and Joe played ball together, and he was catcher when Joe was pitching, played basketball together and generally into everything there was to do as partners. After high school Ralph went to college and after graduation he went to work for the Tennessee Pride Sausage Company, and by then we were home with four small children running everywhere. Now, Ralph understood big families and he "dug" country life from experience; and when he came to visit, he always brought (he knew that flowers was a long way down the list of things we needed) bologna. I am not talking a big hunk or a few slices but the whole enchilada, the big stick, about a foot and a half of the good stuff. What are friends for? I have forgotten 99 percent of the gifts that I have received through the years but on my deathbed, I will remember the bologna. Thank you, Ralph, for being a friend and the big stick! Lesson: Pick your friends and you will never go hungry!

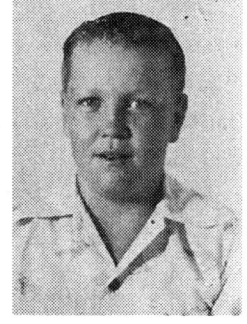

Ralph Wilkerson
"The Bologna Stick Man"

Dan: The Hero

The Buffalo River was always a favorite place for us when the children were in their teens and younger. We went to float the river two or three times a year with friends that had children the same ages as ours. We sometimes had five or six boats full of kids of all ages. All of our experiences on this water was so much fun and wonderful, except this one time. The rains had been coming with regularity and pouring more inches of water than usual, thus making the rapids and water flow much faster and fiercer than usual.

The children were all in the lead and Joe and I were right behind them. Dan Norville and his wife, Rose Ann, were in the rear with some other adults. Shane's boat turned over close to the bank. I saw it happen, and we were coming right behind and she did not come up. We could see her face right under the water about six inches and she was struggling. Our boat caught in the rapids and we could not stop it. Joe jumped out but was fighting his way back and she still did not come up. Dan jumped out right behind her and got to her but could not get her up out of the water. Her bathing suit was hung on a root so he acted fast, tore her suit off, and up she came coughing, spitting and trying to catch her breath; it was terrible to see. By this time Joe had fought his way back and helped get her out. I can still see her face under that water and still have dreams about it. We will be forever grateful to our friend and our hero for his fast thinking and actions in saving our daughter's life. What else can I say but thank you. I never went back to the Buffalo River to float down the rapids again.

Myrtle's Turtle Tale

The children found a turtle on the road and brought him home with them, and we kept him a long time. During this time was our Homecoming at church, and after church my family continued the day with us, visiting and catching up with gossip until night. We had special visitors from Texas. There was this special cousin from Texas that was into oil, and we were very much in awe of him and his success. I was a little nervous since

I had not spent much time with him and did not know him as well as many others of my kin. (I soon learned that he was a true Bailey because he was so very nice and agreeable with all the family.) We had (in the meantime) lost the turtle somewhere in the house and had forgotten about it. My cousin was sitting on the couch in the den with his legs spread out and very relaxed when the said turtle made his presence known by crawling out from under the couch right between his legs. We all got really quiet and my cousin looked down and said, "Well, I'll be dammed!" The whole room exploded with laughter, and the ice was broken for the rest of the day.

Then the same turtle was still here and I was entertaining Joe and Joe Wayne's three children and they were all (seven, counting my four) upstairs in the playroom, when all at once, Milly started screaming and all the other six started screaming and jumping up and down, and I knew we were having another crises. Milly came running down the stairs with the turtle hanging off her index finger and was trailed by excited children. I took her hand and put the turtle on the brick hearth in the kitchen and took a hammer and hit and hit and the more I hit it, the louder the screams. He would not turn loose! I called Dr. Mayfield, and he said he did not know what to do and to "hold on" and he would look it up and call back...Then I thought of fire. In the back of my mind, I remembered someone using fire for some such emergency. I rolled up a newspaper and set it on fire and held up Milly's hand; then she really got hysterical. As soon as the fire hit the turtle's tail, he immediately turned loose and hit the floor. In the meantime, Dr. Mayfield called and said, "Get her down to the office right now." I then called him back, and he said to bring her on because she would need a shot. This did not sit well with Milly either. She was having a really bad day. Her finger turned a pale white and began to swell; but with the shot and a lot of petting, she finally smiled and was ready to go again.

Lesson: Never—Never pick up a turtle off the road and bring him home!

The Goat on Loan for Two Weeks That Stayed Five Years

About the same time as the rabbit episode was going on, we had a "friend" that had a friend who was moving and had a billy goat. Now this friend found out we had a fenced-in backyard, and her friend needed someone to keep their goat for two weeks and assumed we wanted a goat to go with our four kids (pardon the pun.) Of course, we said, "OK" for two weeks. We had never seen these people with the pet problem before and wouldn't you know, we never saw them but the one time when they delivered the animal!

Two weeks went by, then two months, and then two years and, believe me, I really think those people should go back to school and learn to count and study the months in a year. Anyway, the goat became good friends with the children and possibly Joe and me; we got used to having him around.

The goat did a great job of eating around the yard and really cleaning out the flower beds. I do mean cleaning the zinnias, the petunias and when he finished with the flowers, he would sometimes eat some grass and weeds. He always ate the dessert first. Have you ever seen anyone do this? Except me, of course.

Never Run Around the Base on a Foul

We had chickens and ducks that loved to torment the goat. They seemed to know they could outrun him and had great moments accomplishing this feat. The children, on the other hand, had the last call; they would slip up on the chickens and ducks, put a basket or pail over them and squeal with delight around the caught foul, then take the covering off, and chase them until they made it under the house or the shed. These fouls finally learned to hit the underpin as soon as they heard little feet come out the back door. They would ask then, "Why won't the chickens come out anymore?" Lesson: One pet at a time seems sufficient!

Old Loom

Mr. Earl Dunlap was always interested in history and old things and had been collecting for a long time when I first met him. He was a well-read and wise man. He found out that I liked old things too and invited Joe and me over to see his things he had in an old log house he had put up in his backyard. We were still very young, and I had never seen such a wonderful collection of early antiques. He had old World War I uniforms, a Civil War uniform, all kinds of lanterns, and what you would expect to find in such a old log home. He let me borrow an old medical book from the Civil War era that told when the correct time and way to "bleed" a patient, when necessary to amputate a limb, etc. It was an amazing book.

He also told me he was selling an old loom he had sitting up in the middle of the room. He asked me if I was interested. But, of course, I was! Joe was doubtful because we didn't have any excess money since we were still struggling to get started with farming. Mr. Earl said, "I tell you what, I paid forty dollars for it years ago, and I will sell it to you for that exact amount if you want it!" Of course, I wanted it! He told me its history and I wrote it down.

The loom I have in my house belonged to the Hendersons, Medlins, and Brigances before Jasper Emison bought it for his wife. The Brigance lady made four Confederate uniforms on it. Mr. Brigance's daddy said his wife made them and some coverlets also. Mr. Earl said he bought it from Mrs. Raymond Henderson's granddaddy.

The loom is in my log house now but is not put together for lack of space. The log house is so small; the loom would take the whole floor space to set it up. But never you mind, I know it is there and love knowing it is there, set up or not!

Trip to Europe with Mame'

Of all the trips that I have ever made, the one to Europe with Mame' stands out in my mind. This trip was only a year before she died, and I had all this wonderful time with her and seeing her happy and surrounded by all the amazing things that the countries had to offer.

The trip actually started two years before we left Bells on the bus to catch the plane. Julia Wells was the Girl Scout leader and I was the helper. Julia has always had such a great mind and visualized us taking the girls on a trip that they would never forget and one that most of them would not ever have the opportunity to go on. She said, "Why don't we take them to Europe?" I knew then and there that we were as good as on our way.

The plan was to have squash and turnips in the field for two years to pay for this excursion. This was hard work, but the girls stuck to it and picked squash every other day of the season and in the fall cut and hauled turnips to the trucks waiting for them. They threw rotten squash and turnips at each other and complained about aching muscles, but we made it to Europe, not costing the girls a penny, except their spending money if they wanted anything to bring home.

We saw seven countries in twenty-one days, and these girls learned more than they ever could have in a classroom in that time. They flew in a plane for the first time, saw Buckingham Palace with the Queen driving in the gates, Westminster Abby, Hard Rock London, rode the underground, London Bridge, had a Rhine River Cruise, saw Zermatt and the Matterhorn, and played in snow, saw Florence and Pisa, Rome and the Vatican, Sorrento and Capri and the Grotto, Ann Frank's hideout in Amsterdam and the list goes on and on. Our girls' eyes were opened to the world and I think is one of the greatest things that they could have done. All this because their leader, Julia, had a vision for leadership and the ability to carry it out.

Mame's Death: May 21, 1977

I do not have the vocabulary nor do I think there are any words in the English language to express the devastation that Joe and I felt when our daughter, Mame', was killed in a car accident. I can only say a few words that only someone who has been through this agony will understand the depth of sorrow. It breaks your heart and takes your very breath away. You can never be prepared for it. You can never do a thing about it. It is this quick shutdown, and the finality of it, and your helplessness, that blows you away. You are presented with this and there is no answer and no way out of it.

Mame' was our first born. This says a lot for a mother and father. We had been married five years and had long awaited her birth. She was a laughing, bright, and happy girl. She loved life, her family, and her friends.

We were having a Sunday School Class party on the patio at our house when her date came to pick her up. We had never allowed her to go out in a car with a date before, but (there is always a but) they were having a class party in Brownsville and we let her go. She was not quite sixteen. Only a few weeks to go. The boy she was with was her first boyfriend, and we knew they were fond of each other and understood how important this night was for them to go to the party together.

They went through Bells to watch her cousin, Vince, play ball for a while. She was a big fan of sports and especially when this cousin was playing. From there, they left for the class party; and when turning into the drive, they were hit on the side by a car driven by a drunk driver that came over the hill without any lights on. When they called us, I thought they had it all wrong. I kept saying, "It is wrong; they have it all wrong; it's wrong." I could not accept this fact. No way! I won't go into details.

The boy she was with was not hurt too badly outside but was in turmoil inside, which is worse. None of this was his fault, and we tried to let him know that we did not blame him.

180

When we were in Switzerland, Mame' bought several beautiful handkerchiefs, and I had used them to trim a dress for her for a party she went to; we buried her in this dress.

Our world as we knew it stopped and never really became the same. The damage is permanent, and the whole that is left never is refilled. Our outlook on life is different. It puts things in a whole new perspective. I hope this has made better people of us. We certainly know more about what is important in life now. "Baby, we love you!"

Mame's Quilt of many Colors

Upon the death of our oldest daughter, Mame', I had pondered as to what to do with her clothes. I had seen so many people keep their loved ones' possessions, only to have them deteriorate and get musty and brown with age. I did not just want to throw them away because they were too good for that and, to tell you the truth, I did not want anyone else wearing them.

After my father died, the women in the family and friends made a quilt of the ribbons from Daddy's grave, one for me, and one for my sister Betty. The ribbons back then were real ribbons and were not paper or synthetic like the ones now. This gave me the idea of making a quilt of Mame's things and, therefore, all in one item that I could keep fresh and remember the things she used to wear. I had a few of her baby clothes and scraps from school dresses I had made her while growing up. So I had some scraps of her things through the years that were important to her or to me that meant a lot to us. Some of the things I used were baby dresses, kindergarten dress, tops to her shorts or jeans, and then her Girl Scout uniform. I made this quilt with the Lafayette's Orange Peel pattern, which got its name supposedly when at a ball, a young admirer picked up an orange peel that he had peeled and eaten the fruit, and she took it home and made the quilt pattern to imitate this peeling. The quilt turned out well and I love it, and it will be a family heirloom for my children and grandchildren to cherish.

The quilt that was made for me from my father's ribbons was used on my mother's casket as a drape, much like the flag is used on our servicemen's caskets as a gesture of honor to the deceased. I have requested that in my casket a quilt be placed over my feet, and it does not have to be a good one, just one as a remembrance of my love for the craft. Another thing about my mother's casket: Richard brought Mama's favorite fishing pole and leaned it against Daddy's quilt. There was something about this that seemed just right.

Mame Lou's "Quilt of Many Colors" made by Myrtle Leggett Emerson from Mame's clothes after her death

Milly

Our youngest daughter has always been full of mischief, to say the least. She was a tiny little baby and always sick a lot. She had pneumonia when she was six weeks old. Then as the years went by, she became stronger and stronger and stronger still. She has always been thin and wiry, and full of energy. She pulled every trick that could be pulled and stayed in a usual state of entertainment to us. She always had some sort of pet in her arms. It did not have to be a tame animal and was likely not to be. A pet rabbit, squirrel, turtle, and she tried snakes, but I drew the line there. As she grew older, the babies and small children in the family or friend's youngsters always wanted Milly to play with them and entertain them because she just had a way about her that was pleasant and gentle to the smaller ones.

As she got into middle school, she played on the high school basketball team for six years on the main team, starting in the seventh grade. She played with Shane on the team for four of these. She got out on the floor and stole the ball, and Shane stood under the goal and Milly fed it to her and in it went. Milly shot from the outside. She put her whole self into this game and really made her mark there. She was the player of the year for West Tennessee for the girls. We were very excited over this because she had worked for so many years and tried so hard and came up as a winner!

Then when she was in the 10th grade and was on the basketball team, one of the girls on the team they were playing pushed Milly down, hitting her head so hard and her neck was cracked. She was unconscious for a long time; and when she woke up just before the ambulance got there, her eyes were unfocused and she could not talk. The attendants put her in a neck brace and took her to the hospital, and it was a long time before we heard from the x-rays that told us her neck was not broken but they kept her there for a few days for observation. This was a very stressful time for the whole family.

After this happened in the game (and it looked deliberate because the girl that hit her was mad because Milly kept stealing the ball), Shane and other team members all made certain this girl never had a chance again to get the ball.

Milly's House

The log house that Milly lives in has a very interesting story behind it. It was originally the Williams' homeplace, this being her children's ancestors on their father's side. The last member of the Williams' family to live there was Mr. Zab Williams and he was Louise Hart's grandfather. When we first looked at the house, it was covered with cypress boards, forming a siding that kept the rain and bad weather off the logs, thus providing protection through the years They were almost perfect, allowing for some places that were not covered well. The house held a few surprises in little things, like old bottles and a few old pieces of furniture. The decision was made to move it onto land across the road and so it was dismantled and numbered. It was decided that more room was needed than the house provided, so a full basement was added and a dog trot between the two main rooms were separated, thus making a large entry. The two main rooms had an upstairs to them. The original stairway was salvaged for the living room and new ones made out of old wood for the entry. The separated rooms made for a high ceiling with an open half going across the back. When the basement and the hall were added, then the kitchen on the back, the floor plan allowed for almost 5,000 square feet of living area. The L-shaped back was closed in for a screened porch with much room for outside use.

When the house was put up and the kitchen put on the back of the main rooms, we knew that the logs were of a different wood and probably at a different time period, but the family knew nothing about how this happened. One day, a member of the Walnut Hill Church (not far away) came upon an old paper that stated Mr. Zab Williams had bought the original Walnut Hill Baptist Church that was a one room log house to attach to the back of his log house for a kitchen. This made a great kitchen space, allowing for much room to put large tables and old cabinets bought to go with the age of the space. I hope they have the blessing before meals at least in the church kitchen.

Wide poplar boards were put down and stained to look old and long narrow windows the size of period windows and a red tin roof put on for good measure. But the story does not end there. The house was built on the exact spot where the old Jackson School sat, and the drive up to the house was not changed from the old school days. This is the same building that my Aunt Bettie Bailey taught in.

The house was then covered with cypress boards yet again with insulation between the logs and the siding. The raw logs line every room, and the doors were old doors found from older homes of our times. The three fireplaces are large and the one in the kitchen is a walk-in one.

Most people now want everything new, but the ones that love old things have good opportunities to help preserve our heritage and keep our founding days alive.

Dreaded Snake Stories

I have had so many experiences with the dreaded snake through the years and am really not as afraid of them if I see him before he sees me! If I see him, no matter how big or small he is, he really does not have a chance to get in even one "strike." (pardon the pun.) Some of them have been mentioned in previous pages but I have them collected here in one place and in perspective. The first encounter with "the big one" was this huge chicken snake my dad kept in the corncrib to catch the mice and the rats. No one was to even think of harming him because he saved many bushels of grain that Daddy had worked so hard to gather to feed the livestock in the barnyard. Now one of my jobs was to get some corn from this crib to feed the horses, cows, and chickens. (I had to shell the corn for the chickens.) I put off this trip into the "snake's house" until my dad had to do a little sound prompting, saying the snake would not hurt me. I know that I did not look like a mouse or a rat, but I still did not trust a hungry snake. After all, I was just a kid! I literally ran in and out as soon as possible and sometime saw him sleeping on a rafter or on top of the corn pile...'Nuff said.

The most frightening one to me was one I found in the middle of the night in this house. (I had heard of this but did not believe it but I tell you I am a believer now!) I got up late one night and went
in the bathroom and started to sit down and something cautioned me to look back. Did I see something moving? And, sure enough, there the creature was with his head held

high out of the commode and his tongue doing lightning darts and his eyes staring straight at me! I screamed (yet again) until I was so hoarse I could not talk, and Joe thought I was dying and could not believe his eyes. I'm sure at this time of night, the sight he beheld made him think he was still asleep and having the nightmare of all nightmares. He couldn't find anything to kill the critter with and went outside to get a curved stalk cutter and told me to stay and watch him. Watch him?!?! I had seen him enough, thank you! Joe reminded me he may get sleepy and get in my bed. My throat was so sore the next day I could barely talk. Joe thought there was some good to come out of every situation.

One more and I will move on to greener pastures. I had a cousin that helped me some when the children were small, and I was in the fields helping Joe with the farm. She was an older cousin and we all loved her dearly and did not have a problem until one day she was cleaning some in the house and was fluffing the pillows on the window seat. She picked up one pillow and was shaking it up a little and looked down, and there was this little snake coiled up. She had disturbed his nap under the pillow and he was not happy with her at all. I was afraid she would never darken at our door again. She was so frightened and we had to promise her that he was an orphan.

Third Black Book

First Three Pages

March 7, 1997 – This is the third such notebook I have started in the last four years. The first one, I managed two pages; the next one only one and this one, I plan to communicate at least a little more. This is only a paper for thoughts and memories to give my children and grandchildren a little perspective as to what I am, who I am, and what made me so.

My earliest memories are of Mama and Daddy when I was about five. I hear people say they remember things at a much earlier age but, alas, I cannot. I remember the house (before modernizing) and the "old house," the barn, the chicken houses, Mike's house, and, of course, the "outhouse." There was at one time a carport with a side shed that, for some reason, never stood long. I think it had brick siding on it. (The asphalt kind.) The shed part had a dirt floor; there are pictures of the barn. The "old house" had two rooms, a long porch across the front. Daddy used to hang the hams from the rafters and line the Irish potatoes down on the floor. Lime was sprinkled over them to keep them from rotting.

The house was old gray clapboard that was never painted. Betty and I had a playhouse behind it. We "canned" grass and berries for vegetables and fruit. We canned wood chips for meat, imitating Mama canning sausages, loin chops, etc.

When we killed hogs, we had to preserve it quickly. Sausage would last several months in cold weather hung in the rafters of the "old house" along with hams. Most people have never heard of canning meat, but Mama did this on a large scale. The hams were salted down in a large wooden chest; salt lined the bottom, then a layer of hams, bacon, then a layer of salt and alternated until the huge box was full. The meat could not touch each other inside the box. It would spoil if this happened. There was a preservation procedure of rubbing the ham or shoulder in a "sugar cure" mixture that

Myrtle Rose Leggett Emerson

kept them for a year or more hanging from the rafters.

The hen house was by the garden fence that completely enclosed the garden. Mama planted running beans on this fence. The garden was planted from early spring until late fall starting with English peas, radishes, mustard greens, onions, potatoes, and later tomatoes, beans and peas, etc.

The "outhouse" was behind the chicken house. I will not go into details, except to say this was a good outlet to use the outdated Sears catalog.

The chicken house was by the garden. Poles lined the back for the chickens to roost on. One side was lined with nests, made like petitioned shelves with a section for each laying hen to have her own little nest to lay her eggs and to hatch her little ones. Cleaning the chicken house was the pits and literally "for the birds." (Pardon the pun.)

There was a "running pen" in front of the hen house for the baby chicks. A section housed off for lights to keep them warm until they got their feathers. This pen had chicken wire all around it. We had a round trough that fit on a fruit jar filled with water for the chicks and put this top on the jar; then we would turn it upside down, and the water would fill the trough and stop before running over the rim.

Mike's house was beside this. Between the hen house and the "old house." (More on this later)
The clothesline was in front of all this. At one time there was a fence from the garden that ran in front of the "old house" and met up with the pasture fence by the barn.

The well house was inside this fence closest to the house. This was after we got running water. I can remember going outside to the pitcher pump and getting water to bring in the house. There are pictures of the barn. The ground there has leveled off now, and it used to have a bank on the far side of the barn next to Aunt Olive's house. It had a shallow pond that lay beside the barn. A gate opened to the main road right in front of the barn. A "Z" shaped opening was to get from the house to the barn and did not require a gate. There was a pasture behind all this that contained about three acres and then another fence to separate the pasture from the farmland. The strawberry patch was the first field there.

Joe Took Care of the Entire Garden with Just One Sprinkle

We always have a terrible time with our yard. The flowers are either eat-up with weeds or the bugs are having Thanksgiving dinner every day by going from one flower to the next, eating buds and leaves.

One spring I had just finished weeding the flowerbeds and was so pleased when I saw those dreaded Japanese beetles having a picnic on one of my rose bushes. I knew that in a matter of a day or two, all their friends, relatives, and in-laws would be eating on the tender buds and blooms. I was exhausted and my wonderful husband of almost 55 years said he would take care of the bugs. Lucky me!! I went inside to take a shower and when he came inside he said, "All done!" Lucky, Lucky me!!

The next day, the greenery started to look sick, and I thought all they needed to complete the whole process was some water. I got out the water hoses we had (about 25 would be a pretty good estimate). I got those sprinklers going and we were all set with the yard.

The next day, the green stuff was drooping their heads, and the flowers were

185

beginning to droop down to their stems. What was going on? I checked the sprayers: yes, one for bugs, and one for weeds. Only thing wrong, the weed sprayer was still out because Joe had not put it up. Now there is a puzzle that added up to four in a hurry!

My story ends right here. I want you to decide what you would have done right at this moment. Did you add this up to two and two made four? I forgave him and he was nicer than nice for a few days. Although I will admit that his memory is shorter than mine.

Just be patient and things will be all right; then you can try to convince yourself that two and two equals five; and if you can do this, you just solved a problem here...!

Shane's Joy Ride to Ashville

My daughter Shane is generally an unpredictable person. You never really know what she is thinking and rarely what she is doing. She was visiting here two years ago and her family was in Ashville, North Carolina. The two oldest children, Rebecca and John, were in camp and the youngest, Flora, was with her husband, Fenner. She wanted to get there to them yesterday. We checked buses and planes and nothing there until the next day or so. She was talking to our cousin Pat, and Pat told her that she knew a friend that trucked things that way and she would check and see and would call back. A few minutes later the phone rang, and Shane was told that there was, indeed, a truck going through Ashville the very next morning around five. There were a few little catches though.(Isn't there always?) The truck was an eighteen wheeler and the driver unknown. Pat had heard that he was ok. Talk about checking credentials! So the next morning we took her to Alamo to the said place, and sure enough that truck was a knock out! It looked like it was a block long and tall enough to knock stars out of the sky.

The driver was grinning from ear to ear, and I was thinking we were in over our head this time. They left just waving and grinning and off they went! She said that the truck went within twenty miles of her destination, and Fenn met her there and that the driver was so nice and only stopped twice all the way and flew the rest. They listened to country music and sang along a little, and she took naps and had a relaxing trip. She will never forget that ride or the favor from the cousin, the truck owner, and the driver. Thank you so much whoever you are! I love you!

Working in the Fruitvale Store—First Married

I had never had a job before except the cotton and cornfields and the homework around the house. When Joe and I were first married, there came occasions when the hired help in the Fruitvale Store was sick or on vacation or during busy times, and I was elected for this duty. I just simply loved it! There was no dirt getting all over me or bright sun making me so hot I could not breathe or chopping or picking until my hands and arms were about to fall off. I was in heaven (most of the time). I got to wait on people I knew with very few strangers coming in. I sliced bologna to put hot sauce on and laid between two crackers to sell for a snack. I sold yard fabrics for the ladies to make dresses and brooms and mops for the industrious wife and candy for the kiddies.

You name it and we had it! You see advertisements now where the salesman is all dressed up and so brassy and bragging, you will never believe a word he says. But, believe me, if you needed it, Ollie Boyd's store had it, and if they happened not to have it, why you simply did not need it! You could buy clothes, hats, shoes, unmentionables and socks, combs and brushes, nuts and bolts, hammers and nails, roofing, meats and veggies, flour and butter, salt and sugar, plows and harrows for your field, and then sit back and have a coke, then get your mail without even leaving the room.

Some people were casual and easy to please, but every once in awhile, I got a bummer. I had this one man that came in for a pound of bacon, and I got the slab of meat out of the ice box and sliced off what I figured to be a pound, and it turned out to be slightly over this amount. I told the gentleman that it was just a slice over a pound and he very sternly told me, "I told you a pound and that is what I am paying for!" Now, I believe in budgeting as well as the next person, but there are limits, you know. My first thought was to maybe take out two pieces, but one look at this fellow and my better judgment was to take out one piece and weigh it again for it may just need half a slice taken out. I was ready for this ballgame to end!

At the end of the day, we put oil on the floor and swept everything clean. The oil kept the dirt on the floor from trailing on things, and the farmers high top work shoes and boots brought in what you may call clumps at a time. It was either sweep it out or plant cotton on it!

Myrtle's Jobs in Life

I have had many "jobs" in my life. The most important being a mother and wife. I only finished high school; thus, I do not have a way with words as much as I would like. I can think of things but do not have the vocabulary to put my feelings down eloquently. Although I have kissed the Blarney Stone three times, (and it is a wonder that I do not have some serious disease it was so slick from so many smoochies), but have not seen any immediate results.

When we were first married, Joe and I worked very hard just to make a few ends meet. That first year living with my mother and picking cotton "out" and more or less living off her generosity. Then Ollie hired Joe to feed the cows for him at three fifty (that is dollars) a day, and he provided us with the old house we lived in for about 12 years. I painted the house three times while Joe was in the fields and did lots of papering and painting to make it inhabitable. Our four children were born while we lived in this relic.

In about 1964, I started drawing a plan for my dream house and played with it until we built in 1969. Most of the planning was done on an old quilt in the backyard under a shade tree watching the children play. We started the house in January of 1969 and moved in the first day of June in the same year. There are many mistakes, and I know that most fell on my shoulders but it is ours and we love it. I had some problems in the kitchen, (or the brick mason had the problem) where I was having a brick enclosure made for the stove and a fireplace laid with a brick wall. I knew that this would really show up and wanted it to look just right, so I handed the bricks to the mason one at a time and showed him which side to face out. We managed to remain friends, but it strained him to smile at me for a while. He finally admitted that it looked great.

My quilts have always been special to me. I grew up under them that my mother had made. Then I began making them and putting them out at a fair pace even with the children and the farm. It should not have been a surprise to Joe when I would ask him what he thought about me going into the antique business, which I knew nothing about but loved it all. He agreed and I started out with Carl Yarbro with a booth in the old Franklin building downtown Jackson and it was slow go for a while. I was upstairs with this amazing girl that became a good friend named Charlene. She really had the talent and soon moved on and started her own shop that has now turned into a village of shops with her many talents evident. When Carl moved to the shopping center on the bypass, I moved with him and started sewing pillows, throws, runners and stuffed animals, etc. out of ragged quilts that were beyond repair. This really took off and then I added things made of tapestries and silks, etc. I could hardly keep up until the stores started selling them cheaper than I could make them. I had to move on to something else to survive the competition. I started making sculpted Santas on two liter bottles and painting and selling them. Joe started making stands out of wood for me to cover with old worn quilts and jolly faces and adding raw wool beards and old ornaments hanging off him. These started to sell well and then *Southern Living* did a four-page article with lots of pictures and they really took off then. I had one to go to Nashville to the Christmas party the "Governor" was having for the Capitol people. I sold several out of state with some going to New England and one of these was on the front page of a newspaper up there two years ago. This spread and got too much for me, and I finally quit making them after Christmas of 2009. I never cut a good quilt. Some of the old ones, given me for rags, I sat and mended them back to usefulness. I did repair a few for dealers in New England and one for a museum there. I love sitting and working on these wonderful objects. I had four of my quilts exhibited in the "Three Stars" show in Jackson that was advertised as best antiques in West Tennessee. This was a thrill for me because there were printed pictures and written articles in this amazing book that I treasure for my things and also for all the wonderful things that they found here where we live. It was fantastic to see these treasures that fellow West Tennessee people had.

Of course, the first quilts were made for the sole objective of keeping the family warm and their toes from freezing. Some of these old quilts are cherished today, not for their beauty but for what they represent and the comfort they gave to people that really needed them back then. After people began to have more luxuries in life and didn't need many quilts on the beds, the women (and some men that made them and put a completely new perspective on the looks and makes of them) turned to making some "Sunday" covers that were color-selective and design-conscious and were very good on the eye. This was a way to let loose their creative talents and satisfaction. In other words, they became works of art and are considered art today. Some of the older ones are very artistic also. Give some women a pile of fabric and a needle and thread, and you would be surprised at some of the art that emerged.

One last job that I still do is working for United Foods in Bells. One of my friends works on the packaging designs that go to the salesmen that show them to groceries stores to show them exactly what the plant is selling and how good they look. My friend called me one day, I don't know how long ago but maybe 20 years ago, and asked me if I could help her for about two weeks with making the brochures she needed. I was told that I could do it on the dining room table. Of course, I told her to bring it on! I am still doing these brochures today; in fact, I just sent some labels in yesterday and am waiting on another order any day. It takes up both my utility rooms, using the freezer as a counter and the shelves for supplies and an enormous cutter on one wall.

One of the most amazing jobs was to work at school as a teacher's aide when Milly started to school and I no longer had little ones at home every day. I worked for a while at the high school with a great teacher and we only had a few students at the time. This was a great experience for me. We worked with students that had special needs and we did our best to give these needs to them. I had playground duty also. When one of these wonderful children showed any progress at all, it went straight to my heart. I also worked some at the county school and made great friends there.

Some days they would not have enough teachers or aides at Alamo to work with the slow students and I especially loved this place. There was one colored boy that was big for his age, but he was so gentle and sweet and we really got along well together. He could not remember Myrtle Rose so I asked him to just call me Miss Rose, which he always remembered. After a few years since I had worked there, I saw this special boy on the street in Bells, and he came running up to me and hugged me and backed off and said excitedly "Miss....Miss....Miss.....Miss FLOWERS!" I told him I certainly was Miss Flowers and honored to be so. Such are the gifts we receive in our lives, if we are lucky!

The Children's Outlook

As I've been writing down my thoughts and feelings and collecting memories from adult cousins, aunts and uncles, I never thought what might be on the children's minds or what they may recall about growing up in such a complex family. We were all on a trip together and doing a lot of riding on buses, trains, and airplanes, and the idea struck me that maybe they had some things to contribute to our imagination. I gave them some blank pages and a pen and had them write some thoughts they had buried in their heads about growing up. They, indeed, did have something to say and started writing page after page and sending them to me. Some of their pages were about when they were very small and things that had happened that I had forgotten. (Which could be about anything right now at my age.) I decided they deserved their "two cents worth" too and have jotted them all down knowing that someday they can read this family record and be a part of it by having their memories recorded to read after they have begun aging. Who knows, one may even be the new Hemmingway or Alcott. Well, I can dream, can't I?

Betty, My Sister and Her Family

I do not feel that I can adequately write the story of my sister and her family. She is unable to write it herself, and I could never have a complete family story without hers. So here goes...

Betty and Russell Stephen Cooke, married in 1951 right before she graduated from Bells High School. They lived with us for a year or so before getting their first house. Russell worked for Alamo Construction Company for many years and had already started working there when they got married. When they had their first child Steve, Russell was drafted and went to Korea during that war. He saw many terrible things while in Korea that really had a dire effect on him for many years. Steve was a tiny baby, and he and Betty stayed on with Mama and me while their husband and father was away. Steve was so tiny and so used to being spoiled by Mama, Betty and me that he was not used to being around a male figure and did not greet his dad with smiles and hugs. This same thing happened when Joe went to Berlin and Mame' and I were with Mama. No males around and everything went "topsy- turvy" when suddenly, there was a constant presence of a male in the house. This all smoothed over, and things went back to normal and the young couple moved to Alamo to themselves. Betty went to work at the corset factory there and soon advanced in her job to floor lady.

Back to when Steve was born...Daddy was in the hospital for six weeks and we found out that Betty was to have a little one. Mama wanted to wait until Daddy got better to tell him so he would feel like celebrating and be happy over the good news, but somehow the timing got away from us. He was not going to live much longer; and when we decided he needed to know and told him, we are not sure he understood because by this time he was not communicating with us.

Russell's parents were very strict and religious people. Very staunch in their beliefs and "lived what they preached." Russell was the youngest of five children and, being the only boy and the youngest, had a very noticeable effect on him. Ha! He had all the makings of his strict father in him, but through the years and after he began to be himself again after the war, he was a very loving and attentive father. He was a great brother-in-law to me, and I especially appreciated him when we lost Mame'. He seemed to know what to do and how to talk to Joe and me. You do not forget that kind of kindness. I learned to love his parents and respect them. Mama and Pa Cooke were, indeed, a big part of our family until they died.

Barry was born and then Richard. Russell and Betty had three fine boys to love and be proud of. I can truthfully say they are three boys that anyone would be proud of. They have always shown great respect to their parents, Mama Pig, and Joe and me. They continue to care for their mother today better than any sons I have ever seen care for a mother, especially now that she is in an assisted living home and looks forward to them coming for a visit or a ride in the country for a while.

Russell, Richard, Barry and Steve Cooke

One of the things that the Cooke family always enjoyed so much was their house on the Tennessee River. All through the years, friends and neighbors have celebrated the Fourth of July with them. The number of them grew and grew through the years. We have seen as many as 300 there at one time. People from the family, Cairo community, where they lived, Cypress, where Betty grew up, and Bells, where she went to school, and neighbors there on the riverbanks. They always had a live band and one celebrity; the drummer was a musician for Johnny Cash at one time. There were couples dancing and children running around, some on the pontoon boat roaming up and down the river and older people patting their feet to the beat of the music. Multiple tables, laden with food, the fish fryer spewing out fried catfish as fast as the men could batter it. Every car of people was bringing bowls and trays of meats, vegetables and many, many desserts. It was a sight to behold!

The three boys are happily married, and Betty and Russell have three grandchildren and four great-grandchildren. Steve's daughters are Jennifer, a lawyer in Jackson with two daughters, and Sarah, a schoolteacher with two boys, and all are beautiful and good-natured. Richard has a daughter, Elizabeth, in college.

Russell died with cancer this year (2010) after a brief illness. He is buried in Cairo Church of Christ Cemetery with his mother and father and other family members gone before him.

A Note from Their Son, Richard Cooke:

One of the best love stories I have ever seen or heard. Dad was in the hospital about a month before he died; he had been there for about a week with Barry at his side continuously. Steve himself was at the hospital undergoing tests for heart problems. I took off work for the week to help take care of Mom the best that I could. It was like a Saturday morning I asked Mom would she like to go see Dad and, of course, she said, "yes." Since her stroke, she does not walk very well or long distances, so I loaded up the wheel chair so I could roll her up to Dad's room in the hospital. When I opened up the door and rolled Mom in the room, Dad had the kindest words that anyone could ever say after 50 plus years of marriage, "There comes my baby."

Brought tears to my eyes.............*Richard*

Uncle Tommy Leggett and wife Pearl Acosta at Betty and Russell Cook's Fourth of July party

The Unaware Clown

Shane was playing basketball and, boy, were we ever interested and not paying much attention to anything else. Milly and her friends were sitting down from us and watching too. One of the girls pointed to me and started laughing so hard. I knew I could not be the object of her humor being a "big old mama with jeans" and not dressed in the latest *Vogue* designs. But, sure enough, soon the whole (do I call them a drove?) shebang of girls were laughing and causing the ballgame to look like it was of no significance at all to anyone. The whole crowd was soon looking at me and pointing and generally bursting at the seams. Joe finally looked over at me and he too started laughing; and when Joe laughs out loud and shakes like jelly, I know there is something going on. He finally, HEE, HEE, HEE, says, "Your lipstick is smeared all over your face." I told him right quick that I didn't have lipstick on and that my lips were chapped, and I had used lip balm with no color. HEE, HEE, HEE, "Then it must have been a miracle because your lips, your chin, and up to your nose and back is bright red, not counting the smear almost to your ears on both sides." I looked in my purse and sure enough, there was my balm, Cover Girl bright red lipstick in glossy! What is there to do but HEE, HEE, HEE myself and grab a Kleenex to wipe and wipe until the lipstick is almost gone, but now my face glows from so much scrubbing and wiping. Oh, well, we won the ballgame and had a few laughs and isn't that what is important? Lesson: When you buy lipstick, don't get the darkest, reddest or the glossy kind just in case your mind goes blank!

One Week in My Life
Myrtle Leggett Emerson

I thought it may be interesting to record one week in my life that proved to be one more headache. If all my weeks were like this one, I would probably be in outer space at this very moment.

It all started on Thursday, February 23, 2006.

—I broke my pelvic bone a month ago and have had X-rays and MIR's until I am exhausted and am sure the doctors are tired of looking at my skeleton. Am better but worse; spinal shot in two weeks; —Aunt Pritchett is in the hospital with pneumonia and can't swallow.

—Pat has a knot in her stomach and will have x-rays next Tuesday.

—Jimmy Hallman had a pacemaker put in this week and just got home today from a stay in yet another hospital.

—I am starting four Santas that I have sold and hope I can get them all made on time.

—Have had snow the last two weekends off and on, and it gave the kids a boost of energy that was a sight to behold!

—Little Roe had a bad wreck with Andrea and the kids in the car. Roe in Vanderbilt Hospital with broken back, leg, ankle, and ribs; you could tell the truth by just saying he is basically "all shook up!" It was a very bad wreck. The little family was on their way to church to hear their cousin William preach and slid on some ice. Andrea unconscious but home now; children with cuts but home.

—Jody and Joe fishing lots and catching lots and being generally happy with their lot.

This is one week of very versatile happenings and enough to make your head swim. Big families have big rewards and sometimes huge problems. That's life!

The Not-So-Happy Pet Story

We had at one time a bird dog that we had raised as a pup to hunt quail with Joe and Jody when he got older. Jody went outside to feed him and lingered long enough to taunt him, and the dog turned and jumped on him and literally chewed his mouth inside and made deep cuts with his teeth on his cheek. I saw him crying out the window and ran outside, and he was lying on the ground with his face completely covered in blood and I thought his eyes were torn. And I panicked! Joe came running out after he heard both Jody and me screaming and said, "Go in the house and call Dr. Mayfield! He will be home because it is after hours!" I ran inside and could not get the right number and called two or three people who were most definitely not the doctor. I finally got it right and could not talk but just cried and sniffled, and wouldn't you know that Dr. Mayfield knew who I was and said, "Myrtle Rose, calm down and tell me just what is wrong!" I did and was told to get him to the office quickly and he would meet us there. We could not tell where the blood was coming from but could see one of his eyes by this time, and the inside of his mouth was hanging out and blood running. When we finally got to the doctor's office and laid the child on the exam table, everything began to go black, and I heard the doctor tell Joe to put me in a chair before I hit the floor. That's all I remember until it was all over. Jody had to have the stomach shots every day and, believe me, they were bad. Somehow everything began to clear up and we were getting back to normal. The good Lord was with us.

Lesson: Never, Never feed a bird dog and try to play with him while he is eating.

The Roaring Tornado of 2002

We have had tornadoes and then tornadoes, but the one of 2002 really did a job on us in Fruitvale. It was late in the afternoon, and the television had cut off all regular programs to focus on a large and dangerous front coming straight at us. They started naming the highways and even small communities in its path and among them was Highway 79 and Fruitvale. Joe and I never really panic much with these warnings but do pay attention to them.

I know of one such time when the children were small and we could see the clouds forming and dipping in the Northwest, and we put the children and drove in the car into the empty silo on the road, then two more cars pulled in behind us. We got out and could see the huge funnel in the north and that was the one that went through my sister, Betty's backyard, throwing things through her windows.

We remembered that one as we looked out the back door in 2002, when everything started to feel a little strange and Joe said, "We need to go and get in Milly's basement!"

We hurried over to Milly's and by this time everything was very still and eerie looking, like something out of "Twilight Zone." We rushed in the hallway, and things began to hit outside and the wind was unbelievable. We got to the basement just as limbs and debris began to hit the house. It did not last long, and then the rains began to take over like a play and it was their turn to go onstage. We knew there had to be a lot of destruction and we began to panic!

When things slowed down, Joe and I drove to see about where we stood in the catastrophe. We went to the highway through much debris and could not get on Highway 79 for the wires and poles and trees on the roads. Joe got out of the car and said, "We will have to go back the way we came." He heard someone saying, "Help me, help me!" We found one of the girls who lived on the highway in a ditch; the funnel cloud had hit her house and she had been holding on to the bedpost. It ripped her gown off and made her airborne, throwing her into the ditch. Joe helped her out and got her in a car behind us with some of her family to take to the hospital.

We could not get to Fruitvale, so we went around Midway and took the long direction toward home. We got to Highway 20 on 412 and ran out of gas. We tried to call the nursing home, where my mom was and our phone was dead. The phone in the station was out, and we could not get any gas because all the electricity was cut off.

I could see the way to the nursing home was blocked; we were stranded. We knew that Milly and her children were ok, but we did not know about Jody and his family and did not know about Mama. After a long frustrating wait, Barry (Betty's son) got through to the station and told me that Mama was ok and had already gone back to sleep and that we could manage to get to Alamo on 412. I do not remember how we got gas to go home on.

We went through Alamo and came to Cypress from the north. We still did not know if we had a house. We went by Jody's and they were ok, so we picked our way home and then could not get down our drive, but the house was standing. Gerald Skelton's shed was in the tops of our trees and limbs and whole trees down and lots of unrecognizable items strewn all over, but THE HOUSE WAS STILL STANDING!

By this time it is three a.m. and we finally lay down; then at six o'clock, the phone rang and I was told that Mom had been moved to the Alamo Nursing Home since they were afraid that section of the Bells Nursing Home may not be safe because of wires, etc. and that side was hit harder than the rest.

I hurried to Alamo because I knew that Mama would be upset when she woke up and did not have her regular nurses that she was used to and, sure enough, she was very weak and disoriented. We could see that she would not last much longer, and we sat with her through that day and night. About 12 p.m. she was trying to talk and I could not hear her and called the nurse who told me she was hallucinating. About three o'clock to early morning, she had a glazed look to her eyes and could not focus. She died about 11 a.m. that day.

We had a funeral with very much grieving in the next week and I could not get to the Fruitvale store and up Highway 79 all that week. They cleared the road by then; and when we drove down it, I could not believe it. The tornado had taken three tenant houses that were just shacks but not still in use and also on that road, it took the big barn and an old set of field scales.

At Fruitvale it had taken the store and set the old blacksmith shop off its foundation and destroyed yet another set of old scales, but not much damage to the sheds around there. Another barn by the big barn was also flattened. The big barn was very old and we had it filled with family things and antiques that I was saving for our children. The roof was sitting down in the back, but the front was halfway down and we could see so many things inside. We were afraid to go in because it was so shaky and unstable that it was not worth the risk trying to salvage anything we could see. That barn had been such big part of the Emerson family for so many years and is dearly missed by us all. The store was such a big part of the whole community and was like losing a dear friend, if not a family member.

A Cow Named Myrtle

We all are pleased when someone brags on us or pays us a compliment. Even the most common things like "you look well today" or "you sure are in a good mood." I was paid a most unusual compliment one day. (I am assuming it was.)

Joe and I went to a cattle sale on the grounds of the most beautiful home you could imagine. The home of the Stonecipher family; Mary Ann Stonecipher is one of the best interior designers around. There was this huge tent, big as a circus tent with seats all around, a platform with railings for the cattle to be brought up for auction. There were big tubs with cokes, tables with sandwiches, cookies and desserts with all ages of people there to buy cattle and have a good time. Mary Ann and Bitsy and I had a ringside seat that day. I knew they wanted to sit longer than we usually do, and we watched them bring in cow after cow. Not paying too much attention at first, the men brought this huge red heifer and said what a fine specimen she was and bragged on her beauty and said, "Her name is Myrtle Rose." Well, it took me a minute for this to sink in, but I realized that this cow being named Myrtle Rose and my name being the same was no coincidence. My friends were all laughing and the men selling the cow were evidently in on the conspiracy because they were all laughing too. I knew who was behind this escapade right off. Those Stonecipher boys were right about the fine specimen, but the beauty part was off because I know a lot about myself and know for certain — I am no beauty! This was great fun and I was even printed in the book with name and all, but I can't remember if they used the cow or me in the picture. It was great fun and once in a lifetime party, but I will get those boys one day...
Thanks for the memories.

A Thief in Our Mist

After Grandma Annie Emerson died and Uncle Pete (Malcolm's brother) married and moved out of the homeplace, it was left empty for many years. The house had many family heirlooms in it, and there were some that we really wanted to keep but could not get any of the family to say they could be moved. Each one waiting for the other to give the go ahead to empty the old house. Joe had bought the land where it sat, but we did not feel we had bought the contents and they belonged to the family and not just us, so we would not go and get any of the contents. One day we went to see about the cotton on the farm, and there was a white truck with Jackson license backed up to the door and men taking things out and putting them in the truck bed. Joe started to pull up and they ran and got in the truck and sped out to the road, with us following them, and we couldn't catch them and they got away. We went back to the old house and discovered that the men had taken the "Civil War gun" and the family clock plus some of the silverware and we don't know what else. This prompted the family to give the go ahead to take some of the things left in the house. These things were not worth much to anyone else, but family heirlooms are to be kept and loved and cherished and to pass on to the next generation. I have never felt that an heirloom I have is actually mine, just mine to cherish during my life for safe keeping for the next generation behind me. So I hope that I have left a message here to everyone to hold on to the family things; and if you have to sell or give away anything, let the new things go even if they are more valuable than things you inherit. Feelings and continuality mean more than expensive new things you may have. Of course, this is just my opinion, but in the long run, I believe that it is the right way to go. Nuff said...

The Coffin

Having been interested in old things most all my life, I could not pass up an interesting piece I saw in an antique mall in Knoxville, when we were there to see a UT football game. Joe and I had walked and walked around the mall and had not seen anything we thought interesting or good, when I saw this 'ole coffin in a corner of a booth..."NO!"... he said. "We are not buying that thing and carrying it home!"... OK...We walked some more and that old coffin just kept calling my name, and so I went back for a second look and this second look made up my mind. I had to have it! I read the tag and it said, "Take me home and I will make a great coffin table!" This just put the icing on a cake. Now this is what is called "selling with advertisement." Just a few little words made this item a real conversation piece.

Actually, I never did mean to use it in the house, but I had children and grandchildren that just loved Halloween. Why not have a real piece of Halloween cheer? The casket was shaped like the early ones that are narrow at the top, round out a little for the shoulders and then taper off narrow on the bottom and dove-tailed on the edges and all that good stuff.

Joe knows when he is beat and that an antique is not up for debate, so we loaded the casket in our (then) station wagon that was full of suitcases and four children, and the only place to put it was window level on top of the back seats. I have to admit, it was a little uncharacteristic of things you usually see in a car going down the road. Cars passed us with stares and pointed fingers and you could tell that the pointed fingers were saying, "Look at that, Daddy; look at that, Aunt Lucy!" Joe sat low in his seat and the children were having a ball with all the craziness.

On Halloween, we put the casket on the porch with lighted lights and have a skeleton hanging inside and turn off all the other lights, and it really puts some "zing" in Halloween decor. Note: Always look for the unusual and humor, and you can find it in the most unusual places and oddest things. Just keep an open mind and after that, be especially agreeable to your husband. It took awhile for me to work enough for forgiveness on this one (but it was worth it!)

Our New Granddaughter

I suppose that people who get to the age of Joe and me think that their days of having grandchildren are over. We already had Rachel, Maggie, Kayley, Silas, Olivia,

Rebecca. John John and Flora. We were all settled down with these remarkable grandchildren when Milly came home one day and said, "Guess what! You have a new granddaughter and she is 16 and her name is Chelsey Katlin Harris!" We thought it was a joke and we laughed but soon discovered that she was, indeed, telling us the truth. She was a classmate of Maggie's, whose father had left and her mother had died when she was about eight years old. Her step-grandfather and grandmother had raised her and the grandmother died and shortly after, so did her step-grandfather, leaving her with no one that could keep her. She was distraught to say the least, and Milly had taken her into her home and very soon made her officially a member of her family. We were overjoyed when we found out that this was, indeed, the way it was. I do not mean to brag...but...our Milly has a heart as big as Texas! Don't you know it?

Fishermen in My Family

We certainly had our share of fishermen in our family. Daddy Jim Bailey fished until he couldn't walk. The last few years he started out having to take one man with him to get him in and out of the boat and bait his hook, then take the catch off the hooks for him. After that, he got worse and took two men with him to perform these tasks. I really don't know how two men could do this, for he was so big, stiff and clumsy that it was a miracle he didn't turn the boat over or fall totally out of it.

Then along came my mother and Uncle Burhl after Daddy Jim's generation. Uncle Burhl loved the deep-sea fishing and he often took my mother with him on these trips to the ocean. My mother loved fishing for anything with fins and even the catfish with his smooth belly. Ponds, rivers, backwater, you name it; if it was water and had a chance of having fish, she would stand for hours even without catching much. If you happened to go with her, she had the best seat in the boat. We were informed of this before we left home. She had to have the boat positioned right where she thought the fish were hiding out and she was usually right. The big stumbling block was, you did not dare catch more fish than she did and "woe unto you" if you caught the biggest one!

My dad loved fishing too, and his favorite spot was the Dee Webb Camp past Halls going toward the Mississippi River with the blackest dirt and the stickiest mud in the world. The mud would literally pull your shoes off your feet when walking through it. Huge cypress trees lined the banks of the water and huge stumps jutting out of the dark water and it even smelled like fish. My dad hung this huge catfish that ran up under these stumps and he couldn't get him out, and not to be out-maneuvered, Dad jumped in the water and got down and got that fish by the gills and drug him to the bank. Ironically, with all these fish tales swimming around, my mom would not eat a bite of one. She caught them, she dressed them, she cooked them by the big numbers, but she never tasted one of them.

This line of sport knows no age in my family. Now Joe, my husband, and Jody, my son, will ignore anything else and get that pole out and take to the streams. Then there is Joe Wayne, my cousin, that is either with one of them or off with someone else in the family. I was told a few years back that if we had a good boat, we could go fishing whenever we wanted to and to just look at that beauty that just happened to be for sale! You think they fooled me? Well, they didn't about the boat, but my getting to go was the "hookup." I went one time when Joe and Jody had all these hooks lined up in the front, and I sat in the back of the boat with my pole and fished where they had just drug 15 lines through. Needless to say, I did not get a bite. Well, boys, I'm still waiting for my fishing time to arrive!

Dallas Versus Fruitvale

I guess you have to be of a certain age to really relate to this tale. Way back when— there was an early TV show called "Dallas," on a ranch called South Fork with the main character, villain, macho man called J.R. Well, someone, probably with good reasons, shot J.R. and for weeks on end, the producers of the show kept the whole country on edge guessing: "Who shot J.R.?" And, believe you me, that everyone and their cousins watched this show because there weren't too many options at the time.

The day before Thanksgiving, I was in the front of the house trying to get at least one coat of grime off the glass door, when there was this loud noise out back that was a very different beat to anything I had ever heard. I went through the house to the back and met Joe, dragging his leg and leaving a trail of blood behind him with his pants leg saturated in the red stuff. I panicked! Nothing new there. He said something flew out from under the lawn mower, where he was grinding leaves off the yard getting ready for the forty people coming for the holiday meal. He sat down on the brick steps, and I pulled down his sock and blood spewed up with every beat of his heart. What was I going to do? I knew the first thing was to try to slow the blood flow, and I tied a cloth above it tight and this did help. I ran to the phone and called Milly and told her to get Shane (who was visiting) and get over here pronto and not drag their tracks and that their daddy was hurt and it looked bad. Shane is a doctor and she took one look at it and said, "Daddy, you have been shot!" She had seen so many gunshot wounds in New Orleans in the hospital where she worked that she recognized it right away. I had not seen the hole in the other side of his leg, but the bullet had gone through his lined jeans, his hunting socks, and his leg and was very scary to see. When we realized what had happened, we all panicked. She used a syringe and forced medication in one side of his leg and it came out the other. Anyway, I won't finish all those details, but you get the picture.

We knew that we had to report this because of all the children and our grandchildren that were always here in the community. We had the Sheriff and duties and the Game and Wildlife Official here for hours, and they found the bullet lodged in the lawn mower. The bullet that we had thought came from a 22 rifle turned out to be shot from a pistol and was a very much larger one than we had thought. It was so powerful that after going through Joe's leg it had made a big hole in the metal of the lawn mower, but enough to stick your little finger in.

Our "Dallas" story is not over, for we have not found out "who shot J.R." yet, but they will. Larry has offered to send the Texas Rangers up to help, if necessary, but I don't think we will need them but thanks, Larry; you are a life saver.

Guess this ends our version of this story but does show that Fruitvale is right up there with Dallas and South Fork when it comes to mysteries! But we may need the Texas Rangers that caught the lady who shot her husband and got away with it; her alibi: "I didn't know the gun was loaded."

CHAPTER 9

Joe and Myrtle's School Years
School in the 40's

When I was in grammar school, things were surely different than they are now. No buses, no paved roads, no cafeteria, to name only a few differences. Betty and I walked to school about a mile away. This did not seem such a distance if the sun was out and it was not hot, cold, raining or snowing. How many days do we get like this in a year's time?

We started out from our house and with a skip and a hop, we would be at the Spraggins' house and pick up Joe Wayne and Sarah Lou. When Joe Wayne walked to the door, Aunt Olive (his mom) would grab him and with a comb, put the longest, tightest curl right down the center of his head. You see, he had naturally curly hair that made this all possible. This made Joe so mad; and as soon as we were out of sight of their house, he would take his fingers and go to work on that curl until it was just a mass of tangles and he had a completely new masculine look. (or so he thought). Personally, I like the curl since my hair did not have a turn in it and even permanents did not do a good job, nor even give me a resemblance of curly hair. It seems the boys always have the luck when it comes to curly hair.

An Escapade at the Old Fruitvale School

Joe tells about one of the escapades that happened at the old Fruitvale School when he was a little boy attending there, the first through fourth grades. Miss Gladys Stewart was his teacher for school, and Mrs. Wilson taught the Sunday School Class on Sunday there for church in the same building.

The school is close to the railroad tracks, running behind the school, and Highway 79 in front of it. One day at recess, the little schoolmates were running and playing without a care in the world when one of them spied something lying in the gulley behind the schoolyard. They all ran to see what was going on and "low and behold," there lay a body of a man. Now this was a thrilling break from their tame games they were used to, and they all were really excited! (And more than a little scared.) They thought the man was dead and this spooked them even more! Can't you imagine the expressions of shock, surprise and the looks they were passing among each other! And horror! I'm sure there was much shrieking and ooohhh's and aaahhh's!

They went running inside as fast as they could to the teacher who came out to examine the unfortunate soul, only to find a drunk man passed out in the gulley. How unfortunate for the students to have seen this at such a young age. Maybe it taught them a lesson too because I know Joe never forgot this and I'm sure he isn't the only one. If we look hard enough, we usually can find some good out of many bad things.

Grade School at Bells

In fourth grade we had a wonderful teacher that had been traveling over many states and had seen many things. Once she came home with a medicine bottle full of water from the Atlantic Ocean. I stared and stared at this bottle and could not imagine seeing such a wonderful sight. By the time my children were walking well, they were swimming and had made at least one trip to the ocean. Times have changed so much in 73 years!

In this same class, we had a magazine contest to see who could sell the most magazines to raise money for the school. I worked and worked and sold the most for the fourth grade and was overjoyed! I had won the prize! Now what was it? I was handed an ice cream on a stick and by the time I got it, it was half-melted and I was sent outside to eat it. It was dripping and the rest of the children did not have one so I had to leave the room. I went out the door and sat on the steps and by this time cream and chocolate were running down my arms and on the ground. I did not enjoy that stick of ice cream one bit and promised myself I would never sell another magazine for anyone. The next year I was raring to go and to see how many I could sell.

Joe's First Day at the Big School

Joe has always been shy and quiet. I always heard that opposites attract and this was certainly true with the two of us. When he got to the fifth grade in school, he had to start to Bells to the big school because they closed the small one in Fruitvale. Horrors! I remember the first day he came into the classroom there. I already knew him from visiting the Woodsons in Fruitvale since they were kin to me and we visited often. Joe would come to play with my cousin Ray and we soon became a threesome. We became friends at an early age. So when he walked into that room, I knew he was scared to death. He would sit in his chair for hours and not move all day for several days unless completely necessary. Youth finally got the best of him, and he began to make friends and play on the grounds at noon and recess time. I noticed—boy, he sure was cute!

*Joe Silas
Emerson
About 1948*

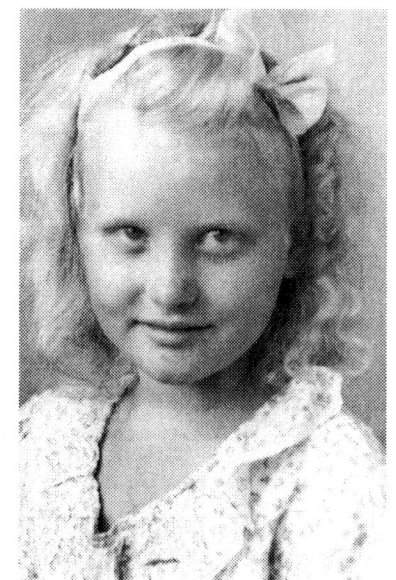

*Myrtle Rose
1946*

Joe's Teen Years

Joe started driving at a very young age. By the time he was 15 years of age, he was working for Ollie in the summer months full time driving trucks to the fields, carrying the hands from one field to the other or carrying produce from the fields to the fruit shed. He drove a big truck with cows or pigs to take to the stockyards in Memphis and to the butchers to sell in stores. He drove to Dyersburg and Newbern to pick up cows at this age too. One of his jobs was to go to Memphis and get fertilizer for Ollie to use on his farms and also to sell in the store. When he got the fertilizer home, he would deliver some of it to the nearby farms to the local men, saving them the trouble of unloading and loading again all over.

When Joe and Bill were young, their family took yearly trips, and sometimes more often, to St. Louis to see the Cardinals play baseball. (Joe is in the den right now watching this ball team play even as I write.) They usually went with the Woodsons. That is, with my Uncle Dutch and Aunt Louise and cousin Ray Woodson. They have always been avid Cardinal fans and to this day root and shout for "their team." They had many stories about their sport adventures at St. Louis. I really felt left out because I was the only member of the Emerson family that had never been to a ball game in St. Louis. Now it is different because I, too, am a fan.

Joe and Bill had this bird dog named "Champ." He was more like a pony, he was so big. He looked fierce but was a honey of a dog. His appetite was a wonder. You threw him a biscuit and it went straight to this stomach. Throw food in his mouth and he just swallowed it whole. He could eat a bucketful of food in the blink of an eye. Anything edible that you wanted to get rid of, you just "threw it to Champ."

Tweens to Teens

Joe and Bill really looked a lot alike when they were young. You might say they looked a lot like twins. I would see them with their backs to me and would not be able to tell one from the other until they took a step. Their stance was so different that when they walked, you would think they were no kin at all. They are a rare set of brothers. Now they never squabble or have disagreements and talk like they are extensions of each other. I don't think this was the case when they were growing up, but you can't have everything!

Ollie let them have pets, cows, etc. on the farm. They had this heifer that was having a calf and both boys were so excited about this. Can you imagine their delight when not one, but two calves, popped out and started trying to stand up???!!! I know this is not something that is rare, but it was for two eager boys that had never seen this happen.

The most favorite pet of the whole family was this old (I could say ancient) bird dog named Sally. Sally hunted with the boys and followed them around so long she was just an extension of them. When Joe and I married, Sally was so old she was staying most of the time in the house by the pot-bellied stove in the front room. She didn't lie down just any old place but resided in the door to the dining room right between the stove and the wall. The shortest way to the kitchen and back door was through this door, and heaven and earth would not move her out of the way. You could take the long route or you could simply jump, hold onto the open door and hop over old Sally because she was in her spot and in her spot she stayed.

Joe in High School

The boys that are "cool" and sharp now had nothing on the boys in the fifties. In fact, the old boys invented cool and carried out their invention with a flair. Joe decided he would look better as a blonde so he went to the drugstore and bought a bottle of peroxide. Blonde had not made it to every other head at this time. You saw only a few self-made blondes back then. Well, this bottle of peroxide proved to be very potent, and Joe's hair was white as snow and then some. He got it cut in a crew cut and it stood straight up on top of his head, and speaking of heads, he turned a few!

Mr. Crider didn't think much of it, but what was done was done and what could he do? So if you get away with one thing, why not try another? When this (finally) all grew out, he decided he would try another "look." This turned out to be the fabulous *Mohawk* that I have seen recently on boys on TV that were being hustled into court for one crime or another. Well, Mr. Crider could not abide by this display and sent him home for a day or two and then called him back and tried to forget it. There was about a month before the *Mohawk* could be trimmed drastically and the new growth almost hid it. You notice I said, "ALMOST."

Joe loved his sports. We did not have a football team. Only the Alamo team in Crockett County had one. Baseball was his favorite and he did a great job with it. He was the pitcher on the school team from his freshman year until he graduated. He played American Legion ball with the Humboldt team, and we have two balls with which he pitched no hitters. This was an advanced team over high school baseball. He loved basketball and excelled with this too. At one game in Dyersburg, he made 33 points in a district tournament. He still loves the sports and the TV in giving him lots of entertainment with football and basketball and watches all other sports with enthusiasm now.

Joe Silas Emerson

The Fifties

When I was in my teens, Elvis ruled. I really don't believe there will ever be another voice and man like Elvis. I know he was not a good actor but who cares as long as you could look at him and hear him sing a good love song! I still watch these old movies when they come on TV and listened to the recordings as long as I had my hearing. I think the two things that I miss more with this disability are hearing my grandchildren when they talk and laugh and listening to my music. Music just used to make a bad day good or a worried mind relax. I really liked all kinds of music; country, jazz, romantic or even opera. The Three Tenors are awesome. Then, of course, there was Patsy Cline. Could she sing or what? When she would sing *"Sweet Dreams,"* I would swoon.

Now the best place to hear Elvis and Patsy was in the drug store sitting in the ice cream chairs by the matching table and drinking a Cherry coke with peanuts in the bottle and Joe sitting on the other side in front of me. Now that was living! We would end up there after a movie if we were lucky enough to get the old red Studebaker. Bill, Joe's brother, was two years older and we usually ended up riding with him or going in the old field truck, but it didn't make any difference. Bill was an okay guy and never complained because he usually had June with him.

The movie was only 35 cents and the cokes a nickel so it was a no lose situation. Remember the Pepsi slogan that went "Twice as much for a nickel too! Pepsi Cola is the drink for you! Nickel, nickel, nickel, nickel." This was Coke's competition but back then, Pepsi had a hard time selling against the king "Coca Cola."

One of our classmates actually rode in that famous "*Pink Cadillac Convertible*!" She had just started college in Memphis, and she and two of her friends were standing on a corner waiting for a bus when this pink convertible drove up with two boys in it, and the one driving asked if they wanted a lift. They replied immediately that they were okay for the bus when one of the girls whispered, "Does that look like Elvis to you?" At that instant they recognized not only the car but the handsome guy driving had these awesome sideburns to kill. There could be no doubt about it! There was the famous *Elvis Presley* asking them if they wanted to ride with him! In they jumped into that pink machine and off they went. He took them to their dorm and waved bye and they stood ready to faint from the experience! Bet you can't beat that one even on a good day!

Back then most of the movies were westerns and nothing but westerns on Saturday. But soon they started having these horror movies that I could not stand. The very worse was *The Mummy.* I'm not talking about today's standard of a scary movie, but from the fifties view, that made this movie really bad. Our gang was at a friend's house for the weekend and walked to the theater to see this movie. I sat with my head covered with my hands most of the show and was scared to walk back to her house in the dark afterwards. In war pictures, I had to do the same thing. I finally just quit going to these movies. Who wants to be scared out of their wits anyway? Nowadays, I think it is everyone; even the children watch scary cartoons. Cartoons???

About twice a year we would all pile in one car and go to Jackson to a movie, and we really thought that we were moving on up. We were very privileged teens, or so we thought. You don't miss what you never had. You know, I never thought about not having money or a car or extra clothes. We just got on our bikes and rode off. If we got hungry, one of our mama's would give us a chicken leg or some cornbread and a cool glass of tea and we were off again. We had fun, baby! Kids don't know how to play these days. We used to play Chess in the gym every day after lunch and play baseball on Sunday afternoons if we did not go fishing or listen to music on the radio.

When we went to ball games for the school, we would meet the bus at Bells High School and go from there. Dan Norville's brother, Barney, drove the bus. He kept the bus across the road at his dad's, Oliver's place, until just before time to leave and then drive up to the school where we would all be lined up to go, scrambling to get on the bus first. The first ones on could get closer to the back of the bus which was very, very desirable. Joe and I were privileged that Dan Norville was a good friend, and he rode across the road with his brother and sat on one back seat and saved the other one for Joe and me. You see, it always pays to have friends in high places!

Pictures of Joe and Myrtle taken in a dream last night

School in Bells in the 50's

In the beginning of my high school days, the gym was underground, under the classrooms on the west end of the building. It was very small and had about two rows of seats on each side. Mr. Crider was the coach and principal then. It was very crude and you could tell you were under ground level.

The old stage had a wine velvet curtain in front of it, and I always thought it was very beautiful because velvet was one thing that I had just had no connection with. I loved to rub my hands on it and feel the smooth warmth of it. I don't know what happened to these wonderful yards and yards of fabric. (Probably burned). How I wish that I had this piece of yesterday. I have spent years looking for old velvet to use in crazy quilts and have not had much luck. Only small pieces here and there.

The science rooms were directly over the gym. It had these huge windows just lined up on one side. It was a pretty good jump to the ground, but there were a few of the boys that tried it when our teacher was occupied or out of the room. They usually headed to the gym to shoot a few loops or out behind all the buildings for a puff or two. Many things happened in this class. One boy, I'll call him John, (not his real name) used to go to the pencil trimmer right by the door and pretend to trim his pencil and when the teacher turned his back, he would just slip out the door. When the teacher called his name, it went like this: "John, John, John !!! Where is John?" The look on his face was one of wonder and question.

When I was a junior in high school, I received a State Degree in Home Economics. I loved this subject with cooking, sewing and general home topics. I did not especially get along with the teacher. We all made these suits that had to have zippers in the skirt, and I finished mine and also put in a few for those who did not like this particular job. When we were graded on our performance with the zipper, I got a B and all the others I put in got an A. This did not sit well with me.

There was one pool to swim in at this time and it was a public pool in Humboldt. Several of us would go over there on weekends and sometimes at night for a swim. We went often and all my friends learned how to swim and dive, etc. Alas, I did not, so I went to FHA camp three years in a row and took lessons from our swimming teacher and still did not learn to swim. I have always had this fear of lots of deep water. When we were on vacation with friends with a good swimmer, she finally taught me to float on my back. By this time I had four children and they were all swimming all around me...Nuff said!

High School Days

When we were still in high school, I was mostly confined to the house and fields. Joe had this old truck and his "work" would bring him by our house. He always had a case of cokes in the back of the truck. I never had even one coke, and here he was with continual cokes when he wanted one. This was a sore spot with me. I always had only a glass of water; this somehow infuriated me. This was before I learned that everyone in life did not live alike.

Basketball, softball and baseball were the only sports we had in high school; thus, they were very important to the students and faculty. There were plenty of schools that we competed with. We went to Spring Hill, Mason Hall, Yorkville, Woodland Mills, Dresden, Gleason, then the county schools: Alamo, Maury City, Friendship and Gadsden. For two years Joe pitched and Bill was catcher. Joe played five years in all. I played high school softball and basketball but not too well. Everyone teased me and said Mr. Crider took me to the games to keep Joe happy. He must have been because he knew how to throw a ball, hit with a bat and knock a hole in the goal with a basketball. The cheerleaders were very entertaining although their skirts were much longer than they are now. I remember the usual cheers like—gimmie a B,—gimmie an E,—gimmie LLS, and then there were some they cheered a long time before the coaches really "heard" the words. Like ABCDEFGHLLLLLLLLLL yes, we're gonna win!!! I thought for a while we were going to be cheerleader-less for sure!

Myrtle Rose Leggett
Graduation Picture

Joe Emerson
Graduation Picture

Basil Jerome Crider, Principal of Bells High School - The man who helped raised me whom I greatly respect

Joe Silas Emerson and Myrtle Rose Leggett
Graduation

Joe Silas Emerson with his
peroxide hair and crew cut

Our gang - 1954

Courting in Fruitvale in the Fifties

Things were sure different when it came to courting in the fifties than it is now. Everyone did not have a car or truck or any wheels as a matter of fact. We were lucky if we even knew someone with wheels that would run and a parent that would let us all pile in and ride around with them. I did not have such luck but Joe was never without transportation. Never mind that on some nights when we were dating, we had to go to

206

Bells to the movie in an old two-ton field truck. We got there and saw the same movie the favored ones saw and had as much or more fun. Geeze, Louise, it's the company you keep!

At this time Joe and his brother Bill had an old red Studebaker car that sometimes we got to court in. Bill, being the older, would drive, and Joe and I would sit in the back seat on double dates since there was one car, and ONE and ONE did not give us two here. Bill and June were cool about it even though by rights they were two years older and probably should have had first go at the old car.

The boys had found this old T-Model horn and put it on the Studebaker, and everyone knew when we were coming before they saw us because the old horn went ooooooooooga! ooooooooooooga! It sounded like a horn with a very bad cold and a bad accent to boot!

Evening in Paris

Now they have Chanel, Diamonds, Lancôme, Sensuous, and many, many other perfumes that lure the nose to lure your brain into telling you that you would really be "in" to smell like their brand. How true this is, I do not know. But in the 50's the really true scent was *Evening in Paris,* a perfume that could be purchased in any dime store or department store in the country. Believe me, it was very potent! This is one case where more is definitely not better.

All us girls had some of this perfume in the Cobalt Blue slender bottle that was shaped a lot like a heart. I had almost forgotten about this "must have" from my teens until a few years ago, I found a bottle still full of the fragrance. Nothing would do but to buy it and I really cherish this memento from yesteryear. I don't wear perfume today but if I did, I would probably douse some behind my ears and have comments on my "new" fragrance and where in the world did I find it! I would probably reply with" Good gracious and sakes alive! Don't you know it is a secret formula?"

Great Mistake of Teen Years

Our teens now think that we are too "square" or too old to imagine how they feel about things now or understand the pressures they are under to maybe do the wrong thing. When a teen in my family does something that I really am disturbed about, I try to think back about what these pressures can get you into.

One particular thing that I went through, when a high school senior, was a trip to Humboldt one night with a car full of girls. As we were coming into Gadsden later, the girl driving said, "Let's go over the overhead bridge on the wrong side," and laughed. (There was at this time a big bridge over the railroad that made a big hill.) We all told her no!! She was driving and went over the hill on the wrong side and just before going over, turned out her car lights. When I think of what could have happened, I can't even comprehend it. Now they just ring things up as hormones. I suppose this is true because there is a certain age in there we all do crazy things. I did and I am sure most people do this at that age. We have to let them make their mistakes just like we did and trust in God for protection.

CHAPTER 10

Fabulous Kinfolk

Kinfolk

All the families that I am kin to are very different. I've heard one tale that was recorded and a lot of it came through the Leggetts. One was saying that they were kin to Jesse James; and though there is no proof of this, the personalities of the older ones when I was young, it could have well been true. It was not hard to imagine this and I really don't believe this one. Is it true or lore?

One tale I know to be true is that Uncle Ben Leggett's grandson is the *"Brooks" of Brooks and Dunn* from Country Music fame.

Another true one is that a Bailey cousin works with the reality show, *Extreme Home Makeover Edition*.

We are a cousin to *Dixie Carter* and have this one traced and very proud to have this connection to someone that I admired so much.

But these are not people that "made me" what I am. (This could be good or bad.) The farmers formed my main personality. Although we have several doctors and a few lawyers, I was never formally educated to use expressive words or to have social graces. We all need to be satisfied with ourselves and love others for whatever makes them happy.

Jon and Julie Bailey graduated second and third in their class at West Point.

Two of Mama's brothers were colonels in the Army. Colonel Lawrence D. Bailey, a pilot in World War II, and Colonel James Bailey, MD, along with nephew, Colonel William H. Bailey, MD USAF was a Flight Surgeon and served in Iraq (see résumé).

Margaret Bailey has a PHD, Larry Bailey, Vassar, Inc., as Director of Air Force Programs, Peter Erik graduated from West Point in 1988 and went on to graduate from Harvard University with a MBA Degree in 2005. This is one example of one family's accomplishments. Other families are scattered throughout this book. I used only one here to show what can be done with one family with the desire to go for it! Peter is a cousin of the afore mentioned Baileys.

What kind of world would we have if everyone were a doctor, lawyer or farmer or entertainer? Pretty unbalanced, it's a "live and let live" world, and each person can be what he or she wants to become. We need to do what makes us happy, and this happiness will make us more productive and useful in the world. There is a saying, "If you don't love yourself, don't expect anyone else to love you!"

John Paynter getting West Point diploma from President George W. Bush - 2006

Kix Brooks of Brooks and Dunn (Country Music)

Dixie Carter, Actress

Col. William Bailey - Iraq

Buster, Elizabeth, Betty and Myrtle Rose
Leggett - 1940

The Buster Leggett Family - 1944

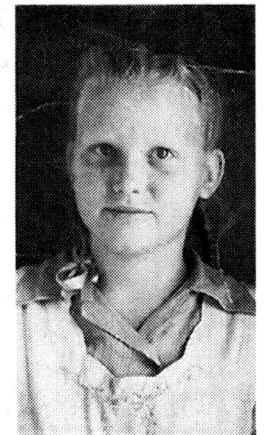

Myrtle Rose Leggett

CHAPTER 11

Myrtle Growing Up

Cotton-picking Cotton Sack

Joe Silas Emerson

The old cotton sack was a dreaded thing. It never got enough no matter how hard you picked or how many of the fluffy stuff in the cluster of briar-like needles that you put in it. A big sack would hold fifty pounds or more when full, but as soon as it was emptied, you got it, "you had to fill it again." Mama was a super cotton picker. She would not slow down for anything. This, on top of the fact when I was really small, I would ride her sack and she was pulling me and the cotton. Funny that I did not think of this at the time but remember it as if it were yesterday. Sometimes I even took a nap with her working so hard. It never ceases to amaze me at the work she did for all of us, never thinking about herself.

After growing up some, I was given my own little sack made from a fertilizer sack. At the time these were made of heavy cotton, more like canvas, and probably came from the Bemis Mills. Mama took the sack and added a wide strap to go over my shoulders and was expected to fill this with my share of the white stuff! The straps were made of wide cotton because if it were narrow, it would cut into your shoulder. I really felt big at first with my own sack but the novelty soon waned, and I was dreaming of those rides up and down the rows without a thought, except maybe what was for lunch or if the water in the jug was still cold.

My little cotton sack was small in comparison to Mama's six footer. I was expected to fill my sack by the time she finished hers. Of course, hers would hold about 50 to 60 pounds and mine 5 or 6, but she was always proud of mine too and encouraged me to think big when it came to pounds of cotton. We always tried to have a bale in the wagon by Saturday night because it was a grand affair to ride that wagon of cotton to the gin in Bells and jump off and take in a movie. Saturday night at the movie was almost certain to be a western with Roy Rogers and Dale Evans, Gene Autry or the Cisco Kid. Before the main show, we had the previews of the following week and a short newsreel that gave some of us farm families the only world news we had all week. Joe was usually there at the movie, and we would sit together and see the movie at least two times while Mama and Daddy bought groceries and feed supplies for the chickens and barnyard animals to last all week. Of course, Joe did not ride a bale of cotton to the movies like I did. He had a truck that he could drive before he could see out the windshield. No one seemed to bother with driver's license so much then. If you could see out the windshield and hold the vehicle on the road, you were a driver, man!

Back then there were no sprays or any way to get rid of the bugs and worms. The bugs I could take but the wiggly worms just made my flesh crawl and my mouth scream. These critters were especially plentiful down in the bottom fields. The ground was richer and more water to make the stalks tall. Now tall to a grown person may be scary, but to a child these stalks looked like trees, and they were just covered in those black and white-striped devils. When one got on me, especially on my neck, I would go into hysterics! No matter how many there were, you could hear me in the next county. I still have this "thing" about any kind of worm. It is very simple—I just don't like that part of nature. When we first got married, Joe would bait my hook when we were fishing, but as the years went by, this little favor just waned and waned until it just went into oblivion. I may be a country girl, but I turn into a "city girl" when the worms crawl out.

We had our lunch in the fields and they were the highlight of the day. Mama would fry up a chicken or sausage and biscuits and have a gallon jug of tea. We had regular picnics every day sitting on a full cotton sack and resting with each other. Come to think of it, farming ain't so bad, is it?

We were in the fields from early spring to late fall or early December. It was some kind of goal to be out of the fields for Thanksgiving.

When we were chopping the cotton, Mama would tell us to "scrape the whole top of the row" so we would get the new seedlings of grass and weeds before they had a chance to grow big and harder to chop out. This did not make sense to me then but, of course, now it just seems the only thing to do. Mama chopped with her back bent all day and came home with supper to fix, then breakfast in the morning and dishes and clothes to wash. *Wonder Woman* in the comics had nothing on my mother!

Can you believe we ever had time to clean house and wash? There was not much time for that. Betty helped Mother in the house and I went outside with Daddy. This suited us all. I loved the outdoors, and Betty loved the house and that was one thing we never argued about. It was lovely having one thing not to fight over. I helped Daddy with feeding livestock and mowing the yard. (push mower with blades that went over and over instead of around like the ones we have now. No motor, just plain old elbow grease.) We had horses, a cow, pigs, chickens, roosters and all kinds of animals. I loved feeding them, but milking the cow was something I had just as soon forget. They say that milking a cow is like riding a bicycle in that when you once learn, you always know how. Not so with milking a cow. Daddy always said when I got through milking that the bucket was not full, the cow's bag was still half full and the ground around the bucket looked like it had snowed. I think he was trying to tell me something, don't you? There was corn to shell for the chickens and livestock. There were tubs to keep under the drain of the house to catch the rainwater for washing. This was really necessary before electricity and running water was put in.

New Dresses in the Forties

We went to Bells on Saturday if we were not chopping, picking cotton or canning out of the garden, etc. We bought flour and groceries and grain for the animals at the old Tri-County or the U-Tote-Em stores. Mama bought two twenty-five pounds of flour at a time. She used so much flour because she cooked all our food, and we always had biscuits every meal.

There was a double meaning to the two sacks at a time flour. These sacks that it came in were printed in flowers or plaids and lots of different designs of the time. One sack would not make a dress for me or Betty; therefore, it took two for one dress. We got our biscuits and one of us got a dress, making a double dip out of each purchase. Sometimes Aunt Virginia and Mama would buy one each of the same design and make Gretta one this time and one for me the next purchase.

When we were smaller, we could get a dress with sleeves if the twine holding the sack together did not pull holes in the ends and have to be cut off. We examined the ends closely before we bought to be sure we got the most for our money. All these costumes were made alike to save fabric. Just a front and a back and two sleeves.

I was in the eighth grade when I got my first "store-bought dress" and, boy, was it pretty. It was pink with white stripes and I could draw you a picture of it today. Mama took me to Alamo to a little dress shop there, and it took the longest time to decide which one to buy. The dress had a "fish tail" all around it at the waist, and I wore that dress until it totally wore out and tore off my body.

Friends When Growing Up

I had two very dear friends when growing up and am so fortunate to still be able to call them dear friends. We get together even now and, "wonder of all wonders," our husbands are great friends. This makes for some good times that I cherish.

Gracie Jo Edwards lived just over the hill from me by the church, and Gretta Ann Leggett was my first cousin and lived just in front of our house down the lane. We rode bicycles up and down the road together and spent the night with each other all our growing-up years.

Jo married my first cousin; Joe Wayne Spraggins and Gretta married a wonderful man, Roe Nell Hughes, from Alamo. The six of us go out to eat and laugh and talk about old times.

This is one of God's gifts to us. We are very fortunate to have each other.

Myrtle Rose Emerson, Gretta Ann Hughes and Gracie Jo Spraggins

Barrel of Rainwater
By: Myrtle Rose Leggett Emerson

When Uncle Doode and Aunt Virginia were living in Fruitvale in the old house there, they had a huge barrel that they caught rainwater in. We were there one hot, summer Sunday afternoon when Gretta and I were about eight years of age, and Brenda Kay was not old enough to get into much trouble at that time, and Betty thought she was too old for things like this tale.

I am so sorry, Gretta, but I just have to tell this one. 'Ole Gretta and I were outside in the sweltering heat, and no swimming pool for us back then, not even running water for a run under the hose. The barrel was full of water and it sure looked good. So we stripped down as far as we dared (this house was right beside the road) and jumped right in that cool barrel of H2O. We, of course, could not keep our screams down low enough not to alert the adults that we were into something. Sure enough, out they came, and Uncle Doode was upset and he was not a man to get unnecessarily alarmed about anything. You see, the water had been sitting there for a spell and had these tiny wiggle worms in it that Gretta and I had not taken the time to notice. They were soon to be mosquitoes and not something to be splashing in our faces, let alone our whole bodies. Thus ended a great idea, "down the drain" (pardon the pun). We were washed off properly and dried, but we sure felt cooler and refreshed and it was really worth it. But I have to admit it was not "Cool Clear Water, water, water" as the song goes.

Growing Up

When I was about six years old, my great-grandmother Delifate died. I had always called her Granny and she is in several of the pictures that I have of Mama's family and also in some of the older ones when she was young. She is the first dead person that I ever saw and I was really afraid to go into the room where she was laid. Mama and Daddy thought that I was old enough to learn some things about the "real Life" so I went with them in the room at Granny Bailey's house and stood for a long time looking at her and studying what I saw.

She was in the front bedroom on the right as you went in the house off the porch and I was against the east wall by the window. She looked so good to me that I thought she could not really be dead. I was much impressed and she was in my thoughts for a long while after afterward and, to be truthful, I can still see her in her casket. We all missed her when she was gone. She was older and did not talk much by that time. I could remember she had slowed down so much that you hardly knew she was in the room but was much respected by all.

About this same time of year, Betty and I started taking piano lessons from Mrs. Henderson. Her grandson is the pharmacist in Bells now. I never really took to the lessons and would not practice until the day before the lesson. I was supposed to practice an hour or at least a half hour every day. Betty was breezing through them and her playing sounded lovely even to me. Mrs. H would shake her head when I played and say, "Why can't you play like Betty? She has such a soft touch and you look like you are trying to kill the instrument!" She did teach me the basics and I learned that on church songs I could just play the right cords she taught me and could play any of the church songs that had flats. I never learned to play sharps.

Gretta lived down the lane in front of our house and I "built" me a play house just across the church road and into the lane on the right. The lane was lined with all kinds of trees on either side of it and at this spot the rain had washed a place out that was about waist high of me. I dug out little shelves to put my play dishes and goodies on. I cooked grass for greens, sticks for meat, water for tea and the little balls on the oak leaved for potatoes. I had lovely meals there and never tired of "my house." About half way to Gretta's there was a Mulberry tree that I just loved it when they ripened. I could eat them and fix them into my menu in the playhouse. This is called checking out all your resources.

Another good resource was for good food too. Joe Wayne and I found the greatest place to eat mustard greens and cornbread. On Aunt Olive's place there was a tenant house down past her house from us where Robert and Izora lived. They were colored people that worked for Uncle Theron. Izora would cook all morning and have a pot of greens and a skillet of cornbread about eleven o'clock. This is about the time we started getting hungry and our dinner time would be after eleven so we would go in and eat with Izora and Robert. It took our mamas' awhile to figure out why some days we had just completely lost our appetites. These meals were cooked on an old iron cook-stove and I don't know why but those greens and cornbread had a barrel of flavor in them.

One summer, Uncle Theron, hired this big bulldozer to dig a pond for him between his house and ours. How convenient can you get? We sat and watched them dig day after day and dreamed of the swimming and fishing. Right after they finished with the pond, it rained a gully washer. Well, the water was so thick with mud that you could almost cut it with a knife, but that didn't stop us! We played and played in that muddy water and when we finally came out we looked like mud men and could hardly walk but we were two happy kids.

From the time I had started talking good, Betty and my parents started to complain that I was not paying attention to anything they said. By the time I was ten it became evident that I could not hear right. I went to the doctors until I was twelve and he said that if I had my tonsils out, I would be fine. At this time this procedure cured anything. So, I went to Old Webb Williamson Hospital in Jackson for the long surgery. He did this without even an aspirin and I thought I was a goner for sure. Mama kept waiting and waiting for me to get better and of course I did not. When Joe and I got married one of the first things we did was take a trip to Memphis to see Dr. Shea. He told me at the time he could help nine out of ten people and I was number ten.

When we were in eighth grade, we had our class trip and it was the first time I had been that far from home. The Capital, the Hermitage, and the Pentagon looked so wonderful and were so above what I have ever seen. After that and in the same year, I took a trip to Florida with my grandparents, so that was a great year for me.

Since my dad and Ray's mom had brothers in Louisiana, we all decided to give it a shot and go down and visit them. There were three of them and four of us that rode in Uncle Dutch's ford. We got almost to Brownsville and Daddy realized he had left his billfold at home and this did not get out trip off to a good start. Uncle Dutch had no alternative but to turn around and get the dreaded billfold for it took both his and Daddy's billfold to get us down there and back. Neither could handle it by themselves. That was a long trip in that old car but we got there. It was a small town called Napoleonville.

Uncle Ray, Aunt Eunice and Uncle Tommy (he was not married then) lived on one side of the street and Aunt Pearl and her parents on the other. They lived in one of the now famous Shotgun houses that are so popular now in New Orleans. The men decided to go to the local honky-tonk and get some beer. They took Ray and me with them. I had never seen anything like it and it really had stuck in my mind. Ray and I sat and watched with big eyes. The men soon saw they had made a mistake and rushed us out of there. There was this citrus tree on the neighbor's yard right on the lot line to Uncle Raymond's. We were informed that we were not to touch this fruit. It looked like a mixed lemon and orange they called nectarine. I had never seen one and my mouth was really watering.

The second night we were there, the grownups were out front on the porch. Ray and I could not stand it any longer and we just snuck over there and got one of those suckers. We ate it where we stood and it was just like heaven on earth. I have thought about this for years and still repent for this deed but still don't see how it could have possibly been avoided.

We formally made it to high school and were in our second year of typing when our favorite teacher, Miss Taylor, gave us this long typed out page and told us that we could not pass this course until we had typed it perfectly. Let me tell you… there were some nervous people sitting in those chairs. We bent over and went to work and started over and over and finally (I was sitting by Joe) got to the last word and said, "All I like about finishing a perfect paper is the period at the end." Joe, being himself, reached over and punched the first button he saw and that was that. Do you think that this deed is to be forgiving? I have been married to him for almost 55 years and I still see that finger coming at me.

Growing Up in Cypress

Betty and I always knew what was under the old makeshift table made from an old crate on the back porch. It had a cover all around it to the floor. This was made out of old feed sacks. In the back of this on the floor were two or three old vinegar jars (the gallon size) with dark liquid in them. We figured out soon enough that two were blackberry and one was strawberry homemade wine. Never think you are "pulling one over" on your children—more than likely this last sentence would be truer if reversed.

We had this tough grass in the yard that Mama called "yard grass" and the hand mower would not cut it. You see, we had one of those old push mowers without a motor. It was run strictly on elbow grease. To get rid of it, we had to get our hoes and scrape the yard around the back steps and the well house, where the wringer washer was after we got electricity.

We washed our clothes in a washtub with rainwater that drained into these tubs off the house. This required a washboard and lye soap that Mama made. The wringer washer was a great invention; and when we finally got one, it really helped us out at the time. It had a dasher to clean the clothes and then all you had to do was put one piece of clothing at a time through the wringer and then run them through a tub of rinse water. This rinse water had "bluing" in it that gave the clothes a cleaner look. Then the clothes were run through the wringer once again and then were ready to hang out on the line to dry. You see, the term "wash day" really meant what it implied. It took all day to wash and get the job done. Of course, when they dried, you had to go out and bring them in, fold and iron them. Up until I was about ten years old, we had to heat cast iron irons and press the clothes with this. When the iron cooled a bit, you had to place it back on the stove to proceed with the business at hand.

We did not have electricity in our house until I was about eight years old. We had running water put in the house at about the same time. We were really moving up and along and making great progress. These two improvements really did a lot to enhance our lives and make things so much easier on us all; we still had the old "outhouse." Electric lights really did a lot for me because I loved to read and in getting my homework. But on the upside of no electricity, we always went to bed early with no distractions like a TV or telephone and at this time, we didn't have a car.

Home life was the most important thing in our lives at that time, and I really think we could all use a little more of that now. We would not need so many medications nor trips to the doctor to settle us down. Times change and people have to move with time to survive and we all want to survive, but we need a dose of home life thrown in to balance things and keep our minds clean.

Growing Up Leggett Style

It was so easy for me to grow up in the Leggett household and was so evident that my mom and dad really loved each other and my sister Betty and me. This never figured in my thoughts because it was just there, a fact plain and simple. I know that my parents had disagreements but, you know, I never witnessed any of them. There was really not much trouble to get into. The kind of trouble we had was getting the cotton fields clear of weeds and grass and then getting the white stuff on the wagon ready to get to the gin. Then trouble with getting the corn patches finished or picking strawberries for a nickel a quart unless you "capped" them. As time wore on, the price for one of this kind went up to a dime a quart and you could really make money at this price. We did not have time to get into trouble. By the time the work was all done, we were about fizzled out ourselves.

I just loved the rain then and still do because of all the good memories I have of the wet stuff from childhood. About the only time we were not working in the fields was when we got a good downpour. If it was not raining cats and dogs, we just got under a big old oak tree like all the animals did to keep reasonably dry. The big drops started falling and we were running for the house to knock it off for a while. If we were lucky, it would be too wet to go back to work until the next day.

A big rain always meant company coming in for everyone was rained out, then out came the popcorn and the radio turned up loud with people just glad to see each other (Sometimes neighbors and other times kin), but after a really big storm probably meant all these at one time.

The rainy day always brought us fried chicken and mashed potatoes or one of Mama's famous pies or cakes. The old wood cookstove was always ready to accommodate hungry kids and adults alike.

I don't remember too much about when I was very small. I do recall liking to catch butterflies and run through mud puddles and I would love to do this today if I could move fast enough. When I was around five years old, one of my favorite games was to catch butterflies. I have a picture of me under the old apple tree with one of these under my hand. The picture is hand-colored. This was done for several years before colored film was so popular and dated these images to within a few years. The people that did this took the black and white picture and lightly applied the colors over the top of the image. They made a pretty blue dress and red apples on the trees. Aunt Eunice made this picture of me. We also have one of Joe as a baby that was done with the same procedure and made a beautiful likeness for family heirlooms.

The simple things can sometime be the biggest and the best. You probably do not recall the old song, The Best Things in Life Are Free, but there is so much meaning in this phrase. A warm bed in winter; a cold glass of tea in summer; a smile from someone you love; the feeling you have in the church you grew up in; the warmth that goes through you when you are with your family. These Are A Few of My Favorite Things! The old songs have so much meaning if you will just listen to them with your heart and let your mind absorb the words.

Jack Randall: A Special Cousin

Jack was the second son of my mother's sister, Olive G. and Theron Spraggins, who brought such a beautiful joy to the whole family from the very beginning. We all knew he was special, but it took one or two years for the doctor to give us any name to his sickness. He thought that Jack had a brain tumor and that he would not reach an age much over his teen years. With no MRI's or machines to "see" the problem or medications to use, sometime they simply guessed what the problem was. We do know that Jack lived until old age and was a very strong and agile man until his death.

How we all loved this brother and cousin. He was like having an eternal, enthusiastic child around. Always eager to see me, his face would light up at the sight of me and always gave me a big hug. My mother was strict with my time, but running to play with Jack at the end of a long, laborious day was always allowed after all the chores were done.

My mother and two of her sisters received 25 acres as a dower when they married. These dowries of land each in a row, bounded by a country road on one end and Cypress Creek on the other. Her two sisters were Olive and Edith Carmen (Pritchette). My mother's land was the far west; Olive's was in the middle and Pritchette's on the east end. Across the back end of Cypress Creek sprawled acres and acres of my grandfather's (Jim Bailey) land.

Maybe because I never had a brother was the reason I was so attached to Jack. He was always so innocent like a child even in his old age, and everyone loves the innocence of children. I only know that he had a special place in my heart.

Jack Randall Spraggins

We did not have much at our house, but we did have an old upright piano that someone had given us. The irony that I learned to play church songs by ear is so enormous as I have grown almost completely deaf. Nonetheless, Jack could hear me play the piano. Some felt that his inability to talk meant that he was deaf, but he proved them all wrong. He loved the slow church songs that had easy rhythm and slow chords. I was always playing with him by irritating him and starting to play something like "St. Louis Blues" and he would push my hands off the keys. Sometimes he would just completely knock me off the bench. He thought when I hit the floor that it was very funny, and I would always exaggerate my fall and bounce a time or two. He loved the songs like "Sweet Hour of Prayer" and would move his body back and forth with perfect time to the music; he completely relaxed at this time. My love for a fast tempo in my teen years was completely alien to him. The slow tempo seemed to ease all the frustrations of a young man trapped in a mind that failed him and let the music soothe the pent-up feelings. When I would finish one of his favorite songs, he would take my hands and place them back on the keys and look at me and tell me with his eyes that I was to start over send play it again.

He really loved me but when his little sister, Sue Carol, was old enough to walk and talk, she became the love of his life and actually was the only person that could make him do what she wanted him to. She was very bossy with him, and he delighted in her when she pointed her little finger at him and said, "Jack Randall, you get right back to this house!" He would only laugh at her, but he always did as she told him to. I think about this and believe that he was reacting to innocence of a child and saw her and loved her because she was so small and he so big and tall.

Jack had his kidney removed and was just coming back to his room, where the family was all waiting. The doctor came in and said everything went well and that he would check back later. Joe Wayne said, "Doc, you better tie him to the bed or something because he will get up." The doctor had told the family to keep him still and quiet. The doctor told Joe, "Man, I just took out his kidney! He isn't going to move anywhere for a while," then left. Before he got to the nurses' station, Jack woke up and stood straight up in bed waving his hand round and round. That doctor learned something new that day for sure.

Then one day Joe and I were in charge of Jack and he wanted to go to Bells and get a snow cone. These were something new that had come to Bells and was a soft ice cream in a regular cone. I tried to tell Joe that we had Jack and had to take care of him, but he said it would be all right. We parked by the bank window straight in and there was a car on each side. We got out and I said, "Maybe I should stay with Jack." Joe's answer was that we would be gone only a minute since it was just down the street. When we came back, Jack was standing with one foot on the top of Joe's truck and one foot on the top of the car parked next to us straight up and his arm reaching for the sky and twirling his hand round and round. The bank window was filled with smiling faces and people on the street had stopped to see the show.

Jack was famous for his acrobats. He had perfect balance and would not only try all kinds of tricks but would succeed. His most famous act was standing with both feet on one arm of a rocking chair, standing erect with both arms up in the air and twirling a fly swatter on the top of his index finger.
He would do this while everyone was screaming for him to get down while he was laughing with such glee until Sue showed up and had no mercy on him. I can just see her now walking in the door with the screen door slamming and screaming, "Jack Randall, you get down this instant!!" He would laugh at her too...but he would get down. We would all take a breath of relief and be happy that once again Jack didn't fall and get a concussion; somehow, he never did. Twirling and slow music were his way of relaxing.

When he was twirling something, he would rock back and forth as though he had a silent song with rhythm that he would follow without missing a beat. One of his favorite "twirlers" was a pencil and cup. For hours he would sit and rock with the rotating cup, then suddenly he would move to the next phase and continue the tempo of the swirling, never missing a beat. Slowly creeping closer and closer to any light bulb he could reach and finally so close that he would pop it. The sudden POP followed immediate darkness that thrilled him. Once again, there was laughter. He knew we were entertained by his antics and loved being the center of attention.

I believe that taking off all his clothes was his favorite theatrical thing to do. In the southern culture in the 40's, this was, indeed, a mock of the Puritan beliefs of country life. He had no humility for his actions. He loved to go to the bridge between his house and ours in his birthday suit and stand on the very edge of the planks with his toes hanging over the side and watch the water running under the bridge, especially after a big rain, all the while moving back and forth, back and forth. His favorite foods were R.C. Cola, turnip greens and Cheerios; in fact, that was all he would eat! The R.C. truck would bring these drinks to the house for Jack by the case to help Aunt Ollie out some. I will never forget visiting this icon of my childhood many years later in a nursing home, where he roomed with his mother, who was by this time deaf and still so very protective of him. When I would go in and he was asleep, she would always tell me to go over and be sure Jack was not cold and that his legs and arms were covered with a blanket. If I went into the recreation room and they had him there, he would do as he always did as a boy and come up to me and rub his cheek up and down over mine, showing me that he remembered and loved me. When I would try to leave, he would take my hand and pull me back into the chair and I would sit a little longer with him. He meant so much to me and was a very positive influence on my life. I LOVE YOU, JACK.

Mr. Reggie and Two Delinquents

Mr. Reggie was an older man when Joe Wayne and I were about eight and nine years old. Joe and I were sitting in the old mulberry tree not far from the road, when we heard Mr. Reggie coming with his horses and wagon. When he got within ear shot, Joe shouted, "Hey, Reggie!" Mr. Reggie looked all around and up and down and was very puzzled. As he moved on down the road, I hollered, "Hey, Reggie!" This really did cause the old man to hesitate and look again, finding no one around; he looked very disturbed. When Aunt Olive found out about this, she gave Joe a good lick or two and sent me home. When she told my mom, I really paid the price for my mischief. We had a good lesson in respect, and on that one I will admit that we deserved all the bad vibes we got. I know that I would be very upset to find that any of mine had done this deed. What would people think?!?!

The said Mr. Reggie was plowing his cotton that was already knee high, and Joe Wayne came right behind him down the rows on his horse. Mr. Reggie told him to get out of his field and take his horse with him. Joe made the mistake of telling him, "You can't make me." The old man told him to get off the horse and he would show him. Joe got off and Mr. Reggie knocked him down. Joe said, "You better not do that again, old man!"—But he did.

Myrtle's Childhood...

My childhood memories are still with me after all these years. It seems I can recall my earlier years and can't seem remember where I went yesterday. Betty, my sister, and I had the usual relationship of siblings with three and half years separating us. I always wanted to hang around her and her friends and was the "pest" to her. Now we are best friends and very close. One instance stands out in my mind was when she was in high school, she had some friends over. We had had our usual misunderstanding before the dashing scholars arrived. We had bedrooms upstairs and mine was right over the living room where the group were gathered. Did I mention we had no indoor bathroom? I had the standard "chamber pot" and I waited until the laughter downstairs began to peak and held the top of the object up over the bottom and dropped it with more force than necessary. Well, there is no mistaking the sound of the impact of said object when clashed together! The room went very quiet! Mama gave me a good sound lecture but it was worth every word I endured.

Then there was the time Betty was upstairs and angry with me and I was heading up the stairs and she threw a pair of shoes down at me, hitting me right in the face, but I still think I got the better end of things!

Uncle Ed Hallman had a two-seated coupe car with a rumble seat. He would let us sit in this little back seat on the outside of the car and would ride us up and down the old dirt road. This had to be in dry weather so he wouldn't get his "baby" dirty. We thought we had died and gone to heaven and wanted to go by all the neighbors' houses so they could see how grand we were. Our two minutes of fame, so to speak.

In the corn crib there was this huge chicken snake that Daddy would not let me near him. Not for my sake, mind you, but for the snake's safety. You see this fellow ate the mice and rats that came into the barn, and we lost almost no corn because of him. He was humongous and really long.

We had a radio but this was before TV. Mama listened to *Search for Tomorrow* and Betty and I would listen to *Howdy Doody*. At night Gabriel Heater gave the news. This was our entertainment. The programs all shut down at midnight and some before. We had to work hard but we played hard too. We had playhouses inside and out. One of my favorites was under a big weeping willow by the back door. I am still partial to willow trees. We played cards, jump ropes, marbles, hide and seek, red rover, tag, etc. When we finally got some time off from work, we children all up and down the road got together and played. We grew close to each other because we communicated and did things together and depended on cousins and neighbors as well.

Once upon a Wrestling Match

I know that you recognize my cousin Joe Wayne Spraggins by now. I want you to know right now that MOST of these escapades were HIS idea. Do you believe me? OK. One Saturday night when we were in high school, we had some spare time and just had to find something that we had never done before ...We had heard that the wrestling matches in Jackson were really something to see or, as we found out, seeing was only half the story. We went to this old gym somewhere on a backstreet and found the said match about to start. We went in and found a standing place (the seats were all taken and half the standing room). Now I had been around cigarettes all my life, but a room full of smokers puffing at the same time is something a little more complex. If you could not smell this cloudy mess or feel it smart your eyeballs right out of your face, you might think you had gone straight up to the clouds in the sky. That would be right before a thunderstorm because there was nothing soothing about the air in there. There were several paper sacks with "refreshments" in them, but we ignored all this and wanted to see the great fight. Two oversized men came into the ring and pranced around like ballerinas. When the bell rang, they were like raging bulls and fought like animals, or so I thought, until one swung at the other and he fell like he had been hit by a boulder. Then I knew that somehow they were putting on a show and enjoying every minute of it. This was very entertaining but was the beginning of our wrestling watch career and also the end of it, too. Mama did not know where we were. Goes to show that sometimes you just have to see things to believe them.

One Long and Two Shorts

You would have to be of a certain age to know exactly what the heading of this page means. To the older ones reading this, you know for certain that this is the ring of the telephone that signaled who the call was for and ours at the Buster Leggett home was one long and two shorts. When calling someone on your line that were usually close neighbors, you would turn the handle on the side of the big oak phone and twist it around a few times, hesitate and then turn it two short turns and it would ring the Leggett house. Someone would have two shorts, someone would have two longs or one long and one short. If you wanted to call someone on another line, you simply called the operator and told her the person you wished to talk with and she would connect you to them. One of the bad problems that we had with this system was that anyone on your line could pick up the phone anytime it rang no matter who the call was for and "listen in." (as the phrase went for this imposition).You had no secrets and if you did, you certainly didn't talk about it on the phone. One of the favorite pastimes of our youth was to tell some story we had fabricated over the phone to see where it wound up and who forwarded the fable. If we had known then about all these cell phones and what you could do, we would have thought it was a piece of science fiction, because when our phone was hooked up and we could communicate with other people anywhere close, we were amazed at the convenience of the contraption. It was a miracle in itself at the time.

We lived then and now with the old saying that what you don't have you don't miss and this is true. Also true is the quote "you don't miss the water until the well goes dry" and this is also true when the TV messes up, the cell phone plays out, or they're out of strawberry ice cream at Baskin Robbins. Most things are simply the state of our minds at any certain time.

Our Mike

Mike McLemore was a man of color that Daddy hired to help him on the farm. He was a very gentle man although not educated. His manners and the know-how of doing the right things seemed to come as natural to him as breathing. He had not been there long before he was as one of the family. We depended on him and he on us. Daddy built him a one-room house out back of our home. It only had enough room for a cot, stove and a small dresser. I've seen doll houses with more square footage than this mini-house. He was very neat and clean in his appearance. Always clean-shaven, even just to go out in the fields. We washed his overalls and shirts for him. I was very young when he came to live with us. He ate his meals in the kitchen at the cabinet while we were eating at the table. Mama and Daddy tried and tried to get him to eat with us and he would not. Mike always cleaned his plate and always complimented Mama on the meal even if it was leftovers or something that we found out he really didn't care for. When he finished his meal, he always stacked his dishes and wiped off the cabinet where he had eaten. I really don't know what we would have done without this man to help us, especially after Daddy died and we were trying to make ends meet. He did lots of heavy work that Daddy was not able or strong enough to do. The diabetes kept my dad from having much strength and he was often sick.

Mike had a girlfriend, whose name was Aileen. He went to see her every Sunday afternoon and she was a very gentle, sweet woman. After I had my children, she would come see me and the babies and we all loved her, too.

Joe and I moved Mike's house down the road to Fruitvale to the house Ollie had fixed for us. We rolled it down the road a few feet at the time using four large logs; two under it and roll it the length of these and then placing the other two under, taking the first ones out and going a few feet before starting the procedure all over again. We put it behind where we were living at the time After we built our present house and rented the old one, one of the renters let a trash fire get out and the little house burned to the ground. I had it full of antiques that I had planned to fix up and use.

Mike had a bad stutter. He was very conscious of this but after he had gotten used to us, it was a little better. He could not get started with his sentences but after he finally got the first word out, he then ran through the words like a freight train. When Daddy hired him, he told him if he ever came home drunk, he would have to move out. I think he did come home in this condition one day, but he stayed because by this time he was one of our family.

Playmates 'Till the End

Things were pretty tight at our house when it came to extra dollars or even cents to spend on toys or something we did not have. It is pretty much summed up with the phrase, "If you can't eat it or wear it, you don't need it." This was not too bad because I had the perfect mom and dad and was very happy in my childhood. As I have said before, Joe Wayne Spraggins was like a brother to me, and we acted accordingly by fussing and fighting with each other and generally having a good time.

Uncle Theron always brought Sue, Joe, and Sarah neat gifts when he came home from his work out-of-state. Joe Wayne had driven a truck up and down the roads when he literally had to stand up to see out the windshield. Six or seven would probably get close to his driving years. It looked like the truck was coming down the road by itself. All this and I don't think he ever had an accident. While me, on the other hand, took the car to Gretta's house to show her my new puppy and ran in a ditch, missing a creek by inches. It was my first time behind the wheel with no one with me.

Joe Wayne and I were cousins, our mothers being sisters. We are both Bailey stock, which made for big bones and strong features, (and bullheaded) plus extra big feet. We did not have long hours to play for all the work that we had, but you better believe we made good use of those hours we did manage to get. We were never bored. Joe Wayne was one year older than me and big for his age, but he didn't have anything over on me because I gave him a "run for his money" on size and determination.

One day Joe and I were playing with his BB gun. We were out by a shed with tin siding and top, and he shot at a bird on the roof and the BB bounced off the tin and hit me in the navel. I screamed and screamed at him like he had done it on purpose and told him, "I will never play with you again!" I didn't until after lunch that day. To make this story a little more believable, the BB did make me shed a drop or two of blood. For his side of the tale he claimed, "I didn't do it! It wasn't my fault." I would not need a law degree to win my case on that one.

In the sixth grade (he was in the seventh) Joe got a horse. I mean a riding horse, not the kind that pulls a plow. We had never seen one of this kind before. We rode that horse all weekend and I was so sore I could not sit, so Mama took me to the doctor and I had broken the end of my tail bone and had to sit on a pillow for weeks at school or stand up. Did I ever get teased for this one. I was humiliated.

When we got to high school, Joe had a car. I mean a real car and no one had a car in high school back then. I was a regular passenger in that car. One day we decided to go to Jackson to the airport without telling our parents of these plans. We got there and were leaning on the fence watching the planes as planned, when Joe looked at me and said, "Myrtle, why don't we just go up in one of those they rent?" Sounded good to me at the time. I know that most of you cannot remember those itsy bitsy planes back then but, believe me, they were SMALL! Anyway, we went up and the wind was blowing us about like we were helium balloons; it scared me to death. I know it did Joe, too, but don't think for a minute he would in a million years admit it. I can understand why sometimes when people get off the plane, they kiss the ground and may have done just that if I weren't so wheezy and wobbly on my feet.

Then there were the times we went riding around in his car. He loved speed and driving fast, but it was not my cup of tea. This is one of the brother-sister arguments that erupted. I did not waste any time telling him on this particular excursion that I wanted him to slow down and not "fly" the car. After repeating myself several times, it was the last straw for Joe. He pulled off the road in front of Dr. Mayfield's house and told me that I could ride if I wanted to, but if I didn't, get out and walk; I rode. Yes, he won that one and it did not take us long to get home. His foot got even heavier on the gas, just to show me who was boss.

I had always wanted something with wheels. Anything that got you somewhere you did not have to walk. I was approaching my teen years. (Does this sound familiar to any of you?) Joe was driving the car, the truck, the tractor and here I was walking and walking and walking some more. We had run the wheels off his scooter and I didn't even have that anymore. We finally got a black Mercury car and I would be driving in a few long years. That is when my bubble burst in the paragraph above and I was sitting on my side in the ditch.

Joe Wayne Spraggins
1947-1948

Pulley Bone

True love can be expressed in different ways. Flowers, candy, love letter, etc. When I was about 11 years old and was at my Uncle Dutch and Aunt Louise's house having dinner with my family, Joe was there eating with Ray and we had been batting eyes at each other since he started to school in Bells. Aunt Louise had fried chicken, much to the delight of us all. She could really fry up a scrumptious platter of fried chicken. The platter went around the table and got to Joe and he picked up the pulley bone. Aunt Louise teased him and said, "Joe, don't you know that Myrtle Rose likes the pulley bone better than any other piece of chicken?" Well, wonder of all wonders, he put that ole pulley bone down and got another piece instead! I knew then that he did not have a chance in the world. A girl can just tell these things!

Another Brother Named Ray
Ray McDonald Woodson

As I have mentioned, Joe Wayne Spraggins is like a brother to me. Although I officially have only one sister and no brothers, I still have yet another brother named Ray McDonald Woodson. He was named after the old doctor that delivered him. He lived down the road from Joe when he was growing up and they were good friends and still are. His mother and my dad were brother and sister and we visited them often.

Our families would sometimes swap out work in the fields to "visit" if these two words could be used in the same sentence; however, work and being together we did. Before Ray and I were big enough to chop cotton all day, we were playing around a water hole in a low place in the field and Ray said, "I heard that if you muddy the water, the fish would all come to the top." We had our hoes with us and began to push them back and forth, making the water thick with mud and, sure enough, a fish or two really did come to the top and in our excitement over our find, we yelled and screamed with joy. Our parents thought one of us had been hurt or snake bit and came running across the field like a house on fire. When they discovered the cause of all this, they became so angry I thought for sure we were going to be strung up a tree! Uncle Dutch wanted to whip us but our mothers came to our rescue! He really put a damper on our little escapade. Remember, never underestimate the power of a mother!

Then there was the time that the Woodsons came to see us just before Christmas and the weather turned ugly and they ended up staying with us a week on through the holidays. Santa brought me this amazing doll with eyes that open and close. I was so thrilled and loved that doll instantly. Well, it had rained the night before and the tubs under the drain of the house were full of water and old Ray just decided he would just give that big baby doll a bath! Sure enough, when she dried off, her face began to crack. I still may take this to court because I still have this doll and she still is disfigured on her face. Then I get to thinking that if the doll had stayed perfect, would I remember that Christmas morning as much without the famous bath? I think not! I would not have this tale about her and probably would have discarded her long ago. I still have to think upon this, Ray, before I forgive or thank you. Don't tell anyone but I still love you!

One other tale about Ray when he still lived in Fruitvale was on a Sunday afternoon when he, my Joe, and I were playing in the front yard when we saw all these cars and people going out in the field, not far in front of the Woodson house. We decided to investigate and see what in the world was going on and had noticed that several of these folks had dressed in all white. We saw that they were gathered at the old pond there out in the field. The three of us sat down on the bank and watched as a preacher baptized these white-clothed people one after another, while the crowd sang hymns and prayed. This was a colored baptism not unlike one Cypress Church had a few years ago because we had several of my family that were baptized that day in Anna and Stephen Bailey's pond near their house. Almost everyone in the church and more were there to encourage the moment. It was a very inspirational ceremony, just like the one I saw so many years ago. A while back, there was a colored artist that was selling his work, and he had this beautiful painting of a baptism that he finally sold me after I begged and begged for it. Every time I go by this picture, I feel inspired by it and the memories it brings back to me. "Good times make good memories."

Ray McDonald Woodson

Sisters Playing House Imitating Their Mother

*Betty Ann and Myrtle Rose Leggett
Taken at Bailey Homeplace, 1943*

My sister Betty and I had a playhouse behind the "old house." We imitated Mama by "canning" grass and berries for vegetables and fruit. We "canned" wood chips for meat imitating Mama canning sausages, loin chops, etc. Mama canned lots of meat back then. It was the only way to preserve these cuts of meat.

The only part of the pork we did not eat were the chitterlings. Mama was famous for her "souse" that she made from the hog's head. If you have never tasted it, you do not know what you are missing. None of the women in the community liked to make it so Mama always ended up with all the hog's heads. You boiled and boiled it until it literally fell apart, then pulled all the meat off the bone and broke that into tiny shreds then putting it into a mold. (a bowl or something with big openings so when it gelled it would slide out the top.) Then she put a plate or saucer on this and a brick on top of the plate, all to press out the unwanted juices. It would come out in a perfect shape of the container and had congealed and when cooled, would cut into thin slices that we would fry until brown and cracked into pieces. It was and still is my favorite "sausage" that is flavored with salt, black and red pepper, etc. Yum Yum!

Song and Dance

Most of the music I heard in early years was country ''country.'' One being "Old Dan Tucker" that went like this with a lively jingle to it——

Old Dan Tucker was a mighty man,
washed his face in a frying pan
Combed his hair with a wagon wheel,
died with a toothache in his heel.

Now I really gave this song a lot of thought when I was very little and could not for the life of me figure out how this man could accomplish these unreal feats. He must have been a mighty man like the first line insinuated.

Another song that was one of my dad's favorites was Ernest Tubb singing, "Wabash Cannonball." All of us in those days just dreamed of going to exotic places, like other states. Other countries were just outside our imagination and the train was the way to go back then. This song suggested all the things a train could do for you back then and had a very lively beat to it that made you feel good and could well imagine these things happening to you.

Another old song is "Stay a Little Longer." It goes something like this............

Play all night
Play a little longer
Dance all night
Dance a little longer
Pull off your coat
Throw it in the corner
Don't see why you don't stay a little longer!

Starting to School at the Big School in Bells

It was a major step for me to start to school in the third grade with so many in my class that I did not know anyone but Jo and Gretta. There were so many rooms and the halls were so long and scary! I would never learn which room was mine without following someone else! But, oh, wonder of all wonders was the restrooms! Indoor toilets were something I had not grown up with and when I saw those stalls, (can you believe doors on them all!) I thought I could put up with anything just to know they were there.

My teacher was Miss Lilia Montgomery, and she knew just the right things to say to you and so understanding that it did not take me long to fit in. I made new friends that year that are still some of my best friends in my whole life. You really know your schoolmates after all the years in school with them. No secrets by the time you graduate.

The school bus that took us to Bells was good for only the best of weather. The roads were dirt and in winter they were a continual line of ruts, mud and water. On these days one of the dads in the community would take his horses and wagon and pick us all up and take us to school. By the time we got there and ate lunch, you got it, it was time to go home again. The men had a wagon that was literally a covered wagon like in all the western movies. It was not a joy ride; I'm telling you it was all bumps and knocks all the way, but the canvas top kept us dry and the wind off in rainy and snowy days. People were always trying to go through with their cars and ended up sliding in the ditch. You had to hope that the nearest house had horses or mules to pull your vehicle out of the muck. After the deep, slushy roads, we finally got some gravel put down and, boy, I thought there was nothing in this whole world as great as those passable roads. Gone were the covered wagons and the school bus was on a run.

The Prom Dress from Memphis

Well, the time came for the prom at Bells School and my sister Betty wanted a beautiful dress for this very special occasion. As we all know, the kids rule on most things that came around. So Mama, Daddy, Uncle Arthur and Aunt Jewell took Betty to Lowenstein's in Memphis in pursuit of the perfect prom dress. The ladies were soon engrossed in the rows of formals and completely forgot about the male escorts. Daddy and Uncle Arthur were soon discussing the disadvantages of being their gender and getting tired of just waiting and waiting, and Uncle Arthur looked at Daddy and said, " I'll kick you and you can kick me...!" Sometimes it is better to use your imagination to finish sentences rather than to write them down.

No Warts in Cypress

Mr. Charlie Porter had another talent that I know most of you will laugh at this tale. All I know is that I had so many warts on my knees that I was totally embarrassed for anyone to see them. Mr. Charlie would spit on his finger and rub those warts and in about two weeks, those eyesores just fell off completely. This feat was also performed and worked the same way on many folks back then. I know you don't believe this, but I saw it and it happened to me. I can't explain it...only record it!

A friend of mine, Tina Gray, confirms this type of wart removal. She said she had some on her fingers and her dad would put his hand in his pocket for a few seconds, then reach for her hand and rub the wart. After a week or two, the wart was gone completely. Many years later, she asked her dad just how he did that. He told her it was an old trick and that he put his hand in his pocket and rubbed a coin. (probably a penny) and some element in the coin would react and remove the wart...It Works! There were no warts in Cypress or...community!

My Aunt Bettie
By Myrtle Rose Leggett Emerson

I realize that so many pages of this book have been centered on Bettie Elizabeth Bailey, but my personal link with her has not been mentioned yet; and if everything was written about her that we all knew, well there is yet another volume to be written.

Aunt Bettie was my grandmother, Lou Myrtle's sister. They married brothers, James and John Bailey. Lou Myrtle had a hard life with Jim as you have probably already read by now, but Aunt Bettie's story is a nightmare. I don't really feel I have the right to display all her problems here on paper. She was blind and she was a battered wife, which may or may not have caused her blindness that was passed off as reading too much. Here, I will not agree, because if reading caused blindness, then I am doomed to blackness at any time now.

She only wore black, long-sleeved and floor-length dresses that she could hem herself. She was so short and tiny; no store-bought dresses would fit her. I once sat with her as she hemmed her dress and asked her if she wanted me to help her with it and she replied in a solemn voice, "Why?"... Why indeed. So you see how independent this old woman was. I can do this by myself and my blindness has no cause for me to have someone help me. I can't tell you how much I admired her at this moment; to have that attitude and that confidence was amazing.

As we have mentioned before, the iron fence around the old church at Cypress, I remember remnants of this old fence and I also remember a big rattle snake hanging across it with many rattlers. Evidently the snake was dead already but was told by an old timer at the time that he would hang there until it thundered and then would be declared dead and would be thrown away. This old fence is gone now, but I have plans to replace that fence in my lifetime, if the church permits me to. I will dedicate it to my daughter Mame' that was killed just short of 16 years of age. Aunt Bettie raised money for the original fence there and collected penny by penny to pay for it and with a hen or rooster thrown in to help out. She was an original ancestress and I greatly admired her more than anyone.

Hog Killing

In the winter, we had hog killings for the community or family. It had to be very cold so the meat would not ruin and would cool so it stiffened up and could be cut up easier. The people would start coming in before the sun came up, and the men would start the process of killing and hanging the hog in the barn upside down to drain out the blood.

The women started the fire under the iron wash pot with sticks and pieces of stove wood to boil the water to wash the skin of the hog clean. After this was done, the water was thrown out and the pot was used for the squares of fat the women trimmed off the lean. This fat was boiled until the squares of fat were swiveled up and brown. This was strained out of the liquid lard (they were called "cracklings") and was used in cornbread. The cracklings were so crisp and good, we popped them in our mouths like popcorn and, boy, was this good! The Old Country Store in Jackson still uses this method of making bread and people from all over come to eat there and taste this delicacy.

The workers would stay all day. After the hogs were scrapped of all hair and dirt and the lard cooked, the women would prepare lunch for the bunch at noon for family and friends. This day took a lot of work, but no one seemed to mind because it became almost like a holiday talking to people that they loved and cared for. There was always a lot of laughter and bonding going on at these occasions. The children were delighted to have a whole day to play with friends while the adults were so occupied.

In the afternoon, the lean slabs of meat were cut into pork chops, backbone, shoulders, hams, and the trimmings from this were ground into sausage and stuffed into long, narrow bags of domestic making for round slices to fry with eggs or make sandwiches with mustard and biscuits.

The hams and shoulders were either rubbed down in sugar cure and hung from rafters or put into huge wooden boxes with salt to preserve them with side meat in the same box. A layer of salt was laid in the bottom and then a layer of meat that could not touch the other cut. This was repeated until all the meat was completely covered in salt and would last all year without ruining. The meat had to be washed off to get most of the salt out before cooking.

This is an old process that people do not do now and it is a lost custom of country people. There may still be a few that do this, but I don't know of any...more the pity!

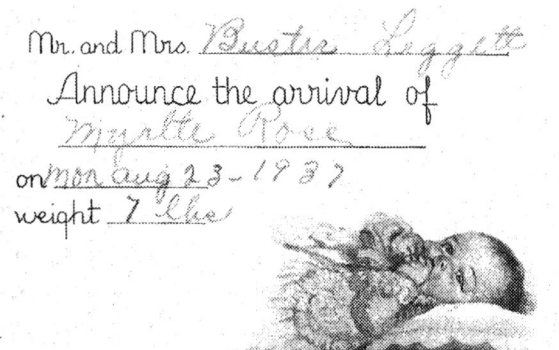

**Birth announcement
Myrtle Rose Leggett**

**Emison School House
Painted by Myrtle Rose Emerson**

**Sisters, Betty Ann and Myrtle Rose
Leggett - 1945**

Leggett Cousins Front row: Thomas, Gretta, Betty, Ray Back row: Clara Jo, Tommy, Della, Annette, Rosalie, and Myrtle Rose

Bailey Grandchildren
Myrtle Rose, Betty Ann, Thomas Marion,
Jimmy, Joe Wayne, Sue Carol, Vera, Peggy
(baby) Bill, Della, Annette, and Susan

Lou Myrtle Forsythe Bailey and
daughter (my mother) Mamie
Elizabeth Bailey Leggett

Lewis McLemore, Charlie
Musgraves, Joe Emerson (on
truck) and Malcolm Emerson
(weighing cotton) – 1957

CHAPTER 12

Mama made this one

"Virginia Reel" Made by Elizabeth Leggett – Myrtle Emerson's mother

Quilts: My Passion

Quilts Are a Lot of Things to Me

When I came home from school all my years through twelfth grade, I got under Mama's quilting frames in the winter months for lots of reasons. First, it was the warmest place in the house. The pot-bellied stove was in the bedroom, and the quilting frames were in the middle of the room that took up almost the whole room. At night Mama would roll the frames up to the ceiling on hooks just for that purpose, so we could move around getting ready for bed. I got my lessons under these frames with a quilt "put in." When I finished with the books, I liked to just lie there and watch Mama's hands glide across the underside of the lining, guiding the needle back up to the top of the coverlet. It went up and down and up and down making thousands of tiny stitches to complete the quilt. Another thing I liked about these covers was they kept us warm and snug in the cold winters when the fire in the old stove got low in the night.

I remember falling down a bank of snow going to the bus and breaking my arm. We did not know at first that it was broken, but it hurt so bad and I crawled under the hanging quilt by the fire and cried, but watching Mama's hands running along the lines quilting stitch by stitch with needle and thread was very comforting for me to watch this.

After we got gas heat for the house, Mama began to make quilts as an outlet for her talents. She was a magnificent quilter, making small stitches and even rows and, believe me, this is not an easy thing to do. But the most amazing thing about her work on these quilts was her sense of beauty in both design and color. She would start to make one and pick out the fabrics to use, and I would really have my doubts until she finished the product then I realized she really knew her stuff because her quilts were unique in style and color coordination; she was an artist. Her hands had done heavy men's work in fields, yard, barnyard, garden and home, but they still did this amazing, tedious work that told the world "there was more to her than met the eye." This was only one of her many talents, but I know that it was her favorite and later it also became mine, too.

I think these experiences with the quilted cover in my youth gave me so much pleasure that it stuck with me into my adult life, and I made these covers a major part of my livelihood. It could be called a "passion" or simply a "hobby." Whatever it is, it is very endearing to me.

Antique Business

I was in the antique business for more than 25 years. I started out in the old Franklin Building in Jackson with Carl Yarbrough. I was really green about business, and Carl and his family were so great to me and helped me get started and stayed with me until I quit around 2004. When I began to buy and sell antiques, quilts were my main source of trading goods. I bought any size, make or age as long as it was done well and had special features such as color coordination or visual appeal. If the quilt was beyond repair, I made runners, place mats, pillows, and stuffed bears, etc. with them. I repaired the ones that could be saved and sold them. I never cut a good quilt or one that could be repaired.

Later on, I made "Father Christmas" with the ragged quilts or from old family pieces. At one time, I did repair work for a small museum in New England. They would send me tattered quilts and I would repair and return them by mail. I also had some quilts in a shop in Maine for a while until the shop closed.

Sometimes I would go to a quilt show and sell quilts. I also did demonstrations on quilting at different places and one of these places was the Ames Plantation.

I have had a good run with this textile since it has been with me all my life and through many changes of my preference. When I first married, I thought the cross stitch and appliqué were dreams to have. I had so many patchwork ones that the change seemed good. Then later

Olivia and Father Christmas made from ragged quilt by Myrtle Leggett Emerson

on in years, the patchwork again took first place, but then as I have aged, the older ones are my favorite.

I helped with the Girl Scouts as long as my girls were in it and one year, we had each girl make her
own block and the finished cover was beautiful!

Times change and we change and see things a little different at each turn.

"Gibson Girl" Feed sack quilt displayed in the Brooks Museum in Memphis

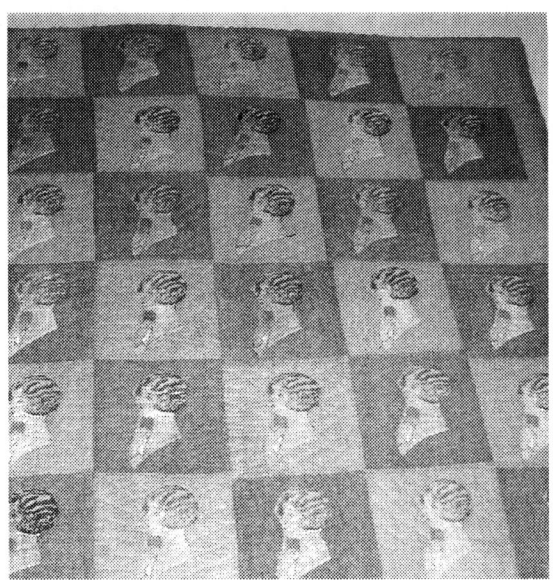

Quilts in the Brooks Museum in Memphis

I was particularly thrilled when I got a call from the Brooks Museum in Memphis wanting to send a curator to our house to see if I had any quilts that might qualify for an exhibit they were having on quilts from Tennessee. The gentleman they sent was very nice and very knowledgeable about quilts. I had never seen anyone know as much about these items before and certainly not a man. He looked at my collection and took his time and commented on several, and in the end he had picked out four he really liked and was having a hard time with his decision because he only had room for three in his show. One he decided on was one very, very old and possibly a Civil War Era covering. The other two were considered to be folk art and not as old. I was amazed at some of the ways he had to determine his opinion of the different textiles. He would rub the fabric and "feel" what it said to him and he picked up one and he asked me what I thought it was lined with. I told him I thought it was either Lindsey Woolsey or flax and he was of the opinion that it was Lindsey Woolsey. The way he reached this fact was by smelling of the quilt. This was the first time I had seen this technique used for evaluating age and quality of a fabric. We had such a nice visit, and I had gained a new insight on my hobby and found a "kindred spirit" as well.

The old quilt that I mentioned above was a quilt that I purchased from an individual that said the quilt was her great-great-granny's chicken quilt. I told her that was nice but it really looked like an eagle on a mountain and I was told right quick that it was her great-great-granny's Chicken Quilt. I said OK. But the authorities thought it was an eagle, indeed, and just may be a political quilt of its time; and since it was made by a Black American, it was very good. It was frayed around the edges and very, very fragile.

As for the other two quilts, they were in the folk art category and not near as old. The second one he picked out was a snake quilt. Whoever made this covering had a great sense of color and design, not to mention a sense of humor. It was made with the "Rocky Road to Kansas" pattern, but the curved lines of patches were turned to make a crooked line diagonal completely across the whole quilt and at the top of each snake heads were appliquéd onto the crooked lines with a forked tongue embroidered at the mouth and at the bottom of the "snake," long pointed tails were added. This, with a green background, giving the reptiles a natural habitat look.

The last quilt was Gibson Girl heads from flour sacks cut out and put on crude yellowed cotton and had lumpy filler and long stitches. I was amazed at this choice, for I had been just given this quilt. At an auction one day I had bid on a better quilt; and when I won the bid, they just threw this one in just to get rid of it. I just washed and folded it and put it away, I suppose just waiting for the museum to call me about it!

The museum made note cards of the snake quilt and sold them in the gift shop. One of these is pictured in this book.

When I was young at home with my parents, the best place in the house was under the quilting frames. We had an old pot bellied stove in the bedroom-den and the quilting frames barely fit between them. In winter I would come home from school and get my lessons under the frames and watch my Mother's hands move slowly over the quilt as she made stitches. These quilts were at the time used to keep us warm in winter and for "pallets" under the shade trees in summer. Later on my Mom made them for pleasure and for her grandchildren. She was a brave and talented woman. My Dad had diabetes and at that time was very bad. Mom did most of the farm work, kept the house and cooked hot meals for her family.

Myrtle Rose Emerson, 2009

My snake quilt made into note cards at the Brooks Museum in Memphis

Plaque on the wall in the Brooks exhibit An e-mail I sent telling them why I loved quilts so much.

Displayed in Brooks museum in Memphis – Antique eagle on a mountain black American – Civil War era

Myrtle Rose's Witch she made for Halloween

Father Christmas made from ragged quilt by Myrtle Leggett Emerson

Stop the Press!

I suppose it is just human nature to want to see our names in lights, on a billboard, on the screen. I suppose we all like our names anywhere but maybe the public restroom walls. I know that I have had a few good times with seeing my work in different papers and things. Not anything important or glitzy, but just plain old reading.

My first experience was when the *Commercial Appeal* in Memphis did an article with pictures on needlework and quilting. I was in my thirties at the time and really green around the gills as far as taste was concerned. I did not know anything about the world of decoration except the things that my hands could turn out with a needle and thread.

I had two different stories come out in *The Jackson Sun* about ten years apart. The first one was almost a duplicate of the one in the Memphis paper with a few more words and pictures. The second was more in line with my obsession with old and new quilts. By this time they were a major role in my sales in antiques. This antique business really started because I had an overflow of quilts and other old things; and if I ran across something I simply could not live without, well, something had to go!

The *Tennessee Magazine* did a spread on my quilts, samplers and pillows, etc. This came about in between the ones with *The Jackson Sun*.

My *Father Christmas* was featured in *Southern Living* magazine one November in the *Christmas* issue and my business really took off there. A good friend, Mary Ann, whom I had made the first one for out of her husband's grandmother 's ragged quilt, was the key to this article. She also helped me get one in the *Governor's Mansion* in Nashville. This was really an experience for me to have the interview and all the photos made. We made a party out of it and several friends came over and we all just made a day of it.

I suppose the last time was a good finale for my five minutes in the limelight. Several antique dealers and men and women in the field got together and had a show at *The Carnegie* in Jackson that ran for several days in Jackson and made a wonderful book called *"Three Stars of Tennessee—-with a focus on Western Tennessee."* This book is well-done and very informative for the antique lovers. They featured three of my quilts in this show with one of my samplers. You meet so many wonderful people at these things like this that love the same things you do and inspires you to do more with your knowledge. While there one day, there was a schoolteacher who came through with her whole class, and she asked me to talk to her about the quilts there. It was so inspirational to see these eager, little faces looking at me and listening to my words and a wonder that they could be so interested so young. They especially liked the *Snake Quilt* that I had there. They pointed their little fingers and laughed at the crooked snakes all over the coverlet.

I suppose this seems like it makes me narrow-minded, and I will admit that I do possess a passion for these quilts and old things, but they do have to go backstage when it comes to my family and friends. I really do believe in "first things first."

Grandmother's engagement ring,
antique – Mississippi

"Broken Star" made by Broxie Marlowe,
Maggie Emerson's sister

Say hello to
FATHER
CHRISTMAS

By LEA SCHNEIDER
features@jacksonsun.com

With a twist of this and a dab of that, wrapped in the fabric history of the South in the form of a quilt, Father Christmas becomes quite real at the hands of local artist Myrtle Rose Emerson.

At her home in Fruitvale, she has a workshop where she incorporates all kinds of items from our countryside: okra pods, twists of vine, blooming weeds and cotton. All of these materials become a life-size sculpture of Father Christmas, or Santa Claus.

Emerson is featured in this month's Southern Living magazine in the Tennessee edition. A story and photos about her can be found in the Tennessee People and Places section.

"It has certainly been interesting," she said of being featured in the magazine.

"She is real creative and is a real good person. She deserves everything that they put in her crown," said Calvin Murphy, co-owner of Yarbro's Antique Mall on Carriage House Drive in Jackson.

Emerson sells her Santas at the mall.

Her creations change with a whim and with the materials on hand. She has sculpted Father Time and Uncle Sam Santas and even an orange University of Tennessee Santa.

It takes her 14 to 22 hours to create one Father Christmas, depending on how elaborate a sculpture is desired.

"One woman wanted me to use black on them. I had some quilts with black in them and they turned out to be really elegant ones. One wanted a really satiny quilt. Every (Santa) has a different look and a different feel," she said. "I once used a 1960s wreath and took it all apart and used the 1960s decorations with the quilt."

One of her first large Santas was ordered by her longtime friend Mary Ann Stonecipher. That Santa, made years ago and still gracing the Stonecipher home this holiday season, was the link to Southern Living.

"When I first saw one at her house, I said 'I have got to have one,'" Stonecipher said. Her

Please see SANTA, 3C

Find out more

Local artist Myrtle Rose Emerson's Santas can be seen and purchased at Yarbro's Antique Mall, 350 Carriage House Drive, in Jackson.

She can also be contacted directly for Santas, or to place a custom order, but only through her e-mail at myrtle007@msn.com, because she has hearing difficulties.

The Santas vary in price depending on the size and how elaborate the decorations are. A smaller Santa can range from $300 to $350, and a larger Santa can sell for $450 to $850.

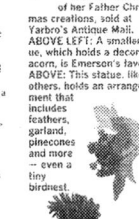

AT LEFT: Myrtle Rose Emerson of Fruitvale shows off her Father Christmas creations, sold at Yarbro's Antique Mall. ABOVE LEFT: A smaller one, which holds a decorative acorn, is Emerson's favorite. ABOVE: This statue, like others, holds an arrangement that includes feathers, garland, pinecones and more — even a tiny birdnest.

Photos by KATIE MORGAN/The Jackson Sun

Myrtle's article about Father Christmas

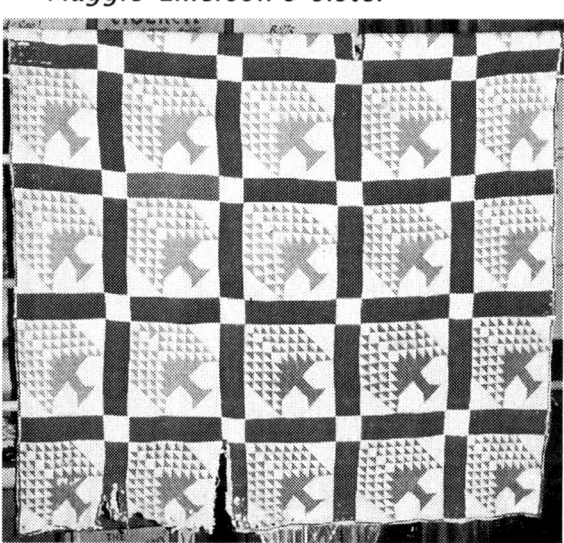

"Tree Of Life"
Emerson Quilt – 1850 – 1860

"Tree of Life" Bailey Quilt
1840 – 1950 or Civil War

237

CHAPTER 13

Cousin Tales

I'm My Own Grandma

If you are old enough, I know you remember the old country (and I do mean country) song, *"I'm My Own Grandpa."* When I was very young back in the middle ages, I tried to follow the words to this tune to see if it was really possible, and I suppose I will never know now because it would take Einstein to figure it out and he is no longer here. I got lost when his uncle married his first cousin by marriage and they had two kids, then he married his second twice-removed to be close to his brother's third wife's sister-in-law's father's half-brother—Strange!

There were eight children in my mother's family and eight in my father's family. That makes thirty-two aunts and uncles. Now if they all had three children each, that would make me first cousins to forty-eight people. Now I am at the age where all these forty-eight cousins have children and suppose they have three children each. This, my friend, comes out to one hundred and forty-four second cousins. Now all these forty-eight cousins had spouses, right? (and some two or three but who is counting). This makes ninety-six second cousins, instead of the original forty-eight. The ninety-six cousins and the one hundred forty-four second cousins, plus the thirty-six aunts and uncles, you have a whiff of what my family is like. Oh, but I forgot to count spouses for the one hundred and forty-four second cousins, but you know this computer will not be able to print a number that big, will it?

This is just an illusion of what a big family can entail and why it takes so long to figure all this out. If you are looking for everyone, you would need to take a job as a mailman just to send out invitations to a reunion and kill a whole herd of cows just to have hamburgers to feed them all. Now as I have this all "thunk" through, guess I'll just stick to the usual subjects and not let my mind do too much wandering from now on. I wouldn't want you to think I was the family dummy, would I?

Paw Paw
By Jill Emerson

Paw Paw was telling Lori and me about the first time he rode in a car from Fruitvale to Jackson. He told me this years before he died and right before he moved into assisted living. It took most of the day to get there because the roads were bad and not very direct to Jackson. Along the way they would have to stop at ditches to get water for the radiator because the engine kept overheating. Back then that was a common thing to do because the service stations were so far apart from each other. The radiators could not have been too clean and were probably packed with mud in the bottom. Crude, but still better than the old horse and buggy.

Memphis Cousins
By Myrtle Leggett Emerson

Mama had two double first cousins that lived in Memphis. They lived not far apart, close to South Haven and the Mississippi line. These cousins were Forsythe sisters that married Bailey brothers. Our trips to Memphis were the only "long" trips that I made until I was fourteen years old. One of the households was that of Marie and Ted Mayhall. I was very close to them, for they had three children: Mary Ann, Betty Jo, and Teddy that I was close to in age and they visited us often. Mary Ann, being exact age as me, Jo, and Teddy coming along some years younger.

Prudence married Dave Teal, and they had boys that were a bit older than me; and when we visited, they were old enough to be moving around town and basically not there. Our families were entwined through their love of Cypress Church and our Homecomings, where they came each year bringing their entire families and we Baileys opened our homes, enjoying fellowship with our Memphis kinfolk.

Daddy Jim's brother, Dr. Conrad Bailey, lived not far from the Mayhalls with his wife, Thelma. She was his nurse before she became his wife. I remember the house had a round torrent on one side, and the house was filled with antiques that I loved even as a child. Most of the Bailey family pieces were in this house. I remember the silver and marble-topped bedroom suits and beautiful glassware in every room. When Dr. Bailey died, these things were either given to Thelma's family or put out in the driveway for "give away." I went over and got the old bowl and pitcher that Dr. Bailey had promised me, and there was an old black bonnet that belonged to Grandma Delifate that I think Aunt Pritchett got and that is all I know of what was salvaged from the big two-story house. I was young and newly married and did not know much about antiques at the time, only that I loved them and especially things that my family had used. I really hated to see these things get out of the family but did not know how to prevent it. I only hope that they are with someone that will care for them and love them and treat them with respect.

Dr. Bailey had a clinic in Memphis and Mama went to see him there several times and I may have too, but it was always while I was too young to remember. He was so kind and gentle and loved all of us unconditionally. His personality was completely opposite from my grandfather's whose was unbending and forceful in his dealings with the family.

Aunt Prue, as we called her, was so gentle and sweet, that I never heard her raise her voice of complaint about anything and, believe me, she had plenty to shout and gripe about. Uncle Dave had a personality a lot like the husband of her sister, Myrtle, and did not treat her as I thought he should, but he was good to us when we visited and made us feel welcome.

The Teals lived in a typical house of the times. It was very roomy with a front porch and big rooms. It looked to me like it was probably built at the turn of the century, give or take a few years. Uncle Dave had a good job working in the post office for many years. He was an intelligent man but lived frugally without many unnecessary things. This was evident, especially in his bedroom that we were not allowed to enter, and the door was usually locked against any intrusion. So now I suppose you know the goal of all the visiting kiddies was. Right, we just HAD to see what was in that room. One day while we were there and Uncle Dave was away, Aunt Prue delighted in opening that door and letting us in to look all we wanted. I was shocked, scared, enthralled and curious all at one time. There were guns of all kinds, bow and arrows, stuffed animals of all sizes, cabinets full of old relics that were men things and more than we could take in. We were not unhappy when we were shown out back into light and polished and cleaned rooms. We never asked to go in there again. Now at 73, I would love to take a second look and see if what I remembered was still there.

When we would visit Uncle Dave and Aunt Prue, he would always make home-made hot tamales for us. We had never eaten them before he started this. He made them outside on a fire and they were rolled in corn shucks and cooked piping hot. (That being two kinds of hot, one heat hot and two, hot pepper hot). Two hots made for one smoking gun! After only one bite, you felt that you would just go poof—and burn away into smoke! Talking about food, Aunt Prue was a super chef. She could cook like you would not believe. She took great pride in her table and everyone profited from her endeavors.

Aunt Prue could not talk plain. I had a very hard time understanding her, even young, because my hearing was already on the way to silence even then. I soon discovered that I did not have to know every word she said because her mood, treatment of us, her heart-full love broke any barrier that may have been there. She was always jolly and put everyone before herself in all her dealings with people. Truly an angel there!

As the years went by, I saw the Teal boys less and less. One day getting off the bus from school, I saw these black motorcycles parked right by our door with these boys dressed in black and it scared me at first. Then I heard Mama calling for me to hurry up and greet my cousins from Memphis. I could see she was beaming and very glad they were there. I realized who they were and went running to hug each one. They stayed with us to eat and talk. (Mom always had food for anyone that cared to come by.)

Now I have nephews and a grandson that love motorcycles, and they are no longer a novelty to me. It just proves that we are comfortable with what we are used to and think nothing of it. But I will admit that I am a little scared yet of these machines, only because I worry about injuries to the ones I love riding them.

Story of Aunt Prue
By *Betty Jo (Mayhall) Trakimas*

My Aunt Prue was my mother's only sister, and I will never be able to express in words how much she means to me and how much I loved her. I knew Uncle Dave probably loved her, but he never showed that love with kindness and affection. I know he loved me and Teddy and Mary Ann because he was good to us and even helped me through my 9th grade Algebra by tutoring me. He was self-taught as a hobby.

I spent hours with him in his garage, filled with motorcycles and tool equipment. He had a Harley along with expensive things. As interesting as he was, Aunt Prue was our much-loved relative and was the one that showed us love and respect and was like a second mother to us.

Everyone always said that Mary Ann was just like Aunt Prue and maybe so, but I am the one that every year plants flowers in my yard like her, and I always love still "talking" to her as I work in them, prompting the lovely blooms all summer.

I only wish that she and her boys had been shown more kindness from him to make home life more pleasant for them.

Short Story of David and Pruedence (Bailey) Teal
By Roy Teal, Son

A young man recently leaving the army traveling across the country via RR box car, arriving at the rail yard at Pine Bluff, Arkansas, and upon exiting the car, was pursued by a railroad agent who if caught him, would have put him in jail or worse. The young man sought refuge in a shop and the man in the shop sent the agent in the wrong direction, then later confronted the young man, "HOBO." He had a good heart and took the young man home with him. His wife "Florence" had a boarding house, and the young man was given a meal and a place to sleep. The young man was David Teal; the man in the shop was "Uncle Will Forsythe." Aunt Florence was the other character, thus far. There were others there that you may have known or heard of – Council Forsythe; Clarence Forsythe; Perry Forsythe; and later a lady named Bettie Bailey and her two daughters, Marie and Prudence. This is where Mom and Dad met.

An incident occurred in 1969 when Dad drove into his drive; two Blacks were at the back of our property, drinking beer; both (a man and a woman) attacked Dad and stabbed him, then left him for dead. Dad did manage to wound the man in the yard before they left. When he recovered some of his strength, he went into the house, got his pistol and followed them about a block and a half before he encountered them again. He attempted to hold them until the police came; however, the woman approached him with a knife and after he warned her (and she could see he was armed), she resumed her threat, and he shot her. The man approached Dad and tried to wrestle the pistol away from him.

The police finally arrived and arrested Dad and the Black man. Dad was taken to the hospital, and they operated on him to see if any vital organs were wounded. He spent two weeks in jail until we could make bond to free him.

Dave Teal, Prudence, Edward, Clarence, and Roy

In 1971, he was on trial in Memphis, charged with first-degree murder. Otis Higgs, a Black judge heard the case; and after the trial, the jury found Dad guilty of involuntary manslaughter, with no punishment recommended. The Black judge opted to sentence him to eighteen months in the penal farm. Dad served nine months.

We had to relocate Mom and market most of their possessions. Mom passed away in 1973 and I took care of Dad until his death in 1981.

Susan (Bettie) E. Forsythe Bailey

By Betty Jo Mayhall Trakimas, granddaughter

Susan Elizabeth Forsythe was born 6 Dec. 1872 to Thomas Jefferson Forsythe (born 13 Feb. 1853; died 27 Feb. 1891) and Sibela Ann Lewis Forsythe (born 21 Jun. 1852.) They were married 16 Nov. 1871.

My grandmother told me she never did like her first name, so she just decided to change it. It was not done legally in those days. She said she liked the name Bettie, so thereafter she was known as Bettie Elizabeth Forsythe. She was adamant about the way it was spelled also – just a little bit different!

Bettie was the oldest of their 8 (possibly 10) children, born 6 Dec. 1872

Willie Jefferson Forsythe (Uncle Will), born 19 Feb. 1875

Ella Florence Forsythe, born 1 Jul. 1877

James Epperson Forsythe, born 20 Dec. 1879

George Bradford Forsythe, born 21 Mar. 1882

John Christopher Forsythe, born 8 Jun. 1884

Perry Leonard Forsythe, born 9 Feb. 1887

Lou Myrtle Forsythe, born 25 Nov. 1889

It is possible, and probable, that twins were born 21 Jul. 1891. They are only identified in my records as T.J. and S.A. Forsythe. It is not known if they survived. I also believe Ella Florence died young. My written information regarding all this was handwritten by my Aunt Prue.

Note: Thomas Jefferson Forsythe (the father) died in February 1891, when Myrtle, the youngest, was 15 months old and Bettie, the oldest, was just over 18 years old.

Bettie Elizabeth Forsythe married John Edward Bailey on 3 Jun 1900. John Edward Bailey (born 16 Jul. 1872) was the son of N.C. Bailey and Mattie (Thomas) Bailey. It is known that John married a woman from Arkansas before he married Bettie. I do not know what became of her. John Edward Bailey died in November 1905, when my mother, Lula Marie Bailey, was 14 months old. The three children of Bettie and John Bailey were:

Prudence Hathaway Bailey, born 24 Feb. 1901

Poston (son), (I do not know his middle name), was born next and died around the age of 16 months.

Lula Marie Bailey, born 9 Sept. 1904

Prudence (Prue) married David Alexander Teal 13 Dec. 1925. They had 4 sons. One son, Cecil, died at birth.

Note: Poston Bailey and Cecil Teal are buried within a few feet of each other near their mother and grandmother, Bettie E. Bailey, at Cypress Methodist Church. Prue and Dave's surviving sons are:

Edward Alexander Teal, born 9 Oct. 1926 (lives in Boston area).

Clarence Bailey Teal, born 10 Jun. 1929 (Clarence died 8 Jan. 2009).

Roy Alvin Teal, born 9 Jan. 1931 (lives in Calico Rock, Arkansas).

Lula Marie Bailey married William Theodore Mayhall 14 Feb. 1936 in Memphis, Tennessee. They had three children:

Mary Ann Mayhall, born 15 Mar. 1937, died Feb. 1998.

William Theodore Mayhall, Jr. born 23 Mar. 1939 (lives in South Haven, Mississippi)

Betty Jo Mayhall, born 9 Jul. 1944 (lives in Carmel, Indiana)

It is important to note that my grandmother told me Brother John was her "favorite" brother. He married a woman named Alice and they had two children. (They lived in a small house on the land next to where Syble lived and where J.C. and Louise Forsythe live now.)

John and Alice both died at a young age, sometime between 1906 and 1910, leaving their two young sons without parents or a home. I was told they died of tuberculosis.

My grandmother, who was recently widowed and with two young little girls of her own, Prudence and Marie, took both her nephews into her own home and raised them into adulthood as her own sons. Their names are Vanden "Doc" Forsythe, the oldest, and Council Mayo "Uncle Scottie" Forsythe. Both of these men lived their adult lives in Dallas, Texas. Council lived in Mt. Pleasant, Texas, for a long time before moving to Dallas with his wife, Annabelle, and their three children: Edwin, Sandy and Candy.

"Doc" married Hazel (she was from the Humboldt area) and they had one son, Theo, who married Liota, raised two children and lived in Dallas. "Doc" died suddenly in the early 1960's of a brain aneurysm.

Bettie E. Bailey, with the help of her two daughters and two nephews, owned a little house and farmed a small plot of land across the road and down just a bit from where Lucille Bailey now lives (used to be Arthur and Jewel's home). She also taught in a one-room schoolhouse at Liberty Hall for forty years. When she was forced to retire because of blindness, the State of Tennessee paid her $33 a month. That is all the money she had to live on.

She started going blind in her early to mid 50's. Council was wealthy and took her to many specialists in many cities, but in those days, they did not know what was causing her blindness. One doctor told her that if she had all her teeth pulled, it might help. Desperate, of course, she said "Okay." Losing her teeth did not help a bit, but she never expressed any bitterness about that – or her blindness, for that matter. She did say many times how she could not tell daylight from dark, even if you were to shine a bright light directly into her eyes. She called it living in a dungeon of darkness.

Because she had no money, she was forced to live with each of her two daughters, Prue and Marie, and her only sister, Myrtle. She had her own bedroom at Prue's house and she had her own bedroom at Myrtle's, both next to a bathroom.

Because she had to share a bedroom with her grandchildren at Marie's house, and Marie had to work at the grocery store helping her husband, Ted, in the daytime, Bettie only stayed with them perhaps three months out of the year. In the spring, she would always want to go to Myrtle's so she could better plan the events for Homecoming in June.

As I write this, I realize there is a treasure trove of information I have about her life and all the lives she touched so deeply and so memorably. I also realize I need to write all this down.

I always felt closest to my grandmother, for whom I was named, than any of my other relatives. She spent time with me and mentored me. She gave me insight, courage and confidence. Without a doubt, I know I would not be who I am without her influence and guidance on my life. I will always love her so dearly and admire her more than anyone I have ever known.

I tell my students, and I believe it to be true, although my grandmother was blind many years before I was even born, she was able to see better than anyone who had their eyesight. Bettie E. Bailey saw what was important about any person – their heart. She had no prejudices or perceptions of people. They talked with her freely because they knew she would not judge them and they needed her wise counsel. I wish the world were full of the likes of this great woman.

May she rest eternally in peace.

Bailey Cousins

Colonel Lawrence D. Bailey
By Susan Bailey, daughter

Daddy had his civilian pilot's license before he volunteered for the Army Air Corps. Uncle Burl and Aunt Louise let Dad live with them while he went to college and, as I understand it, Daddy had been in love with flying since he saw a "barnstormer" fly over Crockett County. Dad worked at the pharmacy and took flying lessons while going to Memphis State and living with Uncle Burl and Aunt Louise.

We also have the telegram Daddy received accepting him into the rank of cadet with the Army Air Corps. What we always heard was that Daddy wasn't old enough to join the Army Air Corps. The only readily available evidence of his birth was the family Bible, where his name and birth date were written in pencil. He so badly wanted to join the Air Corps that Aunt Pig erased his birth date and made him a year older so he could join!!

Mom and Dad met here in San Antonio on a blind date! (She had been going with a Texas Aggie, who joined the Army and was shipped overseas.) They only knew each other for 6 months before they got married, "but it was a different time then," she says. (They actually would have been married even earlier when they had a date set, but Daddy's leave was canceled.) Mom had left the University of Texas just before getting her degree and was living in a rooming house here in San Antonio, while she worked for Braniff Air Lines in reservations and at the counter.

I will always remember what a fun-loving couple they were...they had a great time together and really loved each other. As tight as money was, they made time for themselves, getting us a babysitter or when I was old enough, leaving me "in charge." They usually went to the Officers Club on base.

Dad's friends always called him a great pilot – but a terrible navigator! He could do anything with an airplane but was not a navigator.

I remember once when he came back from Washington, D.C., he and his friends sat in the living room, railing about how "they don't want pilots; they've got monkeys flying those things!" He and several others had been invited to DC to discuss their interest in becoming astronauts!! (If you remember, they did have monkeys in the original spacecraft. And there was no "flying," as everything was controlled from the ground. Real pilots wouldn't have anything to do with it until finally someone convinced NASA to at least put a window and a "stick" in the cockpit so it looked more like a plane.)

We have all of Daddy's flight logs from his service career, as well as his many awards and "efficiency ratings" through his career.

Mom's mother died right before Mom's 16th birthday, which affected her greatly. She always said, "My mother was a saint." And we think our mom was too. Like Dad, she came from a small farming community in South Texas, where her parents had moved for her mother's health. She had two sisters but also had a very large German family (both on her mother's and father's sides). Her aunts and uncles and cousins were all very special to her, as the girls had stayed with them many times when their mother was ill. We (Mom, Dad, and the four of us) stayed with them, too, when I had the measles one Christmas, and when Dad was overseas and we didn't go with him, etc.) Family was equally important to both Mom and Dad, and we loved visiting in Tennessee and going to see Mom's father at his ranch in Los Angeles, Texas, and her family in Pflugerville, where her parents were from originally.

Mom's parents truly valued education, and all three girls went on to higher education. Mom studied home economics; Julia became a teacher and Frances became a nurse.

Dad retired as a colonel from the US Air Force after a 30-year career. He served during WWII as a pilot instructor, flew the Berlin Airlift, had special duties during the Cuban Missile Crisis, oversaw the building of flight lines in View Nam, and served at the Pentagon. Along the way, he finished his college education, graduating from the University of Nebraska.

Us Kids – Our folks continued to value education. Even though there were four of us, it was never a question of whether we would go to college: it was "where will you go to college," even with three girls. How they managed it is unbelievable. We know they sacrificed greatly to make that happen.

Janie graduated from the University of Texas and began her career teaching. She learned the restaurant business later, starting off with a counter in a drugstore, then her own shop in Boeme, Texas, and now thirteen years as owner of Janie's Pie Factory. She's won numerous awards across the country, including first places and Best in Show in the professional category for bakers and chefs in the Nation Pie Contest.

Peggy did her undergraduate studies at Michigan State, then studied at Penn State University, and received her Doctorate Degree in Psychology from Michigan State. (That's where she met and married her husband Jack, who was a professor of political philosophy.) She is now a hospital administrator (Title).

I also studied education and taught for a short time before joining Armstrong World Industries in Human Resources. Worked for them for almost 30 years as Human Resource Manager at manufacturing locations, Manager of Training and Development, and Manager of Employee Communication – living at various locations across the country.

Larry went to South West Texas State, where he studied biology. That's where he met Jeanie, who was studying education. He began working for the State of Texas in water quality, moved on to work for the Federal Government, achieving the rank of a Senior SES Officer. Larry and Jeanie gave up their positions with the Federal Government and Virginia schools and moved back to Texas to be closer to Mom and Jeanie's mom.

The Next Generation – Janie's boys, Ry and Justin, graduated from the University of Texas. Ry has a career in the financial field; Justin is a civil engineer.

Larry's sons graduated from Texas A&M. Kevin is currently working for the State of Texas, and Brandon works in IT for the Organ Donation Alliance. Kevin met his wife, Allison, at church and started dating while in high school.

Peggy's daughter, Ele, is teaching college in New York. Her son, Jon, and his wife, Julie, graduated second and third in their class at West Point. Both served in Iraq, were promoted to Captain, and are currently stationed at Ft. Hood, Texas.

The Newest Generation - Larry's son Kevin and his wife, Allison have two children: son, Bryce and daughter, Raya.

Peggy's son, Jon, and his wife, Julie, have one child, Jack.

Depression Years in South Texas - South Texas was almost a desert, and people weeded by any way they could. My grandfather (Mom's dad) didn't have enough money to pay for his wife's funeral bill (for example) and had to borrow for that. My step-grandmother (his last wife) was a widow, not far away, in the next county. She had to keep a shotgun by her side because of the itinerants and not having enough food for herself and her two children. Granddad had been raising a few cattle but had to kill them (government program), and they were buried instead of being given to the hungry people because government men stood by to be sure this was carried out right.

There was a lot more, but the older people do not want to talk about it. Everyone had boarders to try to help make ends meet. They taught us a tough valuable lesson for the next generation about strength and perseverance and faith and family.

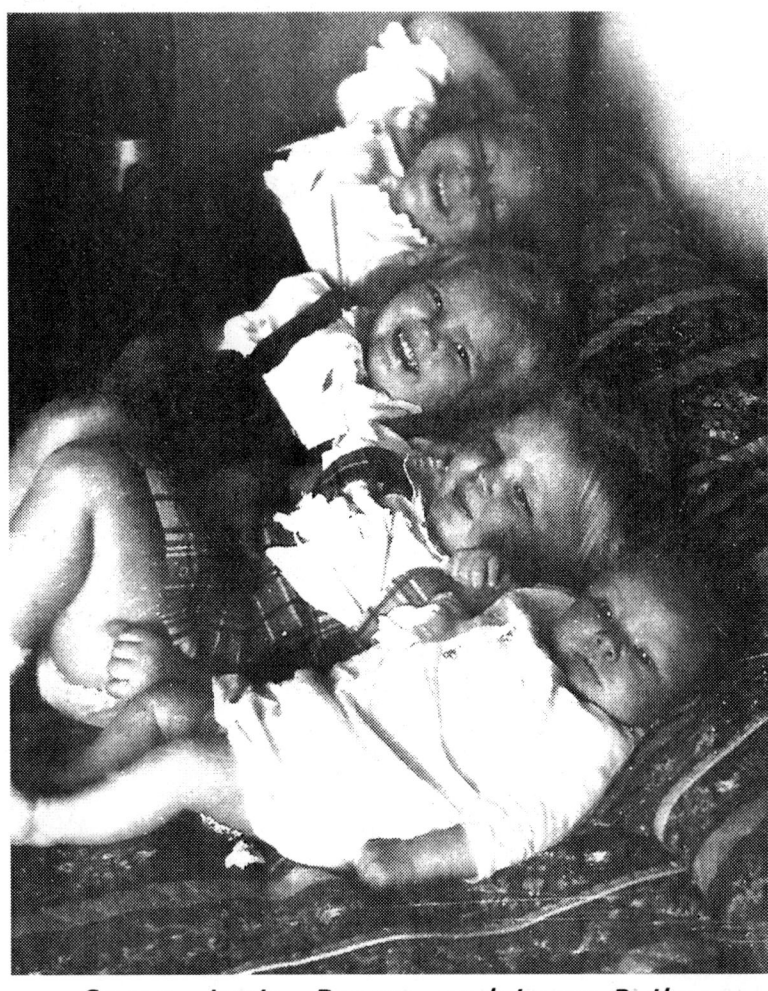

Susan, Janie, Peggy, and Larry Bailey

Uncle Lawerenc and Aunt Ruth

Front row: Kathy Bailey, Susan Bailey, Eli Paynter, Peggy Paynter, Janie Bailey, Myrtle Rose Emerson, Barbara Bailey Steed, and Jeanie Bailey

Back row: Patricia Cummins, Rye Pickard, Joe Emerson, Michael Steed, Larry Bailey, Jerry Steed, and Justin Pickard

Mama Pig – My dad and mother thought the world of your mother. She did so much for him when he was growing up, and you could see his eyes light up when he was going to get to see her and Granny Bailey. She and Granny were just special to the four of us. I loved spending the night with Aunt Pig. We would talk for hours before falling asleep. Granny was the first to "let me drink coffee." Probably one-third cup and the rest milk and sugar but, nonetheless, made me feel grown-up.

There is a story about Daddy Jim that is told in this family. He was a very controlling man, especially with his family. Granny pretty much did as he told her. After he died, she went out and bought a handmade crocheted bedspread from one of her friends and said it was the only thing she ever bought without him telling her she could.

One of the more tender stories is when we were all in Tennessee from Texas and Lawrence Welk was on TV and he asked Granny to dance with him, with a house full of kinfolk there.

One way that Mama showed her love for my dad was to name Janie after him. Janie's name is Lauren Jane.

Granny's House
By Barbara Bailey Steed

—Love, warmth, family, laughter, good time.
—Daddy Jim knocking on the wall when he wanted Granny.
—Daddy Jim calling every one (grandkids) of us before leaving and giving us each a $1.00 bill.
—Granny's flowers—the garden, the hydrangeas, helping her plant the petunias in front flower bed—fragrance of petunias automatically takes me back to Granny's house.
—The swings on the front porch and swinging with people—relaxing—talking—sometimes just swinging. Watching who would drive by and wave—usually a relative, the mailman.
—Running and rolling down the hill in the front yard.
—Magnolia tree in front yard and when it was in bloom.
—The gas pump by garage.
—The garage with Daddy Jim's car in it—last car white with plastic covering from dealer on!
—The front steps of porch of house—wooden porch.

—Dining room—china cabinet with lots of mementos in it—the buffet that was always covered with dessert.

—The big table full of family and wonderful home cooked meals—delicious—good times.

—Playing canasta at the dining table.

—The back porch—crates of soft drinks, RC Cola! Grape!—freezer.

—The kitchen—cooking—washing dishes—Rainbow bread!

—Aunt Bettie's room—having to walk through there at night to go to the bathroom. The big radio in room! The door to the outside from that room.

—The big front room—visiting with my father when Daddy Jim was ill and in the hospital bed and remembering Daddy Jim asking Dad, "Are you the man they call Frog?"

—The attic—friends inside room with books—accounting.

—Playing up there with cousins (Strip Poker)! No, it didn't get past one bluff!!

—The big windows—going out onto the roof.

—Living room with fireplace where during winter had big fires and warming up against fire. The room (closet) next to fireplace and stairs to attic—kept all the preserves—heard it was used for "time outs" with Dad and his brothers and sisters.

—Walking to the pond behind Granny's house.

—Just the excitement driving to Granny and pulling up to house.

—The tears when leaving.

—Combing Granny's hair, her sweet smile—cooking—making biscuits in morning—Lard!

—Granny's bed in living room. Her nightstand—lamp and Bible and glass for teeth.

—Granny's laugh.

—The TV—Daddy Jim couldn't hear well and coming into the house hearing the TV on so loud.

—The couch in living room where if you slept there—Granny would snore!

What I hold on to the most is that Granny's house was a gathering place for everyone, especially after Homecoming. It was a home full of love, warmth, laughter, and generations.

I cherish the memories of Granny's house and am grateful for my family. It just cannot be put into words - it's something in my heart and I am sure in the hearts of the rest of the family. Granny's house was special in, oh, so many ways!

Favorite Memories of Granny
By Janie Bailey

I was thinking about Granny's and my favorite memories are:

—The smell of her house. (we never had a fireplace.)

—Getting up so early and having "coffee" in the kitchen while she straddled that wood stove and cooked.

—I loved gathering eggs and I remember Daddy cleaning fish out back and finding eggs in them one time. Running down to the mailbox and, of course, swinging on the porch, and fighting for the fried pies, and watching Aunt Betty chew. (after hearing that all of her teeth were pulled to bring back her eyesight?)

—I dearly loved all of the aunts and uncles and cousins and each trip was fantastic. I still use notes Aunt Pig sent me as markers in my cookbooks and when I come across them, I always smile and look up.

Granny Bailey
By Jimmy and Jean Hallman

Right after Jean and I were married, we went to see Granny Bailey and Aunt Bettie. We went back to Aunt Bettie's room and she asked Jean to sit on the bed with her. Then she asked her if she could feel her face. After rubbing her face, she began to describe her exactly. When we left, Jean couldn't believe it had happened and was always kind of leery of being in the room alone with her.

Granny's Garden
By Peggy Bailey

My best memory of Granny and Daddy Jim's house was going with Granny to see her flower garden. It was beautiful – seemed large, fragrant and full of beautiful blooms whenever we were there. Even on hot summer days, it was a great spot. There were huge butterflies that also must have loved the place!

Granny Bailey (Lou Myrtle)

Thoughts of Granny and Daddy Jim
By Richard Cooke

I remember being up at Granny's when Jody was around five and we went fishing in the pond behind the house. It was just a real small pond, something to water a few cows, I guess. I remember Jody catching a catfish so big Mama Pig put it in a 5 gallon bucket and the tail stuck out above the top of the bucket. It would probably go above

10 pounds.

I remember the clock that was above Granny's bed; I would love to see it again. I also remember her using the thunder mug late at night when I would spend the night with her and Mama Pig. It was mounted in a straight ladder-back chair. Mom and Dad would go out on the town and I would stay with Granny and Mama Pig. We had fun by playing dominoes. Mama Pig had bought the peg board game that I have now and we would all try to beat the board. Mama Pig finally learned how to do it. Sometimes I get it out and see if I can still do it.

Granny always kept a case of New Grape sodas in the kitchen. I remember asking for one and they said, "No, they belong to Granny." I keep some at home now for myself. Do not ask me for one either!

I remember sleeping up there and Daddy Jim would call out in the night. I was really afraid of him.

Mama Pig was up there one night cooking supper, and the grease caught on fire. I grabbed the skillet and put it in the sink. I didn't know you should not put water on a grease fire. It caught the curtains on fire. We almost set the house on fire.

I remember when Daddy Jim was dying. I remember asking Mama Pig what was wrong with him. She told me he could not make water. I said, "What do you mean?" She said, "He could not go to the bathroom." I often wondered since then if he had prostate cancer or something. I didn't really know what he died from. I know years later Uncle Arthur had prostate cancer.

Bailey Cousin – Annette Wheeler, Joe Spraggins, Jeff Bailey, Bill Bailey, Vera Bailey, Pat Cummins, Betty Cooke, Jimmy Hallman, Myrtle Emerson, Sue Clark, and Sarah Spraggins

Austin Paynter, Avery Paynter, Flora Elizabeth French, Jonie Paynter, Jody Emerson, Rebecca French, Shane French, Pat Cummins, Larry Bailey, and Joe Emerson (Picture bottom right page 251)

Homecoming
By Sheila Holt Swearington

I was playing with Janice Bailey Shelton and Johnny Bailey at the barn next to Lucille and Steve's. They had a hayloft and we tied the horse up below, and our goal was to jump out of the loft and land on the horse!! Where were our parents???

Homecoming really became important to me when we began having the get-together on Saturday night at Mama's. The first time we did it was June 1970—38 years ago. The first year we had hamburgers and hot dogs and had about 40 people. It was NOT planned until that morning—it became an annual event and we have had more than 100 there.

And, of course, the year Pat Cummings fell in the aisle at the church. Who can ever forget that??

Leggetts and Baileys Front: Kay Cooke, Gail Cooke Middle: Merlin Leggett, Virginia Leggett holding Silas Emerson, Arthur Bailey, Burhl Bailey, Rebecca Davis, Louise Woodson, Kayley Mame Emerson, and Mama Pig Back: Lonnie Leggett, Dot Bailey, Betty and Russell Cooke, Vera Bailey, Barry Cooke, Myrtle and Joe Emerson, Jody and Kristie Emerson, and Pat Cummins

The entire church was laughing!! Sandi Forsythe Roddie was behind her and just looked down and poised as could be...walked around the pews and went up the side aisle and NEVER looked back!!! Meantime, Pat and Janet were still looking like idiots, trying to get up out of the floor!!!

(Above)
Front: Burhl Bailey, Marie Mayhall, Dr. James Bailey, Edith Smith, and Arthur Bailey

Back row: Elizabeth Leggett, Syble Holt, Dorothy Lowery, and Lerlene Forsythe

Homecoming
By Syble Holt

Prudence Teal stayed with us one time with her three boys for Homecoming. Roy Teal ran the chickens off their nests and they laid their eggs all over the yard scattered everywhere. Roy (quite mischievous) tied a rope to the churn and rolled it down a big hill—my mother had to retrieve it.

The 8th of June is my daddy's (John Christopher Forsythe) birthday. I was 6 years old the first time that (Homecoming) occurred and I remember that day so vividly. Daddy was in the bed sick and couldn't go to the Homecoming. Mrs. Etta and Pearl Evans brought a ton of food (leftovers) to feed all of us—six of us kids, plus Mama and Daddy.

I was named Syble after my grandmother, Syble Forsythe.

The First Time I Saw Council
By Janice Bailey Shelton

Johnny Bailey, (Texas) Shelia Holt, and myself, (Janice Bailey) were at my grandparents' (Arthur and Jewell Bailey.) It was a hot and very dusty day. We decided to make mud pies in this very large, dusty, bald area. Mud pies turned out to be three Mud Babies. (Covered head to toe.) Up drives the largest car Shelia and I had ever seen in our lives. Across the front of the car were long horns – horns wider than the car. He saw us there and blew an OOGA horn. (not a car horn.) We looked like deer in the headlights – only our eyes shown. He got out of the car laughing as hard as any human could laugh. Then the three of us were carried to the water hosepipe and washed in our clothes. Council never forgot that sight as long as he lived.

Aunt Myrtle's House
By Kelly Parsons

One of my fondest memories is of coming up to stay at my cousin Mame's house and going to Mama Pig's with the other cousins and playing in the house and climbing her trees and eating anything she made us.

Another great memory is—we'd go to Aunt Myrtle's and go upstairs and climb out on her roof and jump off till we got in trouble or we would play her old record player "VICTROLA" until we got in trouble.

We'd go to the Emerson "Grandparents" and play and to Myrtle Rose and Joe's first house.

Homecoming
By Randal Holt (grandson of John and Alice Forsythe)

When I was 8-10 years of age and lived in Cypress Pond, Aunt Bettie would always come to the Homecoming and stay a few weeks and visit different places. Of course, everyone worked in the fields. (No locked doors.) I would come home from school and there would be Aunt Bettie alone in the house – maybe in the kitchen getting a drink of water. Blind in a strange house...making herself at home.

The other memory was the little black suitcase that smelled of peppermint and snuff. She always had peppermint candy for the kids! Her visit was almost as good as "Christmas." For her snuff, she used a small wooden brush. When I was 10 or 11, every spring I would take small limbs from the Black Gum tree, trim off the bark – chew the little knob end to make the little wood brush—I would always try to have 10 or 12 for the year and gave them to her when she came to visit after Homecoming.

Bailey Family Reunion – June 23, 2002
Front: Olivia Rose Hart, Silas Austin Emerson, James Wheeler, Bob Cazort, Kayley Mamç Emerson, Mary Wheeler, MaeBeth Wheeler, Bailey Cazort, Elizabeth Cooke, Houston Cazort, Maggie Leigh Hart, Gail Cooke

Middle: Stephen Cooke, Gracie Jo Spraggins, Gina Cazort, Anna Bailey, Joy Cooke, Janice Shelton, Myrtle Emerson, Patricia Cummins, Betty Cooke, Russell Cooke, Kay Cooke, Annette Wheeler, Sybel Holt, Louise Forsythe
Back: Lucille Bailey, Andria Wheeler, Harvey Shelton, Joe Emerson, Joe Spraggins, Barry Cooke, Arthur Wheeler, Richard Cooke, Jeff Bailey, Jody Emerson, Ronald Holt, Stephen Bailey, Jimmy Wheeler, Larry Bailey

Front: Myrtle Emerson, Pat Cummins, Annette Wheeler
Back: Jeff Bailey, Betty Cook, Joe Spraggins and Larry Bailey (picture left)

After Elizabeth "Mama Pig" Leggett's funeral – Front: Steve Cooke, Bill Bailey, Betty Cooke, Vera Bailey, and Myrtle Emerson Middle row: Richard Cooke, Barbara Steed, Susan Bailey, Milly Hart, and Annette Wheeler Back row: Jody Emerson, Barry Cooke, Jimmy Hallman, Jeff Bailey, Pat Cummins, Shane French and Larry Bailey

Mama Pig (Elizabeth Bailey Leggett)
By Russell Steven Cooke

Her Lot in Life – Mama Pig did not speak fondly of being raised in her mother and father's house. Jim Crow Bailey was a hard man who felt that boys worked hard and contributed, plus they could pass along his lineage. Girls, on the other hand, could cook, clean, wash clothes and were not much of any use beyond the reason already mentioned.

Mama Pig often spoke of cooking the meals for her whole family and the workers from the saw mill. I do have to admit I did enjoy her cooking, and she was particularly adept at making desserts. She lived a long life on the diet of salt meat, biscuits, gravy and pie. It is important to mention that she only had two teeth to chew with for a long time. When those teeth were finally pulled out and she got false teeth, Mama Pig refused to wear them unless she might be going to visit someone.

As a child, her days usually began well before daylight when she would rise from bed to start the fire in the stove to cook breakfast. Breakfast usually consisted of salt pork, eggs, a large bowl of gravy and biscuits. After breakfast was eaten and the dishes were cleaned, they would begin to prepare for lunch. The fire was restarted in the stove, and vegetables were placed in big pots to slow cook for lunch. It was at this point her other regular chores began.

I was visiting Mama Pig one day when she told me that Granny Bailey had burned down the smoke house. She, Kay and I went up to see what had happened. While looking over the smoldering remains, I noticed an old coal stove lying on its side in the ashes. Mama Pig began talking of all the hours she had spent heating up water on that stove to wash clothes. She would wash clothes for her four brothers and father who worked at the sawmill. Mama Pig would also wash the clothes for her mother, three sisters and herself. This required her to start a coal fire in the stove, draw the water from a well, heat the water, wash the clothes on a scrub board, rinse them in fresh water heated on the stove, hang them on the line to dry and then do the ironing. Can you imagine washing clothes next to a stove all day in a small room in the hot summer without a window to let in fresh air?

Arthur was there that day and I asked what he was going to do with the stove. He told me it would be thrown into the ditch out behind the pond. Arthur was more than happy to let me have it, and I took it home that day in the trunk of our 1972 Ford Maverick and cleaned it up. Today I use this stove in my shop and think of all the hard work my grandmother once was required to do to keep her family clean.

Clothes on Her Back – There are not many pictures of Mama Pig, when she lived with her mother and father. Cameras were a luxury and pictures were taken only on special occasions. The few photos that survive show a slim, lanky girl, usually in the same dress and often barefoot. Mama Pig told me she had a good dress and a work dress and usually saved her shoes for school and special occasions. Often her dresses were made out of flour sacks, plus most of their clothes were handed down from one child to the next as they were outgrown.

People They Took In and Fed – I wish there was a complete list of people who came to live with them over the years. There were a number of family members who needed a place to live. Buster's half-brother, Tommy Leggett, stayed with them while he went to high school in Bells. For a short time, Granddaddy Leggett lived with them until he moved into a home in Bells across from the ball field. When Buster's brother, Raymond, left for the army, his wife, Eunice Leggett, lived with Mama Pig. She told me they never turned away anyone who was hungry. Mama Pig often told me how she would add more flour to the grease to make an extra large bowl of gravy, cook a few more biscuits and add another bean to the pot for whoever showed up. Most of these people lived within walking distance.

I would pick Mama Pig up once a week at the nursing home in Humboldt, and we would ride around through the countryside and she would tell me of her life. She would often ask why I wanted to know about what had happened to her, and I told her it was important for me to know who she was because she had been a very important part of my life and the lives of so many people. Most of the stories that follow are short snippets of stories she told me or ones I experienced with her.

A Boy and His Horse – There was a particular young man who Mama Pig went to school with in Gadsden and, I am sorry to say, I cannot remember his name. One day he rode a horse to a young lady's house down the road from Mama Pig's home. Olive and she saw this, and there were some hurt feelings involved even though Mama Pig told me she had only spoken with this young man a few times. Giving the situation some serious thought, Mama Pig and Olive decided to take the boy's horse and ride it back to Gadsden. Well, they did and walked back home, but the young man also had to walk back to Gadsden after he had visited with the other woman. It was probably a three to four mile hike for all the parties involved. She was 86 years old when she told me this story and still felt bad about doing it.

Graduating and Basketball – When she graduated from high school, Mama Pig went to Jim Crowe Bailey, her father, and asked him to send her to nursing school. He told her that he did not think it was right for her to become a nurse and would not send her. You know that was a different time in this country, but you got to think he did send a son to medical school and another son to pharmacy school. Mama Pig thought about it for a while and saw she needed to be able to support herself and went to him and asked if she could go to school and become a beautician. Mama Pig told me that he said, "No daughter of his would be washing and fixing other women's hair." You have to wonder how much potential she did have? She graduated number two in her high school class and played basketball on the first Gadsden team that went to the state tournament. She told me that they were carried there in cars of the families, and at one point, food was short and they were given a basket of fruit to eat. Mama Pig told me her father never saw her play basketball and that he made her arrive late for her own graduation, where she was to give a speech. Because she had arrived late, Mama Pig was embarrassed to go up on stage until someone came down and got her so she could get her diploma and give her speech.

She really loved basketball and was pretty good at a young age. Mama Pig played Varsity Basketball at high school at Alamo in the 9th grade and became a starter on that team. In the 10th grade, she transferred to Gadsden High School and she had to sit out a year because she had played Varsity Basketball as a freshman. She never liked old man Conley because of this. As I said earlier, her father never saw her play basketball, plus he never picked her up from practice or a game. Mama Pig had to walk from

Gadsden to their home at night sometimes with one of her brothers. Even as she got older, Mama Pig would watch professional basketball on TV each Sunday afternoon. One Sunday, I was picking her up to take her to Jackson for lunch with the family, and she made me wait until the end of the game. The Los Angeles Lakers with Shaquille O'Neal were playing against Karl Malone. Mama Pig said, "Look at them picking on that little guy." (Referring to Shaquille O'Neal.)

Running Off To Get Married – Buster borrowed a car from someone in the community and I believe it was Ira Webb. The two of them took Floyd Webb and Olive (her sister) with them and went to Kentucky to get married. The car was an open car, which only had a top and no window. Mama Pig told me it rained the whole way up there and that Floyd asked Olive several times to marry him at the same time Mama Pig and Buster got married. When they came back to Cypress, they stayed in the same room with Buster's sisters. Mama Pig told me this was no way to spend a honeymoon or young married couples special time together.

A Story Told by My Mother (Betty Leggett) – When Mama Pig was first married, she and Buster lived for a short time with Buster's mother and father in a house close to the church. They then moved to a shack behind Ira Webb's house and I do mean shack. It was a simple home with two rooms and a back porch. They slept on a quilt they rolled out on the floor at night without pillows. Each morning when they got up off their simple bed, she would roll up the quilt and place it on a little wooden shelf hanging on the wall. My mother was born in this house on the floor. One day after my mother was born, Daddy Jim and Granny Bailey came to see them and saw their living condition. Upon leaving, Daddy Jim asked Granny if they thought they could give Buster and Pig some pillows to use. My impression is that Jim Crow Bailey was one of the more well to do men in the county at this point.

As Buster Lay Dying – When Mama Pig was 36 years old, Buster died with complications due to type one sugar diabetes. He was one of the few people in the late 40's and early 50's able to get insulin. Mama Pig once told me that Buster loved pie more than anyone; and if she did not watch out, he would eat a whole pie in no time. There was not a way to check to see how much insulin to give a person back then and you just had to guess. Buster's diabetes was out of control and he was sent to the Baptist Hospital in Memphis where he lay in a coma and unresponsive. Mama Pig did not have any money and could not afford to buy anything to eat. She stayed by his side for three days without any food. On the fourth day, a woman saw that she had not eaten and gave her an orange. She told me in later years it was the best orange she had ever eaten. If I could have met this woman, I would have given her a big hug if she were alive today. You know, I think she must have been an angel from heaven sent by God to help a person in need. Sometimes we are too proud to ask for help. In Memphis, Mama Pig had an uncle who was a doctor and in Crockett County, she had a daddy who owned a lot of land and a sawmill. The items we keep to remind us of loved ones and the past always amaze me. Mama Pig kept the needles and syringes she used to give Buster shots until we moved her to the nursing home.

Buster's Quilt of Many Colors – People did not have much back then and they tended to keep everything and use it until the item was worn completely out and then use it some more. There were many flowers placed on Buster's grave. Each flower arrangement had a broad, colorful silk ribbon wrapped around it. I always found it hard to understand how people as poor as most of these people were could give so much of what little they had. Well, the women in the community got together and gathered all the ribbons from the flowers laid on Buster's grave. They took these ribbons and made two quilts. I have one of these quilts and Myrtle Rose has the other. I have often thought of Dolly Parton's "Coat of Many Colors" song and our quilts of many colors made of a short life of loving and caring for people who Buster and Pig came in contact with. I often feel that I fall short in comparison to these wonderful people.

Don't Swim in the Cow Pond – Directly east of the house and barn was a small watering pond for the cows Mama Pig kept when I was young. It was constantly muddy and not more than four feet deep in the center. One day Bubba Webb and Greg Reasons came by to play with Barry and me. They were a few years older and seemed to challenge more of the authority figures than I was accustomed to. Mama Pig told me before we went outdoors, "Steve, you and Barry had better not go skinny dipping in the pond." How did she know what we were about to do? I still can hear Greg saying, "Ah, she'll never know we went swimming; don't be a chicken." Well, that just put fire under my butt and here we went. About the time we got stripped off naked and in that muddy soup of water, here comes Mama Pig around the corner of the barn. "What do you boys think you are doing?" Well, Greg and Bubba got an earful and were sent home. Barry and I had to get cleaned up under a water hose and then placed under house arrest for the rest of the day. I don't think we played with Greg and Bubba much after this, and I did realize "who was boss."

Trading Eggs at the Store – Mama Pig had an old Mercury automobile, which I believe was a 1948 model. It was long, tall, and dark with big round fenders. It had a well-used musty smell that came from years of use as transportation for the family and for whatever had to be moved on the farm. I remember thinking it looked like an army tank I had seen on TV. Whenever we went some place, she would let me push the button on the dash, which was the "starter button." When she was still trying to make a go of farming, Mama Pig had a hen house and sold some eggs. Things were pretty tight financially for her at this time. One day, she took Barry and me to Bells to sell some eggs. There were two very small grocery stores east of Bells High School on the opposite side of the road. Mama Pig went in the first store and they would not buy any eggs from her. They told her most people did not like brown eggs anymore because they only wanted the white eggs. At the next store, they had eggs lying in a basket filled with straw, and the owner told her he did not need any that day. Her voice had a pleading sound, almost desperate, and I was uncomfortable with what was going on. She did not push but seemed to have a way with words when talking with the store owners. The owner finally agreed to trade for items in the store. I don't remember everything she got, but I do remember she got us a giant twenty-nine cent bottle of Canada Dry ginger ale. Whenever she took care of us, Mama Pig wanted to make it a special event.

I was four or five years old when for the first time, Mama Pig sent me out to gather the eggs. The hen house was located behind the house in a line with the smokehouse, the house that Mike lived in, and the old house where she and Buster lived when they first bought the property. Their old house was only two rooms with a front porch, and years before had used logs to roll it around the newly completed house so they could use it as storage. Well, she sent me out to gather the eggs; and as soon as I went in the hen house, an old hen flew onto my head and scratched me up. I could not get that old hen off me as I went running to the house. Well, she felt so bad about the situation I did not have to gather the eggs for a long time. Thank goodness, when she started working at the Winter Garden, she got rid of the chickens.

Buying the New Car – When I was eight years old, Mama Pig, Barry, and I went to look for a new car. We rode to Jackson and went to two different car dealerships. One was the Ford dealership located on Airways Blvd, close to downtown, and the other was the Mercury dealership that was across the street. We looked at a black Mercury, which I didn't like and a Ford Galaxy 500, which was brown and white and had the largest motor available at that time, 352 cubic inch motor with a four-barrel carburetor. She looked at me and asked, "Steve, what do you think I ought to do?" Even at eight, my first thought was she needs someone advising her other than a kid. My inclination was to go with the pretty car with the big motor. Well, we went home in that Ford, which was long and low and on the way home, she said more than once, "I cannot drive this thing slow." We went back a week later to do some paperwork, and this time we took my mother with us. The car manager told my mother that Mama Pig drove a hard bargain because the 'ole Mercury she traded in had a cracked head, and she had gotten the better of him on the trade-in. By the time she got rid of the Ford, it was completely worn-out. The old Ford was not worn out because of the number of miles she traveled, but because she had driven it only 30 miles per hour on the back roads and hauled everything she could. When I would crank her car, smoke would roll out the back, and the air behind us looked like we were spraying for mosquitoes. The cloth top was falling in, the paint was bad, and it smelled like a combination of fishing worms, fish, and mildew. It was a vehicle you wouldn't want to take out on a date.

The Night the TV Blew Up – Mama Pig had an old TV, bought sometime in the late 50's. Her TV screen was about 14" and was contained in a large box. It was black and white and the screen was always snowy. We would always watch the story during lunch and Ed Sullivan on Sunday night. Richard, Barry and I were spending the night with her one weekend, and Barry and I had already gone to bed in the front bedroom. She and Richard were in bed in what we considered the TV room. The picture tube exploded and shattered the safety glass. Smoke filled the room and scared Mama Pig, who got us out of bed, worried there was going to be a fire. I slept through the whole thing. She was afraid that the house would burn down and we might be hurt.

Fishing – The woman would rather fish than eat. She loved to fish whenever and wherever she could. An amazing thing about this...she could not stand to eat fish. When we caught enough, they were always left with families around the community. There was a black family who lived down from the church on what was then a dirt lane. They didn't have very much and lived in a small four-room house. No matter how small the fish or how few we had, she would stop there to leave them the fish. If the family was not at home, we would then stop at Miss Pearl and Miss Effie's houses to leave them the fish. We never dressed the fish beforehand, and both families were always grateful for what we had to leave. Mama Pig was always willing to help those she saw as less fortunate.

She received as gifts over the years several fishing tackle boxes that all went unused. Mama Pig preferred to carry her fishing tackle in a gallon ice cream bucket and I believe the brand was Turner's ice cream. This bucket contained hooks, line, weights, and a few corks. She would also carry a

five-gallon bucket to place the fish she caught in and, depending on the time of year, it would contain her bait. Fish bait took the form of what was available at the time. She partially liked what we called "weed worms." Taking a sharp butcher knife, she would walk down the ditch banks and cut these weeds that had a large bump located in the growth joint and there you would find a worm, which was great bait for bream. Her fishing poles were some of the worst you have ever seen, but in her hands, they were very effective. Her pole of choice was a cane pole, which would allow her to get as far from the bank as possible. Isn't it funny how fishermen on the bank want to get as far as possible from the bank and those in a boat like to get as close as possible to the bank. She would typically fish with one or two cane poles and threw out a spinning reel line, hopefully to catch a catfish. Her favorite fishing ponds were Ferguson Pond and the pond up from Fruitvale, owned by the Henderson family. She also loved to fish at Humboldt Lake off the bank of the west side close to the road. When I was a kid, she and I would walk to Cypress Creek, which ran just behind the house. There was a deep hole that kept water all year and a few fish to be caught along with a good supply of snakes.

Going Fishing With Pig – One summer day when she was about 65 – 66 years old, I carried her fishing to Reelfoot Lake. We rented one of the lake boats that was a cypress canoe, which had a Briggs and Stratton motor and had a drive shaft running through the bottom of the boat. The lake is shallow and, at that time, there were still stumps that you could get hung up on with your boat. The boats would not go very fast (at the best 4-5 miles per hour) and when you got hung up on a stump, you just rocked the boat until you floated off.

I had Mama Pig in one of these boats on the backside of the lake fishing in the tall water grass. One of the things about her that didn't change during the course of her life was she could not catch a fish sitting down. When she hung a fish, she always stood up. This is all right unless you are in a "Canoe." The snakes were particularly bad that summer day and she hung a nice crappie. At that same time, a large water snake came toward the boat, her catch and us. I wish I had a video of her standing up and beating that snake with the end of her fishing pole. The snake was 4-5 feet long and would have made us hurt ourselves if it got in the boat. The boat was rocking and she was screaming and I was praying that I was not going to get an early bath. Luckily the snake turned away and we did not overturn.

We fished for 8-10 hours that day and feasted on bologna sandwiches and peanut butter and crackers. Of course, we washed our hands in the lake before eating. She did hang a large bass later that day, but it got off because I had bought cheap leader line for the poles and she let me know it. It was a great day.

The Great Snake Hunter – Mama Pig could see snakes when no one else could. In her lifetime, she killed more than her share of snakes, for someone who was deathly afraid of them. She always kept a cotton hoe by the front porch and one under the back porch at the ready, to dispatch a venomous or non-venomous reptile to their just rewards. She said that there were a lot of snakes around her house because of Cypress Creek that ran behind her house.

I Never Saw Her Wear a Hat – I never saw her wear a hat. She always wore a bonnet when she was outside. A bonnet serves several purposes in its functionality: 'keeps sun off your forehead, face and the back of your neck. If she was in the field working, mowing the yard, or fishing, she was wearing that old bonnet. I believe Myrtle Rose has it now. I can see it clearly and was much a part of her as Matt Dillon's hat on "Gun Smoke."

Mama Pig – Only having a stove-top and a single oven, it was hard for her to cook for 20 or 30 people. The kitchen at that time was only about 8 x 10 feet containing cabinets, an old wooden table with four chrome, springy chairs. She had an old Philco Ford refrigerator that I believed to be the first one ever made!! As she prepared food for the holiday event, the food was placed on the porch covered in whatever to keep the mice out because it was cooler there. She would also make and freeze pies because she could make them several weeks in advance.

Holidays were very special when I was young. We looked forward to them with high expectation of a most wondrous event. The following question must be asked: Why were these events so special compared to the holidays I experience today? Mostly, we didn't celebrate much in those days except at those special times. People today go out to dinner or to a movie, perhaps to a concert or somewhere special frequently. A holiday was looked forward to for months in advance before the big event occurred. In essence, there were only three, which were truly celebrated. Easter came early in the year and we were just beginning to plant our crops when it came around. Thanksgiving was tremendous because it was at the end of cotton picking, and we needed a break from the fields. Often when Thanksgiving arrived, we would be through with picking cotton and had begun pulling bolls. I will discuss pulling bolls another time. And then there was Christmas with the tree, and Mama Pig always decorated the tree with popcorn balls, made with popcorn, peanuts, and molasses.

What made Easter Special? Dinner at Mama Pig's house! – I will describe the house of my grandmother's, as it was when I still lived at home. It was a small frame house built by my grandfather with the help of some carpenter in the community. Some of the lumber came from my great-grandfather's saw mill. The bottom floor had one bedroom and a living room with a butane floor furnace, a front room with a small fireplace that was not raised and was very shallow, a small dining room and a very small kitchen.

There was a stairway in the front room that led to an upstairs with a bedroom on each end of the house with a hallway running between them. The wall and ceiling were covered with pine wood floor and ceiling and a crude cabinet running along the outer walls under the windows. These were the rooms occupied by my mother Betty and her sister, Myrtle Rose, when they were children. There were storage areas behind doors in the walls that I was afraid of when I was a child. Also, there was a storage area off the stairs in this area where Mama Pig kept all kinds of decorations for Christmas and a few toys.

Easter – The first thing you noticed when you hit the door was the smell. It was the most heavenly smell in the world. The smell of homemade yeast rolls would waif through the air, drawing you back to the kitchen to beg for just one to tide you over 'till the feast began. There would be ham, boiled, not baked, sweet potatoes, black-eyed peas, corn on the cob, and always red Jell-O with two cans of fruit cocktail poured in. Mama Pig would begin baking at least one week before, and there would be a sideboard with buttermilk pies, chocolate chess pies, country chess pie, homemade boiled custard, caramel cake, and the bunny rabbit cakes as the centerpiece.

The Bunny Rabbit Cake – The Bunny Rabbit Cake was very special to all the kids and to Mama Pig, especially. She so enjoyed seeing the excitement of the children and watching them play and eat her specialty desserts. The cake had a round body that looked just like a rabbit. She baked the body in a round bowl so it looked like a round-bodied rabbit. The head was baked the same way in a smaller bowl. Mama Pig would cover the rabbit with white icing and coconut. The eyes and nose were jellybeans and the ears were made from paper, cut and colored by her to look like long rabbit ears.

Boiled custard was made very carefully and slowly. Can you believe it? I didn't get the recipe and may never taste this rich dessert ever again. She kept it in a gallon jug with a piece of wax paper covering the top and a rubber band holding the wax paper on. Remember this point because I will tell a funny story later. The kids got a small cut-glass cupful, filled up as many times as they wanted with a cap full of Watkins' vanilla flavoring added to each glass. When I was helping clean out her house (when we had to move her to the nursing home), she had me take out the three whiskey bottles she used for flavoring for the adults when they wanted it. The bottles in question were over half-full and the date on each was from the early 1960's. She told me her brother (Frog) brought them to her and asked her to make him some boiled custard. Mama Pig moved out of her house in 2000.

She discovered the plastic Easter eggs when I was about 12 or 13 years old. She would place some candy in half and have the grand prize of a quarter in a special egg hid somewhere in the yard. Today, we can't get excited about a hundred dollars, but back then, a quarter was a lot of money. A candy bar was a nickel, a bag of chips was a dime and a coke was only a dime if you had a bottle to turn in at the store. Back then, the bottles were always reusable and required a deposit. It was her great joy of the day to watch the kids running around the yard trying to find those Easter eggs. As the kids all got older and lost interest, she missed the Easter Egg Hunt the most, of all the festivities.

Bailey homeplace (new one)
Front: Myrtle Rose, Lou Myrtle, Betty
Back: Elizabeth, Cyrus, Evelyn, Virginia

When she was about 70 years of age, I decided it was time she had some help with the holiday preparations. I would get to her house at 6 A.M. to help her get ready. She would already have the desserts, but I would help with making the dressing, cooking the ham or turkey, setting the table, mixing the Jell-O or just cleaning the house. It was during this time that I decided to learn how she made the special foods we all enjoyed.

History and Thoughts
By Jim Bailey (Jaybird)

After college (1971) I went into the military for a few years, one of which was in the DMZ in South Korea where I froze my a_ _ off.

I am married and have been blessed with 7 great kids. The youngest one is in her 2nd year of college. The first three were boys and then came the four girls. We have four grandchildren and two are in the oven waiting to be delivered in 2011.

I am currently with University Hospital in San Antonio and hoping to retire next year. My job is Director of Operations for Detention Health Care Services, which means I am responsible for providing medical, dental and mental health care to approximately 4,600 adult inmates and about 400 juveniles.

So many great memories from Tennessee:

—Hearing Daddy Jim pound the wall with his cane to get Granny to come in and clean the chewed tobacco that he spit on the floor and bed.

—Freezing frogs in Granny's freezer. Attempting to see if frogs could come back to life after being frozen. Granny found no humor in this stunt, as she called it; Daddy Jim just looked down at me and said nothing, which was his way of showing he was not happy. Can't remember which one of my parents gave me the belt.

—Picking cotton even though the sack was taller than I was.

—Fishing trips with Aunt Pig and Uncle Arthur and catching my first snapping turtle.

—Constantly eating great foods, especially at Homecomings.

—Watching Granny make biscuits from scratch on the old wood burning stove.

—Hanging with Larry and Jeff.

—Hospitality of everyone when we came to visit.

—Sneaking out at night from Granny's house and running down the road to Uncle Arthur's to meet   up with his kids, hoping not to get caught.

There were so many that when I started thinking about them, I become saddened because so many of our great kinfolks have passed on to a better place and I truly have missed them — *Jim Bailey (Jaybird)*

Other Bailey Stories
By Myrtle Rose Leggett Emerson

Dr. Conrad Bailey was Daddy Jim's brother, who lived in Memphis most of his life. He married and divorced and then married Thelma Shoemar, who was a receptionist in his Memphis office. He had an office and clinic and was the doctor for the Illinois Central Railroad. He got free trips and other perks from the railroad company. He was a World War I veteran, having fought in France and Germany. When the war was over, he came home and his dad, Nathaniel Columbus Bailey, died that same night. The death was due to a heart attack at the old homeplace behind Jim and Myrtle's house. Dr. Bailey died in Memphis of a heart attack and was buried in the Cypress Church Cemetery. When Betty and I were small, he carried Mama and us to see his office. When we were ages 9 and 11, we rode the train to Memphis and visited with Dr. Bailey and he sent us back home to Bells by train. This was very entertaining for us to go alone and on such a rare visit out of the county. It was our first train ride too.

Uncle Arthur was sick and upstairs in the bed, and Uncle Frog was outside getting some stove wood when a great bolt of lightning hit the house over Uncle Arthur's head, splitting the rafters into right over him. Uncle Frog was knocked down and the stove wood was scattered all over the yard. The family all wondered what kept it from setting the house on fire or killing the boys. They were very thankful that no more harm was done.

Donald Harrison Bailey had TB and there was not much to be done for it but a change of weather and "taking of the waters." I am not sure who it was that took Don (as he was called) to Biloxi, where he stayed for a year before he died January 25,1915. On the trip down to Mississippi, he had a green jar with a metal top that he carried water to drink on the train. I am lucky to have this bottle and cherish it as a family heirloom.

After Jim and Myrtle's children were married, Daddy Jim sometimes would want to visit for some reason or other. He would pull the car as close to the door as it would go (never mind what he had to drive over to get there) and would sit there in the car and blow and blow the horn until the family all came outside to pay their respects. This frightened the very small ones and they were afraid of him. I learned early that there was nothing to be afraid of but to not expect much attention from him.

Jewell and Arthur Story
By Lucille Bailey

Mary Jewell Leggett and Arthur Bailey had known each other for a long time. One day when she was a young girl, Granddaddy Leggett took her down to Jim Bailey's saw mill in a buggy. Jim was Arthur's daddy. Her hat flew off and Arthur ran into the field to retrieve it. He brought it back to her and that is how their romance started.

Later he took her fishing at Reelfoot Lake, and she stood up in the boat and fell out. She pleaded for him to help her so she would not drown. He told her to stand up and walk to the bank. (and she still married him!)

Uncle Arthur and Aunt Jewell eloped. They told Aunt Dot that they were getting married and did not want Granny and Daddy Jim to worry so they had a plan: Aunt Dot was to wait long enough for them to "get on down the road" far enough away so no one could catch them before the wedding was over. The plan worked and the parents were not too happy over this new development but what could they do?...Right?

Granny Bailey
By Della Faye Bailey Coughlin

The old porch at Granny Bailey's house was the scene for many adventures. Ask any family member what they remember about Bailey doings, and the porch will automatically come to mind. For one thing, it was so big and cool in the summer when we all congregated there.

One of these escapades was on a sunny afternoon, and Myrtle Rose and I were on the porch when a car full of boys passed and we both stood up and waved and danced around like they were our best friends that we had not seen in a coon's age. They went on down the road a piece and turned around and started up Granny's drive, coming at us. We got scared and panicked and ran inside and made Granny come out and deal with them. She thought it was so funny and teased us about it; she took care of those boys in a wink. It was so easy to get ourselves into a corner in those teen years, much like today's youth. Some things never change.

Buhrl Jefferson Bailey, My Dad
By Buhrl Jefferson Bailey, Jr.

Buhrl Jefferson Bailey was born on September 8, 1919. He was the second son of Jim and Myrtle Bailey. No one has ever told us how Daddy Jim and Granny came up with the spelling; most don't know about the silent "h." Dad's stories of his growing-up experiences in Crockett County were few. He did say he got his nose broken playing football at Alamo, having to walk to school, getting lost in the bottom and all the hard work.

When he graduated high school, Daddy Jim offered him some land or money. Dad chose the money and went to Memphis to attend the University of Tennessee Pharmacy Program. He graduated with one of the highest grades at the time. A story from school was when a chemistry professor accused Dad of cheating and took him to the dean's office, where he was given another test that he "aced." The professor could not imagine anyone could make 100 on his test. Dad graduated UT Pharmacy and had to wait until he was 21 years old before getting his diploma.

Driving around Memphis, he would point out where he started work at Cleveland and Union, or Madison. He was working on Summer Avenue when my mother, Louise Woodall, and her father came in and Dad caught her eye with his "red hair." Both said it was love at first sight. Dad sent the delivery boy to follow her home to see where she lived, but he turned around at the Wolf River. Mom was a social worker and returned to the store a few days later. They soon ran off to Covington and got married in 1934. They built a house at the edge of Memphis in Stonewall Heights, now considered "Mid Town." They opened Bailey Drug Store about four blocks west of their home.

During the time before the war, both brothers and sisters came to stay at the house for weeks, training, or going to school. Mom and Dad had a pull-out bed they all used. Mom and Dad kept the bed, taking it to Grand Valley in the 1980's. I even used the bed when I was hired by the State in East Tennessee.

Dad was drafted at age 34 and was stationed at San Diego, California, in the hospital pharmacy. He was drafted into the Navy, but the Navy furnished the medicines to the Marines. Mom would talk about riding the train out to see him. Dad had to sell the store while he was in the service. Then he was shipped out taking a boat to the Pacific. He talked about it being the only ship around and going to bed, waking up in the middle of hundreds of ships. He landed on Iwo Jima and talked about the Flag Raising. His chief told him, "Don't worry about taking your gun; just get on the beach." After Iwo Jima, they were sent to and made the landing on Okinawa. He stayed on Okinawa until the war ended. He really never talked much about the war, but my sister remembers him dreaming about it. (Rough)

After the war, Dad opened the Bailey Drug Store on Broad Avenue that he owned and operated until about the early 1980's. Vera Lynn was born in 1946 and I (Buhrl Jefferson, Jr.) was born in 1949. During our early years, we all enjoyed water skiing, golfing and fishing.

Dad and his group of friends would charter a bus three times a year and go fishing at Panama City or Destin, Florida. Their trips would last from Friday through Sunday nights. The biggest fish we have a picture of was a grouper that weighed 179 pounds and a grouper's head that weighed 110 pounds, the rest eaten by sharks on the way up. Dad also enjoyed taking us on vacations to Florida but said he would never move down there because you would get "blown away."

Dad enjoyed Memphis, coming home to Crockett County, Grand Valley, and his three grandchildren. He stayed in good health until his stroke in 1998. Dad stayed at Vera's until the middle of January and passed away at the Bells Nursing Home on February 3, 1999. He was a good husband, father and grandfather.

Buhl J. Bailey, Pharmacist
By Vera Bailey O'Neal, daughter

My dad, Dr. Buhrl Jefferson Bailey, Sr. always had a sweet tooth. He said it started in his childhood when his mom would bake a basketful of sweet potatoes. She would then put them on the back porch for the kids to eat. It was their candy.

He would go back home whenever he had a chance. We would leave Memphis after he closed the drug store at 10:30 p.m. and Mom would drive. Dad always told us stories about his childhood during the drive. He would tell us about the oxen pulling the logs out of the fields, feeding the chickens and going out in the chicken house to collect eggs. All the children had "chores." He also would tell us about walking to school in the cold, rain and snow. We found out later that he and Uncle Arthur had a car. We all laughed about that.

We never missed a family reunion. Family was very important to him. My brother Jeff and I talk on the phone several times a week. Our parents set a good example of how family life should be.

A lot of people did not know how competitive Dad was. In the Senior Olympics, he won hundreds of medals—golf, basketball, shuffleboard, horseshoes, and track and field events. His favorite pastime was golf in the morning and fishing in the evening. When we would go fishing at Grand Valley in the evening, he would not go back to the house until he had caught the most fish. After a few times of watching the sunset and the light at the pier coming on, I got wise and would fish without bait so he would be the one with the most fish. He had a great and loving life. We were all blessed to have had him in our lives.

Burhl Bailey

Memories
By Della Fay Bailey Coughlin

My earliest memories were standing by Granny's fireplace, crying because I had to go to the hospital and have my tonsils removed. She picked me up and loved me and said she would go with me and hold my hand. When they came and got me, Granny went with me holding my hand. When I woke up, she was still holding my hand. (While I was sleeping, I dreamed I was Dick Tracey tied to an ironing board, floating down a river!)

Annette and I stayed with Granny while Mother was helping Daddy in the fields; this meant we were always there and went where Granny went. Trips with Granny and Daddy Jim were not always pleasant; I had to sit behind Daddy Jim, (cars were not air conditioned) and he spit tobacco juice out the window; and even when my window was up, his juice blew into my face. One of these trips, we went to pick up Lawrence at the Jackson airport into where he was flying his plane. When he came to the car, he was upset because he wanted to make a "perfect landing" in front of his daddy. He didn't think it was a good landing, but we all thought it was perfect!

Mother and Daddy, Granny and Daddy Jim took a trip to North Carolina to see one of the boys. (I think it was Lawrence.) They left Annette, brother and me with Dot. I was going to start school and had to have my shots. Dot was not old enough to have her driver's license, but she took a big log truck and drove on the back roads to Bells and I got my shots.

James and his family were at Granny's for a visit, when Barbara came walking down the road and asked if she could eat lunch with us because Granny was cooking leaves. (In the south, better known as greens).

After a meal at Granny's in the summer, we all ended up on the front porch. Lawrence and Ruth were sitting on the steps looking out over the fields, when a sawmill worker got out a plow and his wife got in front of it. He hooked her up and she started pulling the plow with him, holding the plow up! Ruth was horrified! Lawrence laughed until he cried and told Ruth, when he retired, they would move back to Tennessee, where he would farm and she could help him with the plowing.

The old Liberty Hall Schoolhouse had not been used in years and it was turned into a community center. In the summer, all the neighbors got together with the women, bringing their best dishes of food, and after the meal, the men made homemade ice cream. Our county agent came out and taught us how to square dance. In the winter, we continued the dances and learned different kinds. Daddy Jim would only dance with me. He never asked, just came and stood in front of me and held out his hand. This was after Granny quit dancing. In their younger days, Granny would get all dressed up and they would go far and wide to dances, but by this time in their lives, she was no longer able to dance.

James came home from overseas and brought presents for all the family. Mine was a grass skirt. When I got too big to wear it, I tied it around my head, like a long wig. I made Ray Woodson pull me in a red wagon all around the yard and said I was "Princess Nila." (I needed a slave.)

I remember Daddy tearing down the Old Bailey homeplace. It was a log cabin, and in it was old furniture, including a spinning wheel that belonged to his grandmother and great-grandmother. I asked to keep the spinning wheel, and he just looked at me and asked, "What are you going to do with it?" Then he threw it on the fire.

I have to talk a little bit about Aunt Bettie. Having Granny and Aunt Bettie was wonderful. Aunt Bettie would come and stay with Granny in the summer and then go back to Memphis for the winters. I did not know for a long time she had another family and that she was not all ours. Every time I went in, she wanted me to come and get in her lap so she could see what I had on. She would make a big fuss about my shorts and tops that did not come to my middle. Aunt Bettie would ask me to walk her down the road to a certain bush and pick her some small twigs for her "snuff brushes." She always knew when we were there. People came from far and wide to see her. She had friends and family that loved her. Aunt Bettie loved Cypress Church and loved Homecoming and worked very hard to make it a success.

Shopping trips were a hoot with Granny, Mother and Aunt Bettie. One of the trips to Gadsden, Mother and Aunt Bettie were still in the store. Granny, Annette and I went to the car and it was hot and I said, "I wish I had a Push-up." Granny wanted to know what that was, and I explained it was an orange sherbet with a stick in it to push it up the paper tube it was in. Granny said she would go into the store and get us one. When she came back out, she was doubled over with laughter and told us she went in and asked for a "dynamite."

In the spring and early summer, we all were busy picking strawberries, chopping cotton, etc., but when the crops were "laid by" we started having family get-togethers. When we were at Aunt Pig's, there was a huge oak tree by the fencerow between the yard and field. We almost dug the tree up, making tunnels for our little cars. Myrtle Rose had a big surprise for us. She took us to the garden and to a little mound in the soft dirt; she uncovered a nest of small snake eggs. I could not wait to get out of that garden! I have often wondered if they were real snake eggs, or if she wanted to just scare us!

When we were at Uncle Doode and Aunt Virginia's, they had some of the largest oak trees I have ever seen. Uncle Doode always came out in the shade and smoked and listened to the St. Louis Cardinals.

While visiting at Aunt Evelyn's, we always wanted to walk to town, with the older ones taking care of the little ones.

I spent the night at Gretta's in the cold of winter. At bedtime, everyone got ready for bed and then started putting on two pairs of socks, coats, and toboggans. I asked, "Where are we going?" and they said, "To bed!" I found out why, after they let the fire die down and it was cold!

The most embarrassed I ever was at camp is when I was 13 years old. I borrowed Myrtle Rose's black bathing suit. It had one strap that fastened on one side and went around my neck and fastened on the other. I really thought I was something walking around in that suit. The boys and girls were not allowed to swim at the same time, but our lifeguard was an older teenage boy and he was the stuff dreams are made of. After about three days, I got up the courage to go and talk to him. I swam across the pool, put my hands on the top and jump-pushed myself up. I felt the strap give way and my suit peeled down. I never looked up and jumped back into the water, holding my suit up with both hands. I did not know how to get out and hold onto my swimsuit. Someone gave me a towel and I did not go back swimming while at camp.

One bad winter day, Daddy came in and told us to put on several layers of clothes. Aunt Olive had a new baby and Granny wanted to go see them. The roads were not graveled between our house and Cypress Church, so he hooked a wagon up to a tractor and we got in the back and snuggled up under quilts and went to see the new baby!

In the early days of my life in the country, we had no electricity. One long winter, Aunt Pig, Uncle Buster, Betty Ann and Myrtle Rose came and spent a week with us. Aunt Pig had baby chickens and she brought them with her. They laid down those wooden homemade chairs on their sides in a corner of the room for a pen. We had a great time.

My Special Memories of Granny & Daddy Jim
Lou Myrtle Forsythe and James Arthur Bailey
By Patricia Lowery Cummins

My grandfather and grandmother, Jim "Crow" and Myrtle Forsythe Bailey, were a very unique and interesting couple. I was very fortunate that on various Saturday nights I was allowed to spend the night with them. I would always sleep on the fold-down divan in the living room, which was also Granny's bedroom. Daddy Jim always, always stayed in his bedroom/office. If he wanted Granny, he would take the "famous wooden mallet" (which I now have) and hit the wall for her to come in and see what he might want. BUT on Saturday nights when "Lawrence Welk" came on the TV, Daddy Jim would emerge from his bedroom. We would then move the coffee table, roll up the braided rug, and push the chairs back. Then the "Magic" would happen!!!! Daddy Jim and Granny would dance. It did not matter if it was a waltz or polka or other dance, they could do it all. It was a sight to behold!! They never missed a beat and were so very light on their feet, which was so surprising, because he was over 6 feet tall and she was barely 5 feet. They were truly amazing!

As you can imagine, they were both noted for their dancing. I was told that their favorite song was "Alexander's Rag Time Band." When they would walk into a local dance hall, the band would start playing that song. Everyone would stop dancing and let Daddy Jim and Granny have the dance floor to themselves. Mother told me that when they would go on trips and Daddy Jim would get tired, he would stop at a dance hall, and he and Granny would dance for hours while Mother and Aunt Pritchett would wait in the car. Then, when they came out, he would be good to drive all night.

Each year, school would let out for six weeks for cotton picking. On Sunday, Mom and Dad would take me to Granny and Daddy Jim's so I could pick cotton. It would have been way too expensive to have driven me back and forth each day, so I would stay until Friday. What an experience! I was so bad at picking cotton; just ask Lucille Bailey. It was hot, hot, hot and I got tired, tired, tired. I had to get up early and work late. Granny was so sweet, but I know that she and Daddy Jim would laugh and laugh at me. When Mother and Daddy came to pick me up each Friday, I felt like Granny and Daddy Jim were proud to see me go home. I have never had a job in my life that was harder than picking cotton. Amen.

Daddy Jim was also noted for many other things. In case you were not aware, Daddy Jim invented the "drive-through." He would go to Wade Climer's Grocery Store in his car, drive up to the door, and sit down on the horn, big time. Pappy Wade would then come out with 2 gallons of milk and a loaf of bread. Curb service every time!

Daddy Jim would often come to see us. Let me rephrase that: Daddy Jim would often come to the house and sit down on the horn for us to come out and visit with him. I only remember one or two times that Daddy Jim actually came into our home. He was certainly one of a kind.

Another thing Daddy Jim was famous for was his black Ford car. Everyone in town recognized it. It always had a streak of chewing tobacco all the way down the side of the door. He also thought his car was a four-wheel drive truck. He would drive through any bottomland, mud and all, and not think a thing about it until he got stuck! This was before the days of cell phones. Each time he would have to walk several miles to get help, but he never learned!!!

Daddy Jim died in 1968 and after his death, my mom, Aunt Pig, and Aunt Pritchett would take turns staying with Granny on the weekends. At that time I had a candy apple red Camaro sports car. Granny would beg my mother to drive my car. The reason for this was very simple. It was a lot easier for her to get in and out of my car, plus "she thought she looked good in that car."

Granny kept Daddy Jim's car after he died, and she always had the gas tank full and the car serviced. Now Granny could not drive, but she always wanted the car in total working condition just in case one day she might have an emergency and need to drive it somewhere.

What wonderful memories. Our family has been very blessed.

Memories of My Mom
Dorothy Fay (Bailey) Lowery
By Patricia Lowery Cummins

I had a wonderful childhood growing up with such great parents. They were both loving, sweet, and kind. But, most of all, they always put family first in their lives.

As I was growing up, everyone wanted my mom to be their mom. It used to make me so mad! Why did they want my mom; they had a mom! Many years later, I discovered that not everyone had great parents like I did. I thought every child experienced the same love and support that had been given to me. What an awakening!!! How very, very blessed Bailey and I have been.

My dad, James Harlin Lowery, was a very handsome, sweet, sweet, kind man. He would always say "Thank You." It did not matter what anyone did for him; he would always thank them. He worked for Alamo Construction Company for over forty years, and while he was accommodating to all his customers, he was especially helpful to the widow women. He would go out of his way to help them so they could get the very best bargains.

My dad died of lung cancer at the age of 66. As Daddy lay in the hospital dying, he would never let us leave his room to even go get a coke without saying to Bailey, Mom, or me, "I love you." We always knew how very much we were loved.

Until my father died, my mom had never spent the night alone in her life. She was the youngest in the family and always would sleep with someone. As a child, she had her sisters to sleep with. When she was older, she would sleep with Granny; in college, she had roommates; then she married Dad. When Daddy was away, Bailey or I would be home. If her work required that she leave town for a convention, there was always a bunch of girls staying in a room together. So, when my dad died, Mom needed me to stay with her. Everything in her life had suddenly changed. With the help of Aunt Pritchett and Aunt Pig, I stayed with Mom for a year after Daddy died. She hated being alone at night and sleeping by herself!

Mother was the youngest of the eight children. After high school, Mother wanted to become a nurse but was not allowed to because her brothers informed Granny and Daddy Jim that only women with NO morals were nurses. So off to Business College she went, but she always had a longing to be a nurse. After college, Mom and Daddy got married. Mother would later become employed with the Crockett County Health Department, where she worked for 44 years.

When Mother was growing up, she and her sisters had to cater to the boys in the family. One job she had was to wash, starch to the max, and iron Uncle James' white pants until they could stand-alone. He wore these as he rode barefoot on his horse and through the mud to pick up his date.

The girls in the family had to help cook for the men that worked at the sawmill, which was located next to the house. Mother was taught to give these men large portions when she would serve lunch each day. For the rest of her life, when she cut a piece of pie for someone, it would be a fourth of the pie. Daddy would tease her and tell her that we had not been working at the sawmill that day.

It seems that nicknames were a big thing within the Bailey family. Everyone remembers most of the nicknames: Pritchett, Pig, Skinny, and Frog. But I wonder how many can remember Daddy Jim's nickname for Granny? It was Sally. My dad decided that he, too, should give Mother a nickname, so he did! He would very sweetly and lovingly call her "Booger!"

Mother told me stories of all her brothers and sisters. One story about Aunt Olive was how very, very skinny she was. The doctors told her that she must drink a beer each day. She would cry and cry because she had to do this. I don't think that a doctor would prescribe that today.

Another story was when Uncle Arthur and Aunt Jewel got married. There was 16 years difference in Mother and Uncle Arthur's age. So when Mother was about 3, or maybe 4 years old, Uncle Arthur gave her first lesson in telling time. He showed her the exact location of the clock hands for a specific time and told Mother to watch the clock until the hands rested on the proper numbers. At that exact time, Mother was to go and tell Granny and Daddy Jim that he and Jewel had gone and gotten married.

When I was in the second grade, my mother was diagnosed with Boeck's Sarcoidosis, and she had to have part of a lung removed. In the 50's, this was a very serious operation, and she spent about two months in the hospital in Memphis. Daddy Jim and Granny hired a nurse to stay with her around the clock. Daddy was back and forth, and I stayed with Aunt Pig for most of that year. I loved to stay with Aunt Pig. The best thing about getting to stay with Aunt Pig was that she never made me take a bath. (This drove my mother crazy!) Many of my favorite childhood memories were made when I was at Aunt Pig's. I was only 2 years old when Uncle Buster died, but I still remember to this day how much I loved him and how much he loved me. He was such a wonderful man.

One of my special memories of staying with Aunt Pig was when we would go to the movies each Saturday night. It did not matter what was playing. For you see, the reason for our going to the movies was so that Mike, the black gentleman who worked and lived in a little house right behind Aunt Pig's house, could go on a date! We would go by and pick up his lady friend, and then the four of us would to the movies in Bells.

Mike and his date always sat in the balcony. After the movie, we would take Mike and his date back to her home, and then we would get to wait and wait in the car. I guess you could call us "their chauffeur." Whatever we were, I sure did get to see some great movie classics!

Mother loved Black Bottom, and she and I would often walk through this beautiful, thick forest. Daddy Jim taught her to tell how many "board feet" were in each tree. At one time, the biggest tree in Tennessee was located in Black Bottom. Mother had a lot of wonderful memories of Black Bottom, but she always said that it caused a lot of heartache and pain. And so it did, for many of our beloved family members.

When Bailey was about 14 years old, he and his first cousin, Johnny Bailey from San Antonio, Texas, were lucky enough to get to help build the new bridges in Black Bottom. What fun they did have!! Poisonous snakes, slimy mud, monster mosquitoes, and 100-degree temperatures; what more could you ask for in a work place? Needless to say, this experience made for many memories and many tall tales.

Once when Mother was staying with Granny, my little brother, Bailey, who was about 11 or 12 years old at the time, asked Mother if he could go see Uncle Arthur, who lived just down the road. Mother said, "Sure, but don't stay too long." She assumed he would walk or ride his bike, but no! As she continued washing the dishes, she looked out the kitchen window. To her surprise, she saw a cloud of dust, as Bailey was driving off in her car. When Mother questioned him, he told her, "But, Mom, you said it was OK." Mom said she was speechless.

One summer, while Bailey was going to school at Memphis State University, I had purchased a rental house. The yard and house both needed a lot of work. Daddy thought that it would be a great idea for Bailey to help me. Daddy said, "This will be so much fun for you two." It was the hottest part of the summer. We worked so hard; we were worn out, hot and tired. Bailey, covered in dirt with sweat pouring off him, turned to me and said, "Gosh, Damn, ain't we having fun!!" This phrase became our favorite saying. Mother and Daddy wanted us to stay close and we have. They encouraged us to do things together, so we could make wonderful, fun memories.

Mother was so happy when she found out she was going to be a grandmother. Tanner, her beautiful granddaughter, was everything to her. Once while staying with Mother, Tanner flipped over in the front porch swing. It only busted her lip, but as Tanner began to cry, so did my mother. They were both covered in blood, and it took me a few minutes to figure out what was going on. They both were fine; it had just scared Mother so. At age 71, Mother taught Tanner how to do somersaults down the hill in front of the house. Mother would do one, and then Tanner would do one until both were turning somersaults all the way down the hill. To use one of Tanner's favorite sayings when she was little, "Unbelievable!" Mother never got to know her two grandsons, James and Will, but she would have loved them, oh, so very much.

I could never write anything about my mom without talking about Homecoming. Next to Christmas, Homecoming was the most important day of the year. She would work for months getting everything ready. She cooked and cooked for weeks, but the "piece de resistance" was always the peach fried pies. She told me she would make between 200 and 250 each year. (I still have the recipe, if anyone is brave enough to try.) They were definitely one of the highlights for everyone at Homecoming.

Mother loved her family so much, and I think we all felt that love. She was truly one wonderful, special mother. Thank you, God, for blessing us with my mom and dad.

Colonel James Bailey, MD
By Barbara Bailey Steed, daughter

My mom and dad met and married in the Philippines during WWII. My mom's dad was from England and had businesses in England and the Philippines and, with the war; they stayed in the Philippines to help with US. My dad was in WWII, Korean War, Vietnam War, and Cuban Missile Crisis. Dad's last duty was at Ft. Sam Houston, San Antonio, Texas, where he was commander of the 5th Army and Chief of Psychiatry at Beach Pavilion. Dad did not talk much about his experiences in the military, but I do know he held many honors, including traveling with General Douglas Mac Arthur in WWII. He retired and went into private practice and was President of the Bexar County Psychiatric Society for a while. He loved farming and ranching and managed three ranches also. One achievement he was most proud of was an award from The Soil and Conservation District of Texas for the 1995 "Absentee Conservation Rancher" in Region III (he was 79 years old at the time)! Dad's work ethics came from his childhood working in the cotton fields, helping with the sawmill and coming from a large family with many siblings. One story I heard about my dad was that he used to hang sausage in his room at Granny's house and would "check it" when he came back if he had to leave! My father loved Cypress Methodist Church and would always request "Little Church in the Wildwoods" at Homecoming. He did not preach to his children, but he would use quotes from the Bible at times, and he lived a life pleasing to our Lord; that, in turn, was a wonderful inheritance gift from my father.

My mother's life was changed dramatically by living in the Philippines during the war and marrying my father. During her young adult life in the Philippines, she was a heroine in that she saved the life of one of her cousins by distracting a Japanese soldier, helped feed prisoners on the Baton Death March and saw relatives killed. She married my father and soon, thereafter, arrived in the United States, where she had a wonderful life with her family (4 children), traveling and going to the country with Dad.

My oldest brother Bill (William Harold Bailey) is an electro physiologist, flight surgeon and Colonel in the US Air Force. He has been on many missions and served in several wars with the Air Force and has survived being shot down in aircraft three times. His last deployment was in the Iraq War, where he was chief of the medical hospital on the Baghdad airstrip. He has achieved so many accolades and medals...too many to list. He is a brilliant man who served his country and represented his family well. He is married to Kathie Fonken Bailey, who is a brilliant woman. She is a pharmacist and they complement each other academically! Bill has two children (Nancy and Will) and Kathie has three children (Gregg, Jennifer and Sarah).

James Edward Bailey is a hospital administrator in San Antonio and he and his wife, Therese (Hospice nurse) have seven children (Peter, West Point graduate, and wife Shannon, son Patrick), (Tom and wife, Ashley, daughter Reese with one child on the way), (James, who works in television filming). (Genevieve, husband Michael, daughter "Gabby," son Michael, and one on the way), (Elizabeth, who works in education), (Rachael works in the medical field), and ("Meg," who is a sophomore at UTSA). Our family in Tennessee knows Jim as "Jaybird!" Jim was a Major and served in the US Army during the Korean War. Jim is much like my father and does not talk about his service in the military. I do know that he was in the DMZ and served his country well. Jim is a wonderful father and enjoys going out to the country, fishing and hunting. He has four grandchildren and two on the way as I write!

My husband Jerry and I live in San Antonio and are blessed with two children, Carrie Anne and Michael. Carrie is in medical recruiting and staffing and will be relocating to Denver next week. Michael just became engaged to Mary Shelby Ames and will marry in March of 2011. Michael is a geologist, living in Houston and working on offshore Brazil seismic mapping. Jerry is a real estate attorney but would rather be a professional saltwater fishing guide. My father took Jerry out and taught him to hunt, fish, and drive a tractor!

Our family traveled because of the military, but my father always took us to Tennessee as often as he could, which instilled a strong appreciation and understanding of family. Our roots are in Tennessee and we love and feel truly blessed by our entire family there.

William (Bill) Bailey, MD F.A.C.C.
Son of Colonel James Bailey, MD and Nancy Bailey

I have always been involved in critical care cardiology as well as Flight Medicine in the air force and as the director of the critical care transport teams in Iraq and Afghanistan. These experiences have always humbled me about life and my destiny. It has been always an honor to care for the sick as well as the wounded both young and old. I was only one person as part of the whole US and British efforts to help in this war effort.

One time when we were shot down, I passed out and crossed the River Jordan. During that brief time I remember looking up at vague figures that appeared to be Daddy Jim and Granny staring at me! I woke up at that point. Both my mother and father always told me that war was hard to talk about when I asked them about WW II and the Philippines. I, too, now understand and hope that none of our families have to face it. If so, I hope that they can step up just as our forefathers in the past stood up in the long gray, blue and khaki lines before us.

I will always remember standing in a cotton field with my Uncle Arthur and my father Frog. They both told me that farming is a very hard career. I think they were trying to tell me something. I will always remember that they reminded me to "Always choose the harder Right in Life, rather than the easier Wrong."

Therefore, I am closing my professional career as a clinical professor of cardiology teaching at the Brody School of Medicine here at the East Carolina University School of Medicine.

I have and remain very grateful to my lovely and very steadfast wife, Kathie, and children, as well as Jaybird and Barbara, my brother and sister.

We have another brother John C. Bailey, who is a corrections officer working at Kennedy, Texas. He also does some ranching and farming.

Things that come to mind about Tennessee include the following:

—Playing the flute at Christmas church service and wetting my pants, singing "The Old Rugged Cross" and Homecoming and the food.

—Locking Pat Lowery in Granny's closet.

—Shooting off firecrackers and rolling down the hill at Granny's.

—RC Colas and Moon Pies and fishing with cane poles at Henderson Lake with Aunt Pig and her can of worms.

—Fried pies, Aunt Betty, Granny's attic.

—Daddy Jim, spitting tobacco into his coffee can.

—Playing dominoes.

—Going to the Black Bottom.

—Putting chewed-up bubble gum in my brother Jay's hair as he went to sleep and watching my mother cut off big chunks of his hair the next morning.

—Hiding a live chicken in the back of our car as we once drove off from Granny's to go back to Georgia.

—Having overnights at Aunt Pig's and watching Myrtle Rose go out with lots of guys and one that gave her a beautiful conch shell.

—Using her outhouse to go to the bathroom in the middle of the winter.

—Spitting watermelon seeds into my sister Barbara's pony tail.

—Jaybird, freezing little frogs in Granny's ice trays and finding them in my cup of Dr. Pepper.

—Chopping cotton.

—Fishing in the pond behind Steve and Uncle Arthur's house.

—Standing up at homecoming to announce my family.

—Visiting your lovely home, quilts, Mason jars.

—The smell of oil and grease in Daddy Jim's garages.

—Smoked hams in the old smokehouse.

—Watching Aunt Jewel ring the chicken's neck for dinner.

—Aunt Dot's smile and sleeping over at Pat's and always going over to the Dairy Queen (I still love their chocolate-dipped cones.)

—Cousin Larry's unforgettable laugh.

—Holding Bailey in my arms when he was only a baby.

—Sitting in front of Granny's fireplace with the wood fire roaring and just feeling that I never wanted to leave that home! *Love, Cousin Bill*

Uncle Frog (James) Bailey and wife Aunt Nancy

WILLIAM H. BAILEY, MD, F.A.C.C.

CURRICULUM VITAE

SPECIALTY: Cardiology/Electrophysiology
DATE OF BIRTH: 03/27/1947
PLACE OF BIRTH: Manila, Philippines
MARITAL STATUS: Married, Kathie, five children
LANGUAGES: German and Spanish

CURRENT EMPLOYER:
East Carolina University
Department of Cardiovascular Sciences
East Carolina Heart Institute
Brody School of Medicine

USAF, Reservist 433rd AMDS Squadron   Present
COMMANDER–USAF Reserves

EDUCATION:

Tulane University	07/65-06/69
Degree: BA-German Literature & Biology	

Tulane University-College of Medicine   08/72-06/76
Degree: MD-Doctor of Medicine

Baylor College of Medicine   07/1976-06/79
Residency: Family Medicine

University of Texas Health Science Center   07/79-06/81
Residency: Internal Medicine

University of Texas Health Science Center   07/81-06/83
Fellowship: Invasive Cardiology

Baylor College of Medicine/St. Luke's Hospital   07/93-06/94
Fellowship: Cardiac Electrophysiology

Astra-Merck Foundation/American Heart   2000-2001
Association
Recipient of the Cardiovascular Health Fellowship.

U.S. Air Force
Brooks AFB School of Aerospace Medicine
Residency in Flight Medicine   1997
And
C.C.A.T.T. - Critical Care Air Transport Team   2003
Medicine

U.S.A.F. AIR WAR COLLEGE   06/2006-08/01/2007
Air University, Maxwell AFB, Alabama
MILITARY GRADUATE

PREVIOUS ACADEMIC AND PROFESSIONAL APPOINTMENTS:
Central Texas Veteran's Health Care System   04/95-04/2000
Position: Chairman of Cardiology and Electrophysiology

Texas A&M University School of Medicine   05/96-04/2000
Position: Assistant Professor of Internal Medicine

LICENSE: North Carolina and Texas

BOARD CERTIFICATION:
American Academy of Family Medicine	1979-1986
American Board of Internal Medicine	09/15/82 #83727
ABIM-Cardiovascular Disease	11/09/83 #083727

North American Society of Pacing & Electrophysiology 12/13/94 #2338
ATLS   2014
ACLS   2012
BLS   2012

PROFESSIONAL SOCIETIES:
American College of Cardiology - Fellow
American Heart Association - Clinical Cardiology Council
American College of Physicians
International Society for Heart Research - North American Section
American Association for the Advancement of Medicine
American Society of Aerospace Medicine
Texas Medical Association
Society of Pacing & Electrophysiology - North American
Heart Failure Society of America
Reserve Officers Association
US Air Force Flight Surgeons Association
Veterans of Foreign Wars
American Legion

CLINICAL RESEARCH:
Congestive Heart Failure, Trial in Medical Compliance *1999*

Gusto IV-ACS: Trial-Thrombolytic Therapy in Acute 1998
Myocardial Infarction:

INVEST Trial-International Anti-Hypertensive Study *1998*

Valsartan-Congestive Heart Failure Trial: *Sponsor-Novartis Pharmaceutics.*1998
ALIVE - Azimilide Post Infarct Survival Trial   *1998*
MOXCON - Congestive Heart Failure Study   1998

Pacemaker Mode Selection, Trial for Patients with   1998
Sick Sinus Syndrome:

VALUE Trial (Evaluation of long term use of Valsartan)
                                                     1998
The Effect of Serzone on Mental and Emotional Induced Cardiac Ischemia in
Depressed Patients with Coronary Artery Disease   *1998*

Educational Grant to Support Medical Student
Research in Cardiovascular Diseases   1998

Early Field Intervention in Acute Myocardial   1997
Infarction

Anti-hypertensive and Lipid Lowering Treatment   1997
To Prevent Heart Attack Trial

Utility of Simple Spirometry in Predicting the Risk of Bronchospasm During Intravenous Dipyridamole and Adenosine Thallium Imaging in Patients with Chronic Air Flow Obstruction-A Comparison Study   *1997*

Educational Grant to Support Medical Student Research in Cardiovascular Diseases
1997
Educational Grant to Support Medical Student Research in Cardiovascular Diseases
1997

HONORS AND AWARDS:

Outstanding Leadership Award: the 433rd AMDS, Lackland AFB
June 5th, 2010

Co-author of the **Reference Manual for Cardiology**, The Brody School of Medicine at East Carolina University School of Medicine 2010

Air Achievement Medal "For 17 Combat MEDEVAC Missions under Fire - Iraq 2003-2004" US Air Force - March, 2010

Authored the chapter "Critical Care Transport Medicine" for the **USAF Flight Surgeon's Manual** - August 2008

Secretary of the Air Force and US Senate selection and promotion to **Colonel, US Air Force** - April 1, 2008

Invited Speaker for the National Riobamba Medical Conference in Ecuador on "Stem Cell Therapy in CHF and CAD" - April 11, 2008
University of Texas Award "For Outstanding Performance and Lasting Contributions to the Family Medicine Residency Program" Galveston, Texas - June 23, 2007

"Top Performer Award" for Operation Golden Medic - June 2007 Fort Gordon, Georgia: a Joint US Army/Air Force Operation for Combat Medical Evacuation

United States Iraqi Freedom Medal for Combat MEDEVAC Missions 2003-2004 Baghdad, Iraq

Department of the Air Force Commendation Medal "For Outstanding Achievement and Bravery" 5 August 2003 to 14 January 2004 during service in Baghdad, Iraq

VII Asian-Pacific Symposium on Cardiac Pacing and Electrophysiology - Beijing, China. **Invited Speaker, 2001.**

Royal Society of Medicine - London, England. **Elected Fellow, 2000.**

Texas A&M Medical School –
Selected as Preceptor Medical Student Clinical Cardiac Auscultation Series.
 1999-2000.

Distinguished Military Service during Conflicts in Iraq, Saudi Arabia, Nairobi, Kenya, and Honduras.
Awarded-The United States Presidential Citation and Meritorious Service Medal (USAF)
1996-1999.

Military Service in Saudi Arabia during Operations Southern Watch and Desert Fox –
Awarded-The Armed Forces Expeditionary Medal, 1998.

Who's Who In America in Science and Engineering, 1998-1999

For the Development of Cardiovascular Research & Training Programs,
Department of Medicine VA Recognition Award, 1998.

For Outstanding Professional Skill in Leadership and Medical Care, 433rd Airlift Wing,
United States Air Force Commendation Medal and Award, 1997.

For Service during US Military Operations in Honduras, Central America
Joint Task Force BRAVO Campaign Ribbon, 1997.

Texas A&M Medical School
Outstanding Lecturer Award, 1997-1998.

Texas Heart Institute-St. Luke's Episcopal Hospital Recipient of the **Bronze Heart** for Studies in Cardiac Electrophysiology presented by Drs. Robert J. Hall and Denton Cooley, June 1994
Merck Foundation Travel Fellowship for Electrophysiology: Baylor College of
 Medicine, 1994

Best Presentation Award: Texas Heart Institute Cardio-Vascular Symposium: "Role
 of
Radio Frequency Ablation of the Slow and Fast Pathway in the Treatment of AVNRT and AVRT" Baylor College of Medicine, 1993.

"For Contributions to Patient Care and the Support of Medical Education" San
 Antonio,
Texas, **Methodist Hospital Foundation Recognition Award,** 1993.

University of Texas Senior Medicine Resident Outstanding Thesis Award and Publication: "Venomous Vipers: Their Systemic Effects of Envenomation and Therapy," Houston, Texas 1981

The Harold Cummins – "For Studies in the Anatomic Sciences" Tulane School of Medicine. 1976

The Conrad Collins Prize "For Outstanding Studies and Performance in Obstetrics & Gynecology" Tulane School of Medicine, 1976.

The National Institute of Health Medical Student Research Grant. "Neuroendocrinology Study of Prolactin" Tulane School of Medicine, 1974.

Delta Phi Alpha Honors Society and German Consulate Award "For Studies in German Literature and Philosophy" Tulane University, 1967.

Varsity "T" Letter for Intercollegiate Track,
     Tulane University, 1967.

Jody Van, Elizabeth Shane, Mame' Lou, Milly Ann Emerson

CHAPTER 14

Imaginations of My Children and Grandchildren
Shane's View of Family

Growing up on a collage of farms in West Tennessee as Shane Emerson, daughter of Joe and Myrtle Rose Emerson, granddaughter of Pig and Buster Leggett and Malcolm and Maggie Lou Emerson and great-granddaughter of Jim "Crow" and Lou Myrtle Bailey and Ollie Boyd, I wanted for nothing but knowledge and experience. A sense of pride was installed in me that I can only attribute to our Irish heritage. I was deathly afraid of Daddy Jim Bailey but reluctantly gave him the respect that he demanded. In turn Ollie was a docile, yet prominent, part of our family lives. Only as an adult were the myths and legends revealed to me, their individual charismatic personalities and their overt justification for success. Please remember my stories of them are just that, stories of what I remember as a child. Because of our three generation gap, I personally was never affected directly by their actions but indirectly they and their children and grandchildren shaped my life.

Ollie, Mimi and Paw Paw

I remember Ollie as an elderly, frail gentleman. He was always in a coat and tie and a hat when out of the house, but he was always present in the home of my grandparents, Malcolm (Paw Paw) and Maggie Lou (Mimi). He moved into their home when they were quite young. He always gave us money at Christmas. I have very vague memories (mostly the smells and faded pink floral wallpaper) of the old house, but he was always there in the chair, a chair in the corner. I remember Mimi waiting on him with much adoration and devotion. She used to babysit us and I loved the mayonnaise and saltines she served us for a snack. We would mash the two edges together and the mayonnaise would squeeze through the holes like worms, and we would giggle with delight as we licked the sweet mayo and licked up the salt with our tongues. Her biscuits always smelled so good, but they were dry and had flour on top and bottom. Dousing them with molasses cured the dryness; but when Mimi made strawberry shortcake, those biscuits and my taste buds came alive (I remember later picking strawberries at Norris Farms.) I had not tasted anything like it until I had strawberry shortcake at Commander's place in New Orleans. Ella Brennan must have gotten the recipe from my grandmother.

Shane's Memories of Granny Bailey

Again, my memories of Granny are only when she was quite elderly. She still lived in the big house. Daddy Jim was dead and all the siblings divided up days to go and take care of Granny Bailey, or I should say "the girls." My job was to unbraid and rebraid her hair and watch the stories on TV with her while Mama Pig worked on the house and chores. She had never had a haircut, and her tresses were down past her waist and very thin. She always wore her hair in a braided bun and her hair was silver gray. She loved to have her hair brushed while she laughed and talked about Dr. John Dixon on the story *As the World Turns* as if he were her best friend and really I think she had a bad crush on him. She would laugh out loud as she smiled with delight at what a scoundrel he was!

I remember the big, white house with a stairway to the attic-room that had old clothes for us to dress up in and Aunt Dot's old formals that turned us into a princess when we put them on were all a great treat for us.

Anywhere in the old house you could usually smell the homemade rolls she made almost daily. They were wonderful, hot, and dripping with homemade butter. Also a cold glass of milk with a cold slice of ham or cheese.

When Homecoming day came to Cypress, Granny's house was filled to the limit with cousins from all over the country. Most were from Texas, Missouri, Florida, Maine, California and Indiana. I always loved seeing these cousins because I always felt they were so glitzy coming from such exotic places. One I really loved was Candi, who was a model and so beautiful that all us young girls just stared at her and dreamed that she was indeed a princess. There were always carloads of kin from Memphis. It seemed that when the generation before me married or graduated from school, Memphis was the place to go where now everyone seems to like out of state places that we used to only read about.

Shane's Memories of Fruitvale

One thing that comes to mind when I think of home and Fruitvale is the cowboy that lived down the road from us. He was always roping a wooden cow off the highway dressed in a cowboy shirt and jeans and really playing the part. This was topped off with a cowboy hat, wide brim and all. He used to tease my older sister and tell her that he was going to marry her one day.

On the way to Mama Pig's or church, there was a pink rose bank all the way down one side of the road all the way to Sue and Ronnie's. It grew in big mountains of roses crawling all over themselves and runners going out in the road. It was a pretty sight almost all summer.

At our house, we always made cookies for Christmas and other holidays for the shut-ins in the community. I remember especially Mr. Francis Emerson, who lived in front of the store in a big old house all by himself. He was so nice and loved for us to come and see him and bring the cookies. He had a very high-pitched voice and always seemed so lonesome to me.

Then there was Mr. Robert that worked for Daddy. He helped to plant and gather the crops and did odd jobs in-between. I remember going to see him and he was not a shut-in, but we carried cookies anyway because he worked for Daddy. They always had a hot fire in the stove, and they had the linoleum floors with the painted wood showing around the edges just like Mama Pig and Daddy Buster used to have. Mrs. Robert always had on her cotton dresses like Mimi wore. They were always starched and ironed and looking good. One of the differences in Mimi's appearance was that she always wore make up and lipstick. She liked to look dressed up every day of the week.

Getting back to Mr. Robert...he was a dark man with dark hair and because in the comic Brutus (e.g. Popeye) the dark man was associated with being the bad guy, and I had to constantly remind myself that he was kind and friendly. (My family was very fond of this man.) This coming from a blonde-haired, blue-eyed girl where most everyone in our community looked like me. He was so eager for us to love him.

Memories of Mama Pig

By Elizabeth Shane Emerson French

It's funny how one thing can bring all ages of people together, but the oddest thing that brought lots of hours of bonding with my grandmother and great-grandmother was hair. Of course, all females are concerned about hair and how theirs look, but this bond did not have much to do with looks, but simply the closeness and love felt by combing, curling and braiding it.

When combing Mama Pig's hair, I discovered that she had two moles on her head that my mom had on her head and in the very same place. I know this may sound strange, but later in life I, too, have these moles in the same place as the two women before me.

Mama Pig wanted Milly and me to twist her hair after she had washed it into little round flat curls that we attached a bobby pin to hold it to her head until it dried. When we took the pins out, her hair would be fluffy and curly and it looked fantastic. However, when our turn came and she curled our long, thick hair, she used long strands of torn rags and twisted our tresses tightly up to our heads, tied the string ends together; and when it dried, we looked like we had been electrocuted and caught in a tornado. Frizz became a new dimension when Mama Pig took those rags out (never mind that a comb or brush could not navigate those strands of hair.) It looked to her just gorgeous! What could you say but smile and say, "Thank you!"

There was one procedure that pleased us all. That was the French Braids and she could also do a reversed French Braid that left the braided line on top of the hair. This was amazing and both Milly and I can do this now to our daughter's hair. It would stay in for days and we would be delighted that we did not have to comb our hair forever-r-r-r-r!

Another "must do" at Mama Pig's was to wear a bonnet whenever outside. She was preaching skin care from the sun before sunscreen was invented. These bonnets were made especially for us in whatever size was required at any given age. They were made from scraps of cotton left from her quilts or some on sale no matter what color or design. Just so it suited the purpose was all that mattered. Every once in awhile, you would get one that you really liked, but what did it matter, after you put it on, you could not see it anyway. There was only one time that we really wanted our bonnets on and that was when Mama Pig went to the catalpa trees to get the worms for bait for a fishing trip. We had to shake the trees so the worms would fall off the leaves and to the ground. This was bad enough, but sometimes those big, black and yellow juicy critters would land right on top of your head! Hello!!!! But you guessed it; we loved her so much that we would do anything for her.

Mama Pig's house always had a special scent to it. I could always smell good things coming from her kitchen. Something was always cooking. Breakfast bacon left a lingering scent and then usually a pie or cake in the oven or maybe a pot roast or fried chicken for lunch. No matter what time of day, you could hear your stomach groan just breathing in the air.

She would fix us a dishpan full of water and put play dishes in it and give us things to "cook," and we would play for hours with this while she prepared food for the family.

How she loved her yard and flowers! She had a green thumb when it came to growing anything whether it be flowers, vegetables or her yard. She would not have her yard grass growing up and looking haggy. We had to mow it a half-inch high and we tried to tell her that this was bad for the grass, but she kept it watered and it always looked good. Mama Pig always had a good game going for us to play, and she always took time out of her busy chores to play with us. She was a great softball pitcher.

At Thanksgiving and Christmas you could not see her house for the cars and trucks that people came in for the meals with us. They were parked on the side of the road on both sides of the yard. Family and friends, neighbors, women and men that had no place to celebrate the holidays were always welcomed in her door. No one was turned away and no one went home hungry.

Mama Pig always kept this big, cheap jewelry box on the dresser, full of gaudy jewelry for us to play dress up with! We all had our favorite pieces, and sometimes that would be the same one that everyone else wanted and this could mean trouble. We were all a very decisive bunch. Sometimes this called for a referee.

One thing that stuck in my mind was her love for coffee. Now, I don't mean that just any old cup of coffee would do. She liked it STRONG!! As gentle and sweet as my grandmother was, you didn't say much or get into anything until she had her second cup of this stuff down. Then she became human and was ready to go. No one who came in (and there was always someone stopping by) could keep up with her and her coffee. They either drank their cups before they came or waited until they got back home to get thirsty. No sugar, no cream, no nothing, but black, pure coffee went into her percolator or her cup but a little water and lots of coffee. This seemed so strange to me because neither my mom nor dad drank the black stuff.

She used an old back pedal Singer sewing machine to make everything! She made sheets and pillowcases for the beds, clothes for the tables, throw pillows for the couch, dishrags, sausage sacks to stuff the fresh sausage in and so many more things. She was especially good at making curtains. She used it to piece her beautiful quilts. It was an old pedal, one that hummed when she pumped the pedals and the fabric going through at steady pace. She made all kinds of things on this old relic. It is in Mama and Dad's attic now, waiting for me to find room for it to rest.

Fabrics were her mainstay. Her quilts were her outlets. She did most of this by hand. Her quilts were painstakingly sewn with small stitches all across the cover. Every now and then, she would make a wool or heavy cover that we would help her "tie" with heavy threads every inch or so. We would bring the thread through the top of the quilt, then down under and back up through the top, then tie a knot in the threads. The kids could help her do this, and it made a nice warm floor pallet or one to drag outside for a quick nap under the trees.

I remember her hands being so different from anyone else. I could identify her as my grandmother by looking only at her hands. They were worker's hands. They were wrinkled hands. They were toughened hands. They were loving hands that did things for me and everyone that needed her hands for help of any kind. She nursed neighbors through sickness, comforted the grieving, and even delivered children with those hands, and they were something I was proud of and something that taught me so very much.

There was an old screened in porch that was on the side of the house. We children played dolls there and got water out of the old pitcher pump to play house there with toy dishes. The connecting bedroom is where she kept old jewelry boxes filled with costume jewelry that we thought was a king's bounty. We wore those pieces out and broke them up but still managed to play with them.

We would all pile up in her bed by the TV and watch movies until 12 a.m. They just turned the TV off at that hour, and now a lot of people are just getting started watching programs, but you didn't stay up that long back then. Entertainment went "poof" at midnight...

The two upstairs rooms were roughly finished, giving my mom and Aunt Betty a room each. Going up the steps, there was a closet built in the wall where Mama Pig kept her old Christmas things like used wrapping paper and used ribbons and old ornaments. She used these things year after year and thought they were so pretty. It wasted too much money to buy new paper and ribbons each year.

I remember before she got the dishwasher, we had to heat the water to wash dishes on the stove in dishpans. Then pour it in the sink and she believed strongly on hot water for this. Barry, Steve, Richard and I usually did this job, and our hands would be scalded from the continually heated water being poured over our hands and dishes.

Her yard was her pet. She wanted her yard cut to within an inch of the ground and never mind if it was not good for it. It looked "wooly" to her if a blade even dated to grow tall. The closely mowed yard was a good place to hunt for Doodle Bugs. We would find the holes in the dirt and get broom straws and punch in the hole then wait for the straw to wiggle up and down (like a fishing line) and jerk it up quickly and, sure enough, there would be the Doodle Bug, hanging on the end of the straw for dear life!...We would all shriek with delight over this venture. I thought at the time she was just as thrilled as we were over the unfortunate bug, but I now realize her joy was for our joy.

OK, now I have been very agreeable about my grandmother in all these things...but...there was one and only one thing she did that I could not agree with; in fact, it made me wheezy. That was the fishing worms and catalpa worms that she did not use up fishing and would bring them home and put them in the deep freeze for the next trip. I refused to take anything out of that freezer at the time. Now, I can see some merit in this action. Nobody is perfect, but she surely made a run for it!

Fishing with Mama Pig

By Elizabeth Shane Emerson French

On occasion it was my role to go fishing with Mama Pig. Today I would give my right arm to be at Humboldt Lake with her and her fishing pole; however, when I was young, fishing was not my favorite sport but I made the day work for us both.

To start with, we had to make sure

we had an old gallon milk jug with frozen water. As the day wore on, the heat and sun would melt the water, giving us great ice water all day. Next, Mama Pig would select her bait from the old broken deep freezer full of live minnows. She had her minnow bucket to put them in. Because Paw Paw Emerson had an old freezer for minnows, I thought everyone had one. We would pack up the old car with her fishing gear, don our bonnets, pack a quilt, some snacks and our ice jug and be on our way. I always brought a book to read as I easily tired of fishing, but Mama Pig would stay all day long. With my book, I never got bored and she got to fish. Everyone was happy! She would always fish in the water close to the bank, and I soon learned my

Mama Pig and "The Big One" March 1992

role was not only to keep her company but to pull her out of the water if she fell in. She always fished standing straight up, and I recall at least twice this occurred but she was never daunted. Out she came with a little help from me and she would continue fishing while she drip-dried!

Although fishing was her very favorite sport, she would not eat a bite of one. At the end of a fishing day, she always gave them away unless she was having a fish fry for friends or family.

Mama Pig
By Elizabeth Shane Emerson French

How do you describe Mama Pig? An entire book could be written about her. Would it be a tragedy? A comedy? Drama? Most likely, all of the above mentioned. I do not remember her as anything but older. She was grandly wrinkled despite always wearing an old-fashioned bonnet when in the sun. Always putting ponds cold Cream on her face each night. She was thin despite having a diet consisting solely of sugar, butter, a coffee with pies and cakes. She managed to raise a family of two girls despite being widowed in a farming community in her thirties and being mostly abandoned by her wealthy father. She was raised as being the second daughter of James Arthur (Jim Crow Hooker) and Lou Myrtle Forsythe Bailey. (Daddy Jim and Granny Bailey). Their home was one of male dominance and chauvinism. The men were allowed freedom; the women made sure the men were accommodated. She cooked, cleaned and helped raise her younger siblings. Field work was not a stranger to her growing up. According to the tales I grew up with, she fell in love with a lovely man but one who had little ambition and poor health. Not a good combination for a widowed woman in the rural South in the 40's with three mouths to feed. I was told had it not been for Mike, (the colored man) who helped in the 25 acres (that was Mama Pig's dower behind the house), they might not have survived. My mother, Myrtle Rose, was one of her two daughters reared on that 25 acres.

When Mama Pig was growing up, her brothers were sent for their education to universities and medical schools. The kitchen, fields and sewing room were the places of education for my grandmother and her sisters. I cannot decide if she were properly educated for the life that she led or that her "education" took away any choice of lifestyle other than what she lived.

Although some feel that with no formal education and no exposure to the outside world, a human's mind is squelched. My beliefs that even under the thumb of control and not of the learned world, a beautiful mind will come spewing out in one form or another. Although she never understood trigonometry and higher mathematics, she could cut and piece together a jigsaw puzzle of quilt pieces with calculated precision, creating a decorative and useful piece of art. She never fully realized her creative artistic abilities. She could budget on a penny and pick different flour sacks for Mom and Aunt Betty's dresses and with scraps put together the most marvelous kaleidoscope of color in her quilts. She made as necessity, quilts for warmth in the winter, her art.

In her garden again budgeted and calculated to the needs of the family, she interjected flowers that spread, that could be utilized to create the beautiful gardens that I remember as a child. Granny Bailey also had a green thumb, but I don't remember seeing her "playing in the garden" like Mama Pig. This is probably because of her age by then. I have tried to recreate some of her magic in my garden in New Orleans but to no avail. I remember her huge, blue hydragenea bushes in the backyard at the steps to the back porch. We called them Pom Poms. She had beautiful climbing roses crawling up the iron posts on her carport. Every Mother's Day, Easter or other religious holidays, Mom would bring straight pins in the car and we would stop at Mama Pig's on the way to church. Mom would pick and pin a rose to our dresses. She always knew what bloomed when, how to water and fertilize, and always except in the dead of winter had something in bloom. She was able to do what most presidents of Garden Clubs with paid gardeners cannot accomplish.

Another trait she had was being a lovely grandmother. She was strict, but she was always fun. She always put our needs before hers. She made us play outside but supplied a soft quilt in the shade of that old mimosa tree. Later she came out with a tray full of tea cakes warm from the oven. They would have pink and white and green icing and some were pinwheel sugar cookies. This was served with fresh-squeezed lemonade that was as sweet as a bar of candy. You cannot imagine what it felt like waking from a warm slumber on an old worn quilt to those tea cakes and lemonade. "Careful not to spill and bring it in when you are done!" she would say.

She taught us how to swing a bat and I will never forget how she pitched the ball. She opened her mouth in a scowl-like way and threw the ball underhanded, of course. She was always the pitcher for both teams; now I know why!

One of my other 100 favorite stories about Mama Pig is that in the winter if it snowed, Dad would tie a rope to the Red Ryder sled and then at about 10 foot from the sleigh tie the other end to the back of the pickup truck. Mom would sit on the tailgate and take movies of us four children all on the sled, riding down the unplowed country roads. Of course, our destination was two miles down the road to Mama Pig's, where we would warm up on her old floor heater while she made hot chocolate. She made a double boiler with a dish pan and with SUGAR , cocoa and whole milk, which produced a gustatory delight and don't forget the marshmallows!

Her biscuits were also great. She made cheese toast with biscuits and cheese! So yummy! Just as she could piece together a quilt and pieces, she could cut and piece together entire doll villages. She used some combination of flour, water and who knows for our "glue." It must be an early recipe for concrete as they never fell apart, and we had a ball with the sticky mess. This was our indoor activity when it had to be hailing or a tornado to keep us indoors.

A Tribute to Aunt Pritchette
By Elizabeth Shane Emerson French

Personality is not a stranger in the Bailey family. Even having said that, there are those that stand out in my mind. Now I cling to Pat and Larry and Milly for sheer entertainment, but no one stands out like Aunt Pritchette. Her real name being Edith Carmen Bailey. Aunt Pritchette seemed out of this world to me when growing up. In a community that prided itself on Puritan values and to some extent old world trends. She used to take Jimmy and the Emersons and any other cousin that was in that age bracket to Lakeland. (An amusement park east of Memphis.) She saved all her quarters until she had jars and jars of the change. She never spent a quarter but put them up for the Lakeland trip. The rides were set up on the quarter system. All rides and food cost either one quarter or more. You could always tell who had eaten more junk and rode more rides because they were the first to throw up. This was a kind of status symbol to be the first. To get there and back, we rode in the back of the truck with pillows and old quilts to soften the bumpy ride down I-40! Can you imagine that?

My favorite story, however, is that on every Halloween we would get dressed and Mama would drive around Fruitvale and Cypress and we went trick or treating. When we got to the sharp 90 degree corner by Horace Reasons house, Aunt Pritchette would jump out of the ditch dressed as any form of ghost or goblin and run in front of the car. Mom knew to watch for her; it scared us to death but she would always jump around the car like Crazy Motto until we screamed enough and then Mom would tell us, "That is just Aunt Pritchette."We always thought we were going to run over her. When things settled down some, we would roll down the windows and she would have the most amazing treats for us. You could tell that she had spent lots of time picking out just the right things for us. She always had on these long, hairy feet with huge toes. I am not sure who had the most fun, the kids or Aunt Pritchette!

I remember one time after one of those scary nights and Jody was just about three and we all had paper bags with handles and he was such a little guy that his sack was dragging the ground; and when we got home, the bottom of his sack was out and nothing to show for all his trick and treating. You see, it was raining and the bottom of the sack just melted away, carrying his loot with it. The girls decided that they would not share with him because he should have been more careful. Use your imagination as to the end of this tale.

She also used to say the most outrageous things. I wish I could remember some of her antics. Whatever she said was always to push the envelope on what we were taught was right and proper. You could see the gleam in her eyes and the grin on her face as she told tales and made you respond to questions that we knew Mom would not approve of. She was hilarious and always the center of attention. The whole family loved her and especially the kids. Now the children have I-pods, all kinds of games, etc. but they missed the boat not knowing our own Aunt Pritchette!

Milly Remembers
By Milly Ann Emerson Hart

There are so many things that go through my mind about growing up that sometimes they are hard to get them straight. We always had something going and some of the things my parents knew about and some they did not. Of course, I am only writing about what they knew to start with. Some of the things I am writing about may already be in some of the other pages by cousins or siblings. I'm sure we saw them in a different light and may be a little off from other interpretations.

My brother, sisters, Uncle Bill and Aunt June's children always went to Paw Paw Malcolm's every Saturday night. This was very special to all of us, getting away from home and being with our cousins that we loved dearly. I was the youngest of the bunch of eight, and Paw Paw saw that I was not being picked on and had my share of the fun and good eats he had for us. He let us do anything we wanted as long as it did not hurt us or anyone else we encountered. This left us with an open mind to get into some mischief and between eight cousins, there was plenty of thinking going on.

In my family there was Mame', Jody, Shane and me. Our Emerson cousins were Lori, Vince, John and Jill. These are all named in the order of their birth in each family.

I think the favorite stunt we pulled was to kill a snake, and there were plenty of these reptiles around Paw Paw's house since there was a small woods lot and fields behind his house. We would kill the snake and tie his head with clear fishing lines so you could not see his predicament. Then laying him across the drive or road, we waited for a victim; and when they got close enough, we just pulled the line and the snake wiggled across the road and looked good enough to kill again. This was very effective to young and old. I don't suppose there is anyone that would love a snake playing anywhere close. Most of the time the driver of the car would back up and try to run over the slimy thing again to see if he could kill it.

One of the best treats was to go to the store when it was closed and get whatever we wanted to eat. No parents telling us that this or that had too much sugar or it was too close to suppertime to eat anything and ruin our meals. We thought we were being very responsible because we decided to get only what we wanted badly and not overdo and get too much. Weren't we the example of model children? You Bet!

What child of any age has not loved putting coins on the railroad track and getting those flat copper or silver pieces back? We loved to do this and knew most of the train schedules and knew when to put them down and did not have too long to wait for the train whistle and hear the rails groaning and that old train coming on down the railroad track. Choo! Choo!

I realize that this was not very good, but a very bad game to play when our parents were not there, but it sure was fun. We always had a fire in the big fireplace from fall until spring. The bricks on the hearth never got cold. (a good place to warm cold feet) When Mom and Dad would go outside to work, we knew they would not be in anytime soon, and the fire was blazing in the fireplace. We would open the screen and make paper airplanes. Not interesting enough?? Read on............We tied some of Mom's thread on the end of the planes and go up on the playroom steps to the top, then sail those planes right at the blazing fire. When it caught fire, we would yank them out really fast! The one that hit the flames won first. If I saw one of my girls doing this, I would not be easy on them. I still can't believe we did such a dangerous thing.

Emerson conspirators - 1980
John Ollie, Jody Van, Milly Ann,
Elizabeth Shane, Vince, and Jill Emerson

Growing Up...Fruitvale Style
By Jody Emerson

As I look back on my life and the circumstances that "formed" who I am today, it is perhaps both interesting and entertaining to hear from my perspective the people, places and things that played a role in that development. Of all the many places on earth, God placed me in the Joe Emerson family, growing up in Crockett County, Tennessee (Fruitvale - Population 73). As a child you don't have the mental capacity to fully realize, but as I have grown to better understand, I couldn't have been more "blessed" than having been placed in this environment. I was raised by two parents who loved each other and loved me unconditionally. My extended family on both sides were good people that laid an "easy" foundation upon which to grow and mature and fully understand "right from wrong." While I could never recall the millions of events in my life that impacted my persona, I can't help but mention some of the people that played a role in that "molding" process. While there is no way to mention everyone, I'll begin with a few of the most obvious...family and friends alike.

Maw Pig (Elizabeth Bailey Leggett) – I never got the pleasure of knowing my grandfather (Grand-daddy Buster) on my mother's side. I hear he was a very kind, easygoing person that everyone loved. I truly would have liked to know him. I can picture the way he probably would have been by the kind of person I believe my grandmother (Maw Pig) would have fallen for.

Sometimes I believe God mistakenly placed me in the wrong "era" (time) but then, I remember that God doesn't do anything "wrong" and accept things as they are...according to His will. The point I wanted to make was that the "old days" perhaps fit my personality better than "modern times." I like the "old time" traditions, values, principles, etc. I believe that America had its "head screwed on right" in the old days. Not to get off on a passionate tangent, but our country is really screwed up right now. I'm going to stop now before I get totally upset. I'll make this last statement on that subject...we better change our ways as a nation or else we are going down...period. Back to where I was. I like family, simple pleasures, oneness with my maker, etc...some of the things that do not seem to be priorities anymore in our society at large. Even though the old days were laden with hard physical work and tough financial times, I think that forced man to be more reliant on a Supreme authority. Maw Pig, Granddaddy Buster, Granny Bailey, Daddy Jim, Paw Paw and Mimi grew up in this tough but "grounding" era. Must have been gratifying.

While I could literally write a book on the times I spent with Maw Pig, I'll hit some of the high points. I'll tell brief stories starting with a "catch title."

Taega Wums (Tiger Worms)- I'll start off with an amazing story that ranks up there with the best. You can't talk about Maw Pig without talking about her profound love of fishing. I've honestly never known a woman that loved fishing any more than Maw Pig. If Maw Pig had grown up with the resources of say "A *Bill Dance*," she surely would have had the know-how and the heart to give ole Bill a "run for his money." I can see it now in large letters across the base of the TV screen: "Stay tuned for outdoor adventures with Miss Pig of Cypress."

Now pay close attention to my spelling and pronunciation of the following words describing the wiggly, gooey creatures that inhabit the large green leaves of the catalpa (correct spelling) tree. Depending on your upbringing, as these terms are passed on from generation to generation, you would pronounce these larvae in different terms. Daddy and Maw Pig and probably Joe Wayne Spraggins got me to referencing these critters as "Catavie" worms at an early age. The way Maw Pig liked to handle acquiring these bad boys was to watch for the "shotgun pelleted" leaves on the catalpa trees (about the end of June, if I recollect correctly), go out with a bucket, a couple of hoes (the kind you chop cotton with) and as many young 'uns as you could hustle up. You'd shake the limbs of the tree and watch as the sky rained worms for a few seconds. Then, of course, you'd round up the prized ones as they "squirted" green, slimy juice on your hands. Next, you would get the old burlap sack and fill it up with twigs that had clusters of leaves on them, put the worms in the bag and tie it up in a tree in the yard (in the shade, of course.) They would usually live several days this way, and their skin would actually toughen up quite a lot which made them more appealing as the fish would have a much more difficult time "stealing" your bait. I can remember using the same "Catavie" worm to catch 3 or 4 bream if they were "tempered up" properly. I know what you are thinking....sounds like an "art" and you would be correct.

Now we get to the good part of the story. On one occasion, Maw Pig was fishing in one of her favorite holes (small lake about a half-mile west of Bells) when she had an interesting encounter with a couple of young boys that were also trying their luck. Of course, Maw Pig was doing her usual thing with her long cane pole, small bobber, small weight and tiny bream hook. Yes, she was raking them in as fast as you could say, "lickity split." Well, these two youngsters were observing this elderly lady, pulling them in left and right while they were experiencing no luck at all. After a spell, these young "whippersnappers" had had all they could take, so they mustered up enough courage to go and confront this "veteran lady angler" of the fishing world. Now they were familiar with these black and yellow wigglers being used by the intriguing lady and were in a negotiating mood. They said, "Ma'am, could we trade some of our "baits" (slang term for red worms) for some of your "taega wums?" Of course, being the kind, sporty fisherwoman that she was, she promptly obliged. Well, Maw Pig proceeded to slide some of those "baits" that she had just bartered for on her hook and commenced to pulling 'em in again. Well, Maw Pig's new found friends watched again as she reeled 'em in one after another. This entertainment show was simply too much for the lads to swallow. After about thirty minutes of this, the two boys showed back up and very politely asked, "Ma'am, we wuz wundrin if we cud have our baits back." End of a true story...

Christmas Quilts – The second thing I think of when I think of Maw Pig was her love of quilting. I guess she did it all her life; and when you do enough of something, you usually get pretty darn good at it. As far as I'm concerned, Maw Pig was the best. I don't know that much about quilting, but one thing I learned from my mother (also a quilt connoisseur) and grandmother, was that the closer or tighter the stitching, the better. Well, Maw Pig's stitching was very tight.

For several years, I can remember gathering at Maw Pig's house at Christmas and enjoying the fellowship of the family. But you know, if I cut to the chase, the climax of the night was when Maw Pig created a drawing game which ultimately ended up with all of her grandkids (6 at the time) receiving a beautiful quilt as her gift to us. Virginia Reels, Double Wedding Rings, Drunkards Paths, Double Iris Chains, and the list goes on and on. As my sisters, Milly and Shane, and my cousins, Steve, Barry and Richard, would agree, this was probably the highlight of Christmas. We were receiving the heart and soul of our very talented grandmother. Something that she had buried her heart in and was able to pass on to her grandchildren. To this day, the most cherished, tangible things I own are my quilts that were constructed by my family. Don't ask for a selling price because none of them are for sale...period.

Ferguson's Pond – If you ever went fishing with Maw Pig in the 60's and 70's, chances are you went with her to Ferguson's Pond (about a couple of miles north of Gadsden.) I believe this was her most favorite fishing hole of all. Today, I could make a complete aerial layout of the pond and could point out all of Maw Pig's favorite spots. She loved catching bream on a cane pole and you better believe she was doggone good at it. I'll give you a few of her secrets that have stuck with me all these years. Make sure you use a relatively small hook, cover the entire hook (shank included) with your bait of preference and use a bobber that barely will hold the weight of the bait, hook and sinker suspended. Maw Pig had three main fish enticers...common red worms, catalpa worms and don't forget weed worms. My opinion is that if weed worms were available (they are seasonal), she would prefer these wiggly creatures over all others. I tend to agree with her. Weed worms (they come from giant ragweed in the heat of summer) were the best. For whatever reason, the bream really seemed to like weed worms the best. As an added plus, the weed worms were just "tough enough" that they were difficult to steal from the hook. This often led to multiple catches with the same worm.

Don't think you were ever going to throw your catch back into the pond. If you caught it, you took it home. 'Course, when you got home, you had to find someone to give the goods to. This was usually not a problem.

Paw Paw (Malcolm Hooper Emerson) - When I get together with any of my first cousins on Daddy's side, at some point I usually say the following words or some variation thereof: I should write a book on the many escapades about the Emerson clan on Saturday nights at Paw Paw's. I'm not sure when or how it started, but as long as I can remember when we were growing up, we spent Saturday nights at Paw Paw's. Probably came about out of necessity for Mom (Myrtle Leggett Emerson), Dad (Joe Silas Emerson), Uncle Bill (Mack Boyd Emerson), and Aunt June (June Stephens Emerson) to keep their sanity...now you're wondering that was to be taken as a joke or not? Anyway, Paw Paw loved us but pretty much let us do whatever we wanted to. Some of the stories will be "incomplete" to protect the guilty against imprisonment.

Bonfire in the Road - When you are bored as a teenager, what do you do for excitement....why not build a "bonfire" in the middle of the road? Now, granted the roads in Fruitvale, Tennessee, in the late 60's and early 70's were not comparable to Summer Avenue in Memphis, but there was the occasional pickup or car passing through after a night out. We built it in the road basically right out in front of Paw Paw's driveway and Ben and Neever's (Miss Geneva) driveway. Looking back, this was not very smart. I don't know exactly what we were thinking...or maybe we weren't. I think Uncle Bill (about 1/2 mile away) may have spotted the "glow" in the night before Paw Paw even knew about it. I think cousins Vince and John ended up getting a nice "whoopin" out of the deal. I was just praying that Uncle Bill didn't tell Daddy. To this day, I don't know if he did or not; however, it might be safe to assume that since I didn't get a "butt burning" out of the deal that Uncle Bill probably refrained from telling Pop.

"Talking Possum" in the Walnut Tree - While this one falls into the "you had to be there to appreciate it" category, I still can't talk about events at Paw Paw's without including this one. It must have been in the fall because the walnuts were transitioning from green to drying down and falling from the tree. There was a walnut tree on the field and yard border southwest of Ben and Neever's house. John, Vince and I decided it would be "neat" to line the walnuts end to end across the road and hide in the bushes and see what happened when cars came zooming through the thriving metropolis of Fruitvale. We retrieved a few walnuts from the ground but didn't quite get enough to stretch plum across the road; therefore, someone had to climb the tree, shake the limbs and knock more walnuts to the ground. I don't know if we drew straw, played rock scissor paper or called out any minnie-miney-mo, but somehow John came out on the losing end of the venture. Problem is, before we could completely finish up and allow John to get down out of the tree, here comes a pickup truck pulling another vehicle with a chain (this was a very, very common thing back in those days). So here John is stuck up in the tree while Vince and I crouch down in the edge of the soybean field and look on. Brrr....Brrr....Brrr....Balup....Balup....Crack!!!! The walnuts had forced enough slack in the chain and the lead truck jerked hard enough that the chain cracked and snapped right into. Needless to say, the occupants of the two vehicles were not happy campers. This was not a difficult situation for them to figure out and they commenced to search out the perpetrators. It was right at dusk and the leaves were obviously off the walnut tree, so John had nowhere to hide. Yep, they spotted John and proceeded to taunt him. One of them states, "Look, there's a possum in that tree."

John nervously responded by saying, "I'm not a possum," to which the unhappy motorist responded, "Ohhhhhhh, it's a talking possum." True story! I don't think the parents ever knew about this one.

Golf Cart Racetrack – Once upon a time, Paw Paw messed up and bought a golf cart and kept it at his home in Fruitvale, Tennessee, for his grandkids to ride around on. I'm sure it ended up being one of those "What was I thinking" moments for Paw Paw. If you've ever seen Paw Paw's house and front yard, you would understand when I say that it was a great place for teenage kids to "build a race track." We would zoom down the long hill on the north side of the big front yard only to make a sharp left at the base of the hill just before barreling off into the road. The first time or two we did this was no problem; however, after about the 50th pass and after a few rainy spells in the fall, Paw Paw's front yard looked like the Daytona 500 Track in "mud" form. The most fun we had with this operation was for a couple of us to hang onto the bumper of the cart and literally drag behind the contraption until we hit the mighty curve at the base of the hill. At this point, as the driver cut sharply to the left, we would let go and allow the cart to "sling" us sideways tumbling down the hill. I'm telling you right now, this was"mucho funo" for a bunch of teen and pre-teen kids. Yeeee....Haaaaa!

Fantastic Features – Sivad – Do you quite possibly remember these words..."Gooooooood Evening, I am your host, Sivad (Davis spelled backward)...Welcome to Fantastic Features." I remember sitting on the couch not wanting to be on the outside (wanted siblings and/or cousins on both sides of me as I shivered in fright.) Then a movie such as "The Mummy," "Dracula," and "Creature from the Black Lagoon" or "Dawn of the Dead" would come on. I'm telling you....this was exciting torture for a kid! Couldn't get enough of it though!!

Hotcakes – Every Sunday morning (after having spent the night at Paw Paw's) our grandfather would wake us up to the sound of "All right, who's number 1," then a couple of minutes later you'd hear, "Who's number 2" and so forth and so on. This was the Emerson way of ringing the breakfast bell. Paw Paw made good "hotcakes" as he called them with a side of bacon and Dr. Pepper to drink. Talk about a sugar overload!!

Jody Van Emerson, Milly Ann Emerson, and Elizabeth Shane Emerson - 1994

We, however, had no problem working the carbohydrates off. By the way, he offered us up "Brer Rabbit dark syrup, Karo dark syrup or Karo light syrup" from the Fruitvale store. I preferred the Karo light syrup. To this day, I prefer Karo light syrup on my "hotcakes" (if'n I have the choice.)

Olivia Remembers

When I was small, I thought that all boys were older than girls. This was until John was born and he was younger than Mame'.

I remember when Mimi always put bonnets on us when we went outside, and they were made out of old quilts with trim put on them. I would wear them without a fuss, but Maggie would scream and cry and refuse to wear them; she hated them so bad.

When I was really little, my favorite book was Dr. Seuss's Foot Book. It was this book about counting feet and the different sizes and shapes of them. Mimi would always read it to me. I knew every word in that book and I couldn't even read then.

Silas and I used to take all the bikes and tricycles and things apart and try to put them back together again by putting bicycle wheels on the front of tricycles, etc. We came up with some odd looking things, but some of them worked and we could ride them.

Mimi and PaPa did not allow animals in the house. Whenever they would get really busy, we would sneak the kittens in the back door and take them upstairs. It was fun.

Mimi bought a red wagon like the old timey ones for us to play with and she loved the red flyer color. We did not know how much until we took all the different colors of spray paint we could find in the barn and painted it all over with just spray here and there and everywhere. That is when we found out how much she loved the RED wagon.

At Christmas all the kids would eat really fast and go peek into our presents. We could not open them until we had finished our dinner. It was like a race to see who could open their gifts faster and see what we had. Mimi and PaPa always wrapped everything in separate boxes so we would have bunches of things to open.

While Mimi and PaPa were watching TV, we would get behind their chairs and put hair gel and hairspray all in their hair and put bobby pins and hairpieces on them and see how funny we could make them look. It took forever for them to wash it all out!

Another spray paint job was to get PaPa's lumber and spray it all colors; and when he got ready to use it, he sometimes had to paint the whole piece before he could use it.

Whenever Mimi would take pictures of us while we were eating, we would all shove food in our mouths and as soon as she was about to take the picture, we would make ugly faces and open our mouths full of food... Ugh!

Mimi hates frogs. At one of the family dinners, we put a frog on her head and it jumped in her salad! Oh, my!

French's Fables
By Rebecca French

I was bored one day at our farm in Mississippi, so I got out some scissors and took my little sister, Flora, and cut her bangs! I didn't think anyone could notice it, but Mom spotted it right away! Ugh! I thought it looked good myself!

Once my family (John, Flora, Mom and Dad) went to Florida and Mom wanted to make pies, (chocolate and coconut cream). The recipe was from my great-great Granny Bailey. When Mom asked Flora if she knew how to separate eggs, Flora said "Sure." She took one egg, cracked it into her hand, pulled the whites away from the yolk with the other, making it all mix into a yucky mess in her hand. That's one way to do it! Ha, Ha, Ha!

When we were having some work done on our house and the men were blowing some fluffy insulation into the walls, Flora walked up to the men and asked, "Did you get this cotton from Tennessee?" She had just been visiting her family there, and it just happened to be in the fall when the farmers were picking the white stuff there.

John John, being the little "man" around the house, always questioned his mother about her decisions. Most of these doubts would arise when they were in the car traveling. His questions went a lot like this—."Mom, do you know where we are going? Mom, do you have enough gas to get us there?'—Mom, are you driving over the speed limit?—Mom, do you have enough money with you to buy our lunch?"— and on and on the questions would go. Never what you would expect a six or seven-year old to ask, like his toys or his pet, etc.

My Favorite Stories
By John Fenner French, Jr.

I remember we had the most fun in the cotton trailer at Aunt Milly's house. She always had a full trailer waiting for us and we would jump and roll in the cotton, and have "cotton" fights and sometimes even take naps in it. We made a big mess with it too because we would throw it at each other and big handfuls would go out on the ground, but Aunt Milly never fussed at us about it.

Another fun thing for us was riding in the gator at PaPa and Mimi's house. We would always fight over who was going to drive but finally learned that we had to take turns. We were not supposed to drive it fast; but when the adults were not looking, we could make it go pretty fast. There was always 5 or 6 in it all the time, and we would go round and round the house about a million times a day.

The skateboards were fun, too, on the hill in back of Mimi's house. She did not like this much because they went down the hill so fast, and we were always falling off them, or running into each other down the hill, but it was really fun.

My Fun Stories
By Flora Elizabeth French

I am the youngest of PaPa and Mimi's grandchildren and can usually get my way with things from them and my bigger cousins and family. I really don't mean to get into things, but sometimes you just can't help it.

I know we all really loved the cotton in the trailers, and Aunt Milly always made sure we had one when we came to Tennessee. Aunt Milly always had the neatest things for us to do at her house. She usually played with us, and sometimes at night we had scary things to do outside and she was always there with us.

At Mimi's we had a blanket chest full of dress-ups and we always had fun dressing up in fancy clothes and old Halloween costumes. She had old evening dresses for us, too. We took old quilts and blankets and made tents and fairy houses. We always made big messes at Mimi's house.

Kayley Mame' and Maggie Leigh
Combined Words

I can't tell who wrote what in this section but most was by Kayley and Maggie and I see whiffs of Olivia in there, too. I'm sure that Rebecca was in on it although she did write some on her own.

We had this water toy that hooked up to the water hose and it was in the likeness of a gopher. It spewed water all around, and then this gopher head would pop up and really throw the water at us. Our main "act" with this contraption was to pretend we didn't have a clue that the culprit was about to jump at us with gallons of water. Surprise, surprise!

There was this grape arbor behind the barn that had these dark purple grapes and we loved eating this fruit until we were full and then we had some good old times throwing them at each other and making purple stains on everyone's cloth.

Mimi and PaPa cut the labels on top of the chest freezer in the utility room and had to cover it with big sheets of white cardboard to keep from ruining the top of the freezer. We loved using this as an art pad and drew every single space with our writings and pictures so that our grandparents had to change the cardboard every time we came, which was almost every day. We signed our names and drew cartoons and X and O games for hours.

We knew that Mimi was picky about her computer because that was her way to communicate with her family and friends and did not like for us to play on it. When she got busy with fixing a meal or sewing, we would go in the utility room where it was and close the door, and she wouldn't know it for a long time and by then, we were usually through with it anyway.

Dress up was one of our favorite play times. There was a quilt box full of old dresses and evening gowns and Halloween costumes that we could put together any kind of outfit. We put on fashion shows and outdid ourselves. Our favorite outfit was an old, white long dress and we pretended we were getting married and live happily after. (Lots to learn here.) We even had some old high heels that really did a job on our feet!

Mimi was always sewing and we always wanted to sew too, so she would give us squares of fabric and show us how to close up the sides and made pillows. We tried to sell some but they did not do too well. I don't know why!

Maggie and Silas used to be adventurous. They would slip around and build fires behind the barn and "cook" things like frogs. They did gross things with those fires. Halloween all year long!

The gator was and still is one of our favorite things. We got old quilts and pillows and put in the back and rode around and around the house because we were not allowed to get on the road. This went on until there was usually a fight over whose time it was to drive. Silas always considered himself as the main person in the gator because he was the only male in the bunch. He took things in his own hands and hid the keys to the gator and the lawnmowers, which the kids used as "cars" when the gator was ailing. Something else that always picked a good fight!

Mimi has never been a fan of bikinis, especially when one of the grandchildren bought one. Kayley got this really neat suit and it was a little skimpy and Mimi had a fit and said she was going to burn it and Kayley cried and cried...The bikini stayed!

When no adults were watching us, we would get the gator and run it up on this trailer and put dolleys at the end and run the gator off down the end and make it bump pretty bad and shaky. I know now that this was not the safest thing we could play with, but at the time it was fun and scary at the same time.

When we were just totally broke, we tried our hand at a lemonade stand every summer. We set it up in the front of Mimi and PaPa's house and at the time there was not much traffic there. We had some of the neighbors that stopped (We know this now) just out of pity and give us twice the 25 cents we were asking because there seemed to be a depression going on in the lemonade business.

At Christmas time we always had bunches of gifts with our names on them. We would go into the living room and move all ours in one place and in piles. We were not supposed to touch them until after dinner on Christmas Eve but who could resist and, to be honest, we wanted to see if we all had the same number of boxes. Never you mind what was inside, but opening them up was the fun part. But this arranging the gifts made for a faster access to your things if they were all in one place.

We did not think of ourselves as being too messy but once we had some leftover brownies and decided the best thing to do with these leftovers was to have a food fight. Messy, messy, messy! (We were very considerate though! We did go out on the porch for the war!)

PaPa was always a good target for our "games." One of our favorite things to do to him was to catch him unaware and steal his wallet out of his back pocket. Sometime he knew it but sometimes he didn't. (Or he pretended not to know.)

PaPa spanked Silas when he was little because he did a wee wee on Maggie's leg. PaPa had never spanked any of us, and we knew right then and there, this was NOT something that would be tolerated in the Emerson family. I guess it just seemed like a fun thing to do at the time. Silas must have been about three at the time and trying out his abilities.

All of us grandchildren used to take baths together when we were all little and could squeeze in. Mimi would always tell us to be sure and wash our too toos and our boo boos to get clean. That is sure some good advice! Ha Ha Ha!

We always loved to be naked when we were little. Maggie and Kayley proved this one rainy day in the summer. Silas was just a baby and Mimi was sitting on a bench giving him his bottle, and it had just come a big shower and there were puddles of water everywhere. Just behind her, there was a dandy one. The little girls came to Mimi and asked if they could take their shoes off. Sure, it was ok to take their shoes off and wade in the puddle, and Mimi and Silas just might join them wading when he got full. Several minutes passed and the girls got louder and louder just laughing and giggling and Mimi decided she had better investigate. I mean, water is fun but silly fun? What she found behind her was two little naked girls holding hands jumping up and down splashing and dancing a jig in that water! The term, "Give them and inch and they will take a mile" came to mind. Mimi slipped in the house and got the camera, and that picture turned out to be one of the best she ever made. The whole family had to have a copy and many of them are framed.

We loved to wear Mimi's bras and underwear and model them. They were a "little" too big, but who cared and it was good for a good laugh when the family came in.

We always had popcorn in little green bowls when we watched movies at PaPa and Mimi's house. Our favorites were "Matilda," "The Little Rascals," "The Little Mermaid," and many others.

PaPa always had an old freezer full of water and minnows for fishing that he kept in the barn. We were not supposed to bother the minnows. They were very dear to him. My, oh my, but who could resist such a treat at such a small age? We had lookouts on duty when we chased those fish around and around the freezer.

When we were four years old, we had this pink Barbie car at PaPa and Mimi's. There were the two of us and so many other children our age that played in it that it was always broken down. We always fought over who got to drive it first and if that person's time had run out and I think the grandparents were glad when we finally outgrew it. Then Santa brought Silas a dump truck that went a little faster than the pink car, and he was really not very happy to share it with a bunch of girls.

PaPa and Mimi have this huge fireplace in the den and always kept a fire in it. We just loved to throw things in it and, of course, we had been told time and time again that it was a "no no" and too dangerous; however, at Christmas we were allowed to throw the old wrapping paper in it with the adults watching us, but this kind of slowed down the fun of it all. Then, too, the year the chimney caught fire from too much paper and all the neighbors came running over when they saw the flames roaring out the chimney.

We used to play with these long things in the back of PaPa's old Expedition. I don't remember what they were, but we made out like they were guns and we were cops going down the highway chasing robbers and shooting everything in sight.

Maggie got the scissors out one day and decided that I (Kayley) needed a haircut. We hid at the bottom of the stairs in the living room and she cut this big hunk of my hair off on just one side. We combed it around and thought that no one would notice it, but my mom sure did!

We are seventeen and eighteen now and just got back from a family vacation in Europe and had a great time but thought we would jot down some downers that happened while we were away:

...We lost Papa at the airport.
...Got delayed until one a.m. at one airport and hours at another causing us to miss ourNashville plane and having to stay another day.
...Missed the boat in Germany and had to chase it down the Rhine.
...Brought all the wrong seasonal clothes.
.   ...The taxi took us to the wrong hotel and we lost hours.
...Jody got detained at Paris Airport because of Swiss knives for gifts.
...Mimi and PaPa were in the middle of the road in traffic.
...Went to McDonald's in Cologn and Jody walked into a glass wall.
...Ruined half Mimi's pictures by making crazy faces in them.
...A lady started yelling at Olivia, Rebecca, and others in a hotel but did not make anydifference because they did not know a word she was saying. French to them!
...As soon as I walked out the door in London, the wind blew my umbrella inside out. *(Kayley)*

Memories of PaPa and Mimi
By Silas Austin Emerson

As the only male grandson in Tennessee of PaPa and Mimi Emerson, I probably got by with more than my share of trouble. I know that my cousin Olivia and I are close to the same age, and we thought of and did lots of things that were not in the book of things we should do, but in the naughty book instead. If there was anything at PaPa's barn that could be painted, we painted it! Mimi always had lots of spray paint for her Santas, and we loved spreading that stuff on everything. It was so easy to make a mess with it and we could not resist. I know the red wagon was a mistake because we hit a nerve with Mimi on that one! She loved it so much because it was just like the one she had when she was a little girl. The shed walls, Papa's lumber, and the shelves all became targets of many colors.

The Gator was my favorite thing. Maggie and Kayley thought that since they were bigger than Olivia and me, they should be in charge of this vehicle, but we knew how to manage a few tear and sob stories to Mimi and came out with more than our share of "the driver!"

We all loved to go into the kitchen and "borrow" candy and cookies that Mimi kept there; and when she came out to serve us some, we were usually about to pop from all the sugar we had "borrowed."

We used to love to take off all our clothes and play in the water out back and really were bummed when Mimi decided we were getting a little too old for that. The water was just not as much fun with clothes on!

Olivia and I made the strangest things out of old bicycles and tricycles, but some really were fun. It was PaPa's job to try to put them back together and he soon tired of this, so one day he let us know the "hard way."

Now we are all getting more grown up and still love to be together and try out new things on our grandparents. They really don't see as much now on things that we pull, because they are older, but love us all the more.

Joe and Myrtle Emerson and "their bunch" at the Vatican - 2010

Maggie Leigh, Rebecca Emerson, Elizabeth Shane, Jody Van, Kayley Mamç, Olivia Rose, Myrtle Rose, and Joe Silas Emerson

Elizabeth Shane and Milly Ann Emerson welcome Patrice, an exchange student

Jody Van Emerson and sister Milly Ann

Emersons -2009

Front: Flora Elizabeth French, Rebecca Emerson French, John Fenner French Jr.

Second: Myrtle Emerson, Maggie Leigh Hart, Olivia Rose Hart, Chelsie Harris, Joe Silas Emerson

Third: Jody Van Emerson, Milly Ann Hart, Kayley Mame Emerson, Silas Austin Emerson Back: John Fenner French, Elizabeth Shane French

Joe and Myrtle Emerson's Children: Mame' Lou, Elizabeth Shane, Jody Van, and Milly Ann Emerson

Mame' Lou Emerson

Jody Van Emerson, Milly Ann Emerson, and Elizabeth Shane Emerson - 1994

301

In The Cotton Trailer – 2003
Rebecca and John John

"Here's looking at you, Mimi!"
Flora Elizabeth, Rebecca Emerson, John Fenner, Kayley Mame, Olivia Rose, Maggie Leigh, Silas Austin (above)

The Little Red Wagon before the new paint job – 2003
Kayle Mame, FLora Elizabeth, Olivia Rose, Silas Austin, John Fenner (below)

Visiting Paw Paw
Kelsey, Noel, Hannah, Josie, Olivia, Kayley, Maggie and Silas
Standing: Jody, Vince, and Paw Paw (above)

"Filling PaPa's Shoes"
Silas Austin Emerson
1995

"Million dollar grin!"
Maggie Leigh Hart 1992

Cousins at Easter – Rebecca, Olivia, John
John, Rachel, Silas, Kayley, and Maggie

Maggie Leigh and Olivia Rose Hart, Kayley
Mame', and Silas Austin Emerson – 2000

"In the cotton trailer" – 2006
John Fenner French Jr., Rebecca
Emerson French, and Flora
Elizabeth French

Swinging Babies – 2000
Shane holding John John, Kayley, Olivia, Rebecca, Silas, and Maggie

*"Cousin Happiness"
2006*

*Back: Olivia, Silas,
Rebecca*

Front: Flora, John John

*2006 – Front: John Fenner French Jr.,
Maggie Leigh Hart, Flora Elizabeth French,
Kayley Mame Emerson
Back: Olivia Rose Hart, Rebecca Emerson
French, Silas Austin Emerson (below)*

1997 Wedding

*Front: Maggie Leigh Hart, Kayley Mame
Emerson
Back: Shane Emerson French, Olivia
Rose Hart, Rachel Ann Hart, Silas Austin
Emerson*

CHAPTER 15

Cypress Methodist Church the way it looks now

Cypress Methodist Church

My Church, God and Me

In a world plagued by wars, drugs, greed and unease, we can all find peace and guidance in our churches. Our little country church of Cypress is certainly no exception. It's existence has given me hope and peace and happiness for my whole 73 years of life. The existence of Cypress Church came into being through the efforts and faith of many of my forefathers, giving me deeply embedded roots through continuance. This church is the core of this book.

There are many stories and different ages of time and places included in these pages, but everything seems to come back to my beginnings at this small country church just down the road from where I was "brought up" and will always be home to me wherever I may go or wherever I roam. All roads do not lead to Rome to me, but to Cypress Church as each story here at some point has a connection to this place of worship. The church seems to be sowing grain and, "the Seeds are still Growing!" The saying that "Home is where the heart is" and my heart belongs to Cypress Methodist Church.

Church, God and Me

I have tried to think of a way to express what the Cypress Church has and does mean to me. It has been a center for my life since the day I was born; not one quarter of a mile down the road from it seventy-three years ago. This church has been a worship building for so long as described in other pages in this collection of memories. Always a place to worship our God and a place for our community to gather and share their joy and sorrow to make the congregation one body in Christ. It was and is the

305

core of the people of Cypress, Fruitvale, Liberty Hall, some from Bells, some from Alamo and surrounding areas. It makes all these communities one.

I recall that the church did not have a porch when I first knew it. It had evolved from the log structure to a number of different boarded buildings through the years. When you went inside the church, the pulpit was not in the center of the back, where it is now. The choir loft was to the right of the entrance. There is a picture of this seating that I have. You went in straight and then the aisle turned to the right, leaving the pulpit centered on the north wall and the choir behind this.

Included in these papers is a history of the church and the founding of the cemetery fund by Aunt Bettie Bailey.

I started playing the piano at church as a teenager that hardly knew one note from the other but learned a lot as time went by and finally I played by chords and always played in flats. Do not ask me why I could not play sharps. I just simply could not do it; and since there was no music but my piano, I simply changed the sharps to flats and do not know how to do this now, but then I could look at the sharps and know how many flats to play to make the song correct to me. When we got the first organ, it was sitting on the platform on Homecoming Day, and I had never been that close to any organ, let alone play one. The Superintendent stood behind the pulpit and presented the new organ to the congregation and added that Myrtle Rose would now play us a solo on the new organ to demonstrate its many wonders. It never dawned on me to say simply that I could not play an organ, but I turned (I will never forget that song and do not like it to this day.) the page to "Sweet Hour of Prayer," struggled and panted through the whole thing and acted like I didn't know that I hadn't hit too many right notes. The congregation was very quiet for a few seconds and they burst into applause. Bless them all!!

In early church years I recall that it was customary for the preacher to eat lunch each Sunday with a different member's family. This one particular preacher loved ice cream, and the mothers always made an attempt to have some homemade cream just for his pleasure. As soon as he was presented with a bowl of the cold stuff, he would reach for the black pepper and proceed to blacken his dessert with it. I do not remember any certain sermon or good works he did, but I will never forget watching him ruin a perfectly good bowl of ice cream with black pepper.

When I was twelve years old, we had our revival or "Big Meeting" as the old timers called it. The preacher preached an unusually good sermon, or I had paid more attention to what he was saying and I could feel goose bumps all over me and became very agitated and felt hot. I realized that God was calling and talking to me. That was when I knew without a doubt what becoming a Christian was all about.

I had another similar experience when going to Rome with the Girl Scouts and going to an old church where the steps that Jesus walked up to face Pontius Pilate. A wife of one of the Caesars had had these steps moved to Rome. A good friend and I had taken a side Christian tour to the Catacombs and then to see these steps. By the time we got to the church, I was so very tired and did not know what was going on. We got back to the bus and asked my friend what was going on in the old church with so many people crying and crowding around. I had thought it was just another old church to see the architecture. She then told me about the steps story. I stood up and said I was going back across the street and touch those steps. I was informed that the bus was loaded and the driver did not have time to wait for me. I just told them to go on and I was not going anywhere until I had touched those steps. I got off the bus with my friend following me saying, "We have to get back on the bus." We did go back in and we did touch those steps. I once again had those goose bumps and felt God talking to me. I have never regretted "getting out of line" for the experience. Oh, by the way, the bus did wait and never a word was said, and my friend and I had the best day of our trip right there in that old church.

Lesson: Never give up on a feeling that you know is right in your heart. Follow your heart!

Cypress Church History

The deed for the land to build another church was filed on December 12, 1871, at 2:00 in the afternoon. The agreement for the sale between A.C. MC Millan of Haywood County to James Emmison, J.C. Bowls, William Emmison and Daniel Layman, church trustees for the ME Church South at Cypress on the Cagevile Circuit, Memphis Conference. This land was obtained for thirty dollars.

Cypress Methodist Church was organized in 1831 as the Methodist Episcopal Church South. Charter members were James Emison, William Emison, John Emison, Robert Emison, Benjamin Emison, Susan Emison Laman and Daniel Laman.

It had its beginning in a 20' x 30' one-room log cabin that had formerly been used by a Baptist congregation as their house of worship, and it stood a few yards from the present church site of what is now the churchyard in the northeast corner. For some reason, the Baptist congregation had discontinued using it for worship. The Methodists took over the old cabin church, and most of the people of surrounding miles made up the whole of its members and worship services there. Thus, the first Cypress Church began meeting there and the first Cypress Church was built. During the Civil War, the building was used for a sleeping place for soldiers passing through. In later years it burned down, and it is believed to have been approximately one hundred and ten years old then. This is information gathered by Erin Leggett and I believe this to be accurate, knowing how well versed this lady was on history and its facts.

Since this first church of the old log cabin burned, three church buildings have been erected on the very spot where the present church now stands. Erin Leggett remembered quite well the first of those buildings, although it was an old building when she was young.

This first "new" church was only one room in size (35' x 56') but quite large. It had three rows of seats that were only a few feet from the pulpit all the way back to the front of the church and had two doors close to last pew that opened on the front of the structure. The ceilings were high and a choir loft with the pulpit raised on a loft. A door on one side of this dais opened to the backyard and cemetery. The light being brought in was the only light except the kerosene lamps with reflectors that hung all along the walls and the back of the choir loft allowing for night church services.

The floors of the building were wide planks nailed down with square-headed nails. There were never any carpets on the floors.

Erin Leggett was only a child about twelve years old when she first began attending worship services there with her family. She recorded early memories of revivals held there at the end of summer and lasted for two full weeks. The wooden floors were covered with straw in front of the pulpit with a long bench on each side of the straw, which made a "Mourner's Bench" for after the altar call for people to come and pray. This bench was often filled with people praying for loved ones or forgiveness for their shortcomings. The revival was a wake-up call for these country people that were seeking God and the good life for them. The "mourners" that lined the bench on the straw were often moved to shouting and hallelujahs as they were converted, and there was much moving around the church as all the people were moved to express their joy. These members were not embarrassed to show their feelings of exhilaration and joy that moved them when God spoke to them to witness their emotions. What would happen today if we all witnessed in such a wondrous, happy way and showed our feelings bursting out? Would it not be an expression that could show others what happiness God could project into our lives?

Of course, there was the essential fixture in the center of the church. The old potbelly stove that was a source of warmth and comfort in an old building without any insulation or airtight windows and doors. I suppose there was always a little breeze coming through the structure that in the summer months was a plus.

The old church burned to the ground in about 1907. The congregation then built yet another one-room house of worship in the same spot. This later building was considerably larger than the one before it. It was more modern and comfortable. The ceilings were high and the benches had high backs to them, making them pews rather than benches. Still, there was no electricity to light and heat the church, so the oil lamps and lanterns were still a necessity. The purchase of an organ made the services more interesting and entertaining and thus the membership grew.

Mr. John Emerson was a member at this time and he was a talented man. He made coffins, chairs, and tables, etc. out of solid oak and crafted a new pulpit for the new church of this wood. He had a workshop at his home, not far from the church toward Fruitvale. He was very faithful to the church and its needs with his work and his faith.

With a new organ, the music became an important part of the services and there were two teen-aged girls who took music lessons in order to play the hymns. The "old timey" pedal organ was first played by a music teacher, and then the two young girls took lessons and became the musicians each Sunday for the hymns. These two ladies were Ada Goldsmith and Ethel Emerson, who both lived in the community. Erin Leggett was one of the first singers in the choir.

As luck would have it, this building was thrown off its foundation by a violent storm. The men in the church repaired it and services were resumed, but the condition of the building proved to be unstable and was eventually torn down. Membership had grown to the point that finances were soon available for a new church. This one was still larger and more modern than the last. At this time the annual Homecoming came into being, and the funds from this day were a big addition to the regular offerings.

These members will always be remembered for their work and dedication, which is only right. They still have descendents in the church now, and ones that live away always come home to Cypress at some point if only for a visit. With help from the Methodist Conference and much help from Bettie Elizabeth Bailey (Aunt Bettie to everyone, whether kin or not) who went all around the county collecting money for building purposes. She was very successful in her endeavors.

In raising the money for the old church, Aunt Bettie named several ladies and assigned them routes to take and families to approach for donations. She told her "workers" that if the family could not contribute fifty cents or a dollar (money being hard to come by and a penny was worth so much in those days) that surely they could send a chicken to be put in the pot to be sold for pennies. She listed some names that contributed to this fund. They were Mrs. L.C. Craig – fifty cents; James Seth Bolton – one dollar; J.C.W. Nunn – one dollar; Limon Lewis – fifty cents; Lon Lewis – one dollar; J.C. Forsythe and wife – fifty cents; Mrs. Marlow – fifty cents; Sidney Permenter – one dollar; Brad Webb – one dollar; Superintendant Lowery – one dollar; Alice Marcum – fifty cents; Tennie Laman – fifty cents; and Mrs M.J. Williams – one dollar. This collection was in 1919. Thanking one and all, I am your friend, *Bettie E. Bailey.*

While the church building that was thrown off its foundation was still being used, it became imperative that the congregation build a newer and safer building. The church was being used for so many purposes as weddings, box suppers, receptions and even for political meetings; it had to go and was torn down in 1910. Yet another one room church was constructed and was similar to the others but was more modern and quite a bit larger. It did not cost as much since the older church had just been moved off its foundation and the lumber, etc. was still good and was used over in the newer one. Then, too, much of the work was done by church members and even non-members that were able-bodied members of the community. The men did have a professional carpenter to oversee the building. His name was a Mr. Speight.

The people were very proud of their new worship facility, being the third church, and it grew steadily, financially and spiritually.

For many years, the church has been in a circuit with Gadsden, Cypress, Center and Pond Creek, all having the same pastor the Methodist Conference appointed. The parsonage was located in Alamo. Pond Creek pulled away, leaving three churches on the circuit.

For years after this new church was finished, it was used as it was built but eventually partitions were built, making two added classrooms. Soon other improvements were made. The M.Y.F. designed and had made a china plate with the image of the church on the front and a brief history of the church on the back side. Many members still possess these treasured plates.

Brother John Batsel was pastor along the line and had a steeple constructed over the front of the church, but many members did not like it and was finally taken down.

All these years the choir had been on the north side of the sanctuary with the pulpit in front of it.

Another pastor, Brother Graves, encouraged a new carpet and seat cushions with corresponding covers to the carpet, and this was readily installed and a red velvet curtain put behind. They then moved the choir to the west side of the sanctuary.

Mr. Hosea Body donated a huge bell and had it put on a concrete slab to the south of the church. Several older ladies had wanted it to be installed in a bell tower over the entrance to the church, but this never happened. They compromised and put a cross in the bricks on the front over the porch. The entrance lights up and shows the cross for miles and miles.

This brings us to the modern Cypress Church today, where a new gymnasium and kitchen and side porch have been added with much love. The old kitchen has been converted into a lovely pre-school room with the old cabinets from the kitchen re-done and making room for the children's tools. There are Sunday School rooms for the teens over the gym entrance. The kitchen and the gymnasium floors are covered with tables and chairs for the many church meals and cake auctions held there. The seats are sometimes filled to capacity with people having to go to other rooms to eat their meals. We have the ladies making cakes to auction off for different charities or events and they are a wonder to behold – some going for over a hundred and fifty dollars. I've forgotten what flavor it was, but it looked good to a lot of people. We have been blessed with the Cypress Methodist Church...there is no doubt.

I realize that most of the records and personal information about the people have either been lost or probably not even recorded. All we can do is rely on the writings of our older generation and hope they got things right.

The story of the Stained Glass in Cypress Church is pretty much recorded as it happened. We know some of them were added in the last few years and were put up by the same company that put the first one in, and they had records of them with their archives. The later ones were made by this company with the same colors and style of colored glass used in the original ones. Representatives of that company came out and examined the old ones to be sure they matched. All the windows were filled in with stained glass, and none were available to install the colors in. Joe and I put one in over the door coming into the sanctuary on the inside hall looking into the main building,

since there was no place to put a memorial for our daughter, Mame'. When the new gym was put in, there was a small hall connecting it to the old part of the church, and they had to move one old window put in for Dr. James Bailey and his wife, Nancy. There was room for two more when this hall was built. Joe and I and his brother and wife, Bill and June, put in windows for our daughter Mame' and John, their son.

The window story actually began in 1968 when Brother Harold Graves was our preacher, and most of the windows were put in at this date for memorials of different families. The windows came from Memphis "Binswanter Glass Company." The sales lady, Mickey Laukhauf, made more than one trip to Cypress to direct the installation of these beautiful windows.

Dinner plate with Cypress Church on it sold by M. Y. F. to raise funds for church

Personalities of the Pulpit

As much in order as I can, I will record the names of the pastors and the years in which they served.

Rev. Stratton – 1908
Rev. Rudd
Rev. V.S. McCaslin

Rev. Suggs
Rev. O.H. Moore
Rev. E.L. Robinson – 1925 – 1927
Rev. J.E. (James) – 1927 – 1928
Rev. O.J. Smith – 1928 – 1930
Rev. W.S. Cooley – 1930 – 1931
Rev. B.T. Fuzzett – 1931 – 1933
Rev. J.K. Pafford – 1933 – 1935
Rev. B.C. York – 1935 – 1936
Rev. P.T. McClaren – 1936 – 1940
Rev. V.E. Banks – 1940 – 1943
Rev. B.N. Whitehurst – 1943 – 1944

Rev. B.N. Whitehurst was our pastor during World War II and endeared himself to many of his members whose sons were in service overseas by frequent visits to their homes, praying with them and helping in many ways spiritually.

Rev. H.R. Taylor – 1944 – 1946
Rev. L.M. Napper – 1946 – 1949
Rev. E.R. Roach – 1949 – 1953
Rev. John Batzel – 1953 – 1954
Rev. Nelson Wade – 1954 – 1958
Rev. Paul Phillips – 1958 – 1959
Rev. John Clark – 1959 – 1961
Rev. D.F. Dickey – 1961 – 1966
Rev. Tommy Bullock – 1966 – 1968
Rev. Harold Graves – 1968 – 1973
Rev. W.H. Howard – 1973 – 1977
Rev. Claude Bickley – 1977 – 1979
Rev. James Griffith – 1979 – 1981
Rev. Perry Miller – 1981 – 1983
Rev. Joseph A. Gearly – 1983 – 1988
Rev. Richard Carruth – 1988 – 1991
Rev. Richard Haley – 1991 – 1992
Rev. Thomas Perkins – 1992 – 1993
Rev. Harrell Nation – 1993 – 1995
Rev. Brett Blair – 1995 – Dec. 1997
Rev. James E. Bittner – Jan 1998 – 2003
Rev. Terry Presson – 2003 – 2007
Rev. Ben Stilwell-Hernandez – 2007 – 2010
Rev. Derek White – 2010 –

At the present time, those who are worshipping here and serving the Lord are descendents of those members of seventy-five years ago, and who, with their families, try to be present each Sunday in the choir and in the sanctuary. These are descendants of the Emersons... Jones... Williams... Goldsmiths... Boyds... Baileys... Leggetts... Clarks... Crossnoes.. Webbs, and others with many new families joining us along the way.

Cypress Church Assessments 1926-27

ALAMO CIRCUIT
Rev. J. E. JAMES, Pastor
The M. E. Church, South, CYPRESS, Assessed for Preacher
and Presiding Elder for 1926-27---$680.50

We have assessed Members what we felt they were willing to pay. If we have assessed you too high or too low, please let us know. Let every one pay the assessment and we will have no trouble in meeting our financial obligations.

Done by Request of Board of Stewards

L. D. CULIPHER, Steward.

L. D. Culipher	$10	Maud Fergerson	$2	Algie L. Nichols	$5
Ada Boyd	5	Mrs. Susie Laman	2	John Lewis	10
Florence Bodkin	2	Rose Nichols	2	Mrs. John Lewis	5
Maggie Mae Bodkin	1	Maud Nolen	2	Hallum Lewis	5
Annie W. Baldridge	2	Ada Stephenson	3		
		Leva Worrells	1	Total	57

MRS. ROSA PIERCE, Steward

Ruffin Crossnoe	$2
Ina Crossnoe	2
Countice Boals	2
Lullah Emison	5
Etta Evans	5
Willie Evans	10
Grace Evans	2
Blondell Evans	50c
Arthur Jones	15
Florence Jones	2
Elizabeth Jones	2
Pauline Jones	2
Don Pierce	10
Alton Pierce	5
Grace Porter	2
Rosa Pierce	10
Viola Rust	5
Carrie Rust	2
Surene Rust	2
Ewell Rust	2
Mildred Rust	2
James Rust	2
Angeline Rust	2
Garner Emison	10
Alice Stephenson	3
Nelson Stephenson	2
Lessie Selph	5
Willie Tyler	2
Pearl Evans	2
Arena Rust	5
Arthur Sutton	2
Minnie Sutton	2
Ida Sorrell	2
Total	$121.50

CARL EMISON, Steward

Carl Emison	$10
Mrs Iona Blurton	2
C. H. Blurton	5
Mrs. Eliza Butler	3
J. S. Emison	30
Ruby East	2
Beatrice East	1
Martha Forsythe	2
Avdria Fears	1
Auda Fears	1
Pearl Gourly	1
Raymond Leggett	2
W. C. Leggett	2.50
Rosa B. Leggett	1
Jewell Leggett	2
Louise Leggett	1
Clora Lewis	1
Elbert Lewis	1
Hazel Lewis	1
Joe Lewis	1
Sallie A. Permenter	2
Edgar Permenter	2
Mollie A. Permenter	2
Dorothy Permenter	1
Rosa Porter	3
Lucy Porter	3
Minnie Reasons	3
Doshia Stephenson	3
Mattie Pearl Skipper	2
Bessie Lou Woods	2
Mary Butler	3
Mrs. Carl Emison	3
Total	$99.50

J. D. BOYD, Steward

J. D. Boyd	$30
Mrs. J. D. Boyd	10
Minnie Boyd	10
Lorene Boyd	10
Jimmie Boyd	5
Willie Bolton	2.50
Mrs. Clemmie Bolton	1
Etta Bolton	2.50
Mary Bolton	1
Inez Emison	5
Maggie Emison	2
Hess Emison	1
Mrs. Hess Emison	1
Boscow Emison	5
Lester Elkes	2
Maggie Elkes	2
Mary Elkes	2
Maggie Lou Goldsmith	5
Nina Harris	1
Mellie Graves	1
Mrs. Willie Graves	1
Allie Hampton	1
Willie Leggett	1
Ora Leggett	1
Loon Leggett	2.50
F. M. Leggett	2.50
Annie Norville	2
Alson C. Patton	3
Florene Stewart	2.50
William Stewart	2.50
Gladys Stewart	2.50
Cecil Stewart	2.50
Hattie Stephens	1
Total	$123.00

W. W. EMISON, Steward.

W. W. Emison	$5
Gertrude Boyd	2.50
Eula Boyd	2.50
Bettie Bailey	5
Myrtle Bailey	5
Marie Bailey	2
Prudence Teal	2
Susan W. Emison	1
Tempie Follis	2
F. M. Goldsmith	30
Archie Goldsmith	5
Adie Goldsmith	2.50
Clara Bell Goldsmith	2
Broxie Goldsmith	2
J. W. Grant	2
A. D. Grant	1
Doss Leggett	10
Eton Leggett	2
Garlin Leggett	1
Mathlee Leggett	1
Merlin Leggett	1
Mathleene Leggett	1
J. D. Mathews	2
Mollie Goldsmith	5
Martha Spraggins	2
Vina Sutton	1
Loucinda Taylor	1
Joe Lenard Leggett	1
Berl Kenner	2
Jannie Emison	2
Total	102.50

J. L. MARLOWE, Steward

J. L. Marlowe	$5
Ina Marlowe	1
Mary D. Marlowe	1
Edith Marlowe	1
Henry Emison	2
Emma Emison	2
Bernice Emison	2
Renshaw Emison	2
J. W. Mitchell	5
Sarah Mitchell	3
D. A. Crossnoe	5
Margaret Crossnoe	3
Ruby Crossnoe	2
Marjorie Crossnoe	2
T. W. Crossnoe	5
Fletcher Crossnoe	3
Benton Crossnoe	2
Johnny Mitchell	5
Grady Mitchell	1
Eugene Permenter	10
Martha Permenter	1
Annie Emison	1
Ruth Emison	2
Russell Emison	2
Don Emison	2
Homer Crossnoe	5
Martha Willet	3
Luther Mitchell	10
Hattie Mitchell	1
Anna Marlowe	2
Total	$106.00

HOMER L. CLARK, Steward.

Candis Crossnoe	$3
Mosie Dunnigan	2
Sophie Balentine	2
Opal Cole	2
H. L. Clark	10
Lillie Clark	5
Jones Clark	1
Clem Clark	10
Ada Clark	2.50
Rebecca Clark	1
Mrs. Kate Culipher	2
Martha Wright	2
Jeroldine McCoy	1
Ira Webb	10
Aubrea Webb	3
Abbie Webb	5
Mrs. M. A. Webb	2
Vergie Webb	5
James Webb	1
Floyd Webb	1
Fay Webb	.50
Total	71

ALAMO#L01

Cypress Baptism in the Pond

I have mentioned in another story about a colored baptism that I saw when I was a little girl and have never forgotten the sight. We had a very similar event for our little Methodist church here in the Cypress Community. There were a few of the congregation that wanted to be immersed when baptized. The preacher made arrangements with the church members, Stephen and Anna Bailey, to use their pond they have in their yard.

The news got around and there were several people lined up to join the church and decided they, too, would like to become members of the church by being baptized this way. Plans were made for the big day, and some of the members wanted to be immersed and be re-baptized.

When the day came to perform the ritual, there were several people who planned to be there. This brought in family members to be there for their loved ones, friends and interested members of the church and community.

The Baptism of Kayley Mame Emerson by Preacher Terry Preston - 2007

People were in yard chairs, children on old quilt pallets and groups standing together. It was a very emotional afternoon for everyone. It was a joyous occasion and bonding among family and friends. We had several members of our family to be among the ones joining the church. I have enclosed a picture of our granddaughter, Kayley Mame', just before she was immersed in the water. After the ceremony, the crowd lingered and were hesitant to leave such a loving and important occasion. There was a bonding with God, with friends, and with neighbors, with young and old friends and strangers. Truly, one of life's miracles and a memorable occasion.

A Tribute to Aunt Bettie Bailey
(Bettie Elizabeth Forsythe)
with permission from
Sister Mary Frances Cates

Bettie E. Bailey was Bettie E. Forsythe and married John E. Bailey on 3 Jun 1900. Bettie was born in 1872 and died 1974; John was born 1872 and died in 1980. They had three children: Prudence Hathaway Bailey, who married Dave Teal; Lula Marie Bailey, who married Theodore Mayhall; a son, Poston, who died young.

Personally, I heard of Aunt Bettie years before I knew or met her. When I was a very small girl, my Aunt Glen who worked at People's Bank, Alamo, Tennessee, would come and tell me that Aunt Bettie had come from Memphis and came in to find out how I was and wanted her to tell me "Hello." This happened every year and I wondered who Aunt Bettie was. (I think Aunt Bettie is related to me some way, but am not sure how.)

When I was about 12 years old, Uncle Brad Webb invited me to a "Webb Family Reunion." Aunt Bettie was there!!! So I knew Aunt Bettie now. Aunt Bettie was very jovial, telling jokes, great fun, and loved being with us kids. AND SHE WAS BLIND! We young ones helped her to cross the road and back; she was great to be with. After coming back to the house, Aunt Bettie looked at me and said, "Go get me a tablet; I want to write a note to someone." I looked at her for a moment but then did what she asked me to do. When I returned, she took the tablet, tore off a sheet, turned the tablet over, using the back cardboard as a guide, and thus proceeded to write the message. Well!!!

The next couple of times I saw her were at a couple of Cypress Church Homecomings! She was fantastic! She was an emcee of the all-day program each time – singing, introductions, etc. I have always wished I had known her better and would hope others who knew her well would add to this tribute.

I believe it was Sybil Forsythe and Jean Brown who mentioned her sewing and that she could put in a perfect hem and also do other sewing, even though blind. Myrtle Rose Emerson also mentioned the fact and how hard it was for her at first, but she kept working with her fingers in feeling her work until she could do it perfectly. Myrtle Rose also said she had been a teacher when younger and went blind when she was 30 years of age.

When I was home in September 2003, Jimmy Wheeler gave me a copy of the booklet "History of Cypress Methodist Church" by Mrs. D. L. Leggett. I will quote from this booklet about her abilities as a "fund raiser."

Ladies of the Church, doing their part to raise needed funds for a larger church, one of the oldest, and one of the most faithful members, a retired school teacher, who had been totally blind for a number of years, volunteered herself to start raising more funds by visiting in the homes of everyone for miles around, if someone could drive her over the country. This was Mrs. Bettie E. Bailey, who never hesitated to offer her best efforts to help in anything the church committee decided should be done...and, of course, there were many, many who offered to drive her around, anywhere she wanted to go, and she collected a large amount of money...and this "Thank You Notice" was printed in the county newspaper, sent in by "Aunt Bettie" (as everyone called her) which said:

We...the members of Cypress Church wish to extend our thanks to everybody who helped raise the money to build this nice church. We are proud of our people who willingly donated to this worthy cause. Cooperation has come from all over the county. We cannot express in words our love and appreciation to everyone we called on, who were so glad and anxious to have their names placed on our list, for they wanted a part in this beautiful building. Some could not give as much as others, but those who could, certainly did their part.

May God's richest blessing fall upon everyone who donated, and helped in this work, with the help of God, we got our church, so come with us. Remember this is everybody's church. We extend a hearty welcome to all."

Mrs. Bettie E. Bailey, and the Members of Cypress – After this very successful and rewarding experience of raising money for a new church building was finished, "Aunt Bettie" did not rest on her "laurels" but at once began a new, much needed project of organizing a Cemetery Society, whose purpose was to keep the cemetery in good condition.

At this point, we think it would be appropriate to copy another notice sent in by "Aunt Bettie" to be in the Crockett newspaper, *The Crockett County Sentinel*:

NOTICE TO THE LADIES OF CYPRESS COMMUNITY... Some people live a long time in a dead community, "This is because they use so little of life!"

Anyone passing by Cypress Church, and looking toward the cemetery would say...We are traveling through a dead community...but this is not so.

*People at last have begun to see their duty they owe the dead. So, on next Saturday, July 10, 1915, the ladies of Cypress community will meet at the church at 2:30 o'clock for the purpose of organizing a Cemetery Society. We hope to have a full house, so every lady come and lend a helping hand, young and old, married or single. We must not think that if we cannot do great things, we can do nothing. So we will do the little deeds first, and hope they may grow to be great ones in the future, so, everyone come and take part in this work. We trust in the near future we can feel proud of our work. Let God our Heavenly Father be our leader and our Guide, and we will **surely be successful. Much love to the Sentinel and its many readers.**" Signed, Mrs. Bettie E. Bailey*

The Cemetery Society was very successful for a time, and the cemetery was kept mowed and clean. As time went on, it was again in a state of neglect, as there was no money to pay the caretaker to keep it mowed, so once again, our blind, resourceful, and faithful "Aunt Bettie" took upon herself the task of again trying to raise money, and after about two years since the organization of the Cemetery Society, a second notice was printed in the "*Sentinel*", a copy of it as follows:

Notice...A Great Hen Shower... The members of the Cemetery Society have begun their work for the year 1917. We want to complete our cemetery now, and make it a great work. We want a nice fence and it is going to cost a great deal. We want an iron fence, which will last a lifetime.

Now, all that will help, we are going to give you a chance. We can surely tell who loves and respects their dead by their contributing to this worthy cause.

We want every family in reach of Cypress Church, to send a hen to the home of Bettie E. Bailey just as soon as they can. She has coops ready to take care of them, and the next car that is loaded in Bells, she will deliver them there, and place the proceeds in the bank to be added to the sum we now have. I will list the names of everyone who sends a chicken, I ask for one chicken from every house in the county. "Who is it that feels like they could not spare one chicken for this purpose? I shall notify the public if there be such a family in this county!"

It is almost inconceivable, as it seems now, but in those days one dollar was considered a generous offering, and a dollar "went further" than today. So Aunt Bettie, and all the others involved in this project, were very pleased at the response to her plea for a hen...shower.

So she did purchase a section of iron fence, but only for the front of the cemetery, and in all the years since the Cemetery Society was organized, it has never again been neglected or allowed to be overgrown with weeds...today, it is one of the best-kept cemeteries to be seen anywhere. Always on "Homecoming Day" there are contributions sufficient to keep it well taken care of for another year."…. God Bless!

Sister Mary Francis Cates. Kin through McMillans to Rose Belle Webb to me. Picture made in Scotland with Scotts in clan plaids SMFC, toured Scotland and met our Clansmen and Chiefs

Grandma Rose Belle Webb Leggett Ancestors in Scotland before they migrated

Cypress Church

Cypress Church has been the center of the community for generations and generations. Not only for the Cypress community but for adjoining areas all around. Some of the names of these communities are Liberty Hall, Fruitvale, with some from Walnut Hill, Gadsden, Alamo, Bells and many other places near it.

The church has gone through many changes and congregations through the many years it has stood on the grounds. I have found much information on its history from several older people in the community through the years and have tried to combine these sources into a common line. The church has stood through many hardships and has endured by the determination of its members and with help of the hand of God. May it last through many more years to come and lead its people to live better lives and become closer to their creator.

One of the customs that has helped the church to grow and thrive is the annual Homecoming, held the second Sunday in June without fail every year, bringing family members that have moved away "back home."

The *Annual Homecoming Day* at Cypress Church is certainly a joyous day with all the things God tells us are important for a good life: love, friendship, singing and breaking bread with family, friends and neighbors. The worship service, being filled with singing, memorials with pictures on a screen of loved ones gone on before us and telling stories of their lives for inspiration. There is no one in the church that is not connected to someone in this tribute.

The grounds outside are lined with "tables" strung between the giant trees and laden with food that the ladies have cooked using their favorite recipes and their many cooking talents. You will see fried chicken, hams, casseroles and salads, not to mention the many cakes and pies and other sweets. There are iced tea and homemade lemonade to finish all this off. The grass is covered with yard chairs and picnic tables with old quilts used for pallets for the laughing and playing children and babies. People making snapshots and home movies and much hugging and mingling of folks from afar. Locals that are genuinely happy to see each other again and share their love all around. This is the day everyone "comes home" from all across the country, making the name "Homecoming" truly a reality. Almost 100% of the people attending have ancestors buried in the Cypress Cemetery and contribute funds to keep this memorial beautiful.

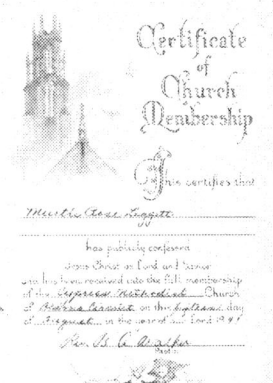

Certificate of Church Membership – Cypress Methodist Church of Alamo Circuit

On church steps, long standing members of Cypress Methodist Church – Bettie Bailey and Etta Evans (good friends since youth)

Cypress Church before remodeling – about 1953

Early Cypress Church before brick one

THIS PICTURE WAS TAKEN ABOUT 1926.
CYPRESS METHODIST CHURCH GROUP.
STARTING WI

1. HICKS BLURTON
2. STERLING PERMENTER
3. ARTHUR JONES
4. RUSSEL EMISON
5. EWELL MARLOWE
6. LYLE SPRAGGINS
7. EARL MARLOWE
8. GARNER EMISON
9. BROOKSIE GOLDSMITH (MARLOWE)
10. MRS. EDDIE EVANS
11. BUCK CALL
12. MRS. ROSIE PIERCE
13. ELIZEBETH JONES (WEBB)
14. DON PIERCE
15. BUD (ROBERT HENRY EAST)
16. HUBERT HALBROOK
17. ARCHIE GOLDSMITH
18. RANSHAW EMISON
19. AUDREY FEARS (CALL)
20. PAULINE JONES (PICKENS)
21. ANN STEPHENSON
22. THELMA HUNT
23. CARRIE RUST (EVANS)
24. UNCLE JONNY EMISON
25. WALTER EMISON
26. BUSTER LEGGETT
27. AUBREY WEBB
28. BEATRICE EAST (WEBB)
29. GLADYS STEWART (GRIFFIN)

30. NELSON STEPHENSON (HUNT)
31. CECIL STEWART
32. OPAL CALL (JACKSON)
33. AUDA FEARS
34. GRACE EVANS (HUMPHREYS)
35. SUREEN RUST (GWINN)
36. LOUISE WILLIAMS
37. AUNT MATT WEBB
38. IDA WEBB (MC.NEELY)
39. LUCILLE WILLIAMS
40. FLOYD WEBB
41. MARTHA SUTTEN (SPRAGGINS)-(HUNGERFORD)
42. EULA BOYD (CLARK)
43. RUBY EAST (TOY)
44. FLORENCE JONES (HAYS)
45. MARY NEAL SORRELL (HAL
46. BELL GOLDSMITH (MARLOWE)
47. DONALD CROSSNOE
48. BLONDELL EVANS (JONES)
49. ANGELINE RUST
50. MILDRED RUST (SHELLABARGER)
51. LOUISE LEGGETT (WOODSON)
52 FAY WEBB (JOHNSON)
53. LEWIS BOY
54. DALTON JONES
55. DUDE (CLARENCE LEGGETT)
56. HERSCHELL EMISON
57. JAMES RUST

CHAPTER 16

Bailey DNA

Bailey (DNA) and Genealogy

By Larry O. Bailey

I have great news; we got a DNA match with the Rhode Island Baileys. We also have proof that Samuel Bailey's (born about 1665 in Newport, Rhode Island) father was Richard Bailey. I want to thank Dr. Scott Swanson, Professor, Department of History, Butler University, and Indianapolis, Indiana. Most of the time line on the Rhode Island Baileys came from his research. I also want to thank Cindy Mize for her hard work and all of you that have helped me over the years. Now maybe the Rhode Island and North Carolina researchers can work together and find Richard Bailey's family in England.— —-*Larry Bailey*

Descendents of Richard "Baily" Bailey

Generation No. 1

2. RICHARD "BAILY"BAILEY was born about 1620, and died bet. 20 Jun 1677 - 01 May 1978 in Newport, Rhode Island.

Notes for Richard "Baily" Bailey:

1664: Richard Bailey met John Clarke in England before the year 1664 and became the best of friends. John Clarke, one of the co-founders of the colony of Rhode Island was sent to England to get a charter for the colony of Rhode Island.

Note: "Richard Bailey probably knew law. He may well have given John Clarke advice on petitions for the RI charter and some of the wording of the final document." (John Clarke and His Legacies, By Sydney V. James, Theodore Dwight Bozeman pages 55,)

1664: Richard Bailey and his good friend, John Clarke and Richard Barnes sailed in the spring of 1664 from Bristol, England to Rhode Island on the ship "The Sisters." (John Clarke and His Legacies By Sydney V. James, Theodore Dwight Bozeman pages 55,85)

1665: Richard Bailey witnessed a deed between Robert Williams of Newport and Robert Morris and Daniel Abbott of Providence, "This first day October 1665. Recorded by & with ye Townes Consent. August 27th; 1678" (The Early Records of the Town of Providence. By City Council, Brennen, William G., d. 1909, Horatio Rogers, Providence (RI). City Council, Providence (RI), page 17)

1668: Richard Bailey, made free of the Town of Newport, admitted freeman of the colony by the RI General Assembly; 29 October 1668 (Records of the Colony of RI and Providence Plantations (Providence, 1856-1865) 2:238

1669: Richard Bailey, Secretary of the Governor and Council of His Majesty's Colony of Rhode Island and Providence Plantations, by their order signed a letter to the Colony of Connecticut; 28 Jul 1669 (Records of the Colony of Rhode Island and Providence Plantations (Providence, 1856-1865) 2:274-278)

1670: Mary Timberlake of Newport (wife of Henry) on record that 30 Jan 1670, she was allowed 15s for a horse hired to New London for Richard Bailey. (Ancestral Lines by Carl Boyer page 439.)

1670: Captain John Greene, Joseph Torrey, Richard Bailey appointed commissioners to meet at New London CT; May 1670 (Smith, Civil and Military List of RI 1647-1800:6)

1670: Richard Bailey, Secretary of the Government and Council of His Majesty's Colony of RI and Providence Plantations, by their order signed a letter to the Colony of CT; 23 Mar 1670 (Records of the Colony of RI and Providence Plantations (Providence, 1856-1865-2: 329-331)

1670: Copy of writ of Governor and Assistants of RI to Mr. James Barker, Lieut. Joseph Torrey, Mr. Caleb Carr, and Richard Bailey "to repair to Narragansett" to find people exercising jurisdiction under pretense of such authority from the Colony of CT; 20 Jun 1670 (Records of the Colony of RI and Providence Plantations (Providence, 1856–1865) 2: 332–333)

1671: Mr. Richard Bailey was elected Attorney General at General Court of Election held at Newport, 3 May 1671; he declined office, and Lt. Joseph Torrey was elected in his place'; 30 May 1671 (Records of the Colony of RI and Providence Plantations (Providence, 1856–1865) 2: 374–375)

1671: Richard Bailey witnessed deed of Thomas Burge of Newport to Thomas Ward of Newport; 29 Jul 1671 (RI Land Evidences 1648–1696 (Providence, 1921; reprinted 1998): 106 (146 in original)

1672: Richard Smith of Newport, merchant, sold Joseph Torrey and Richard Bailey, both of Newport, four acres lying at the pond side in Portsmouth; witnesses John Collins, Francis Simson; 2 Mar 1671–2 (RI Land Evidences 1648–1696) Providence, 1921; reprinted 1998): 31–32) 38 in original)

1673: Richard Bailey appointed by General Assembly part of committee to audit records of John Coggeshall, late Treasurer of the Colony; committee gave Coggeshall an acquaintance; 11 Jul 1673; recorded 4 Aug 1676 (RI Land Evidences 1648–1696 (Providence, 1921; reprinted 1998); 87 (111 in original)

1673: Richard Bailey witnessed deed of Benedict Arnold to the Town of Newport for Goat Island and Coasters Harbor; 1 May 1673 (RI Land Evidences 1648–1696 (Providence, 1921; reprinted 1998): 86 (110 in original)

1673: Richard Bailey witnessed deed of William Brenton, John Hull, Benedict Arnold, John Porter, Samuel Wilburn, Samuel Wilson, and Thomas Mumford to William Clarke, weaver; 25 Apr 1674 (RI Land evidences 1648–1696 (Providence, 1921; reprinted 1998): 112–113 (156 in original)

1674: Richard Bailey witnessed deed of John Clarke of Newport, physician, to Richard Smith of Newport, merchant, of land in Newport; 27 Apr 1674 (RI Land Evidences 1648–1696 (Providence, 1921: reprinted 1998): 44 (57 in original)

1674: Richard Bailey witnessed deed of Matthew Mayhew of Martin's Vineyard (Martha's Vineyard?), son and heir of Thomas Mayhew Jr., grandson of Thomas Mayhew, to Peleg Sanford, Philip Smith, and Thomas Ward, all of Newport, for two western most of Elizabeth Islands; 27 Oct 1674 (RI Land Evidences 1648–1696 (Providence, 1921; reprinted 1998): 108 (150 in original)

1675: Richard Bailey witnessed deed of William Clarke, by attorney Jireh Bull of Pettacomscutt, to John Pierce of Portsmouth, mason; 6 Aug 1675 (RI Land Evidences 1648–1696 (Providence, 1921; reprinted 1998: 112–113– (157 in original)

1676: Matjew Boomer of Newport for one and thirty pounds currant Silver money of New England paid by George Browne of Newport Planter, have Granted Land, lying in Newport, Ten Acres bounded on the north and east by land lately in the possession of Richard Tew, deceased, on the South by land of Peter Easton, and on the west by a highway, the land granted in breadth twenty, rod six and 20 Feb 1676. Mathew Boomer: Wit. Thomas Ward, Richard Barnes, Richard Bailey.

Note: "The witness's above Thomas Ward's will left bequest of 20 shillings to Samuel Bailey and Richard Barne's will left bequest of a piece of gold to Samuel Bailey. Richard Barnes sailed from England on the ship "The Sisters" with Richard Bailey to Rhode Island in 1664."

1676: At the time of King Philip's War the RI General Assembly "voted and ordered, that Commissioners be empowered to take care and order the several watches and wards on this Island, and appoint the places. The persons are, Mr. Walter Clarke, Assistant, Major John Cranston, Mr. John Clarke, Mr. Caleb Carr, Mr. James Barker and Mr. Richard Bailey, for Newport; 11 Apr 1676 (Records of the Colony of RI and Providence Plantations (Providence, 1856–1865) 2:539)

1676: Richard Bailey received legacy in the will of Dr. John Clarke, will dated——, proven 17 May 1676 Newport: "To Richard Bailey a concordance and lexicon to it, written by myself, being the fruit of several years study, and to him a Hebrew Bible and rest of books"; friends William Weeden, Philip Smith, and Richard Bailey were executors of the will; Thomas Ward witnessed the will; (Austin, Genealogical Dictionary of RI (Albany, 1887; reprinted 1995): 46

Note: "Richard Bailey wrote Clarke's will and the subsidiary instructions that went with it; his hand penned them and his mind probably translated the dying man's wishes into sufficiently legal language. By the will he was to receive Clark's books and the concordance to the Bible and the lexicon (probably Hebrew) Clarke had written. And he became the guiding member of the team of three executors." (John Clarke and His Legacies By Sydney V. James, Theodore Dwight Bozeman pages 55,)

Another part of John Clark's will:

Item unto my friends, William Weeden, Phillip Smith and Richard Bailey, I give and devise a certain piece of Land at the Southeast corner of my Orchard to be, and remain unto them and their heirs and assignees forever for the use and uses by me declared in a paper under my hand and seals the said Land to contain in breadth next the street three rod, and in Length six rod. (John Clarke and His Legacies By Sydney V. James, Theodore Dwight Bozeman pages 55.)

Note: The land above that John Clarke gave to William Weeden, Phillip Smith and Richard Bailey was the same land that Richard Bailey's son, Samuel deeded to Captain William Weeden in 1721.

1676: Mr. Phillip Smith and Mr. Richard Bailey, surviving Executors to the last will and testament of Mr. John Clarke, physician, presented a paper to the RI General Assembly wherein they demanded $100 due Mr. Clarke; 25 Oct 1676; RI General Assembly because of questions suspended payments to Sanford and Bailey; 30 Oct 1678 (Records of the Colony of RI and Providence Plantations (Providence, 1856-1865) 2: 558; 3:22-23)

1677: RI General Assembly chose Captain Peleg Sanford and Mr. Richard Bailey as agents for the colony to go to England; 1 May 1677 (Records of the Colony of RI and Providence Plantations (Providence, 1856-1865) 2: 580; Smith, Civil and Military List of RI 1647-1800: 9)

1677: Richard Bailey Secretary of Court of Justices of Peace of Narrangansett; May 1677 (Smith, Civil and Military List of RI 1647-1800: 9)

1678: "And whereas all the writings and papers that do concern the said Court Martial, are in the custody of Lieut. Edward Richmond, who was Clerk of the said Court, should have been delivered unto the Town Secretary, Mr. Richard Bailey, to record in the Book of the General Council, which hath not been done, and the said Mr. Richard Bailey being deceased,

1 May 1678 (Records of the Colony of Rhode Island and Providence Plantations (Providence, 1856-1865) 3:5)

Child of Richard "Baily" Bailey is:

1. Samuel Bailey (Richard "Bailey") was born about 1665 in Newport, Rhode Island, and died between 19 Dec 1728 - 28 Jan 1729 in Westerly, Providence Rhode Island. He married Elizabeth Rogers about 1700

2. Samuel Bailey (Richard Bailey) was born about 1665 in Newport, RI and died between 19 Dec 1728 - 28 Jan 1729 in Westerly, Providence RI. He married Elizabeth Rogers about 1700 in Newport, RI, daughter of Thomaa Rogers and Sarah. She was born about 1677 in Newport, RI and died aft 27 Jan 1729 in Westerly, Kings County, Rhode Island.

Notes for Samuel Bailey: Providence Plantations was formed in 1703. Kings County was formed out of Providence in 1729. Kings County name was changed to Washington County in 1781.

1683: Thomas Ward, Newport; will dated 9 Jun 1683, proven 2 Jun 1690 Newport RI; left bequest of 20 shillings to Samuel Bailey (Janet Fletcher Fiske, Gleanings from Newport Court Files 1659-1783, record 4A)

1687: Richard Barnes, Newport will dated 7 Apr 1687 Executor friend, John Ward. To sister Susanna Loader, 10. To sisters Mary Hydes, Alice Wilkins and Hester like legacies. To Samuel Bailey, a piece of gold. To Williams James 5. To executor, the rest of estate, whether money, sheep etc. Witnesses —William Jannett, John Clarke, John Hulme, Samuel Stapleton. Probated June 22,1687, with inventory.

Note: Richard Barnes and Richard Bailey sailed in the spring of 1664 from Bristol England to RI on the ship "The Sisters". (John Clarke and His Legacies By Sydney V. James, Theodore Dwight Bozeman)

1689: James Mann, Newport, RI conveyed to Philip Smith/Newport RI, for 160 silver money of NE, a certain farm containing 40 acres in Newport, RI; bounded southerly by land of Jonathan Holmes, Philip Smith, Thomas Ward, and Samuel Bailey, westerly by land of James Barker and the highway, northerly by land of Philip Smith, eastwardly by land of Jonathan Holmes; witnesses: John Ward, John (X) Peabody, Thomas Ward; signed James Mann; 13 Mar 1688 (RI Land Evidences 1648-1696)

1702: Proprietors of Newport by agreements dated 12 Mar 1701-2 divided 300 acres of common land into 12 acres parcels: "to Samuel Bailey was laid out in Sachuset Neck twelve acres of land bounded east on Henry Tew land, north on a highway, south on Edward Smith's land on the west on——being his full share only Edward Smith to pass through his land to go to his own land——by an act of Committee for the same; 5 Jan 1702 (Newport RI Miscellaneous Records Book 1:19)

1709: Samuel Bailey, Newport RI sold Thomas Rogers, Jr. 16 acres in Newport, 29 Jan 1709. (Austin, Genealogical Dictionary of RI, p. 369)

1712: Jeffrey Champlin, (Kingstown RI) for L50 New England conveyed to Samuel Bailey, Newport RI all right and title to premises (described elsewhere); witnesses Robert Westcott, Peleg Sherman; 29 Mar 1712, entered 23 Jun 1716 (Westerly RI Land Evidences 2 (1707-1717) 207R)

1712: Samuel Bailey and his family moved between March and December 1712 from Newport RI to Westerly RI.

1712: Samuel Bailey witnessed deed of James Rogers, Westerly, yeoman, to his brother Jeremiah Rogers, Newport, Cordwainer, for love and affection 50 acres in Westerly; 17 Dec 1712 (Westerly RI Land Evidences (1717-1728) 3:14L)

1716: Samuel Bailey witnessed deed of Peter Teft, Westerly, yeoman, to Thomas Rogers, Newport, yeoman, tract of 130 acres in Westerly; 20 Feb 1715-6 (Westerly RI Land Evidences (1717 - 1728) 3: 41L)

1716: Samuel Bailey witnessed deed of Thomas Parker, Westerly RI, yeoman, to Samuel Willberks; 30 Mar 1716 (Westerly RI Land Evidences (1707–1717): 187L.

1717: Samuel Bailey, Westerly RI, yeoman, for 11. NE conveyed to Mr. Arnold Collins/Newport RI, merchant tract in Westerly RI in the Shannock Purchase, 138 acres; witnesses Thomas Draper, Mary Sanders; Mr. Samuel Bailey personally appeared before the clerk to warrant the deed 10 Jan 1716-7 (1716-7 (Westerly RI Land Evidences 2 (1707–1717): 219L

1718: Samuel Bailey, Westerly RI, yeoman, for 238. New England conveyed to Samuel Wilbore, Westerly RI Messuage or tract in Westerly RI 130 acres more or less bounded easterly by Beaver River, southerly and westerly by certain highways, northerly by land of Peter Parker; Elizabeth wife of Samuel Bailey relinquished dower; Elizabeth made her mark; witnesses Daniel Willcocks, Stephen J. Willcocks; 17 Sept 1718 (Westerly RI Land Evidences (1717–1728) 3:13)

1718: Samuel and Penelope Wilbore, Westerly, yeoman, conveyed to Samuel Bailey, Westerly, yeoman, for L200 NE, tract of 130 acres in Westerly, bounded on the east and north by highways, west by land of said Samuel Wilbore, south by land of Thomas Lillibridge; witnesses Daniel Wilcox, —Wilcox; 18 Sept 1718 (Westerly RI Land Evidences (1717–1728) 3: 30 R)

1719: Samuel Bailey and Francis Colegrove witnessed receipt of Thomas Dells, Westerly RI to his mother Sarah Dells alias Sarah Toplit, executrix of the estate of her husband and his father, saying that he had gotten his legacies from his father in full; 17 Feb 1718-9 (Westerly RI Land Evidences 3:77)

1719: Samuel Bailey witnessed deed of William Bentley, Westerly, Cordwainer, to Joseph Hull, Westerly, yeoman, 3 Mar 1718-9 (Westerly RI Land Evidences (1717–1728) 3:23R)

1719: Samuel Bailey witnessed deed of Joseph and Susanna Hull, Westerly, yeoman, to William Bentley, Westerly, Cordwainer, land adjacent Francis Colegrove; 3 Mar 1718-9, (Westerly RI Land Evidences (1717–1728) 3:25L)

1719: Samuel Bailey, Westerly RI. Yeoman, for 5.18.6 New England, conveyed to Thomas Lillibridge, Westerly RI, yeoman, tract in Westerly, 19 ¾ acres, bounded easterly, southerly, Westerly on land of Thomas Lillibridge, northerly upon land of Samuel Bailey; Elizabeth Bailey relinquished dower; witnessed Daniel Wilcox, Edward Popplestone, Daniel Wilcox, Jr; Samuel Bailey appeared before Clerk to warrant deed 25 May 1719; recorded 25 Oct 1731 (Westerly RI Land Evidences 5:302)

1719: Samuel Bailey, Westerly RI for love and affection conveyed to son-in-law and daughter. Francis Colegrove, Jr. and Hannah his wife, Westerly RI a tract in Westerly RI 30 acres more or less bounded northerly and easterly by certain highways, southerly and westerly on land of said Samuel Bailey; 8 Nov 1719 (Westerly RI Land Evidences (1717–1728) 3:32)

1720: Samuel Bailey, Westerly, yeoman, surveyed to Francis Colegrove, Jr. Westerly, for L50 NE, tract of 50 acres in Westerly, bounded on south by land of said Samuel Bailey, west by land of William Petty, north by highway, east partly by land of said Francis Colegrove, Jr. and partly by a highway; witnesses Joseph Woodmansee, Edward Rogers (X); Samuel Bailey and Elizabeth (X) signed; 18 Jul 1720 (Westerly RI Land Evidences (1717–1728) 3:52L)

1720: Francis Colegrove, Jr., Westerly and wife Hannah Colegrove conveyed to Jeffrey Wilcox, Kingstown, yeoman, for 50. NE, tract of 80 acres in Westerly adjoining Samuel Bailey and William Petty; witnesses James Orme, Elizabeth Champlin; Francis Colegrove and Hannah Colegrove signed; 31 Cot 1720 (Westerly RI Land Evidences (1717–1728) 3: 53R)

1721: Samuel Bailey/Westerly RI conveyed to his loving friend, Captain William Weeden/Newport RI a lot which John Clarke had granted to "my father Richard Bailey" in his will dated 20 Apr 1676; 27 Apr 1721 (Newport Land Evidences Book 6: 213–214)

1722: Samuel Bailey witnessed deed of Mary Tucker, Westerly to Judiah Irish, Kingstown; 4 Apr 1722 (Westerly RI Land Evidences (1717–1728) 3: 76R)

1723: Samuel Wilbore, Westerly RI RI, yeoman, conveyed to Thomas Lillibridge, Westerly RI. Yeoman, tract of 20 acres counted easterly partly on Samuel Bailey's land and partly upon Lillibridge's land; Penelope wife of Samuel Wilbore relinquished dower; 6 Feb 1722-3 (Westerly RI Land Evidences 5: 130)

1728: Samuel Bailey and John Colegrove witnesses deed of William (and Mary) James, Westerly to their son, Joseph James, Westerly; 3 Jun 1728 (Westerly RI Land Evidences (1717–1728) 3: 57LR)

1728: Samuel Bailey, Westerly RI, yeoman, for love, good will, and natural affection, conveyed to son Richard Bailey, Westerly RI, one message or tract situated in Westerly, 100 acres more or less, bounded easterly by a certain highway, southerly and westerly by land belonging to Thomas Lillibridge and Robert Lillibridge, both of Westerly, northerly by land of Jeffrey Wilcox of North Kingstown; "I am the true sole and lawful owner of the above premises and am lawfully seized and possessed of the same in mine own proper right as a good perfect and absolute estate of inheritance in fee simple and have in myself good right full power and lawful authority to convey..."; witnesses Joseph Woodmansee, Samuel Wilbore; 28 Jun 1728; Samuel Bailey appeared before Clerk to warrant deed 19 Dec 1728; recorded 27 Jan 1729 (Westerly RI Land Evidences 5:56)

1729: Elizabeth Bailey, widow of Samuel Bailey, granted letters of administration in keeping with laws respecting disposition of intestate estates; 27 Jan 1729 (Westerly RI Court Records and Probate Records 3: 302)

1729: Elizabeth Bailey, Hannah Colegrove, and Francis Colegrove Jr. witnessed deed of Peter Parker, Westerly RI, yeoman, to Joseph Woodmansee, Groton CT; 8 Apr 1719; Elizabeth Bailey and Francis Colegrove Jr. appeared before Clerk to confirm that they had seen Peter and Hannah Parker sign the deed; 27 Jan 1728-9 (Westerly RI Land Evidences: 5: 58)

1729: Elizabeth Bailey, widow of Samuel Bailey, granted letters of administration in keeping with laws respecting disposition of interstate estates; 27 Jan 1729 (Westerly RI Court Records and Probate Records 3:302)

Children of Samuel Bailey and Elizabeth Rogers are:

1 Hannah Bailey b. about 1702, Newport, Rhode Island; m. Francis Colegrove, Jr., 5 Mar 1719, Westerly, Providence Rhode Island.

2 Elizabeth Bailey, b. about 1704, Newport, Rhode Island; m. James Babcock.

3 Mary Bailey, b. about 1706, Newport, Rhode Island; m. Edward Rogers, 22 Jul 1728, Westerly, Kings Rhode Island.

4 Richard Bailey Esq., b. about 1707, Newport, Rhode Island; d. 21 Nov 1780, Richmond, Kings County, Rhode Island; m. (1) Abigail Woodmansee, 25 Apr 1729, Westerly, Kings County Rhode Island; b. about 1708; d. before. 7 Jan 1768, Richmond, Kings County Rhode Island; m. (2) Mrs. Judith (Clarke) Card, 7 Jan 1768, Richard, Kings County, Rhode Island; b. 8 Feb 1742 or 43.

Notes for Richard Bailey Esq.:

1728: Samuel Bailey/Westerly RI, yeoman, for love, good will, and natural affection, conveyed to son Richard Bailey, Westerly RI, one message or tract situated in Westerly, 100 acres more or less, bounded easterly by a certain highway, southerly and westerly by land belonging to Thomas Lillibridge and Robert Lillibridge, both of Westerly, northerly by land of Jeffrey Wilcox of North Kingstown; "I am the true sole and lawful owner of the above premises and am lawfully seized and possessed of the same in mine own proper right as a good perfect and absolute estate of inheritance in fee simple and have in myself good right full power and lawful authority to convey...", witnesses Joseph Woodmansee, Samuel Wilbore; 28 Jun 1728; Samuel Bailey appeared before Clerk to warrant deed 19 Dec 1728; recorded 27 Jan 1728/9 (Westerly RI Land Evidences 5:56); possibly sold to Thomas Wait in 1750

1729: Richard Bailey/Westerly RI married 25 Apr 1729 Westerly RI: Abigail Woodmansee, Westerly RI (Charlestown RI Town Council and Probate Records Book 1:61)

1730: Richard Bailey of Westerly admitted freeman of the colony by General Assembly; (1st Tuesday) May 1730 (Records of the Colony of RI and Providence Plantations (Providence, 1856-1865) 4:436)

1735: Lieutenant Richard Bailey, in room of David Kenyon who refused commission, Charlestown First Company, Third Regiment, Kings County RI Militia; June 1742 (Smith, Civil and Military List of Rhode Island 1647-1800: 92)

1744: James Babcock will, dated 15 Jul 1744, proven 1 Oct 1744 Charlestown RI (Charlestown RI Town Council and Probate Records Book 1A: 117): wife Elizabeth; daughters Hannah Babcock, Elizabeth Babcock, Mary Babcock, Sarah Babcock, all under 18 unmarried; executors wife Elizabeth and brother Richard Bailey of Charlestown; witnesses Daniel Everett, Joseph Card, James Colegrove Jr.

1744: Captain Richard Bailey allowed 6 for going to Newport to defend Town of Charlestown against action by Josiah Greene; 1 Oct 1744 (Charlestown RI Town Council and Probate Records Book 1:65)

1745: Captain Bailey allowed liberty to sell liquor at his house three training days; paid fee of ten shillings; 7 Sep 1745 (Charlestown RI Town Council and Probate Records Book 1:71)

1747: Richard Bailey registered earmark: two forks in the left ear and a halfpenny under the right ear; 15 Mar 1747 (Richmond RI Town Meeting Records and Land Evidences Book 1:6)

1748: Major Richard Bailey, Field Officers of Kings County RI Regiment; June 1748 (Smith, Civil and Military List of Rhode Island 1947-1800: 128)

1750: Richard Bailey/Richmond/Kings County RI, yeoman, conveyed Thomas Wait/Tiverton/Newport County RI, yeoman, for 1600 NE, 100 acres Richmond RI, bounded easterly by a highway, southerly and westerly by land of Thomas Lillibridge and Robert Lillibridge, northerly by land of Jeffrey Wilcox; Abigail wife of Richard Bailey relinquished dower; witnesses Samuel Irish (X), John Webster; signed Richard Bailey, Abigail Bailey (X); 16 Feb 1749-50, Major Richard Bailey appeared to warrant deed 16 Feb 1749-50, recorded 2 Jun 1750 (Richmond RI Land Evidences Book 1:146); possible land given him by his father Samuel Bailey in 1728.

1752: Joseph Woodmansee estate accounts, Mary Lillibridge executrix; payments to Alice Woodmansee, Joseph Woodmansee, Richard Bailey; 18 Sept 1752 (Richmond RI Town Council and Probate Records Book 1:106-107)

1753: Major Richard Bailey appointed in behalf of Town of Richmond to defend suit brought by John Webb against Thomas Rogers, Town Treasurer, at next Inferior Court of common Pleas to be held at South Kingstown the first Tuesday of August; 27 Jul 1753 (Richmond RI Town Meeting Records and Land Evidences Book 1:38)

1754: Richard Bailey supervisor of road crew to mend and repair all highways and bridges beginning four rods west of the northwest corner of Richard Bailey's land that lies to the south of the highway, thence westward to Wood River bridge and all highways to the northward except the highway that runs westward from Peleg Thomas' mill to the north and south highway (Richmond RI Town Councilor, Council Meeting' Council met at the house of Richard Bailey; 1 Sept 1755 (Richmond RI Town Council and Probate Records Book 1:185)

1758: Richard Bailey chosen for grand jury of Superior Court of Judicature to be held in South Kingstown.

1760: Major Richard Bailey Deputy for Richmond in RI General Assembly; (first Wednesday) May 1760 (Records of the Colony of Rhode Island and Providence Plantations (Providence, 1856-1865) 6:250)

1761: Major Richard Bailey Deputy for Richmond in RI General Assembly; (first Wednesday) May 1761 (Records of the Colony of Rhode Island and Providence Plantations (Providence, 1856-1865) 6:283)

1764: Card Foster/Richmond/Kings County RI, yeoman, conveyed to Richard Bailey/Richmond/Kings County RI, yeoman, for L85 RI, 3 ¾ acres in Richmond RI, bounded: beginning at a stake and heap of stone at the southeast corner of said Foster's land, thence running north 14 degrees west bounding easterly by the land of Elisha Babcock twenty rods to a heap of stones, thence running west fifteen and a half degrees south bounding northerly by the land of grantor fifty seven rods and sixteen links to a heap of stones, thence running east two degrees south bounding southerly partly on land of Richard Bailey and partly on land of William Potter Jr. sixty rods and sixteen links to the first mentioned bounds; witnesses Enoch Lewis, Richard Bailey Jr.; signed Card Foster; 19 Mar 1764 (Richmond RI Land Evidences 2: 193-194)

1765: Richard Bailey/Richmond/Kings County RI, yeoman, conveyed to Alexander Case/Exeter/Kings County RI, weaver, for 240 Spanish milled dollars, 50 acres in Exeter RI, bounded northerly on land of William Sunderlin, easterly on land of James Brayman, southerly partly on land of Joseph Hammond and partly on land of James Barber, westerly on Pascopang River; Abigail wife of John Sudnerlin/Execter RI relinquished dower; witnesses —,—, signed Richard Bailey, Abigail Sunderlin; 10 Mar 1765, Richard Bailey appeared to warrant deed——,recorded —April 1765 (Exeter RI Land Evidences Book 10:92-93)

1765: Major Richard Bailey chosen one of two delegates to RI General Assembly; 27 Aug 1765 (Richmond RI Town Meeting Records and Land Evidences Book 2:312)

1765-66: Richard Bailey Speaker of the RI General Assembly Oct 1765 to May 1766 (Website)

1768: Richard Bailey/Richmond/Kings County RI, yeoman, conveyed to Richard Bailey Jr. for 450, 150 acres in two tracts in Richmond RI; the first bounded northerly partly on land of Card Foster and partly on land of Robert Wilcox, easterly partly on land of Elisha Babcock and partly on land William Potter Jr., southerly partly on land of William Potter Jr. and partly on a highway, westerly on a highway; the second bounded northerly on a highway, easterly on Beaver River, southerly on land of Joseph Woodmansee, westerly on land of Thomas Lillibridge; witnesses Hannah James, Clarke Bailey; signed Richard Bailey; 6 Jan 1768, Richard Bailey personally appeared to warrant deed 6 Jan 1768, recorded 6 Nov 1780 (Richmond RI Land Evidences Book 3:260-261); possibly land bought from Edward Boss in 1750.

1770: Richard Bailey and his wife Judah Bailey signed the covenant with Elder James Wightman to found the Six Principle Baptist Church in North Kingstown RI, 31 Mar 1770 (Austin, Vital Record of Rhode Island ——, p, 287)

1770: Richard Bailey Esq. to have license to sell strong liquor in his dwelling house for one year; bailey to pay 12 shillings license money; 3 Sept 1770 (Richmond RI Town Council and Probate Records Book 2:71)

1772: Richard Bailey/Richmond, Kings County RI, yeoman, conveyed to Mary Sunderlin/Exeter/Kings County RI, for 42, 41 acres in Exeter RI, bounded westerly and northerly on land of heirs of William Sunderlin deceased, easterly on lands of Joseph Hammond, southerly on lands of James Brayman; Judith wife of Richard Bailey relinquished dower; witnesses Abigail Sunderlin, Richard Bailey Jr; 19 May 1772, Richard Bailey appeared to warrant the deed 20 May 1772, recorded 30 Jun 1772 (Exeter RI Deed Book 1:216-217)

1774: Richard Bailey/Richard/Kings County RI, yeoman, conveyed to Richard Bailey Jr./Richmond/Kings County RI, gentleman, for 200, 50 acres in Richmond RI, bounded beginning at southeast corner of tract, the southwest corner of land of William Potter, Jr., thence running westerly on a highway to a white oak tree, thence northerly bounding west on a highway until it comes to the land of Card Foster deceased and bounded northerly on land of said Foster and partly on land of Bartholomew Phillips until it comes to land of Elisha

Babcock, thence easterly on land of said Babcock until it comes to land of William Potter Jr., thence westerly bounding southerly on land of said Potter until it comes to northwest corner of said Potter, from thence south or southerly bounding easterly on land of said Potter to the first mentioned bound; Judith wife of Richard Bailey relinquished dower; witnesses Caleb Butler, Joshua Webb; signed Richard Bailey; 24 Oct 1774, Richard Bailey personally appeared to warrant deed 24 Oct 1774, recorded 26 Oct 1774 (Richmond RI Land Evidences Book 3:117–118)

1775: Major Richard Bailey chosen Town Treasurer; he giving in his fees to the Town towards the support of his brother and is engaged; 6 Jun 1775 (Richmond RI Town Meeting Records and Land Evidences Book 2: 363)

1776: Richard Bailey part of committee to determine which freemen are incapable of arming themselves; 19 Feb 1776 (Richmond RI Town Meeting Records and Land Evidences Book 2: 369)

1776: Major Richard Bailey Deputy for Richmond in RI General Assembly; (first Wednesday) May 1776 (Records of the colony of RI and Providence Plantations (Providence Plantations (Providence, 1856–1865) 7:511)

1776: Town store to be moved to Major Richard Bailey, he giving receipt; 4 Jun 1776 (Richmond RI Town Meeting Records and Land Evidences Book 3: 531)

1776: Major Richard Bailey and Samuel Clarke chosen committee to receive arms and deliver them to soldiers raised in this Town; 16 Sept 1776 (Richmond RI Town Meeting Records and Land Evidences Book 3:532)

1776: Major Richard Bailey got order for ~7.4.0 for blankets for soldiers; 3 Dec 1776 (Richmond RI Town Meeting Records and Land Evidences book 3:534)

1777: Captain Richard Bailey Jr. appointed to have care of stores in room of Major Richard Bailey who declines; 5 May 1777 (Richmond RI Town Meeting Records and Land Evidences Book 3:536

1777: Major Richard Bailey Deputy for Richmond in RI General Assembly; (first Wednesday) May 1777 (Records of the Colony of RI and Providence Plantations (Providence, 1856–1865) 8:219)

1777: Richard Bailey of Richmond appointed to procure blankets from his town; 19 May 1777 (Records of the Colony of RI and Providence Plantations (Providence, 1856–1865) 8:254)

1778: Major Richard Bailey et alia chosen committee to implement Act of General Assembly for taking a general estimate of rateable property; 7 Dec 1778 (Richmond RI Town Meeting Records and Land Evidences Book 3:552)

1779: Major Richard Bailey and George Webb appointed to collect Town's portion of State Tax; 5 Mar 1779 (Richmond RI Town Meeting Records and Land evidences Book 3:555)

1780: Major Richard Bailey chosen one of two delegates to the RI General Assembly; 29 Aug 1780 (Richmond RI Town Meeting Records and Land Evidences Book 3:497)

1780: Richard Bailey (Jr) granted letters of administration for estate of father Richard Bailey; he posted bond; 21 Nov 1780 (Richmond RI Probate Records Book 2:297)

1780: Major Richard Bailey chosen delegate to the RI General Assembly in room of Major Richard Bailey deceased; 20 Oct 1780 (Richmond RI Town Meeting Records and Land Evidences Book 3:501)

> v.   JEREMIAH BAILEY SR., b. about 1709, Newport, Rhode Island; d. about 1779, Granville County, North Carolina; m. UNKNOWN, before 1740; b. about 1715.

Notes for JEREMIAH BAILEY SR.:

Jeremiah Bailey was born about 1709 in Newport, Rhode Island. Jeremiah's mother, Elizabeth (Rogers) Bailey probably named Jeremiah after her brother, Jeremiah Rogers.

1775: Joseph Hull Jr. and Susanna his wife, to James Halls, 27A bounded: land in possession of Wm Bently, land in possession of Jeremiah Boss, ye said Joseph Hull, John Tift, Jan. 27, 1724/25. Witnesses: Anne Rogers, Rebeckah Rogers, George Babcock Jr., and Jeremiah Bailey. (Westerly RI Deeds Vol 4 Page 103 FHL film #940,233)

Note: Jeremiah's father Samuel Bailey also witnesses a 1719 deed for Joseph and Susanna Hull. Samuel Bailey's family was the only Bailey's living in Westerly during this time period. Jeremiah's first cousins, Anne and Rebeckah Rogers witnesses on the above Deed were sisters of Peleg and Job Rogers.

1734/5: Jeremiah Bailey's first cousins Peleg and Jo Rogers sold their land in Westerly Rhode Island and moved to Bertie County, NC. At this time I have no documents but I believe Jeremiah Bailey Sr. left Westerly Rhode Island and came with his first cousins to North Carolina.

Note: Some time before September 1750, Jeremiah Bailey Sr. moved his family from Goshen Swamp, NC to the forks of the Yadkin River in Anson County, NC. This part of Anson County became Rowan County, NC in 1753.

1750: Robert Jones 29 Sept 1750 280 acres in New Hanover County on the north side of Goshen Swamp- being the land that Jerry Bailey built a cabin on. (Colony of North Carolina 1735 - 1764, Abstracts of Land Patents Vol.1 by Margaret M. Hofmann, page 250)

Note: Looks like Jeremiah Bailey Sr. was squatting on the Land on Goshen Swamp. Also living on the north side of Goshen Swamp was a John Rogers. Peleg Rogers died in New Hanover County, NC and had a son named John.

1753: September – Jeremiah Bailey portioned this Court for a license to keep ferry over the Yadkin River and at the Plantation where he now lives. Granted security proposed John Whisides and John Dunn.

1753: September – Jeremiah Bailey portioned this court for a license to keep public house at the plantation where he now lives. Granted security proposed John Whisides and John Dunn.

1754: March 22, Peter Aron (appellant) vs. Jeremiah Bailey (appealer) the consideration of the court was that the appellant shall have a new trial this next court the verdict of this jury not being agreeable. (Peter Aaron also had a license to keep a Public House)

The information above came from (Of the Court of Pleas and Quarterly Sessions Rowan County, NC 1753 – 1762, pages 9,11,and 22.)

1758: 25 May – Witness: John Henry and Jeremiah Bailey called for evidence in William Linn vs. William Harrison. (Rowan County Superior Minutes 1:39) page 119 The Frontier Hendricks Vol 1, by John Scott Davenport)

1759: Jeremiah Bailey and the famous Daniel Boone were listed on the Rowan County Militia List. During this time period Rowan County was about as far west one could go in NC. The Rowan County Militia was fighting Indians in the French and Indian War. (1759 Rowan County Militia List, from the Military Collection of the Treasurers and Comptroller's Papers at the North Carolina Archives.)

1761: 4 April, James Carson 320 acres in Rowan County in the Parish of St. Luke on the north side of Grante Creek. James Carson. Wits: John Frochock, Henry McHenry examined by: John Frochock, Surveyer."This is the last date I can find Jeremiah Bailey Sr. in Rowan County, NC."

Note: Robert W. Ramsey, in his book "Carolina Cradle: stated that half of the families living in Rowan County moved east during the French and Indian War 1756 – 1761.

1761: Some time after February 15, Jeremiah Bailey Sr. moved his family east to Granville County, NC, within a few miles of his first cousin, Job Rogers and his son, Peleg Rogers.

1761:On 5 Aug 1761, Gilliam Harris sold 297 acres of land on both sides of Newlight Creek to Jeremiah Bailey for 20 pds. Witness: Britain Fuller, John Bridges, (Granville Deed Book E page 4)

1761: Tax list Granville Co., NC Jeremiah Bailey and two sons (Richard & Jeremiah C.) no blacks listed.

1761: Deed Book E page 62 records a deed dated 24 Dec 1761 from Archibald Graham to John Mann, witnesses by Gilliam Harris, Jeremiah Bailey and Solomon Fuller.

1767: Tax list for Granville County showed Jeremiah Bailey with 2 white polls (himself & Jeremiah C.) and Richard Bailey with 1 white poll.

1769: Tax list for Granville County showed that Jeremiah Bailey with 3 white poll (himself & William & John). Jeremiah, Jr. with 1 white poll and Richard with 1 white poll.

1769: Granville County Deed Book 1 page 326 records a deed on 10 Jun 1769 from Jeremiah Bailey, Sr. to Richard Bailey for 10 Virginia money for 107 acres of land on both sides of Newlight Creek, Witnessed by Gilliam Harris and William Bailey.

Note: Jeremiah Bailey Sr. paid a poll Tax in 1769; he was not listed on the 1771 Tax list of Granville County. Jeremiah Bailey Sr. was not list on the 1771 Granville County Militia. This time period in NC, a male stop paying poll tax at the age of 60, also the Militia requirement was 16-60. With this information Jeremiah Bailey Sr. was born about 1709.

1775: Granville County Deed Book L. page 210 dated 12 Sept 1775, records the sale of 150 acres of land on both sides of Newlight Creek to William Bailey by Jeremiah Bailey Sr. for 20 pd. Proclamation money. Witnessed by: William Jones, Jones Fuller.

1776: April 12 – North Carolina became the first Colony to vote for independence.

North Carolina, The State Record Vol. XXII page 173

1778: OATH OF ALLEGIANCE TO THE STATE OF NORTH CAROLINA

The independent government thereof against George the third King of Great Britain and His successors and the attempts of any other person, Prince, Power, State, or Potentate who by secret arts, treason, conspiracies or by open force, shall attempt to subvert the same and will in every respect conduct myself as a peaceful, orderly subject and that I will disclose and make known to the Governor, some members of the Council of State or some Justice of the superior Courts or the Peace all treason conspiracies and attempts committed or intended against the state which shall come to my knowledge.

Oath of Allegiance of the State of North Carolina and for the County of Granville and the district of Beaver Dam taken by the subscribers and administered, by Thomas Banks. To-Witt:

Jeremiah (his X mark) Bailey Sr.

Note: between 1778 and 1779 no more reference Jeremiah Bailey Sr. and Jr.

1781: Lord Cornwallis' finally surrendered at Yorktown on October 19,1781

    vi. SAMUEL BAILEY JR., b. about 1714, Westerly, Providence Rhode Island; d. about 1774, Richmond, Kings County, RI; m. CHARITY CLOSSEN, 12 Feb 1735, Westerly, Kings County RI; b. about 1716; d. Aft. 02 Jun 1789, Richmond, Washington County, Rhode Island.

    vii. Vii. JUDITH BAILEY, b. about 1717, Westerly, Providence RI; m THOMAS BRAND JR., 17 May 1739, Westerly, Kings County RI; b. about 1705, Westerly, Providence, Rhode Island.

:

EPILOGUE

My Little Black Book

I could never have imagined I could be writing these words down in any fashion at all. I began jotting down a few thoughts in the late 1970's. Then years would go by without anything recorded with pen and paper. In 1997, I began again with a black composition book to record random things I could remember and would think "I want my children and grandchildren to know this!" There was no organized recording—just a paragraph here and there about my children, when the next would be about an ancestor that I had heard my parents or grandparents talking of. Then about a year ago, I began the task of finding all the information I could from older family members and pretty soon the "little black book" began to fill up fast. Last summer (2009) I finally started trying to make some sense of all the scribbles, when Billy Webb, a cousin of mine, published his memoirs; I was much inspired. This lovely man had really done a great job and it hit me that maybe my "little black book" could have more possibilities than I first thought.

I then began a task of greater magnitude and tried to sort things out of all those papers and notes that had somehow been shuffled like a gambler's deck of cards They were all stuffed in a big plastic bag. That was weeks and weeks and hours upon hours ago. I took these efforts to a publisher and they laughed and told me that I had good possibilities, but I had to do a good deal more sorting! (Interpretation...it's a mess). So home I came and once again shuffled, cut, stapled, and pasted. Most of the sorting and rewriting has been done on car trips to visit our family in New Orleans. I work on it down there and back, and down there and back again. In fact, I am writing this final page on Interstate 55, heading back to Memphis and home.

As I wrote this book, I invited the whole family to send some personal stories if they wanted to be included, and I got tremendous responses to this request, getting so much wonderful information about us all. Some people wrote about the same things but had different outlooks on the same situation, making it more interesting on one subject. Some cousins and family did not respond to the invitation, thus leaving out a few lines, but this was their choice and turned out ok. I am forever grateful to those helping me with this in any way, and I had so many to lend time and information. I know that all the facts are not right down the line, for there are things told over and over through the generations losing some of their flavor, and some other flavor thrown in with each set told. But there is always some truth left in there and so I wanted to record what I "knew" and maybe keep the stories as they are in my generation. Many thanks to all of you for your help. I have enjoyed a renewed closeness with so many of you writing this book, and I sincerely hope that this closeness will grow with all of us keeping us close as a family for generations.

This is a record of family ancestors, family stories and, lastly, a sort of biography of 55 years of being married and with the "love of my life" since the 5th grade! That's a lot of recorded years and is still choppy, I'm sure, but is recorded for my family now and their families yet to be born.

These pages contain connections to people you would not believe. With so many in Mama and Daddy's generation, these marriages alone meant many connections to people all across the country.

For all of us now and the ones yet to be born, "Keep the Seeds Growing!"

It is my way of leaving more than our footprints in the sands of time.

Various Documents and Pictures

Grave Pictures are from Cypress Church Cemetery

Ann Louise Woodson, 86

GADSDEN — Services for Ann Louise Leggett Woodson, 86, will be at 10 a.m. today at Cypress United Methodist Church. Burial will be in the Marlow Cemetery.

Mrs. Woodson, a homemaker, died Thursday at her Gadsden residence of heart failure.

She was preceded in death by her husband, W.H. Woodson. She is survived by a son, Ray M. Woodson of Gadsden; a sister and brother, Lydia Williams of North Haven, Conn., and Tommy Leggett of West Wego, La.

For more information, call Bells Funeral Home at (901) 663-2766.

BUSTER LEGGETT

Buster Leggett, aged 40, died August 1st at the Baptist Hospital in Memphis. He had been ill five weeks. Mr. Leggett was a resident of the Cypress community and was a life long resident of this county. He was a member of the Methodist church and had many friends who are deeply grieved by his passing.

Services were held last Thursday at Cypress Methodist church, Rev. E. R. Roach officiating. Burial in Cypress Cemetery with Ronk Funeral Home in charge.

He is survived by his wife; two children, Betty Ann and Myrtle Rose; three brothers, Clarence Leggett of Cypress community; Raymond and Tommie Leggett of Napoleanville, La.; four sisters, Mrs. Arthur Bailey of Liberty Hall community, Mrs. Edward Hannah and Miss Lidye Belle Leggett of Bells and Mrs. Louise Woodson of Fruitvale.

This community was shocked and grieved Saturday when it became known that Col. Lawrence Bailey had died suddenly at his home in San Antonio, Texas. He was reared in this community, had served in World War II, where he was promoted to Lieutentant Colonal. His funeral was to be held on Tuesday, a military band sounding taps. at the close of the service. His many friends and relatives here are grieved at his passing.

Col. Bailey

Services for Col. Lawrence O. Bailey, 56, of San Antonio, Texas were held at 9:15 a.m. Tuesday. Burial in Fort Sam Houston National Cemetery with full military honors.

Mr. Bailey, a retired U.S.A.S. Col. died Saturday, June 2, after a short illness. He was born near Gadsden, the son of Mrs. Myrtle Forsythe Bailey and the late Mr. Jim Bailey.

Besides his mother, he leaves his wife, Mrs. Ruth S. Bailey; one son, Lawrence O. Bailey, Jr. of Austin, Texas; three daughters, Miss Susan Bailey of Appomattox, Va., Mrs. Janis Pickard, III, of California and Dr. Margaret Bailey of Michigan; three brothers, Arthur Bailey of near Gadsden, Burl Bailey of Memphis, and James Bailey of San Antonio, Texas; four sisters, Mrs. Dorothy Lowery of Alamo, Mrs. Elizabeth Leggett, Mrs. Edith Smith and Mrs. Olive Spraggins, all of near Gadsden; one grandson.

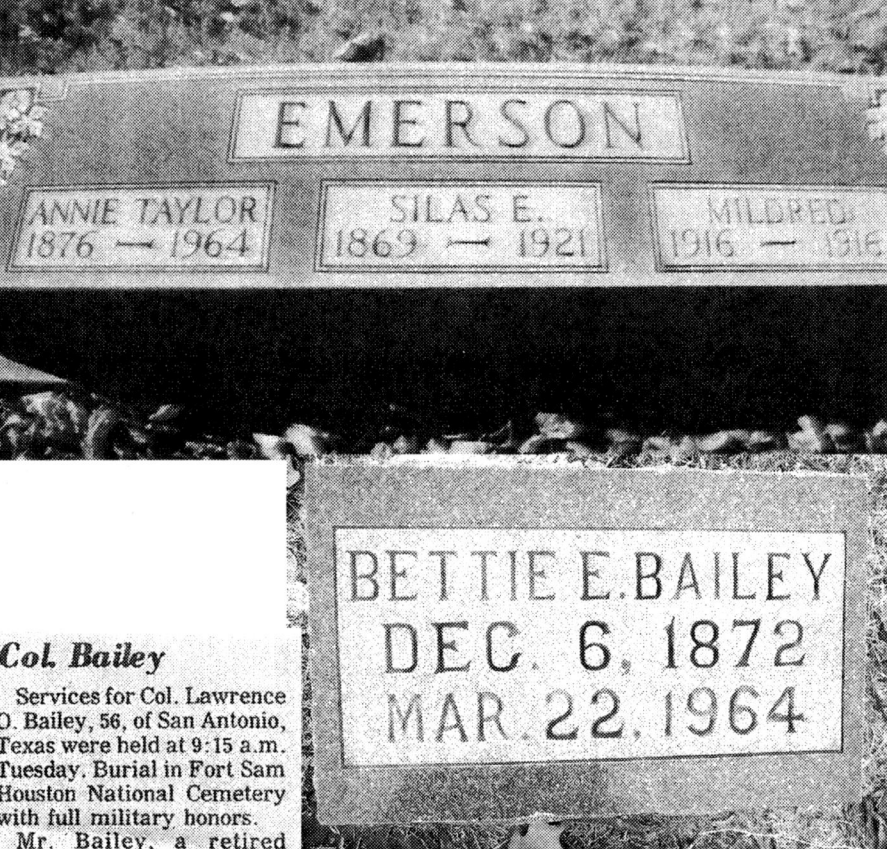

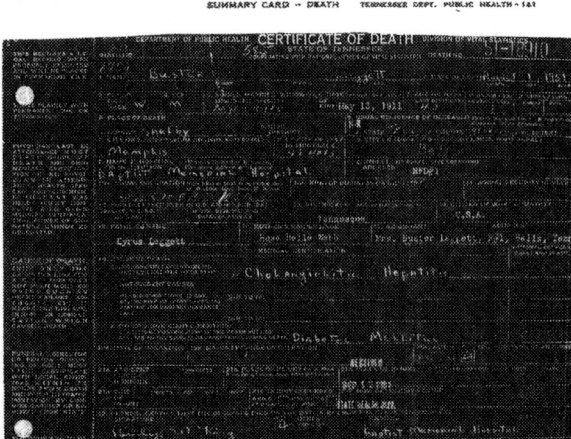

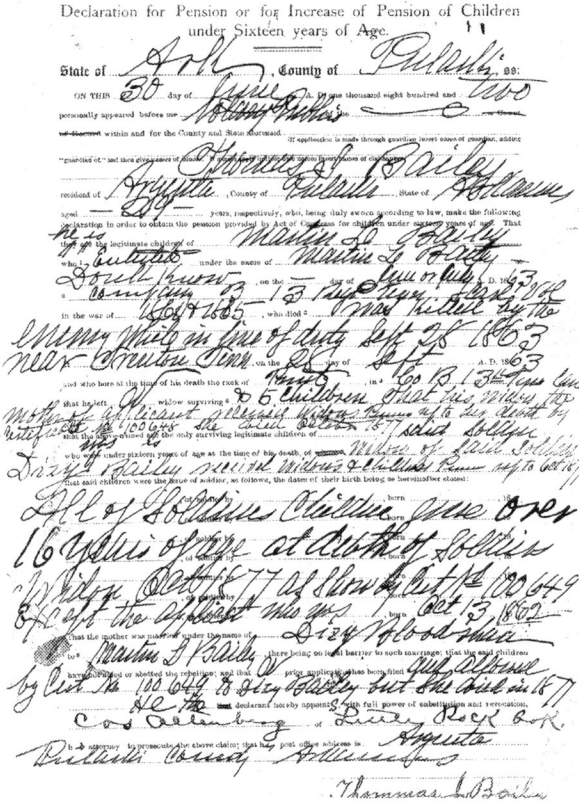

Russell Emerson
Services for Russell Nelson Emerson, 74, were held Saturday at Cypress United Methodist church with Rev. Perry Miller officiating.

Mr. Emerson died Friday morning at his home on Rt. 1 Bells after a short illness. He was a retired farmer; born in Crockett County, son of the late Silas and Annie Taylor Emerson. He was a member of the Methodist church. Mr. Emerson leaves his wife, Mrs. Mable Johnson Emerson; three daughters, Mrs. Pat Sherrod of Jackson, Mrs. Betty Massey of West Memphis, Ark., and Mrs. James Byrum Jr. of Brownsville; two brothers, Malcolm Emerson of Bells and Don Emerson of Murfreesboro; eight grandchildren.

MRS. ANNIE EMERSON
Bells Resident's Rites Will Be Today At 3 P.M.
BELLS, Tenn., July 15.—Mrs. Annie M. Emerson, widow of Silas E. Emerson, died at 3:35 p.m. Wednesday in her home. She was 87.

Services will be at 3 p.m. Thursday in Cypress Methodist Church. Burial will be in the church cemetery with Bells Funeral Home in charge.

Mrs. Emerson was a lifelong resident of Crockett County. She was a member of Cypress Methodist Church.

She leaves three sons, Russell Emerson and Malcolm Emerson of Fruitvale, Tenn., Don Emerson of Muphreesboro, Tenn.; his daughter, Miss Ruth Emerson of Pensacola, Fla.; four sisters, Mrs. Verbie Reasons of Alamo, Tenn., Mrs. Dovie Hopper of Henderson, Tenn., Mrs. Lizzie Nelson and Tenn.; five grandchildren; and seven great-grandchildren.

Don N. Emerson

Funeral services for Don N. Emerson, 82, were held Tuesday, Oct. 15, 1991, at 2 p.m. at Woodfin Memorial Chapel in Murfreesboro. Burial was in Evergreen Cemetery in Murfreesboro. Ronk Funeral Home had charge of the services.

Mr. Emerson, a resident of Murfreesboro and a native of Crockett County, died Sunday, Oct. 13 at his home. He was a graduate of Milligan College, received his Masters from George Peabody College, a former teacher, school administrator and assistant principal of Crockett High School, principal of Hillsboro High School, principal of Culleoka High School, and superintendent of Franklin Special School District. He was a member of St. Mark's United Methodist Church in Murfreesboro. He was preceded in death by a daughter, Sandra E. White, in 1984.

He is survived by his wife, Lavern Riddick Emerson of Murfreesboro; a son, David N. Emerson of Dallas, Texas; a daughter, Donna K. Emerson, of Murfreesboro; a brother Malcolm Emerson of Fruitvale; and 3 grandchildren.

Dave Teal

ALAMO — Graveside services for Dave Alexander Teal, 79, a former Alamo resident, were today at Cypress Cemetery. Ronk Funeral Home was in charge of arrangements.

Mr. Teal, a retired employee of the U.S. Postal Service, died Monday at Fulton County Hospital in Salem, Ark.

He was born in Orange, Texas, and lived in Alamo for several years before moving to Salem. He was married to the late Mrs. Prudence Bailey Teal.

Surviving are three sons, Edward Teal of Abington, Mass., Clarence Teal of Westminster, Calif., and Roy Teal of Brockwell, Ark.; two sisters, Mrs. Ora Mae Ocraman and Mrs. Maggie Huskey, both of Deweyville, Texas; a brother, Clarence Teal of Hartburg, Texas; eight grandchildren and six great-grandchildren.

MEMPHIS PRESS-SCIMITAR, MEMPHIS, TENNESSEE

ILLNESS FATAL TO MRS. BAILEY

vale, Tenn., and Alfred W. Emison, Bells, Tenn.

Services at 11 a.m. Saturday in the Cypress Church with burial in the church cemetery, Ronks Funeral Home of Alamo, Tenn., in charge. Thompson Brothers Mortuary had charge in Memphis.

Member of Pioneer Crockett County Family Was 84

Mrs. Sarah Diliphate Bailey, who was born in Crockett County, Tenn., near Bells, and lived there until she came to Memphis in 1919, died at her home, 101 E. McKellar, at 1:15 a.m. today following a brief illness. She was 84.

Mrs. Bailey was a member of a pioneer Crockett County family. She was a member of the Cypress Methodist Church near Bells, which she first attended as a child when the building was made of logs. She often told of wolves showing up along the road in those days when the family was going to church.

She came to Memphis with her son, Dr. C. O. Bailey, shortly after he returned from France, where he was in the Army Medical Corps, following the first World War.

Besides Dr. Bailey she leaves another son, James Arthur Bailey, of Gadsden, Tenn., and two half-brothers, Bascom Emison, Fruit-

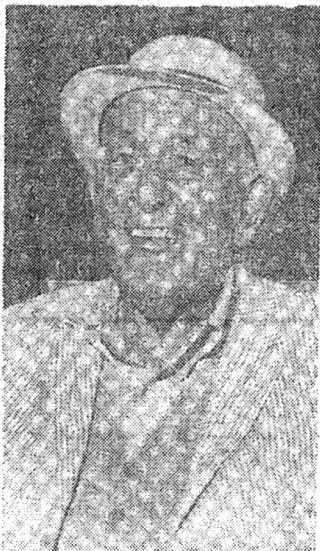

GABRIEL HEATTER

Gabriel Heatter Is Dead At 82

MIAMI BEACH (AP) — Gabriel Heatter, who kept wartime audiences turned to their radios with "there's good news tonight," died today at the age of 82 at the Miami Heart Institute following a five-year illness.

Heatter, whose deep baritone brought the London blitz and the Pacific jungle into American living rooms, died of pneumonia, said son-in-law Ralph Daniels.

The pioneer newscaster retired from his national nightly broadcasts on the Mutual network in 1961. His last broadcast, over a Miami radio station, was May 23, 1965.

Heatter suffered a stroke that partially paralyzed his right side five years ago.

The broadcaster called Winston Churchill and President Franklin D. Roosevelt his friends, and when birthdays rolled around during his later years, often borrowed the British prime minister's birthday quote for his own: "In view of the alternatives, it feels pretty good."

The newscaster used to open every broadcast during the dark days of World War II with "Ah, yes, there's good news tonight," and the news of lost battles and death counts was always saved until later.

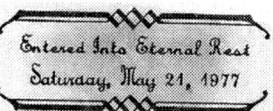

Saturday, May 21, 1977

Mame Lou Emerson

Services for Miss Mame Lou Emerson, 15, were held at 10:30 a.m. Monday at Cypress United Methodist Church with Rev. Paul Phillips and Rev. W.C. Howard officiating. Burial was in the church cemetery with Bells Funeral Home in charge.

Miss Emerson died Saturday night near Brownsville, from injuries she received in an automobile accident.

Mame was the daughter of Mr. and Mrs. Joe S. Emerson of near Fruitvale.

She was a student at Tennessee Academy in Brownsville. She was a member of the Cypress Methodist Church.

She is survived by, other than her parents, one brother, Jody Emerson; two sisters, Elizabeth Shane Emerson and Milly Ann Emerson, both of the home address; grandfather, Malcolm Emerson of Fruitvale; grandmother, Mrs. Elizabeth Leggett of Rt. 1, Bells; great grandmother, Mrs. Myrtle Bailey of Rt. 1, Gadsden.

Pallbearers were: Vince Emerson, Barry Cooke, Allen King, Max Williams, Gary Spraggins, Ross Raines.

Gadsden

Mrs. A. L. Ferguson

visited Mrs. Vivian Clark, who is very ill at General Hospital Sunday afternoon.

Relatives and friends in Gadsden were saddened on the weekend by the sudden death of Miss Ruth James at her home in Memphis. Ruth was the only daughter of the late Dr. and Mrs. F. C. James and was reared in our town. She taught in Gadsden and Bells schools after which she taught in the Memphis school system until her retirement last year. She was a brilliant Christian lady and the traits of fine character she portrayed should be an example for all of us who mourn her departure.

Mr. and Mrs. Charles Bolton and Kay accompanied Mrs. Lucille Hutchison to Ripley Saturday where she will spend several days with Mr. and Mrs. Cecil Hutchison and family.

Mrs. A. L. Ferguson and Mrs. M. D. O'Dell visited Mrs. Nola Cox, Mrs. Lorene Norville, Mr. and Mrs. M. H. Pearson and family in Humboldt Saturday.

As a teacher in Fruitvale school, this writer made a lasting acquaintance with Mrs. Malcolm Emerson. Last week Maggie Lou slipped away after a long illness at Baptist Hospital. Many Gadsden friends and relatives paid tribute at Bells Funeral Home Friday to this fine lady who had endeared herself to so many. She was a stalwart Christian mother, an adoring grandmother, a loyal church member and indeed an upright citizen of the Fruitvale Community. Interment was in Cypress Cemetery Saturday morning.

Mrs. Flora Johnson of Jackson attended Baptist services Sunday and was a dinner guest of Mrs. Chester Williams.

Mr. and Mrs. Milton Nelson left Sunday for two weeks with Mr. and Mrs. Jerry Warren and sons in Lorain, Ohio.

Mr. and Mrs. Frank Smith and Mr. and Mrs. Jesse L. Antwine were at Memphis Funeral Home Monday evening in respect to Miss Ruth James who was buried in Bellview Cemetery in Bells Tuesday.

The Jones Quartet sang to an overflowing crowd at the Methodist Church Sunday evening. At intermission the ladies of the church served refreshments, visitors were welcomed and good fellowship enjoyed. The message in song was outstanding!

Mr. and Mrs. Bobby Lynn

IN MEMORY OF
MR. MALCOLM H. EMERSON
AGE 94

Mr. Emerson passed away in Bells Assisted Care Living, Bells, Tennessee, Sunday, June 10, 2007. He was preceded in death by his wife, Mrs. Maggie Lou Goldsmith Emerson, on February 24, 1972.

Funeral services will be conducted in Cypress United Methodist Church at 10:00 AM, Tuesday, June 12, 2007 with Rev. Terry Presson officiating.

Interment will follow in Cypress United Methodist Church Cemetery.

PALLBEARERS:

Vince Emerson	John Nelson
Jody Emerson	Silas Emerson
Young Chow	Paul Emerson
John Fenner French	

SURVIVORS:
Two Sons: Joe S. Emerson and Bill Emerson, both of Fruitvale, TN; Eight Grandchildren; Twenty-one Great-grandchildren; and Two Great-great-grandchildren.

MEMORIALS MAY BE MADE TO CYPRESS CEMETERY.

DIED

In the Extendicare Nursing Home at 11:05 p.m. Sunday following a short illness

JAMES OLLIE BOYD
Age 90

Funeral services will be conducted in the Cypress Methodist Church at 10 a.m. Tuesday July 6th by Rev. Paul Phillips

Interment in Cypress Cemetery

PALLBEARERS:

Quinton Boyd
James Boyd
Fred Boyd
Ben Emerson
Merlin Leggett
Donald Crossnoe

Survivors: Miss Lorene Boyd, Mrs. Maggie Lou Emerson, Bill Emerson, Joe Emerson and many nephews and nieces

Arrangements
by
BELLS FUNERAL HOME
Fred T. Jones

Garland Harris Leggett

ALAMO — Services for Garland Harris Leggett, 69, will be at 11 a.m. Wednesday at Cypress Methodist Church. Burial will be in the church cemetery with Ronk Funeral Home in charge.

Mr. Leggett died Monday at Cedar Crest Hospital in Humboldt after a short illness. He was a member of Cypress Methodist Church and was employed at Wayne Knitting Mill in Humboldt.

Survivors include his wife, Mrs. Maggie Bodkins Leggett; three sons, Richard Leggett and Bob Leggett, both of Knoxville, and Bernie Leggett of Austin, Texas; a daughter, Mrs. Sandra Anderson of Martin; his mother, Mrs. D.L. Leggett of Gadsden; two brothers, Merlie Leggett of Gadsden and Clifton Leggett of Lexington; three sisters, Miss Bernie Faye Leggett, Mrs. Ernest Richards and Mrs. Ben Yearwood, all of Gadsden; and three grandchildren.

S. E. Emison were read by Attorney J. B. Avery and unanimously adopted. The resolution follow:

WHEREAS, The Almighty, in His wisdom and mercy, has seen fit to remove from this earth our beloved friends and fellow magistrates, Esqs. T. P. Hopper and S. E. Emison; and

WHEREAS, This Court desires to announce to the public, and especially to the families of these deceased, the esteem entertained by this Court for these gentlemen. Be it

RESOLVED 1st, That the families of these deceased have lost a kind, patient and gentle companion and father.

RESOLVED 2nd, That Crockett county has lost two of its best citizens, and this Court two of its worthy members. Be it further

Resolved, That a copy of these resolutions be spread on the minutes of this Court; that the several editors of the newspapers in our county be asked to publish same, and that a copy be sent to the families of each of these deceased.

Nan Overfield, Mrs. Guy Lashlee, Virgil and Cecil Griggs, Camden.

John Henry Emerson

JACKSON, Tenn., April 10—Services for John Henry Emerson, 77, who died Monday at his home near Fruitvale, Tenn., after a short illness will be held Tuesday morning at 11 o'clock at Cypress Church. Burial will be in the cemetery there.

Mr. Emerson, a Methodist, was born and reared in Crockett County. He lacked one day of reaching his 78th birthday.

He leaves four sons, W. R. Emerson of Fruitvale, Hollie Emerson of Alamo, Bernie Emerson of Gadsden and Hess Emerson of Crockett County.

---

her sister, Mrs. Bud Woods.

PUCK AND TUG.

Last week the Sentinel was pained to announce the death of a member of the Crockett County Court—Esq T. P. Hopper. This week we are called upon to announce the death of another good member—Esq S. E. Emison, of district No. 3. Esq Emison was sick only a few days of pneumonia, and his death last Saturday afternoon was a severe blow to his family and wide circle of true friends. He was a good farmer; he stood in the front for good schools, better churches, and for everything that elevated and made better citizens of our people. Sunday afternoon the church would not hold the people who gathered at Cypress to attend his funeral held by his pastor, Rev. A. O. Moore, assisted by Revs. U. S. McCaslin and R W. Thompson. The home, the church, the community, the county, will miss the wise, careful leadership of Esq. Silas E. Emison.

GET INTO BUSINESS—Watkin's 137 products sell to every farmer. If you own auto or team, can give bond, write today for information where you can get territory for selling products of largest institution of kind in world. Twenty million users. J. R. Watkins Co., Dept. 111, Winona, Minn. 1-14-4tp.

EMERSON

MAME LOU

AUGUST 8 1961

MAY 21 1977

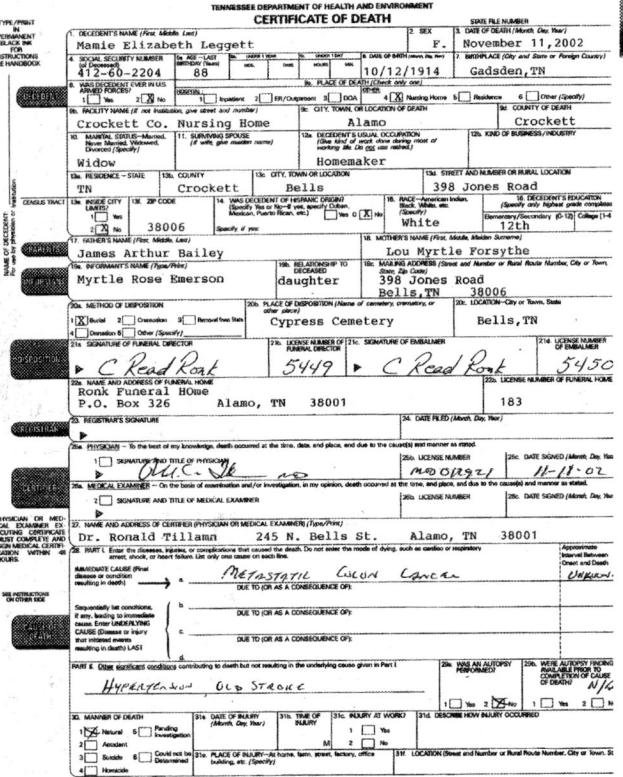

Mrs. Maggie Emerson

Funeral services for Mrs. Maggie Lou Emerson, 64, were held at 10 a.m. Saturday at Cypress Methodist church with Rev. Harold Graves officiating. Burial was in the church cemetery with Bells Funeral Home in charge.

Mrs. Emerson died Thursday night at Baptist hospital in Memphis after a long illness.

She was the wife of Malcolm H. Emerson of Fruitvale. She was born in Crockett County, daughter of the late Archie and Addie Mae Emerson Goldsmith. She was a member of Cypress Methodist church.

Besides her husband she leaves two sons, Joe S. Emerson and Bill Emerson, both of Fruitvale; two sisters, Mrs. Belle Marlowe and Mrs. Brooksie Marlowe, both of Gadsden, Rt. 1; eight grandchildren.

2-24-72

MRS. BETTIE BAILEY

Former School Teacher Dies At Age Of 91

Mrs. Bettie E. Bailey, who lived with her daughter, Mrs. D. A. Teal at 25 East Davant, died at 12:15 a.m. yesterday at the home after an illness of four months. She was 91.

Services will be 2 p.m. tomorrow at Cypress Methodist Church in Bells, Tenn. Burial will be in the church cemetery with Ronk Funeral Home Alamo, Tenn., in charge.

Mrs. Bailey was a scho teacher in Crockett Coun Tenn., for 40 years until 19 She was the widow of Jo Bailey, Crockett County far er who died in 1905. She w a charter member of Cypr Methodist Church in Bells

She leaves another daugh Mrs. W. T. Mayhall of 3 Lakeview Road; a sister, M J. A. Bailey of Gadsd Tenn.; six grandchildren 14 great-grandchildren.

**Margaret Emison Boyd
Obituary**

From an unknown newspaper, Feb 1929.

Margaret Emison Boyd died Saturday at 69 years of age. She was a Methodist. She leaves her husband, James D. (Jim) Boyd and six children: Ollie, Hosie, Oscar, Eldon, Lorene and Mrs. Hom Clark. Burial was at Cypress. Mrs. Gooseman in charge.

Obituary courtesy of Jean Cox Holden.

(Margrett Emison Boyd was born 31 Dec 1859 and died 23 Feb 1929. She was the daughter of Rob and Letitia Bolton Emison, the wife of James David Boyd, and the mother of James Ollie Boyd, Ro Ella Boyd Pierce, William Lonzo Boyd, Elbert L. Boyd, Oscar Boyd, Hosea Herman Boyd, Minnie Azalea Boyd, Lillie Mai Boyd Clark, Flora Lorene Boyd, and an infant son not named.)

Contributed by Jeff Reece

Return to Obituary Index

Return to main Crockett Co. TN web page

© Jeff Reece - 2003

Last updated Friday, 30-May-2003 14:54:49 MDT

Page 15

OBITUARIES

Mr. Castleman

Services for William Lawrence Castleman, 70, were held at 2 p.m. Saturday at Cairo Baptist church with Rev. Bill Coleman officiating. Burial in Pond Creek cemetery. Ronk Funeral Home.

Mr. Castleman died at his home at Rt. 2, Alamo Friday morning after a short illness. He was a retired farmer.

He leaves his wife, Mrs. Georgia Archibald Castleman; three sons, Gene Castleman of Rt. 1, Alamo, Alvin Castleman of Trenton and Owen Castleman of Memphis; two sisters, Mrs. Maude Emison of near Bells and Mrs. Mary Lewis of Brownsville; two brothers, Homer Castleman and Alvis Castleman, both of Brownsville; 16 grandchildren.

Mrs. Emerson Buried Today

BELLS, Tenn. — Services Mrs. Annie M. Emerson, 87, v died at 3:35 p.m. Wednesday her home were at 3 p.m. too at the Cypress Methoc Church, with the Rev. D. Dickey officiating. Burial v in the church cemetery w Bells Funeral Home in char

Mrs. Emerson was a meml of the Cypress Methoc Church. She was the widow Silas E. Emerson who died 1921.

Survivors include three so Russel Emerson and Malco Emerson both of Fruitvale, a Don Emerson of Murfreesbo one daughter, Ruth Emerson Pensacola, Fla.

BELLS — Mrs. Maggie I Emerson, 64, wife of M colm Emerson, died Th day at Baptist Hospital Memphis. Services will b 10 a.m. today at Cypr Methodist Church, with b al in the church cemet Bells Funeral Home charge. She also leaves sons, Joe Emerson and Emerson, both of Bells, two sisters, Mrs. Belle I low and Mrs. Brooksie I low, both of Gadsden.

Physician to discuss tour of duty in Iraq

On Sunday, Aug. 22, at 2 p.m., Lt. Col. William H. Bailey will give a presentation of slides and pictures as he gives an account of his experiences at Baghdad Airport during the Iraq War, where he was the doctor in a tent hospital.

He will give an account of things he saw there and of people living there. He was shot down three times in a Blackhawk. Anyone interested in this is invited to come and meet Dr. Bailey at the Cypress United Methodist Church near Bells. Any questions you may have will be answered by Dr. Bailey during the lecture. He received the Air Force Commendation Medal (Oak Leaf Cluster) for outstanding achievements for performance while on duty as a flight surgeon. Dr. Bailey is the son of Dr. and Mrs. James Bailey of Texas and grandson of the late Jim and Myrtle Bailey of Gadsden.

Dr. William Bailey, a descendant of the Fruitvale and Cypress Baileys, will present a slide show Sunday, Aug. 22, at 2 p.m. about his experiences as a cardiologist serving in Iraq.

Dr. Bailey, the grandson of the late Jim and Myrtle Bailey of Fruitvale/Cypress, is a cardiologist with the Austin (Texas) Heart and member of the Fayette Memorial medical staff. He received the Air Force Commendation Medal (First Oak Leaf Cluster) for Outstanding Achievement for his performance while on active duty as a flight surgeon.

Bailey, who holds the rank of lieutenant colonel in the U.S. Air Force Reserve, was a member of the 447th Expeditionary Medical Squadron, 447th Air Expeditionary Group, 332nd Air Expeditionary Wing based at Baghdad International Airport in Iraq.

He was presented the commendation by Lt. Gen. Walter E. Buchanan, commander of the 9th Air Force and U.S. Central Command Air Fort.

The accomplishments of the commendation read:

"Lieutenant Colonel William H. Bailey distinguished himself by outstanding achievement as Flight Surgeon, 447th Expeditional Medical Squadron, 447th Air Expeditionary Group, 332nd Air Expeditionary Wing, Baghdad International Airport, Iraq. During this period in support of Operation IRAQI FREEDOM, Colonel Bailey displayed outstanding performance by ensuring safe and expedient care to over 600 ill and injured troops in over 45 missions from the Contingency Aeromedical Staging Facility.

"While in Alarm Red conditions following an enemy rocket attack on 30 November 2003, he provided care and treatment to aeromedical evacuation patients in the facility and subsequently rendered critical medical support to 18 smoke and halon inhalation casualties from the attack. On 15 December 2003, he immediately and without hesitation stepped in to provide comfort and medical care to immobilized patients during an enemy ground attack on the installation.

"Colonel Bailey displayed outstanding performance while serving as a Flight Surgeon and Critical Care Aeromedical Transport Team leader providing direct clinical care to 12 severely wounded ill patients during long and arduous aeromedical evacuation flights through an active combat zone.

Unflappable in the face of danger, he again provided rapid response to the staging facility during an enemy rocket attack on 31 December 2003 and ensured care for 12 litter bound troops.

"A proven combat veteran, Colonel Bailey developed intensive care unit protocols and a triage system for the staging facility for mass casualty response incorporating Critical Care Aeromedical Transport concepts of operation. The distinctive accomplishments of Colonel Bailey reflect credit upon himself and the United States Air Force."

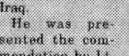

Lt. Col. Dr. William Bailey will present a slideshow at Cypress Methodist on Sunday at 2 p.m. about his service in Iraq.

STATE OF TENNESSEE — CERTIFICATE OF DEATH

Young Cemetery

Mrs. Goldsmith Rites Thursday

BELLS, Tenn. — Services for Mrs. Addie Maie Goldsmith, 83, will be held Thursday at 11 a.m. in the Cypress Methodist Church. The pastor, Rev. D. F. Dickey will officiate. Burial will be in the Cypress Cemetery.

Mrs. Goldsmith died Tuesday night after a lengthy illness in the home of her daughter, Mrs. Ewell Marlowe.

She was born and reared in Crockett County and was a member of the Cypress Methodist church.

She is survived by her husband, Archie Goldsmith; three daughters, Mrs. Malcolm Emerson of Fruitvale, Mrs. Ewell...

TRIBUTE TO MRS. MYRTLE BAILEY

Once again I've been called upon to say "goodbye" to an old, old friend! One whom I'd learned to depend on to share my joys and sorrows for at least 70 years. In our teen-age years we were very close, lived in the same community, enjoyed all the parties and entertainments, Christmas holidays, and other gatherings that country people enjoyed in the "Horse and Buggy" days of long ago.

Since we were so near the same age (only 4 months difference in our birthdays), We attended the same church, were members of Cypress Church for almost 70 years. Then, when we married and started housekeeping, we still lived only a couple of miles apart and in the same community. Both of us reared a large family of boys and girls who grew up together and attended the same school. And so, after knowing Myrtle as well as I do, I feel qualified to write a tribute to her inspirational life. I never knew her to fail to help in giving to any family in need, or to donate a liberal contribution to any worthy cause presented to her. She was "Southern Hospitality" personified, for the door of her large, lovely home was open to everyone, old or young, rich or poor. Her contributions to help beautify Cypress Church were liberal and given often.

I'm sure that now she is wearing a crown with many stars in it, and is now enjoying a well-earned rest given to all of God's faithful children who have finished their work here, and this brings to my mind a comforting poem, copied below.

Beautiful rest for the weary,
Well-deserved rest for the true.
When our life's work here is ended,
We will again be with you.
This helps to quiet our weeping.
Hark! "Angel music so sweet".
God giveth to his beloved,
Beautiful, beautiful sleep.
Mrs. D.L. Leggett

Mrs. Bailey

Services for Mrs. Lou Myrtle Bailey, 90, were held at 3:30 P.M. Saturday at Cypress United Methodist Church with Rev. Jimmy Griffith officiating. Burial in the church cemetery. Ronk Funeral Home.

Mrs. Bailey died Friday at Nucare Convalescent Center in Humboldt.

She was the wife of the late James Arthur Bailey who preceded her in death in 1968. She was born in Crockett County, the daughter of the late Thomas Jefferson and Syble Lewis Forsythe.

She leaves three sons, Arthur Bailey of near Gadsden, Buhrl Bailey of Memphis and Dr. James M. Bailey of San Antonio, four daughters, Mrs. Dorothy Lowery of Alamo, Mrs. Olive Spraggins, Mrs. Elizabeth Leggett and Mrs. Edith Smith, all of Rt. 1 Bells.

23 grandchildren, 30 great-grandchildren and 8 great-great-grandchildren.

Pallbearers were grandsons: Thomas Marion Bailey, Ted Mayhall, Jr., Jeff Bailey, Barry Cooke, Bailey Lowery, Jimmy Hallman, Joe Spraggins, and Jim Bailey.

Mrs. Lou Myrtle Forsythe Bailey

GADSDEN — Services for Mrs. Lou Myrtle Forsythe Bailey, 90, were Saturday at Cypress Methodist Church. The Rev. Jimmy Griffin officiated. Burial was in the church cemetery with Ronk Funeral Home in charge.

Mrs. Bailey died Friday morning at Nucare Convalescent Center in Humboldt after a long illness.

She was a member of Cypress Methodist Church.

Survivors include four daughters, Mrs. Olive Spraggins, Mrs. Elizabeth Leggett and Mrs. Edith Smith, all of Bells, and Mrs. Dorothy Lowery of Alamo; and three sons, Arthur Bailey of Gadsden, Buhrl Bailey of Memphis and Dr. James M. Bailey of San Antonio, Texas.

Page 5

Poet's Corner

From A Myrtle To A Rose

From a Myrtle to a Rose,
From earth to a golden crown.
She's with Jesus, I know,
She's smiling at the sweet, happy sound.

She lived for Jesus while here,
Her love for each one showed through.
We know she's in Heaven, tho' still near,
These words of God's Saint are not new.

I did not know her well, tho' neighbors we were
I would loved to have seen her again.
She showed she was living for Jesus,
Around her there was no sin.

I hope someday to meet you, Miss Myrtle,
On God's Golden streets up above.
I have no doubt you'll greet me without,
And gently lead me into God's love.
(In memory of Mrs. Myrtle Bailey)
Alice Adco

James Arthur Bailey
3-20-1881 CC
12-29-1968 CC

(M)
Bailey 12-26-1907
Grimes

Lou Myrtle Forsythe
11-25-1888 CC
1980 CC

339

In WWII, Bailey risked her safety by helping POWs

BY CARMINA DANINI
EXPRESS-NEWS STAFF WRITER

BAILEY

Nancy Weinstein Bailey, who lived in Manila during the Japanese occupation in World War II and dodged severe punishment for coming to the aid of American prisoners of war, has died at age 86.

She died of heart failure on Monday at Brooke Army Medical Center, said her eldest son, Dr. William Bailey of La Grange.

The youngest of four children born to a businessman and his wife, she saw the city where she was born and raised virtually destroyed by Japanese bombs.

"She witnessed the incarceration of her father in Santo Tomás prison because he was Jewish, and she saw one of her brothers burned in front of her," said Dr. Bailey, a cardiologist at the Austin Heart Hospital.

After the fall of Bataan and the surrender of American troops, she and her brothers saw thousands of American and Filipino prisoners of war on the grueling march to Camp O'Donnell.

Forced to walk nearly 100 miles in the heat, without food or water, suffering from malaria or dysentery, thousands perished.

When Nancy Bailey and her brothers tried to sneak water, rice and bread to some of the men, they were caught by the Japanese and given a harsh slapping.

"My mother said she never had a slapping so hard in her life," her son said. "She said her jaws and face hurt for weeks."

Nancy Bailey rarely could talk to her family about that dark period. What information they gleaned usually was from a cousin who told how she and her brothers would go into the mountains to obtain rice and food.

"All they had to eat was dry rice and dry fish that stank. That's why she never could eat fish again," Dr. Bailey said.

Married to James M. Bailey, an Army combat surgeon who accompanied Gen. Douglas MacArthur on his return to the Philippines, she lived the life of a military wife, raising their children by herself when he was in Korea.

A Tennessee native, Col. James Bailey was the 5th Army's chief of psychiatry before he retired at Fort Sam Houston in 1965. He died in 2004.

"For someone who was a foreign military bride, stepping into the military way of life in America took quite a bit of courage and determination to tough it out," Bailey's son said.

cdanini@express-news.net

MYSA.COM

Keyword: Obituaries
Searchable list of local death notices.

BAILEY

James M. Bailey, Colonel, US Army (RET) passed away peacefully on Friday, September 3, 2004, at Chandler Hospice House in San Antonio, Texas. Dr. Bailey was 87 years old and a resident of San Antonio, Texas since 1962. He was one of eight children born to James A. and Myrtle Bailey in Gadsden, Tennessee. He attended a two room rural school for his elementary years and then graduated with honors from Gadsden High School in Tennessee. He also received medals in high school for his basketball achievements. He was affectionately known by all as "Frog". Dr. (Colonel) James Bailey graduated from the University of Tennessee School of Pharmacy and then continued on in Medical School graduating in 1943. He was commissioned in 1946 as a Captain in the US Army and accompanied General Douglas MacArthur on his successful return to Bataan and Manila, Philippines. He served as a combat surgeon during this time. During his career he also served as a combat surgeon during the Korean Conflict. He then completed a Psychiatry Residency at Fitzsimmons Army Hospital in Colorado in 1954. He served as Chief of Psychiatry at various duty stations during the Vietnam Conflict. He was awarded the American Campaign Medal, the National Defense Service Medal, the Army Occupation Medal (Japan), and the Legion of Merit award during his career. It was in the Philippines that he met his wife of 58 years, Nancy Weinstein. They were married at Fort McKinley, Philippines. They enjoyed a 26-year military career, which culminated in his retirement at Fort Sam Houston in 1965. At the time of his retirement, he was Chief of Psychiatry 5th Army. Following his retirement, he began an active career in the private practice of psychiatry in San Antonio. It was during this time that he also served as President of the Bexar County Psychiatry Society. He retired from private practice in 1995. During his spare time, Dr. Bailey pursued his love for cattle ranching in Falls City and hunting in the hill country and South Texas. This love was engendered from his experiences as a youth in Tennessee where he was raised on a cotton and soybean farm. In Tennessee he was instilled with a strong work ethic by his father, "Daddy Jim". He maintained his desire to be productive even in illness. He received several awards from Karnes County Agricultural Extension Center for the successful introduction of new strains of grasses to South Texas. He was a dedicated member of the Fasching Methodist Church. Dr. Bailey managed his failing health with dignity and taught us as much in his dying as he did in his living. Those generations and friends he leaves behind will continue to embody his character and values. He did more than what the Lord gave him to do. Beloved husband, father and patriot to Nancy Weinstein, spouse of 58 years; his children: William, James, and Johnny Bailey, and Barbara Steed; son-in-law Jerry Steed; daughters-in-law Therese and Kathie; grandchildren: Nancy, Will, Peter, Tom, James, Genevieve, Elizabeth, Rachel, Meg, Carrie Anne, and Michael. He is also survived by his sisters, Edith and Olive Spraggins. The family will receive friends from 6:30 to 8:30 on Monday, September 6th at the Porter Loring Chapel.
GRAVESIDE SERVICE TUESDAY -- 9:15 A.M. FORT SAM HOUSTON NATIONAL CEMETERY WITH FULL MILITARY HONORS
MEMORIAL SERVICE TUESDAY -- 11:00 A.M. ALAMO HEIGHTS UNITED METHODIST CHURCH 825 EAST BASSE ROAD
The Rev. Jack Bush Officiating. Memorial donations can be made in Dr. Bailey's name to the University of Tennessee Medical School Scholarship Fund, Memphis, Tennessee or the James M. Bailey memorial Scholarship Fund for a graduating senior at Robert G. Cole High School, Fort Sam Houston, Texas. Please send these c/o Dr. William H. Bailey, 606 S. Washington St., La Grange, TX 78945. The family would like to express their gratitude to the many doctors, medical facilities and their staff who cared for Dr. Bailey. Special thanks also to his caregiver "Nurse Teofilo" and extraordinary friends Reverend and Mrs. Jack Bush. The family invites you to leave a message or memory at www.porterloring.com by selecting Visitation and Services. Select "Sign Guestbook" at the bottom of the Individual Memorial. Arrangements with Porter Loring Mortuary.

PORTER LORING
MORTUARIES
1101 MCCULLOUGH 227-8221
www.porterloring.com

NANCY WEINSTEIN BAILEY

Born: Oct. 6, 1920, in Manila, Philippines
Died: March 26, 2007, in San Antonio
Survived by: Three sons, Dr. William Bailey of La Grange, James Bailey of San Antonio and John Bailey of Falls City; a daughter, Barbara Steed, also San Antonio; 11 grandchildren and two great-grandchildren.
Services: Visitation beginning at 11 a.m. Friday in St. Pius X Catholic Church at 3907 Harry Wurzbach Road, with recitation the rosary at 11:30 a.m., followed by Mass. Interment in Fort Sam Houston National Cemetery.

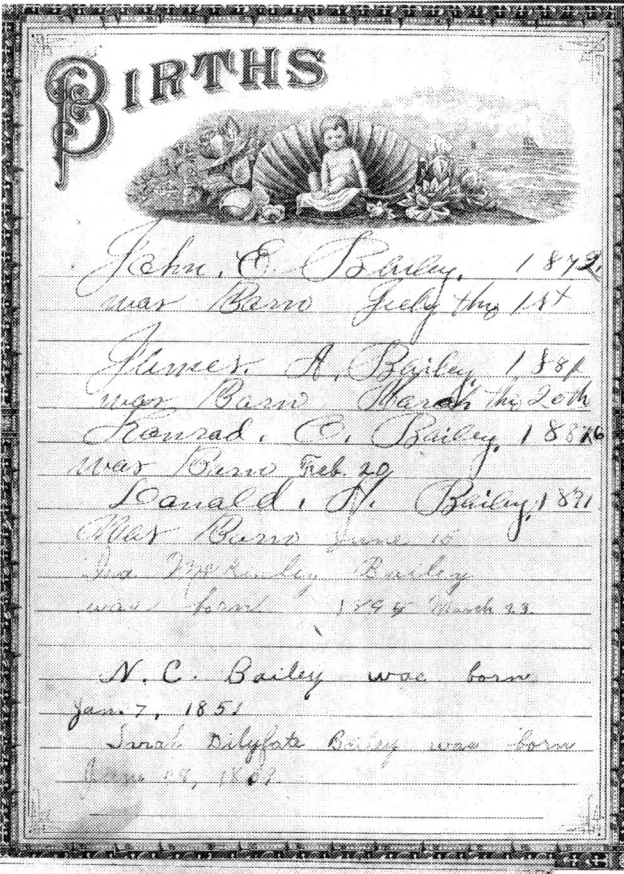

BIRTHS

John E. Bailey 1872 was Born July the 1st

James A. Bailey 1881 was Born March the 20th

Konrad C. Bailey 1886 was Born Feb. 20

Donald H. Bailey 1891 was Born June 15

Ira McKinley Bailey was born 1894 March 23

N. C. Bailey was born Jan. 7, 1851

Sarah Dilyfate Bailey was born June 18, 1861

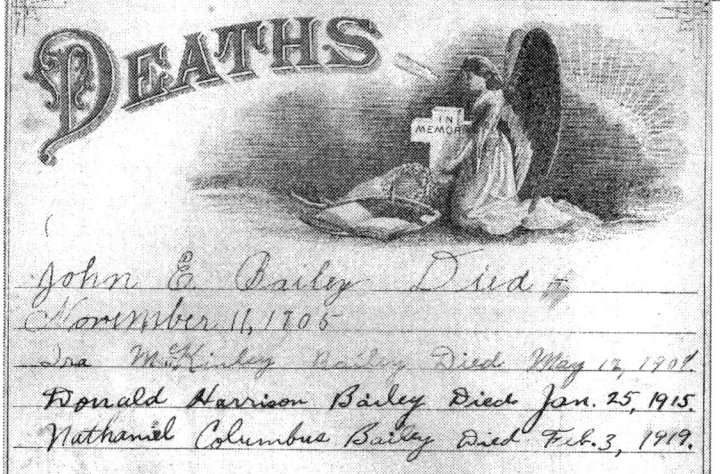

DEATHS

John E. Bailey Died November 11, 1905

Ira McKinley Bailey Died May 13, 1901

Donald Harrison Bailey Died Jan. 25, 1915

Nathaniel Columbus Bailey Died Feb. 3, 1919

Bells, Crockett County, Tennessee

Established as Harrisburgh in Haywood County on April 1, 1826
Name changed to Cherryvliie sometime during 1835
Name changed to Bells Depot on February 11, 1859
Located in Crockett County sometime during 1869
Name changed to Bells on May 12, 1894

Postmasters	Appointment Dates Through September 30, 1971
Daniel Cherry	April 1, 1826
Edward J. Read	December 8, 1843
Calvin W. Cherry	December 21, 1843
Norman P. Cherry	December 9, 1847
Hiram A. Partee	August 22, 1848
Benjamin H. Pyland	October 27, 1860
Hardy L. Wenburn	August 12, 1863
Thomas J. Smothers	April 24, 1869
John J. Farrow	April 20, 1877
A. W. Brooks	January 13, 1879
Mrs. S. C. Winburn	May 21, 1885
Mrs. Mary B. Freeman	April 15, 1889
Mrs. Josephine B. Walker	April 5, 1893
John H. Smith	April 12, 1897
Clayton J. Montgomery	May 16, 1900
William R. William	April 21, 1910
G. W. Bell	June 5, 1914
Clayton M. Dunn	February 24, 1912
Alson C. Patton	March 16, 1918
William R. William	September 1, 1918
Guy W. Mobley	May 24, 1934 (Confirmed)
Russell F. Emerson	March 20, 1959 (Assumed charge)
	March 25, 1959 (Acting)
Warren D. Blackburn	August 19, 1960 (Assumed charge)
	August 26, 1960 (Acting)
Charles A. Whitaker	February 3, 1961 (Assumed charge)
	February 6, 1961 (Acting)

We can furnish for $2.00 electrostats of the site location reports
relating to the Bells Post Office.

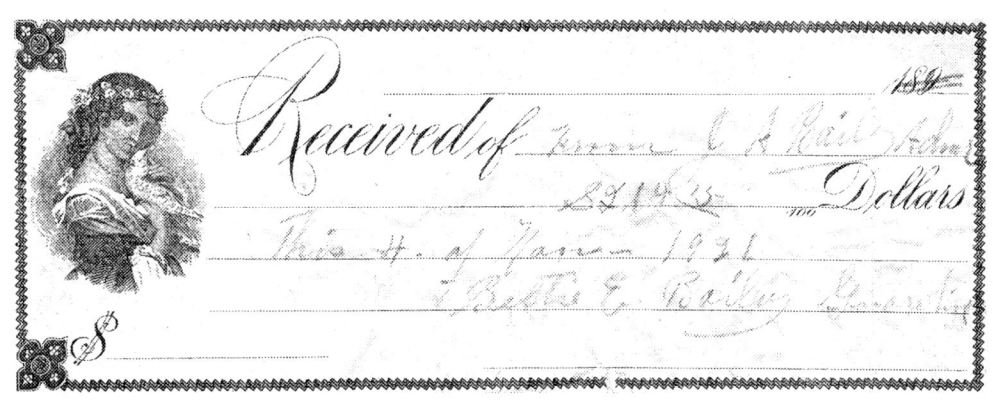

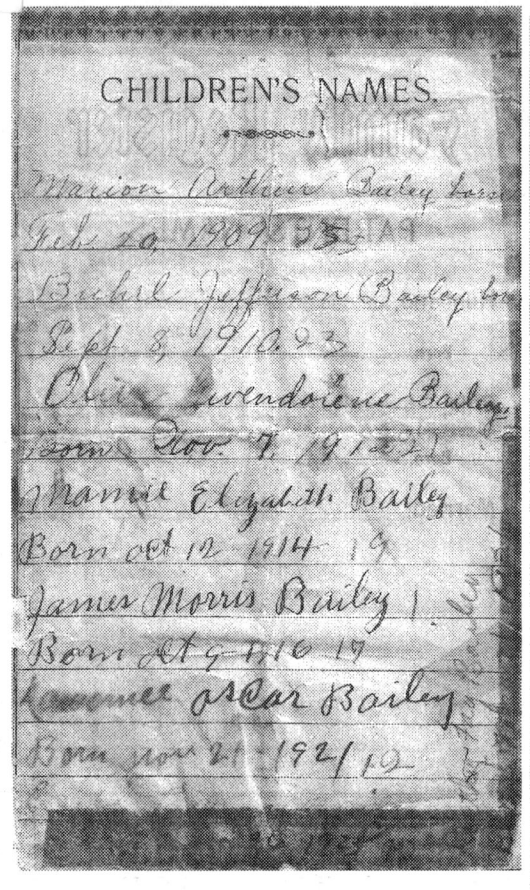

CHILDREN'S NAMES.

Marion Arthur Bailey born
Feb. 20, 1909

Buchel Jefferson Bailey born
Sept 8, 1910

Olice Gwendolene Bailey
born Nov. 7, 1912

Mamie Elizabeth Bailey
Born Oct 12, 1914

James Morris Bailey
Born Aug 1916

Lawrence Oscar Bailey
Born Nov 21, 1921

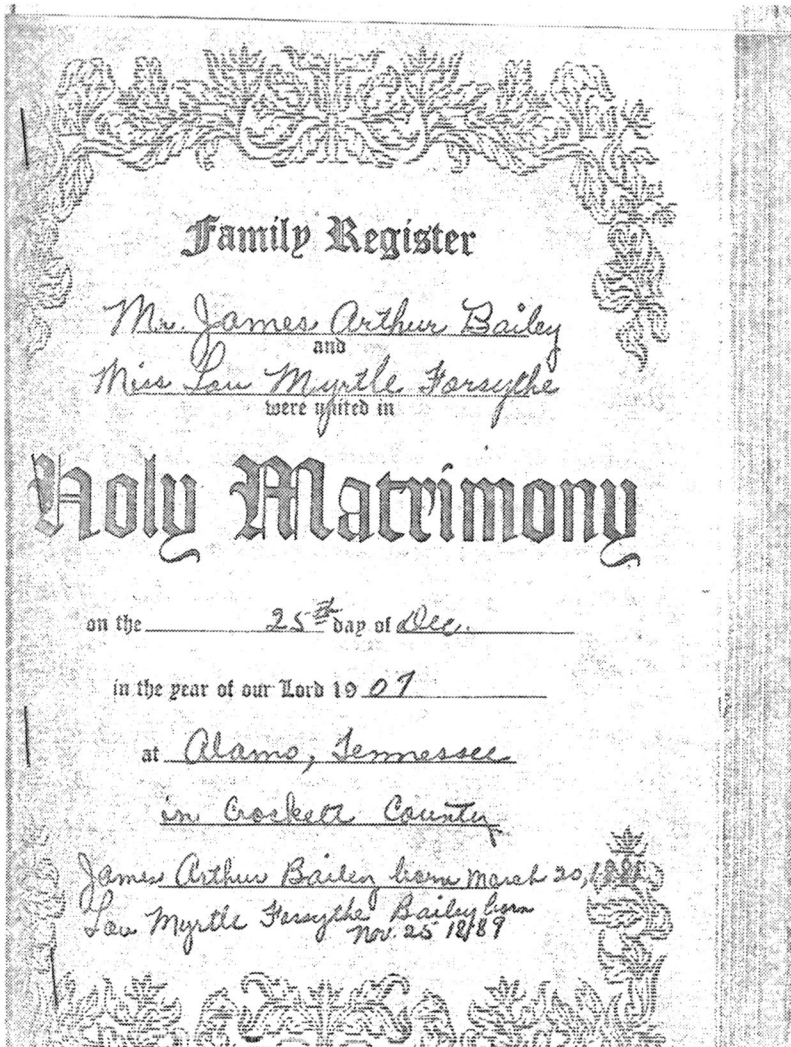

Family Register

Mr. James Arthur Bailey
and
Miss Lou Myrtle Forsythe
were united in

Holy Matrimony

on the ___25th___ day of ___Dec.___

in the year of our Lord 19___07___

at ___Alamo, Tennessee___

___in Crockett County___

James Arthur Bailey born March 20, 1881
Lou Myrtle Forsythe Bailey born
Nov. 25 1889

---

visited Mrs. Vivian Clark, who is very ill at General Hospital Sunday afternoon.

Relatives and friends in Gadsden were saddened on the weekend by the sudden death

Gadsden
Mrs. A. L. Ferguson

of Miss Ruth James at her home in Memphis. Ruth was the only daughter of the late Dr. and Mrs. F. C. James and was reared in our town. She taught in Gadsden and Bells schools after which she taught in the Memphis school system until her retirement last year. She was a brilliant Christian lady and the traits of fine character she portrayed should be an example for all of us who mourn her departure.

Mr. and Mrs. Charles Bolton and Kay accompanied Mrs. Lucille Hutchison to Ripley Saturday where she will spend several days with Mr. and Mrs. Cecil Hutchison and family.

Mrs. A. L. Ferguson and Mrs. M. D. O'Dell visited Mrs. Nola Cox, Mrs. Lorene Norville, Mr. and Mrs. M. H. Pearson and family in Humboldt Saturday.

As a teacher in Fruitvale school, this writer made a lasting acquaintance with Mrs. Malcolm Emerson. Last week Maggie Lou slipped away after a long illness at Baptist Hospital. Many Gadsden friends and relatives paid tribute at Bells Funeral Home Friday to this fine lady who had endeared herself to so many. She was a stalwart Christian mother, an adoring grandmother, a loyal church member and indeed an upright citizen of the Fruitvale Community. Interment was in Cypress Cemetery Saturday morning.

Mrs. Flora Johnson of Jackson attended Baptist services Sunday and was a dinner guest of Mrs. Chester Williams.

Mr. and Mrs. Milton Nelson left Sunday for two weeks with Mr. and Mrs. Jerry Warren and sons in Lorain, Ohio.

Mr. and Mrs. Frank Smith and Mr. and Mrs. Jesse L. Antwine were at Memphis Funeral Home Monday evening in respect to Miss Ruth James who was buried in Bellview Cemetery in Bells Tuesday.

The Jones Quartet sang to an overflowing crowd at the Methodist Church Sunday evening. At intermission the ladies of the church served refreshments, visitors were welcomed and good fellowship enjoyed. The message in song was outstanding!

Mr. and Mrs. Bobby Lynn

Dr. James M. Bailey

From a two-room Tennessee schoolhouse to the fighting fields of Bataan, James M. Bailey passed on life's lessons to his four children before passing away Friday, Sept. 3, at Chandler Hospice House. He was 87.

James Bailey, affectionately known as "Frog," graduated from the University of Tennessee Medical School in 1943. Three years later, he was commissioned as a captain in the Army.

Serving as a combat surgeon, Bailey accompanied Gen. Douglas MacArthur on his return to Bataan and Manila, Philippines.

It was there that he met his wife of 59 years, Nancy Weinstein, whose father owned a business in Manilla.

After a stint as combat surgeon in the Korean War, Bailey completed a psychiatry residency at Fitzsimmons Army Hospital in Colorado in 1954. He served as chief of psychiatry at various duty stations during the Vietnam War and received several medals during his career.

He retired at Fort Sam Houston in 1965 and began a private psychiatry practice in San Antonio, retiring in 1995.

Although medicine defined Bailey's career, it was a love of the land that defined him as a person. As he aged, he went back to farming and ranching.

Bailey was one of eight children born to James A. and Myrtle Bailey of Gadsden. He was raised on a cotton and soybean farm where his father, "Daddy Jim," impressed upon the young boy a strong work ethic.

Besides wife Nancy, Bailey is survived by two sisters, Edith Smith and Olive Spraggins; four children, William Bailey, James and Johnny Bailey and Barbara Steed and their spouses; and 11 grandchildren.

A graveside service with full military honors was held Tuesday, Sept. 7, at Fort Sam Houston National Cemetery.

A memorial service followed at Alamo Heights Methodist Church in San Antonio, Texas.

Memorials may be made to Cypress United Methodist Church.

DIED

In Bells Nursing Home at 1:50 A. M., Sunday, August 16, 1998 following a long illness. Mrs. Marlowe was preceded in death by her husband, Mr. Ewell Marlowe on January 9, 1972.

MRS. CLARA BELLE MARLOWE
Age 89

Funeral services will be conducted at 3:00 P. M., Monday, August 17, 1998 in Cypress United Methodist Church with Rev. Sam Pace and Rev. James Bittner officiating.

Mrs. Marlowe will lie in state in the church from 2:00 P. M. until service time Monday.

Interment will follow in Cypress Cemetery.

PALLBEARERS:

John Pearson	Bobby Marlowe
Leland Marlowe	Nelson Bickerstaff
Joe Emerson	Leroy Johnson

SURVIVORS:
One Daughter, Louise Marlowe Pearson, Jackson, TN, One Son, Edwin Marlowe, Bells, TN, Three Grandchildren, Leland Marlowe, Robin Pearson Gorman and John Pearson, One Great great grandchild, Barrett Marlowe

IN LIEU OF FLOWERS, DONATIONS MAY BE MADE TO CYPRESS UNITED METHODIST CHURCH.

STATE OF TENNESSEE
DEPARTMENT OF PUBLIC HEALTH
NASHVILLE 37219

BUFORD ELLINGTON
GOVERNOR

CERTIFICATE OF DEATH
TENNESSEE DEPARTMENT OF PUBLIC HEALTH FILE NO. 68-035373
DIVISION OF VITAL STATISTICS

DECEASED — NAME: James Arthur Bailey
DATE OF DEATH: 12-29-1968
RACE: White SEX: Male AGE: 87
DATE OF BIRTH: 3-20-1881
COUNTY OF DEATH: Crockett CITY, TOWN: Gadsden INSIDE CITY LIMITS: No HOSPITAL OR OTHER INSTITUTION: Home
STATE OF BIRTH: Tenn. CITIZEN OF WHAT COUNTRY: U.S.A. MARRIED, NEVER MARRIED, WIDOWED, DIVORCED: Married SURVIVING SPOUSE: Myrtle Forsythe
USUAL OCCUPATION: Ret. Farmer
RESIDENCE — STATE: Tenn. COUNTY: Crockett CITY, TOWN OR LOCATION: Gadsden INSIDE CITY LIMITS: No STREET AND NUMBER: R-1
FATHER — NAME: Nathaniel C. Bailey MOTHER — MAIDEN NAME: Sarah D. Emison INFORMANT — NAME, MAILING ADDRESS: Arthur Bailey Gadsden, Tenn.
CAUSE: Cerebral Vascular Thrombosis — 3 wks. Cerebral arteriosclerosis — Not known
PART II. OTHER SIGNIFICANT CONDITIONS: Diabetes Mellitus
AUTOPSY: No
PHYSICIAN — CERTIFICATION: B. V. Maxwell M.D. DATE SIGNED: 1-9-69
BURIAL, CREMATION, REMOVAL: Burial DATE: 12-30-1968 CEMETERY OR CREMATORY — NAME: Cypress LOCATION: Crockett County Tenn.
FUNERAL HOME — NAME AND ADDRESS: Ronk Funeral Home Alamo, Tenn. 38001
DATE RECEIVED BY LOCAL REGISTRAR: 1-13-69

I hereby certify the above to be a true and correct copy of the original record on file in this Department. Valid Only when embossed seal of the Tennessee Department of Public Health and multi-color seal of State Registrar are affixed.

OCT -7 1983

Commissioner

ALAMO, TENN., Dec. 28 192 7

Mr. J. A. Bailey

IN ACCOUNT WITH

Evans & Pinkston Lumber Co.

All Kinds of Building Material

ALL ACCOUNTS DUE AND PAYABLE FIRST OF EACH MONTH.

Dec	12	700 ft flg #2	21 00	21 00
"	"	20 - 12" pilloe blocks	9 00	2 00
"	"	4. 16" "	2 60	2 65
"	26	1 door 2-6 x 6-6	2 65	
"	"	2 pr. ?	1 00	2.5
"	"	2 - 16" pillow blocks	1 90	
"	28	1 window 10x12 8 lt	2 00	
			39 65	

Pd. 12/28/27
Andrew B. Evans

Lumber Reciept Dec. 28m 1927 J.A. Bailey

DIED

In the Sacred Heart Hospital, Pensacola, Fla., Sunday, Sept. 23rd, 1979 following a lenghty illness.

MISS MARY RUTH EMERSON
Age 75

Funeral services will be conducted in the Chapel of the Bells Funeral Home at 3:00 P.M., Wednesday, Sept. 26, 1979 with Rev. James Griffith officiating.

Interment will be in Cypress Cemetery

PALLBEARERS:

Vince Emerson	David Emerson
John Emerson	Dalton Jones
Jody Emerson	Joe Emerson

SURVIVORS:
Three bothers, Russell Emerson, Bells Don Emerson, Murfreesboro, Tenn., Malcolm Emerson, Fruitvale, Nephews, Bill Emerson, Joe Emerson, David Emerson, Nieces, Mrs. Sandra Taylor and Miss Donna Emerson

Arrangements
by
BELLS FUNERAL HOME

Dyer Tenn.
Jan. 30. 1975

Dear Myrtle Rose.
Here is a copy of the letter you ask for. omiting the solatation. Copy.

My mother's maiden name was Lavenia Davis. she was born in the state of North Carolina, but I don't know what County. Her parents were Holland Dutch. That came over perhaps with the first settlers. May have been with the "Pilgrim Fathers" but I can't vouch for that. Mother never had but very little if any correspondence with her family in my recolection. The reason for that in part was because of her choice in marriage. It was contrary to the wishes of her parents.

some of the family married a Congressman. with whom I had coresspondence. But I lost his address by having some letters misplaced Her first husband was a mr. Bird. They left soon after marriage for west Tenn. on Horse back. stopping a little way. from where Godsden is now. There was where her husband met his death in a drunken brawl leaving her with three small children to battle with Pioneer life alone. Her family was those who was wealthy I remember in the summer of 1860 her Brother in law came to where we were living and gave her a small sack of money. said it was her part of the estate. and that is all I can tell you.

Dad.

Margaret Emison Boyd
Obituary

From an unknown newspaper, Feb 1929.

Margaret Emison Boyd died Saturday at 69 years of age. She was a Methodist. She leaves her husband, James D. (Jim) Boyd and six children: Ollie, Hosie, Oscar, Eldon, Lorene and Mrs. Hon Clark. Burial was at Cypress. Mrs. Gooseman in charge.

Obituary courtesy of Jean Cox Holden.

(Margrett Emison Boyd was born 31 Dec 1859 and died 23 Feb 1929. She was the daughter of Rot and Letitia Bolton Emison, the wife of James David Boyd, and the mother of James Ollie Boyd, Re Ella Boyd Pierce, William Lonzo Boyd, Elbert L. Boyd, Oscar Boyd, Hosea Herman Boyd, Minnie Azalea Boyd, Lillie Mai Boyd Clark, Flora Lorene Boyd, and an infant son not named.)

Contributed by Jeff Reece

MRS. ROSA PIERCE, Steward

Ruffin Crossnoe	$ 2
Ina Crossnoe	2
Countice Boals	2
Lullah Emison	5
Etta Evans	5
Willie Evans	10
Grace Evans	2
Blondell Evans	50c
Arthur Jones	15
Florence Jones	2
Elizabeth Jones	2
Pauline Jones	2
Don Pierce	10
Alton Pierce	5
Grace Porter	2
Rosa Pierce	10
Viola Rust	5
Carrie Rust	2
Surene Rust	2
Ewell Rust	2
Mildred Rust	2
James Rust	2
Angeline Rust	2
Garner Emison	10
Alice Stephenson	3
Nelson Stephenson	2
Lessie Selph	5
Willie Tyler	2
Pearl Evans	2
Arena Rust	5
Arthur Sutton	2
Minnie Sutton	2
Ida Sorrell	2
Total	**$121.50**

CARL EMISON, Steward

Carl Emison	$10	
Mrs Iona Blurton	2	
C. H. Blurton	5	
Mrs. Eliza Butler	3	
J. S. Emison	30	
Ruby East	2	
Beatrice East	1	
Martha Forsythe	2	
Audria Fears	1	
Auda Fears	1	
Pearl Gourly	1	
Raymond Leggett	2	
W. C. Leggett		2 50
Rosa B. Leggett	1	
Jewell Leggett	2	
Louise Leggett	1	
Clara Lewis	1	
Elbert Lewis	1	
Hazel Lewis	1	
Joe Lewis	1	
Sallie A. Permenter	2	
Edgar Permenter	2	
Mollie A. Permenter	2	
Dorothy Permenter	1	
Rosa Porter	3	
Lucy Porter	3	
Minnie Reasons	3	
Doshia Stephenson	3	
Mattie Pearl Skipper	2	
Bessie Lou Woods	2	
Mary Butler	3	
Mrs. Carl Emison	3	
Total		**$99.50**

J. D. BOYD, Steward

J. D. Boyd	$30
Mrs. J. D. Boyd	10
Minnie Boyd	10
Lorene Boyd	10
Jimmie Boyd	5
Willie Bolton	2.50
Mrs. Clemmie Bolton	1
Etta Bolton	2.50
Mary Bolton	1
Inez Emison	5
Maggie Emison	2
Hess Emison	1
Mrs. Hess Emison	1
Boscow Emison	5
Lester Elkes	2
Maggie Elkes	2
Mary Elkes	2
Maggie Lou Goldsmith	5
Nina Harris	1
Mellie Graves	1
Mrs. Willie Graves	1
Allie Hampton	1
Willie Leggett	1
Ora Leggett	1
Lona Leggett	2 50
F. M. Leggett	2.50
Annie Norville	2
Alson C. Patton	3
Florene Stewart	2 50
William Stewart	2.50
Gladys Stewart	2.50
Cecil Stewart	2 50
Hattie Stephens	1
Total	**$123.00**

W. W. EMISON, Steward.

W. W. Emison	$ 5
Gertrude Boyd	2.50
Eula Boyd	2.50
Bettie Bailey	5
Myrtle Bailey	5
Marie Bailey	2
Prudence Teal	2
Susan W. Emison	1
Tempie Follis	2
F. M. Goldsmith	30
Archie Goldsmith	5
Adie Goldsmith	2.50
Clara Bell Goldsmith	2
Broaxie Goldsmith	2
J. W. Grant	2
A. D. Grant	1
Doss Leggett	10
Eron Leggett	2
Garlin Leggett	1
Mathlee Leggett	1
Merlin Leggett	1
Mathleene Leggett	1
J. D. Mathews	2
Mollie Goldsmith	5
Martha Spraggins	2
Vina Sutton	1
Loucinda Taylor	1
Joe Lenard Leggett	1
Berl Kenner	2
Jarmie Emison	2
Total	**102.50**

J. L. MARLOWE Steward

J. L. Marlowe	$ 5
Ida Marlowe	4
Mary D. Marlowe	1
Edith Marlowe	1
Henry Emison	2
Emma Emison	2
Burnice Emison	2
Renshaw Emison	2
J. W. Mitchell	5
Sarah Mitchell	3
D. A. Crossnoe	5
Margaret Crossnoe	3
Ruby Crossnoe	2
Margurite Crossnoe	2
T. W. Crossnoe	5
Fletcher Crossnoe	3
Benton Crossnoe	2
Johnny Mitchell	5
Credy Mitchell	4
Eugene Permenter	10
Martha Permenter	4
Annie Emison	4
Ruth Emison	2
Russell Emison	2
Don Emison	2
Homer Crossnoe	5
Martha Willet	3
Luther Mitchell	10
Hattie Mitchell	4
Anna Marlowe	2
Total	**$106.00**

HOMER L. CLARK, Steward.

Candis Crossnoe	$3
Monie Dunnigan	2
Sophia Balentine	2
Opal Cole	2
H. L. Clark	10
Lillie Clark	5
Jones Clark	1
Clem Clark	10
Ada Clark	2.50
Rebecca Clark	1
Mrs. Kate Culipher	2
Martha Wright	2
Jeroldine McCoy	1
Ira Webb	10
Aubrea Webb	3
Abbie Webb	5
Mrs. M. A. Webb	2
Yergie Webb	5
James Webb	1
Floyd Webb	1
Fay Webb	.50
Total	**71**

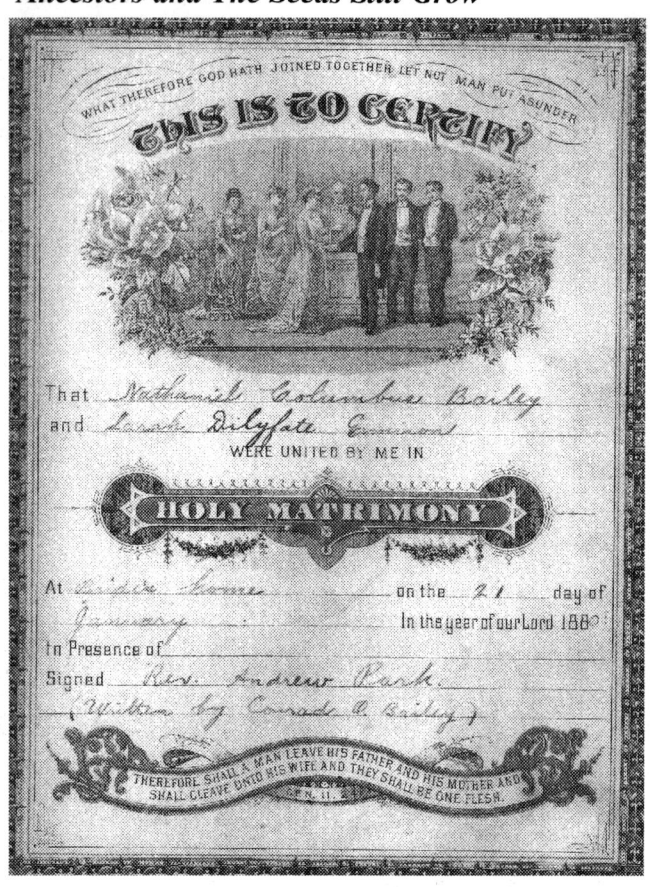

WHAT THEREFORE GOD HATH JOINED TOGETHER LET NOT MAN PUT ASUNDER

THIS IS TO CERTIFY

That *Nathaniel Columbus Bailey*

and *Sarah Dilyfate Emmons*

WERE UNITED BY ME IN

HOLY MATRIMONY

At *Bride Home* on the *21* day of

January In the year of our Lord *1880*

In Presence of

Signed *Rev. Andrew Park.*

(Written by Conrad O. Bailey)

THEREFORE SHALL A MAN LEAVE HIS FATHER AND HIS MOTHER AND SHALL CLEAVE UNTO HIS WIFE AND THEY SHALL BE ONE FLESH.

MARRIAGES

John E. Bailey
was Married

James H. Bailey
was Married Dec. 25, 1907

Konrad O. Bailey
was Married

Darrell H. Bailey
was Married
Ira McKinley Bailey
was Married
Lieut Conrad O. Bailey left for Fort Oglethorpe Ga. Feb. 1918. Returned from France Feb. 2, 1919.

MARRIAGES.

Arthur Bailey Jewell
Leggett Married Jan. 3,
Elizabeth Bailey & Buster
Leggett Married Dec. 26, 1932

Family Register

PARENTS' NAMES.

Husband, *James Arthur Bailey*

Born, *Mar. 29, 1881*

Wife, *Lou Myrtle Bailey*

Born, *Nov. 25, 1870*

Married, *Dec. 25, 1907.*

Original writing of Francis Marion Leggett

$5.80.   April 5   1930

On or before the ____1st.____ day of ____July____ 1930, I, we, or either of us, jointly and severally, promise to pay to the order of J. O. BOYD, FRUITVALE, TENNESSEE, the sum of

____Five & 80/100____ DOLLARS

with interest thereon at the rate of six (6) per cent per annum from June 1st of the year this note bears date until paid; payable at the office of J. O. BOYD, in Fruitvale, Tenn., for value received in fertilizers furnished by said J. O. BOYD for use

on the farm of ____Jim Bailey____ in the County of ____Crockett____ State of ____Tenn.____

The consideration of this note is Fertilizers furnished by said J. O. Boyd as follows:

____ Sacks ____   ____ Sacks ____   ____ Sacks ____

___1___ Sacks Nitrate of Soda   ____ Sacks ____   ____ Sacks ____

I (we) hereby declare and agree that no claim resulting from delayed deliveries shall be pleaded by me (us) in any action upon this note, and it is agreed that I (we) purchased, received and used said fertilizers without any warranty whatever on the part of the seller, save only that the analysis is true and correct as printed upon each bag, and I (we) admit that the said fertilizers have been inspected, tagged and branded in accordance with the laws of this state, and no failure of consideration shall be pleaded by me (us) in any action on this note. Further, it is expressly understood and agreed that the seller has neither expressly nor impliedly warranted the effects of said fertilizers on crops and that I (we) cannot hold the said J. O. BOYD responsible in any way for practical results.

As against this debt I (we) waive for myself and family all rights which I (we) or they may now or hereafter have by virtue of any homestead or exemption laws of this state or any other state. If this note is not paid at maturity I (we) agree to pay all costs of collection, including fifteen per cent (15 per cent) attorney's fees. This note is secured by mortgage on the following described property, to-wit:

To be used under 1/2 acre Cabbage on said farm.

Due ____July 1____ 1930   _____ (SEAL)

Residence _____   _____ (SEAL)

P. O. Address ____Gadsden R. 1.____   _____ (SEAL)

State of Tennessee
County of Gibson

On the 25 day of October, 1865, personally appeared before me, a clerk of House of Record in and for the county and state aforesaid, Dizzy Bailey, a resident of Tennessee in the county of Madison and State of Tennessee, aged 41 years, who being duly sworn; makes the following declaration in order to obtain the pension provided by the Act of Congress approved July 14, 1862. That she is the widow of Martin L. Bailey, who was a private in Company B, commanded by Captain John H. Posten in the 12th Regiment of Tennessee Cavalry Volunteers in the war of 1861. Her maiden name was Dizzy Craig and that she was married to said Martin L. Bailey on or about 14 day of March, 1846, at Mr. Porters in the County of Gibson and State of Tennessee by James Porter, Esquire and that she knows of no record evidence of said marriage except that of evidence a true copy is here attached.

She further declares that said Martin L. Bailey, her husband, died in the services of the United States as aforesaid at Tarpley Grove Church in the State of Tennessee on or about the 28th day of September, 1863 of affects of a musketball by the enemy which passed though his head received while scrimmaging with the enemy. She also declares that she has remained a widow ever since the death of said Martin L. Bailey and that she has not in any manner been engaged in or aided or rebutted, the rebellion in the United States; and she hereby appoints Mr. Wolfshart of Washington DC as her lawful attorney and authorize him to present and process this claim and to receive any orders or certificates that may be issued in satisfaction thereof. She has 5 children at home, Nathaniel 15 years, Mary E. 10 years, Sam 8 years, Newton W. 5 years and Thomas 3 years of age.

Signature of Claimant	Dizzy Bailey
Attorneys	Thomas Porter & Novice McFuel

Personally appeared before me, Thomas Porter and Jasper M. Craig, residents of Madison County and State of Tennessee to be well known as reliable persons, who being duly sworn declares that they were present and said Dizzy Bailey sign her name to the foregoing declaration and that they have every reason to believe from the appearance of the said applicant, and their acquaintance with her that she is the intended person who represents herself to be and know this said deceased recognized said applicant as his lawful wife and that she was so recognized by the community in which the resided; and that they have no interest direct or indirect in the presentation of this claim and they have heard the foregoing declaration read and reconstruct facts set forth therein.

Signature	Thomas Porter
	J.M. Craig

State of Tennessee }
Gibson County } To any Minister of the gospel having the cure
of souls, or any Justice of the Peace for said county: Greeting

These are to Authorize you to solemnize the rite of matrimony and
between Martin L. Bailey and Mrs Lizzy Blalock of
your County, agreeably to an act of Assembly, in such
cases made & provided. Provided always that said Martin L Bailey
be an actual resident of this County; otherwise these shall be null
and void, and not to be authorities any license or authority
to you or either of you for the purpose aforesaid, more than
though the same shall never have been prayed or granted.

Given under my hand at the Clerk's
Office in said County this 13th day of March 1846.
(Seal) A. C. Nimmo Clerk

I certify that I solemnized the rite of matrimony between the above
named parties on the 15th day of March 1846.
(Seal) James Porter J.P.

State of Tennessee }
Gibson County }

I James E. Wood clerk of the County
Court in & for the County & State aforesaid do hereby
Certify that the above is a true copy of the marriage certificate &c
of Martin L. Bailey and Mrs Lizzy Blalock, as remains
on file & record in his office.

Given under my hand and seal of office
at office this 4th day of November
A.D. 1865
James E. Wood Clerk

State of Tennessee, Crockett County

State of Tennessee, Crockett County

CASUALTY SHEET.

Name:

Rank: Company: Regiment: 13

Arm: Cavalry State: Tennessee

Nature of Casualty: Died

CAUSE OF CASUALTY—(Name of Disease, &c.)

BY WHOM DISCHARGED.

DEGREE OF DISABILITY.

FROM WHAT SOURCE THIS INFORMATION WAS OBTAINED.

BY WHOM CERTIFIED.

REMARKS.

DATE OF DISCHARGE, DEATH, &c.

PLACE OF DISCHARGE, DEATH, &c.

Clerk.

GENERAL SERVICES ADMINISTRATION
NATIONAL ARCHIVES AND RECORDS SERVICE

ORDER FOR PHOTOCOPIES CONCERNING VETERAN
(See reverse for explanation)

RECEIPT NO. 8 4492   DATE 12-15-19

SEARCHER

FILE DESTINATION

Department of the Interior,
BUREAU OF PENSIONS.
Washington, D. C. March 6, 1907.

SIR:
Will you kindly answer, at your earliest convenience, the questions enumerated below? The information is requested for future use, and it may be of great value to your family.
Very respectfully,

V. Warner, Commissioner.

No. 1. Are you a married man? If so, please state your wife's full name, and her maiden name. Answer: I was Married to Tobitha Thomas She is dead

No. 2. When, where, and by whom were you married? Answer: I was marred Dec 31 1868 in Madison co By D D Watkins J P

No. 3. What record of marriage exists? Answer: You will find my marriage License enclosed

No. 4. Were you previously married? If so, please state the name of your former wife, the date of the marriage, and the date and place of her death or divorce. If there was more than one previous marriage, let your answer include all former consorts. Answer: Was never married but the one time

No. 5. Have you any children living? If so, please state their names and the dates of their birth. Answer: Dora A Bledso, Born apr 12, 1821, Mattie I Bledso, Born aug 29, 1872, William J. Born Jan 19 1874 Irma V " Oct 21, 1882, Lovina V. Born may 13, 1890 Grace M. Born Oct 18, 1899 Gladys M. Born may 15, 1896.

Date of reply, March 1907.

Joseph M. Bledsoe (Signature.)

In the name of God Amen

I, Dizzy. W. Bailey of the county of Crockett
and State of Tennessee being of sound
mind and memory, and considering
the uncertainty of this frail and transitory
life, do therefore make ordain publish and
declare this to be my last will and
testament, That is to say, First after
all my lawful debts are paid and
discharged, I give and bequeath to my
son Joseph. M. Bledsoe. one half of a
fifteen acre tract of land purchased
paid for by me and deeded to me by W.I. McFar-
=land. And bounded as follows (towitt)
on the North by the land known as the
Elisha Raines heirs, on the west by the
land of T.H. Hollis on the South by
the land of Allen William and on
the East by the land Elijah Raines
and situated in the County of Crockett
and State of Tennessee

Secondly I give and bequeath also to my
said son, Joseph M. Bledsoe an equal share
with the rest of my children in all my
personal property.

Thirdly I give and bequeath to my daughter
Emaly. C Kenner, fifty dollars in cash
over and above the rest of my children
to be paid her by my Executor on account
of her not receiving as much by that amount

in the payment for a horse as the rest of
my children, to whom I have given horses.

Fourthly, I give and bequeath to my daughter Samantha A. the gray horse she now
claims, in addition to her distributive share
with the rest of my children to make her
equal with the others.

Fifthly I give and bequeath to my son
Newton W. the bay filly now claimed by
him to make him equal with my other
children in a distributive share of my
property.

Sixthly, I give and bequeath to my son
Thomas J. the Roan horse colt claimed by
him to make him equal also with the
rest of my children in the distributive share
of my estate.

Seventhly, This will is made by me for
the purpose of making all my children
share and share alike in my whole estate.

Eighthly. It is my desire that my children
not named above (towitt) Sarah A
Nathaniel C. and Mary E to gather with the
rest above named that share equally with
them in the remainder of my estate
not named above

Likewise I make Constitute and appoint
my said son Joseph M. Bledsoe to be
Executer of this my last will and testament

hereby revoking all wills by me made,

In witness whareof I have hereunto subsc=
ribed my name and affixed my seal
the 15th day of November 1875—

Attes N Stop   Dizzy W. Bailey Seal
~ T.I Hicks   her mark

The above written instrument was subscribed
by the said Dizzy. W. Bailey, in our presence
and acknowledged by her, to each of us and
she at the same time published and declared
the above instrument so subscribed, to be
her last will and testament; and we at the
testators request, and in her presence, have
signed our names as witnesses hereto
and written opposite our names our respective places of Residence.

Gadsden Penn   Nelson I. Hess
        "   "   T.I Hicks

Last Will and Testiment of Dizzy W. Bailey 1899 Page 3 of 3

Descendants of

John Emison and Margaret (Peggy) Boals

ଔଔଔଔଔଔଔଔଔଔଔଔଔଔଔଔଔଔଔ

Go to Index

I have chosen to use the Emison spelling in this genealogy report since it is the one in my database. The name has been equally spelled Emerson and Emmerson in the early records of Madison, Haywood and Crockett. The original spelling has not been verified by any researcher, so the choice of the individual families, census takers and record keepers prevailed in most instances.

The origin of the Emison lineage, prior to those immigrants to America, has not been found. An earlier researcher advanced the theory that they were descended from Emer, the first Milesian King of Ireland, who shared the throne jointly with his brother Eremon. After considerable research this cannot be found in any of the Irish records I have collected in my library. A thorough search of my Scottish records have not revealed Emison/Emersons in the clans of that country. This leaves another theory that the Emersons were of Saxon origin and were in England prior to the invasion of William the Conqueror. James I, of England, promoted a massive transportation of English and Scottish people to Ireland in order to dispossess the native Irish Clans of their heritage. Oliver Cromwell, in his destructive march throughout the island, brought in many of his followers, to complete the job of leaving, for the most part, the native Irish landless. It is possible that the Emison and McKnight families found themselves in Belfast, Antrim, Ireland as a result of one of those plantations.

The immigrant ancestor of all the Emisons in Madison, Haywood and Crockett, Tennessee, John Emison, arrived with the family of his aunt, Rebecca (Batty) McKnight on the British Brig, "Alexis" out of Greenock, Scotland. A list of passengers intending to go by British Brig, Alexis, of Greenock to Wilmington, North Carolina included 17 passengers, sworn 29 Mar 1804. Departure date has not been found, but it was probably shortly after the passengers had all signed on. Listed were the family members of Hu McKnight, age 48, farmer, from Belfast, Ireland. Other family members were: James McKnight, age 54 (14), farmer, out of Belfast, Ireland; Batty McKnight, age 36, farmer, out of Belfast, Ireland; Margaret McKnight, age unknown, out of Belfast, Ireland; John McKnight, child, out of Belfast, Ireland; Batty McKnight, Jr, child, out of Belfast, Ireland; and Elizabeth McKnight, child, out of Belfast, Ireland. (Handbook on Irish Genealogy", by Donal F. Begley, transcribed and submitted to the Internet by Alison Davis). The age of James McKnight later proves to be a son, age 14, and the listing of John Emison as John McKnight cannot be explained, but one can only conjecture that it was for passage purpose.

Greenock, Scotland is on the Firth of Clyde in Strathclyde located near Port Glasgow. In 1804, Greenock was a big shipbuilding center, and an important embarkation point for emigrants leaving Scotland for North America and Australia The convenience of Greenock for those Ulster immigrants was the fact that they had only to cross a short stretch of the Irish Sea to enter the Firth of Clyde that would take them up to it's port at Greenock. The Alexis, and other ships sailing from Greenock, would probably have taken a northern route around Ireland until they reached the open sea..

The Alexis would have arrived in America at the mouth of the Cape Fear and traveled the 16 miles up the river to reach Wilmington, the destination of the first leg of the McKnight families' migration to Moore County, North Carolina. The river had many stories to tell prior to the arrival of the Belfast

http://www.rootsweb.com/~tncrocke/family/emison.html   2/18/2005 *immigrants, and it is possible that the McKnights had heard the tales of Edward Teach, "Blackbeard", the pirate, who would sail down from his home at Bath to raid and put fear in the hearts of the settlers. The pirate, Stede Bonet, had been captured on the Cape Fear River, ridding the river of another dangerous individual. The river was navigable by large vessels for about 40 miles above Wilmington. From that point, long boats, lighters and large canoes would take travelers for 100 miles more. However the river, itself, was a dangerous place to travel, with it's fluctuation of water levels, causing logs and sandbars to upset many of it's travelers. Alligators were plentiful in it's waters, and if those dangers were overcome, there was always the thieves who plied the waterways looking for some unsuspecting traveler to rob. By the time the McKnights arrived, there could be seen many plantations built along the river and the town of Fayetteville, about 27 miles up the river from Wilmington was heavily involved in the receiving of goods from inland, and shipping down the river for transport overseas. The Revolutionary War had disrupted the busy activities that had begun to take place before the war, but business was beginning to recover and the river was a busy place.*

The Cape Fear River had it's beginning two hundred miles up it's course in the piedmont area, where the Haw and the Deep River came together in Chatham County. The McKnight's destination could be reached by traveling up the river and branching off into the Deep River, which carried them to Moore County located on the river. This stretch would have used for it's mode of transportation a flatboat, raft, or perriauger, which had been build to navigate the inland rivers. Moore County, was by that time, a settled county, with the majority of it's population Scottish. It was recovering from the Revolutionary War where several skirmishes and battles had been fought on it's soil. Land grants were being issued to those soldiers who had fought in the war, and many of the grants were for land in the newly emerging lands that had been Indian territory prior to 1821 in the western part of Tennessee.

Hugh McKnight is listed in the 1810 and 1820 Censuses of Moore County. In the same vicinity were: Robert Boles, father of Margaret (Peggy) Boals; Andrew Cole, father of Susannah Cole, who was the mother of Margaret (Peggy) Boals; and Archibald Boyd, who married one of the Emison's daughters. Other familiar families who themselves, or their children, were later found in Madison, Haywood and Crockett Counties were: Asa, John, Abraham, Isaac, John Sr., John, Jr., and Jesse Sowell; Thomas, Henry and George Cox; John and Archibald Medlin; Jacksons; Pearce; Perrys; Malcolm, Nevan, and Alexander Clark; Archibald, Alexander, and John Ray; James Freeman; William Coffer; Silva, John, John B., Joseph, Richard, Thomas, Jr., Thomas, William, Benjamin, Elvina, George H., and James Cole; Peter and Murdock Ferguson; Charles Stewart; Flora, Daniel, and Donald McFarland; Archibald and Christian McMillan; John, Archibald and Donald Patterson; Henry Morris, John Baker, Tobias Fry, Warren Jones; John Cates; William Arnold; and Henry Bailey and many others.

John Emison married Margaret Boals, 1820, in Moore County. ..Margaret Boals was the daughter of Robert Boals, Jr. who had married Susanne Cole, c1795, in Moore County, North Carolina. Susanne was the daughter of Andrew and Rebecca Cole. The arrival dates for the Boals and Cole families has not been established, but they were in Moore County prior to the arrival of the McKnights. Many of the Cole families of North Carolina are noted for their pottery which has been a family tradition for many generations. It has not been established whether the Coles of Moore County, were involved in the industry.

The first two children of John and Margaret Emison were born in Moore County, and before the birth of their third child, in 1825, the family had migrated to West Tennessee and settled in the Cotton Grove Community, in Madison County.

The route the Moore County families took to reach their West Tennessee destination could have been across North Carolina to connect with the Valley Pike Road that would have taken them to Long Island

http://www.rootsweb.com/~tncrocke/family/emison.html   2/18/2005 *(now Kingsport) on the Holston River. Basically, their route would have then followed the route that Interstate Highway 40 now travels. The migration from North Carolina tended to take this route. South Carolinians wishing to move west took a route through Georgia and northern Alabama. The exact arrival date has not been determined definitely, but the later censuses record that the third child, Rebecca, born in 1825, was born in Tennessee. This indicates that she was born in Madison County or on the trail after coming into Tennessee. They are said to have settled in another area of Madison county before moving to their final location.*

In 1832, the couple moved to the area located in Madison County, that later became a part of Crockett County when it was formed in 1871. On June 4, 1838, the General Assembly of the State of Tennessee passed an Act establishing the public school system in the state. On June 4th 1838, a record was make of the elected school commissioners in each district of Madison County, Tennessee, and a listing of the parents with number of children attending the schools. In District #1 the following parents, of interest, were listed: Thomas McKnight, 1; Hugh McKnight, 5; and William McKnight, 2. District # 9 had: Kitchen Hathaway, 1; John Carter, 2; James Bowls, 2; John Emerson, 4; Micajah Midgett, 3; Joshua Cozart, 2; and Gray Medling, 4.

After the move to the new area, John Emison went into debt for a large tract of land and died before the debt could be retired. James Emison, the oldest son, went into the stave business, with his mother, and was able to pay the remaining money due on the mortgage. Some of the original tract of land is still in the possession of some of their descendants.

Cypress Methodist Episcopal Church, South was organized in 1831. John and Margaret Emison, their oldest daughter, Susan Laman, son-in-law, Daniel Laman; and five sons, William, John, James, Robert and Benjamin Emison, were charter members of the church. They are all buried in the cemetery at Cypress. The church was placed on the Cageville Circuit in the Madison and Haywood Conference. The first building was a log house 20' by 30'. It remained the main building until 1871, when a plain frame building 35' by 56' replaced it. Trustees at the time of the property deed was executed in 1871 were: A. C. McMillan, James Emmison, J. C. Bowls, W. M. Emmison, and Dan'l Layman. By 1871, the church had been placed in the Memphis Conference.

Following is a four generation chart of the descendants of John and Margaret (Peggy) Boals Emerson. The notes added are those I have written into the records. My original notes would have made the report so cumbersome that it would have been very difficult to follow the general outline of the descent. In addition, it would have taken up approximately 75 to 100 pages. By digesting the notes, I have been able to bring it down to a manageable size. Anyone wishing the complete descent, with notes, can contact me and I will be glad to share a Gedcom file with you. An effort has been made to include the female lines of the children of John and Margaret Emison in this report. It is indexed to facilitate easier researching.

Descendants of James Forsythe

1. James Forsythe (b.1759;d.1831)
  sp: Pharaba (b.1760;m.1783;d.1840)
    2. William Forsythe (b.1784;d.1863)
    2. James Forsythe (b.1786)
    2. Samuel Forsythe (b.1788;d.1845)
    2. Nancy Forsythe (b.1790;d.1858)
    2. John Forsythe (b.1792;d.1850)
      sp: Unknown (m.1814;d.1822)
        3. Pharaba Forsythe (b.1815)
        3. Smith Forsythe (b.1816)
        3. James Epperson Forsythe (b.1818;d.1880)
          sp: Elizabeth Lowery (b.1832;m.1847;d.1903)
            4. Nancy J. Forsythe (b.1848)
            4. Thomas Jefferson Forsythe (b.1853;d.1891)
              sp: Sybelia McMillan Lewis (b.1849;m.1871)
                5. William J. Forsythe (b.1875)
                5. James E. Forsythe (b.1879;d.1906)
                5. John C. Forsythe (b.1883;d.1951)
                5. Perry Leon Forsythe (b.1886;d.1957)
                5. Lou Myrtle Forsythe (b.1890;d.1980)
                  sp: James Arthur Bailey (b.1881;m.1907;d.1968)
                    6. Marion A. Bailey (b.1909)
                    6. Buhrl J. Bailey (b.1910;d.1968)
                    6. Olive G. Bailey (b.1912)
                    6. Mamie Elizabeth Bailey (b.1914;d.2002)
                      sp: Cyrus L.(Buster) Leggett (b.1911;m.1932;d.1951)
                        7. Myrtle Rose Leggett (b.1937)
                          sp: Joseph (Joe)Silas Emerson (b.1937;m.1955)
                          8. Mame' Emerson (b.1961;d.1977)
                          8. Jody Vann Emerson (b.1963)
                            sp: Kristi Kay Hart
                              9. Kayley Mame' Emerson (b.1992)
                              9. Silas Austin Emerson (b.1994)
                          8. Elizabeth Shane Emerson (b.1965)
                            sp: John Fenner French
                              9. Rebecca Emerson French (b.1998)
                              9. John Fenner Jr. French (b.2000)
                              9. Flora Elizabeth French (b.2003)
                          8. Milley Ann Emerson (b.1967)
                            sp: ?? Hart (b.1965)
                              9. Maggie Leigh Hart
                              9. Olivia Rose Hart
                        7. Betty Leggett
                          sp: Russell Cooke (d.2010)

Descendants of James Forsythe

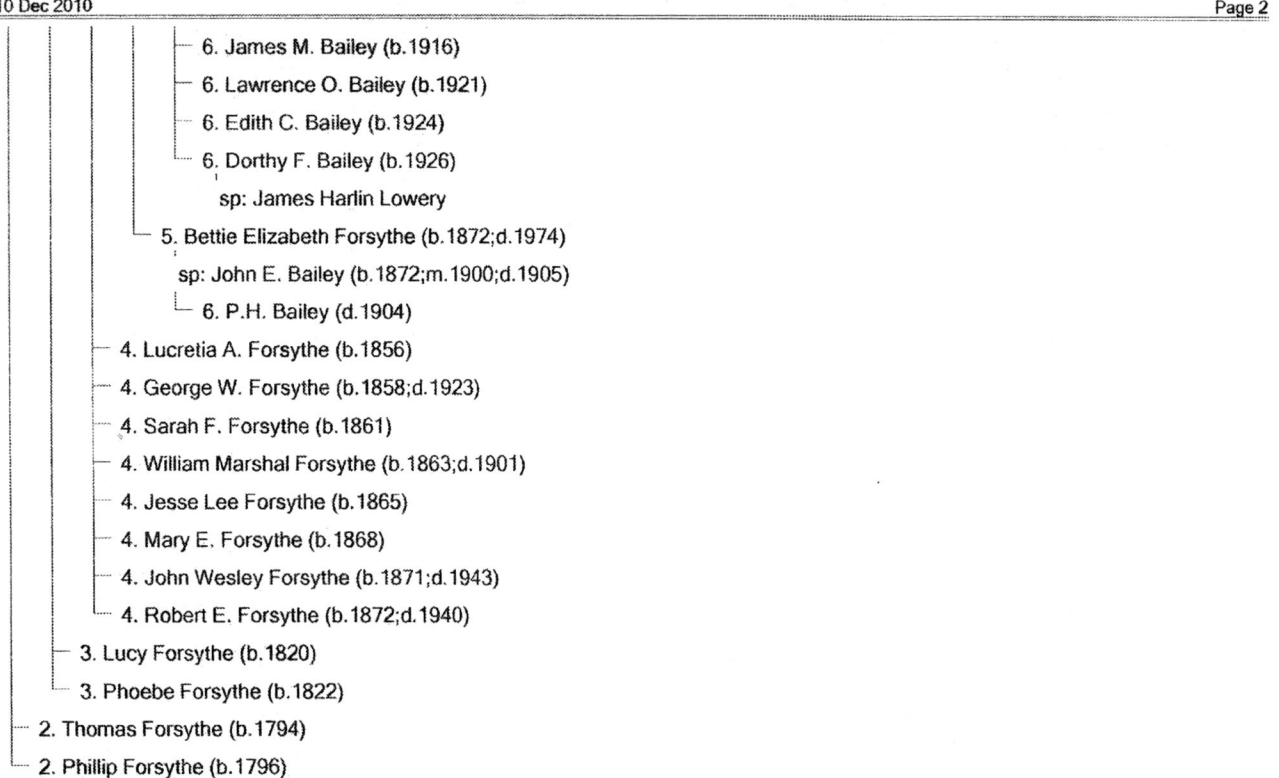

```
            ┌─ 6. James M. Bailey (b.1916)
            ├─ 6. Lawrence O. Bailey (b.1921)
            ├─ 6. Edith C. Bailey (b.1924)
            └─ 6. Dorthy F. Bailey (b.1926)
                    sp: James Harlin Lowery
        └─ 5. Bettie Elizabeth Forsythe (b.1872;d.1974)
              sp: John E. Bailey (b.1872;m.1900;d.1905)
                └─ 6. P.H. Bailey (d.1904)
    ┌─ 4. Lucretia A. Forsythe (b.1856)
    ├─ 4. George W. Forsythe (b.1858;d.1923)
    ├─ 4. Sarah F. Forsythe (b.1861)
    ├─ 4. William Marshal Forsythe (b.1863;d.1901)
    ├─ 4. Jesse Lee Forsythe (b.1865)
    ├─ 4. Mary E. Forsythe (b.1868)
    ├─ 4. John Wesley Forsythe (b.1871;d.1943)
    └─ 4. Robert E. Forsythe (b.1872;d.1940)
  ┌─ 3. Lucy Forsythe (b.1820)
  └─ 3. Phoebe Forsythe (b.1822)
┌─ 2. Thomas Forsythe (b.1794)
└─ 2. Phillip Forsythe (b.1796)
```

Descendants of James Thomas (Sr) Webb

1. James Thomas (Sr) Webb (b.1805)

  sp: Rose Ann (b.1813;m.1832)

    — 2. Mary J. Webb (b.1834)

    — 2. Rebecca Webb (b.1834)

    — 2. William A. Webb (b.1838)

    — 2. Frances E. Webb (b.1840)

    — 2. John H. Webb (b.1843)

    — 2. James Thomas(Jr) Webb (b.1844;d.1922)

      sp: Mary L. McMillan (b.1845;m.1865;d.1900)

        — 3. Julia Ann Webb (b.1866)

        — 3. Mary L. Webb (b.1868)

        — 3. Thomas M.(Bud) Webb (b.1877)

        — 3. Aletha (Tint) Webb (b.1877;d.1959)

        — 3. Willie L. Webb (b.1879)

        — 3. Jesse E. Webb (b.1879)

        — 3. Mose Lee Webb (b.1885;d.1932)

          sp: William Fern Stone (b.1881;d.1921)

            — 4. Johnnie Herschel Stone (b.1904;d.1994)

            — 4. Dovie Louise Stone (b.1905;d.1926)

              sp: Brodie Francis Cates (b.1903;m.1922;d.1976)

                — 5. Rachel Louise Cates (b.1924)

            — 4. Elvis Thomas Stone (b.1912;d.1997)

            — 4. Mary Stone (b.1917;d.1935)

        — 3. Rosa Belle Webb (b.1888;d.1937)

          sp: Homer Cyrus Leggett (b.1890;m.1906;d.1912)

            — 4. Raymond Leggett (b.1907;d.1978)

              sp: Eunice Mary Crochet (b.1909)

            — 4. Mary Jewell Leggett (b.1909;d.1993)

              sp: Arthur Bailey (b.1909;d.1999)

            — 4. Cyrus L.(Buster) Leggett (b.1911;d.1951)

              sp: Mamie Elizabeth Bailey (b.1914;m.1932;d.2002)

                — 5. Myrtle Rose Leggett (b.1937)

                  sp: Joseph (Joe)Silas Emerson (b.1937;m.1955)

                    — 6. Mame' Emerson (b.1961;d.1977)

                    — 6. Jody Vann Emerson (b.1963)

                      sp: Kristi Kay Hart

                        — 7. Kayley Mame' Emerson (b.1992)

                        — 7. Silas Austin Emerson (b.1994)

                    — 6. Elizabeth Shane Emerson (b.1965)

                      sp: John Fenner French

                        — 7. Rebecca Emerson French (b.1998)

                        — 7. John Fenner Jr. French (b.2000)

                        — 7. Flora Elizabeth French (b.2003)

                    — 6. Milley Ann Emerson (b.1967)

Descendants of James Thomas (Sr) Webb

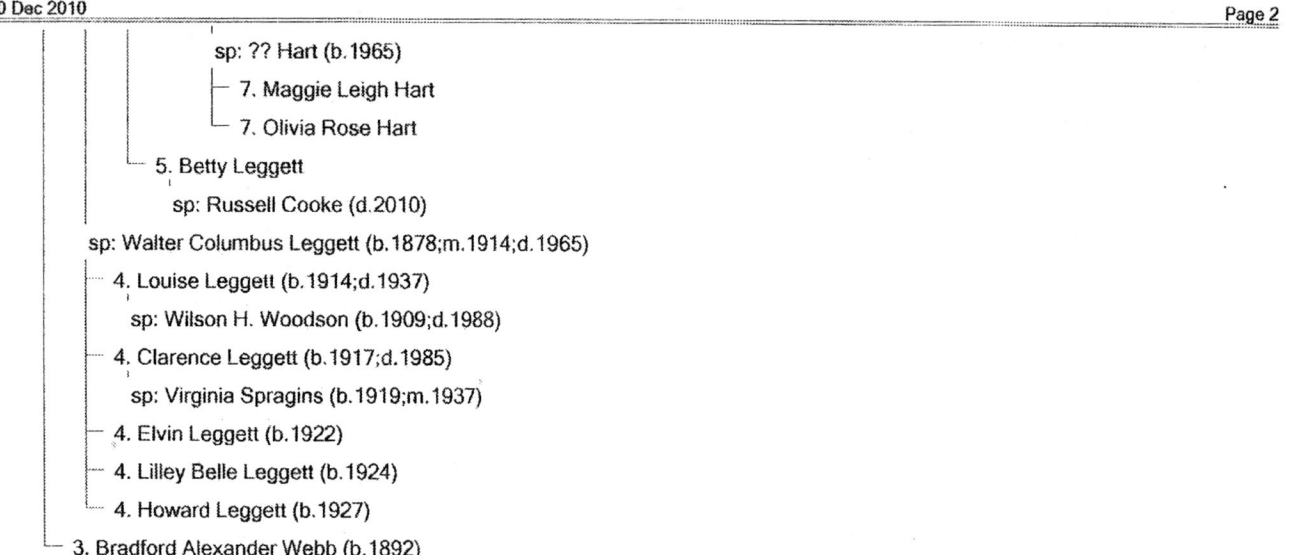

```
              sp: ?? Hart (b.1965)
                ┌─ 7. Maggie Leigh Hart
                └─ 7. Olivia Rose Hart
        └─ 5. Betty Leggett
                sp: Russell Cooke (d.2010)
    sp: Walter Columbus Leggett (b.1878;m.1914;d.1965)
      ┌─ 4. Louise Leggett (b.1914;d.1937)
            sp: Wilson H. Woodson (b.1909;d.1988)
      ┌─ 4. Clarence Leggett (b.1917;d.1985)
            sp: Virginia Spragins (b.1919;m.1937)
      ┌─ 4. Elvin Leggett (b.1922)
      ┌─ 4. Lilley Belle Leggett (b.1924)
      └─ 4. Howard Leggett (b.1927)
  └─ 3. Bradford Alexander Webb (b.1892)
```

Descendants of John Emison

1. **John Emison (b.1799;d.1844)**
   - sp: Margaret Boals (b.1799;m.1820;d.1874)
   - 2. James Emison (b.1821;d.1888)
     - sp: Sarah Bowlton (b.1822;m.1846;d.1899)
   - 2. Susan Emison (b.1823;d.1903)
     - sp: Daniel Laman (b.1815;m.1840;d.1896)
   - 2. Rebecca Emison (b.1825)
     - sp: John Harshaw (m.1850)
   - 2. Robert Emison (b.1826;d.1875)
     - sp: Etishia Bolton (b.1830;m.1849;d.1878)
   - 2. William E. Emison (b.1827;d.1900)
     - sp: Bedie Richards (b.1827;m.1851;d.1864)
     - 3. Sarah D. Emison (b.1859;d.1943)
       - sp: Nathaniel Columbus Bailey (b.1850;m.1880;d.1919)
       - 4. John E. Bailey (b.1872;d.1905)
         - sp: Bettie Elizabeth Forsythe (b.1872;m.1900;d.1974)
         - 5. P.H. Bailey (d.1904)
       - 4. James Arthur Bailey (b.1881;d.1968)
         - sp: Lou Myrtle Forsythe (b.1890;m.1907;d.1980)
         - 5. Marion A. Bailey (b.1909)
         - 5. Buhrl J. Bailey (b.1910;d.1968)
         - 5. Olive G. Bailey (b.1912)
         - 5. Mamie Elizabeth Bailey (b.1914;d.2002)
           - sp: Cyrus L.(Buster) Leggett (b.1911;m.1932;d.1951)
           - 6. Myrtle Rose Leggett (b.1937)
             - sp: Joseph (Joe)Silas Emerson (b.1937;m.1955)
             - 7. Mame' Emerson (b.1961;d.1977)
             - 7. Jody Vann Emerson (b.1963)
               - sp: Kristi Kay Hart
               - 8. Kayley Mame' Emerson (b.1992)
               - 8. Silas Austin Emerson (b.1994)
             - 7. Elizabeth Shane Emerson (b.1965)
               - sp: John Fenner French
               - 8. Rebecca Emerson French (b.1998)
               - 8. John Fenner Jr. French (b.2000)
               - 8. Flora Elizabeth French (b.2003)
             - 7. Milley Ann Emerson (b.1967)
               - sp: ?? Hart (b.1965)
               - 8. Maggie Leigh Hart
               - 8. Olivia Rose Hart
           - 6. Betty Leggett
             - sp: Russell Cooke (d.2010)
         - 5. James M. Bailey (b.1916)
         - 5. Lawrence O. Bailey (b.1921)

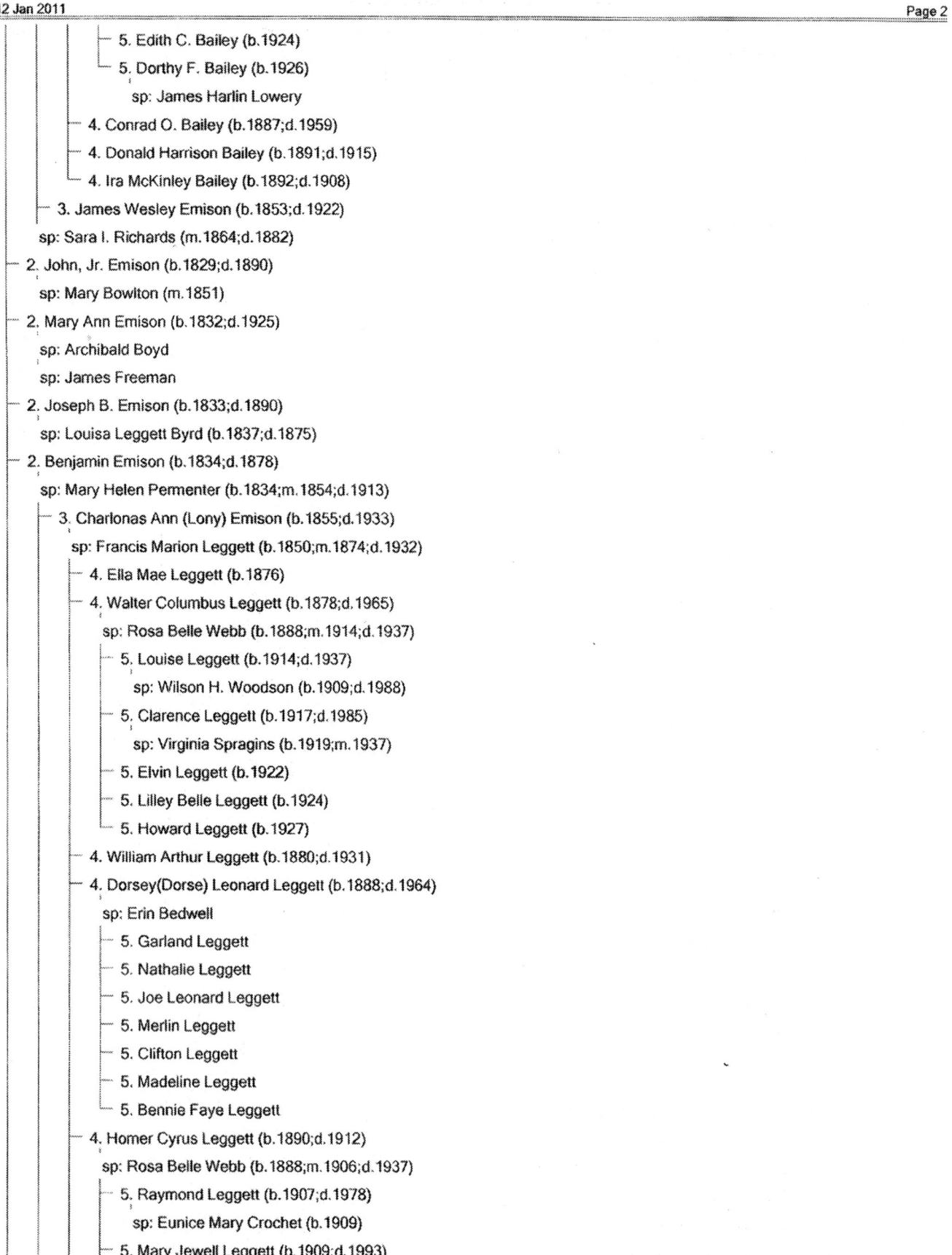

- 5. Edith C. Bailey (b.1924)
- 5. Dorthy F. Bailey (b.1926)
  - sp: James Harlin Lowery
- 4. Conrad O. Bailey (b.1887;d.1959)
- 4. Donald Harrison Bailey (b.1891;d.1915)
- 4. Ira McKinley Bailey (b.1892;d.1908)
- 3. James Wesley Emison (b.1853;d.1922)
  - sp: Sara I. Richards (m.1864;d.1882)
- 2. John, Jr. Emison (b.1829;d.1890)
  - sp: Mary Bowlton (m.1851)
- 2. Mary Ann Emison (b.1832;d.1925)
  - sp: Archibald Boyd
  - sp: James Freeman
- 2. Joseph B. Emison (b.1833;d.1890)
  - sp: Louisa Leggett Byrd (b.1837;d.1875)
- 2. Benjamin Emison (b.1834;d.1878)
  - sp: Mary Helen Permenter (b.1834;m.1854;d.1913)
    - 3. Charlonas Ann (Lony) Emison (b.1855;d.1933)
      - sp: Francis Marion Leggett (b.1850;m.1874;d.1932)
        - 4. Ella Mae Leggett (b.1876)
        - 4. Walter Columbus Leggett (b.1878;d.1965)
          - sp: Rosa Belle Webb (b.1888;m.1914;d.1937)
            - 5. Louise Leggett (b.1914;d.1937)
              - sp: Wilson H. Woodson (b.1909;d.1988)
            - 5. Clarence Leggett (b.1917;d.1985)
              - sp: Virginia Spragins (b.1919;m.1937)
            - 5. Elvin Leggett (b.1922)
            - 5. Lilley Belle Leggett (b.1924)
            - 5. Howard Leggett (b.1927)
        - 4. William Arthur Leggett (b.1880;d.1931)
        - 4. Dorsey(Dorse) Leonard Leggett (b.1888;d.1964)
          - sp: Erin Bedwell
            - 5. Garland Leggett
            - 5. Nathalie Leggett
            - 5. Joe Leonard Leggett
            - 5. Merlin Leggett
            - 5. Clifton Leggett
            - 5. Madeline Leggett
            - 5. Bennie Faye Leggett
        - 4. Homer Cyrus Leggett (b.1890;d.1912)
          - sp: Rosa Belle Webb (b.1888;m.1906;d.1937)
            - 5. Raymond Leggett (b.1907;d.1978)
              - sp: Eunice Mary Crochet (b.1909)
            - 5. Mary Jewell Leggett (b.1909;d.1993)

sp: Arthur Bailey (b.1909;d.1999)

    5. Cyrus L.(Buster) Leggett (b.1911;d.1951)

        sp: Mamie Elizabeth Bailey (b.1914;m.1932;d.2002)

        6. Myrtle Rose Leggett (b.1937) ** Printed on Page 1 **

        6. Betty Leggett ** Printed on Page 1 **

  4. Florence B. Leggett (b.1892)

  4. Norma Irene Leggett (b.1896;d.1970)

3. George W. Emison (b.1860;d.1933)

  sp: Bell Johnson (b.1862;m.1880;d.1917)

  sp: Adernia Brassfield Lipscomb

3. Silas E. Emison (b.1868;d.1921)

  sp: Anna M. Taylor (b.1876;m.1901;d.1964)

    4. Ruth Emison (b.1904)

    4. Russell Emison (b.1906)

      sp: Mabel Johnson Goetz (b.1915;m.1965)

    4. Don Neil Emison (b.1909;d.1991)

      sp: Laverne Reddick (b.1916;m.1935;d.1993)

      5. Sandra Ellen Emison (b.1940;d.1984)

      5. Donna Kay Emison (b.1944)

      5. David Neil Emison (b.1947)

  4. Malcolm Hooper Emerson (b.1912)

    sp: Margaret Lou Goldsmith (b.1907;m.1934;d.1922)

    5. Joseph (Joe)Silas Emerson (b.1937)

      sp: Myrtle Rose Leggett (b.1937;m.1955)

      6. Mame' Emerson (b.1961;d.1977) ** Printed on Page 1 **

      6. Jody Vann Emerson (b.1963) ** Printed on Page 1 **

      6. Elizabeth Shane Emerson (b.1965) ** Printed on Page 1 **

      6. Milley Ann Emerson (b.1967) ** Printed on Page 1 **

    5. MacBoyd (Bill) Emerson (b.1935)

      sp: June Stephens (b.1935)

      6. Lori Emerson (b.1957)

      6. Vincent Emerson (b.1959)

      6. John Ollie Emerson (b.1962)

3. Tennie Emison (b.1869;d.1942)

  sp: Soloman B. Laman (b.1860;m.1885;d.1933)

2. Margaret Emison (b.1840;d.1864)

  sp: William Alexander Webb (b.1838;d.1916)

2. Nancy Ann Emison (b.1842;d.1871)

  sp: Francis Marion Leggett (b.1850;m.1867;d.1932)

  3. Margaret Lavenia Leggett (b.1868;d.1913)

    sp: Tillman Erastus Poindexter (b.1860;m.1884;d.1939)

    4. Viola Poindexter (b.1885)

    4. Theodore Poindexter (b.1886)

    4. India Mae Poindexter (b.1888)

Descendants of John Emison

— 4. Thomas Marion Poindexter (b.1890)

— 4. Librum Erastus Poindexter (b.1891)

— 4. Lilly Equilla Poindexter (b.1893)

— 4. Borce Franklin Poindexter (b.1895)

— 4. Dewey Lee Poindexter (b.1898)

— 4. Maxi Poindexter (b.1900)

— 4. Susan Frances Poindexter (b.1903)

— 4. Bonnie Irene Poindexter (b.1905)

— 4. Tilman Ernst Poindexter (b.1907)

— 4. Aubrey D. Poindexter (b.1908)

— 3. Mary Susan Leggett (b.1871;d.1904)

sp: Joseph LaFayette Gaba (b.1870;m.1891;d.1904)

— 4. Sarah Ann Gaba (b.1892)

sp: E.G. Johnson

— 4. William Robert Gaba (b.1894)

sp: Addie Lee Love

— 4. Jesse G. Gaba (b.1897)

sp: Gracie Howell (m.1916)

— 4. Francis Marion Gaba (b.1899;d.1952)

sp: Lillie Taylor (m.1920)

— 4. Bessie Pearl Gaba (b.1901)

sp: Claude Gourley (m.1923)

— 5. Hester Laverne Gourley (b.1924)

— 5. Frances Janita Gourley (b.1926)

Descendants of John Lowery

1. John Lowery (b.1752;d.1818)
  sp: Winnifred (Winney) Beacham (m.1772;d.1836)
  - 2. Robert Lowery (b.1785;d.1873)
    sp: Nancy (b.1808;m.1807)
    - 3. James Lowery (b.1811;d.1876)
      sp: Nancy (b.1811;m.1828;d.1857)
      - 4. Elizabeth Lowery (b.1832;d.1903)
        sp: James Epperson Forsythe (b.1818;m.1847;d.1880)
        - 5. Nancy J. Forsythe (b.1848)
        - 5. Thomas Jefferson Forsythe (b.1853;d.1891)
          sp: Sybelia McMillan Lewis (b.1849;m.1871)
          - 6. William J. Forsythe (b.1875)
          - 6. James E. Forsythe (b.1879;d.1906)
          - 6. John C. Forsythe (b.1883;d.1951)
          - 6. Perry Leon Forsythe (b.1886;d.1957)
          - 6. Lou Myrtle Forsythe (b.1890;d.1980)
            sp: James Arthur Bailey (b.1881;m.1907;d.1968)
            - 7. Marion A. Bailey (b.1909)
            - 7. Buhrl J. Bailey (b.1910;d.1968)
            - 7. Olive G. Bailey (b.1912)
            - 7. Mamie Elizabeth Bailey (b.1914;d.2002)
              sp: Cyrus L.(Buster) Leggett (b.1911;m.1932;d.1951)
              - 8. Myrtle Rose Leggett (b.1937)
                sp: Joseph (Joe)Silas Emerson (b.1937;m.1955)
                - 9. Mame' Emerson (b.1961;d.1977)
                - 9. Jody Vann Emerson (b.1963)
                  sp: Kristi Kay Hart
                  - 10. Kayley Mame' Emerson (b.1992)
                  - 10. Silas Austin Emerson (b.1994)
                - 9. Elizabeth Shane Emerson (b.1965)
                  sp: John Fenner French
                  - 10. Rebecca Emerson French (b.1998)
                  - 10. John Fenner Jr. French (b.2000)
                  - 10. Flora Elizabeth French (b.2003)
                - 9. Milley Ann Emerson (b.1967)
                  sp: ?? Hart (b.1965)
                  - 10. Maggie Leigh Hart
                  - 10. Olivia Rose Hart
              - 8. Betty Leggett
                sp: Russell Cooke (d.2010)
            - 7. James M. Bailey (b.1916)
            - 7. Lawrence O. Bailey (b.1921)
            - 7. Edith C. Bailey (b.1924)
            - 7. Dorthy F. Bailey (b.1926)

Descendants of John Lowery

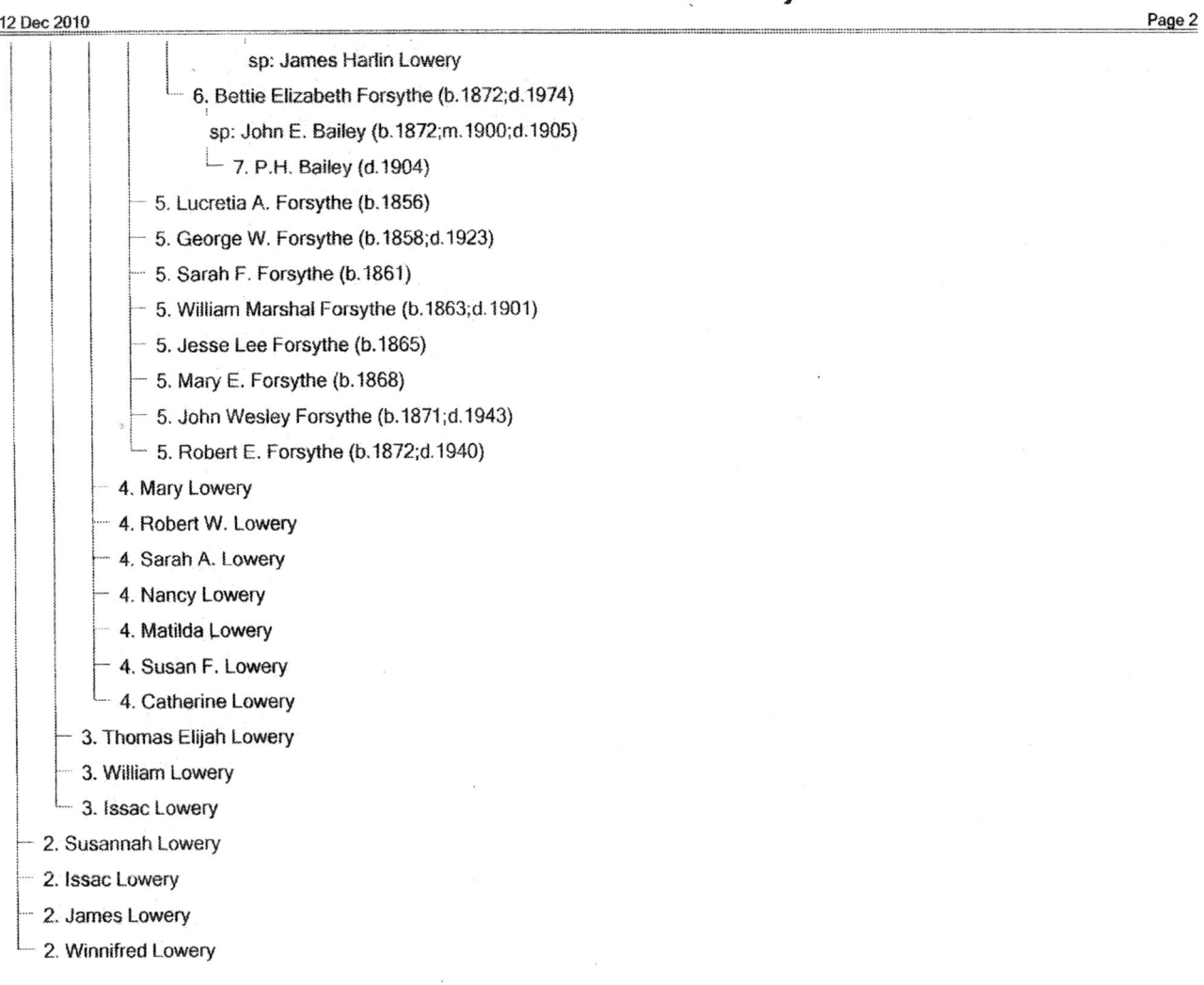

sp: James Harlin Lowery

6. Bettie Elizabeth Forsythe (b.1872;d.1974)

sp: John E. Bailey (b.1872;m.1900;d.1905)

7. P.H. Bailey (d.1904)

5. Lucretia A. Forsythe (b.1856)

5. George W. Forsythe (b.1858;d.1923)

5. Sarah F. Forsythe (b.1861)

5. William Marshal Forsythe (b.1863;d.1901)

5. Jesse Lee Forsythe (b.1865)

5. Mary E. Forsythe (b.1868)

5. John Wesley Forsythe (b.1871;d.1943)

5. Robert E. Forsythe (b.1872;d.1940)

4. Mary Lowery

4. Robert W. Lowery

4. Sarah A. Lowery

4. Nancy Lowery

4. Matilda Lowery

4. Susan F. Lowery

4. Catherine Lowery

3. Thomas Elijah Lowery

3. William Lowery

3. Issac Lowery

2. Susannah Lowery

2. Issac Lowery

2. James Lowery

2. Winnifred Lowery

Descendants of Joseph Craig

1. Joseph Craig (b.1800)

  sp: Cynthia (b.1800;d.1858)

    2. Dizey Washington Craig (b.1826;d.1877)

      sp: Martin Luther Bailey (b.1821;m.1846;d.1863)

        3. Emily Cynthis Bailey (b.1847;d.1912)

          sp: Thomas Wilson Kenner (m.1868)

        3. Sarah Ann Bailey (b.1849;d.1919)

          sp: William A. Winn (m.1866)

        3. Nathaniel Columbus Bailey (b.1850;d.1919)

          sp: Sarah D. Emison (b.1859;m.1880;d.1943)

            4. John E. Bailey (b.1872;d.1905)

              sp: Bettie Elizabeth Forsythe (b.1872;m.1900;d.1974)

                5. P.H. Bailey (d.1904)

            4. James Arthur Bailey (b.1881;d.1968)

              sp: Lou Myrtle Forsythe (b.1890;m.1907;d.1980)

                5. Marion A. Bailey (b.1909)

                5. Buhrl J. Bailey (b.1910;d.1968)

                5. Olive G. Bailey (b.1912)

                5. Mamie Elizabeth Bailey (b.1914;d.2002)

                  sp: Cyrus L.(Buster) Leggett (b.1911;m.1932;d.1951)

                    6. Myrtle Rose Leggett (b.1937)

                      sp: Joseph (Joe)Silas Emerson (b.1937;m.1955)

                        7. Mame' Emerson (b.1961;d.1977)

                        7. Jody Vann Emerson (b.1963)

                          sp: Kristi Kay Hart

                            8. Kayley Mame' Emerson (b.1992)

                            8. Silas Austin Emerson (b.1994)

                        7. Elizabeth Shane Emerson (b.1965)

                          sp: John Fenner French

                            8. Rebecca Emerson French (b.1998)

                            8. John Fenner Jr. French (b.2000)

                            8. Flora Elizabeth French (b.2003)

                        7. Milley Ann Emerson (b.1967)

                          sp: ?? Hart (b.1965)

                            8. Maggie Leigh Hart

                            8. Olivia Rose Hart

                    6. Betty Leggett

                      sp: Russell Cooke (d.2010)

                5. James M. Bailey (b.1916)

                5. Lawrence O. Bailey (b.1921)

                5. Edith C. Bailey (b.1924)

                5. Dorthy F. Bailey (b.1926)

                  sp: James Harlin Lowery

            4. Conrad O. Bailey (b.1887;d.1959)

Descendants of Joseph Craig

```
    ├─ 4. Donald Harrison Bailey (b.1891;d.1915)
    ├─ 4. Ira McKinley Bailey (b.1892;d.1908)
    │  sp: Martha M. Thomas (b.1855;m.1870)
    └─ 4. John E. Bailey (b.1872;d.1905) ** Printed on Page 1 **
─ 3. Mary Elizabeth Bailey (b.1855)
│  sp: George Winn
─ 3. Samantha(Addie) Adeline Bailey (b.1858;d.1940)
│  sp: James Owen Harvey (b.1854;m.1878;d.1929)
│     ├─ 4. Nora Fair Harvey (b.1879;d.1883)
│     ├─ 4. Lillie Browne Harvey (b.1881;d.1958)
│     ├─ 4. Ethel Harvey (b.1883;d.1958)
│     │  sp: Horace Leon Carter (b.1881;m.1904;d.1945)
│     │     ├─ 5. Virgil Leon Carter (b.1904;d.1986)
│     │     ├─ 5. James Wesley Carter (b.1906;d.1906)
│     │     ├─ 5. Halbert Leroy Carter (b.1910)
│     │     │  sp: Esther Virginia Hillsman (b.1909;m.1937;d.1988)
│     │     │     └─ 6. Dixie Virginia Carter (b.1939;d.2010)
│     │     │        sp: Harold (Hal)Rowe Holbrook (b.1924;m.1984)
│     │     │        sp: Arthur Lloyd Carter (b.1932;m.1967)
│     │     │           ├─ 7. Rosalin Helen Virginia Carter
│     │     │           └─ 7. Mary Dixie Carter
│     │     └─ 5. Melba Ethel Carter (b.1917)
│     ├─ 4. Virgil Harvey (b.1886)
│     └─ 4. Bertie Estelle Harvey (b.1893;d.1979)
─ 3. Newton Warren Bailey (b.1860;d.1916)
│  sp: Dora Hartsell
─ 3. Thomas Jefferson Bailey (b.1862;d.1916)
│  sp: Ella Jones
sp: Unknown Bledsoe (b.1824;m.1841;d.1845)
├─ 3. Joseph M. Bledsoe (b.1842)
└─ 3. William Jefferson Bledsoe (b.1844)
```

Descendants of Nathan Taylor

1. Nathan Taylor (b.1820)
   - sp: Jane Prince (b.1832;d.1856)
     - 2. Abraham Prince Taylor (b.1850;d.1910)
       - sp: Mary Asenath Jernagan (b.1855;m.1876;d.1922)
         - 3. Anna M. Taylor (b.1876;d.1964)
           - sp: Silas E. Emison (b.1868;m.1901;d.1921)
             - 4. Ruth Emison (b.1904)
             - 4. Russell Emison (b.1906)
               - sp: Mabel Johnson Goetz (b.1915;m.1965)
             - 4. Don Neil Emison (b.1909)
               - sp: Laverne Reddick (b.1916;m.1935)
             - 4. Malcolm Hooper Emerson (b.1912)
               - sp: Margaret Lou Goldsmith (b.1907;m.1934)
                 - 5. Joseph (Joe)Silas Emerson (b.1937)
                   - sp: Myrtle Rose Leggett (b.1937;m.1955)
                     - 6. Mame' Emerson (b.1961;d.1977)
                     - 6. Jody Vann Emerson (b.1963)
                       - sp: Kristi Kay Hart
                         - 7. Kayley Mame' Emerson (b.1992)
                         - 7. Silas Austin Emerson (b.1994)
                     - 6. Elizabeth Shane Emerson (b.1965)
                       - sp: John Fenner French
                         - 7. Rebecca Emerson French (b.1998)
                         - 7. John Fenner Jr. French (b.2000)
                         - 7. Flora Elizabeth French (b.2003)
                     - 6. Milley Ann Emerson (b.1967)
                       - sp: ?? Hart (b.1965)
                         - 7. Maggie Leigh Hart
                         - 7. Olivia Rose Hart
                 - 5. MacBoyd (Bill) Emerson (b.1935)
                   - sp: June Stephens (b.1935)
                     - 6. Lori Emerson (b.1957)
                     - 6. Vincent Emerson (b.1959)
                     - 6. John Ollie Emerson (b.1962)
         - 3. William Latta Prince Taylor (b.1878;d.1952)
           - sp: Bessie B. Lewis (b.1887;m.1904;d.1975)
             - 4. Hazel Geneva Taylor (b.1907;d.1980)
             - 4. George Penn Taylor
             - 4. Betty Louise Taylor
             - 4. Camalia Taylor
             - 4. Neil Brown Taylor
         - 3. Beatrice Taylor (b.1883;d.1952)
           - sp: Reginal (Reggie) Buckingham (b.1887;m.1908;d.1954)
             - 4. Elijah Prince Buckingham (b.1909;d.1981)

Ancestors and The Seeds Still Grow

- 4. Maylon Buckingham (b.1911;d.1972)
- 4. May Aileen Buckingham (b.1915;d.1944)
- 4. Annie Mildred Buckingham (b.1918;d.1988)
- 3. Cardova (Dovie) Angela Taylor (b.1886;d.1981)
  - sp: Virgil Hopper (b.1883;m.1904;d.1960)
    - 4. Burdon Hopper
    - 4. Bonnie Hopper
    - 4. Mayo Hopper
    - 4. Owen J. Hopper (b.1905;d.1979)
    - 4. Oscar Hopper (b.1905)
- 3. Olive Verbie Taylor (b.1889;d.1975)
  - sp: Alsie Raines Reasons (b.1888;m.1907;d.1951)
    - 4. Truman Reasons (b.1908;d.1972)
    - 4. Douglas Reasons (b.1910;d.1983)
    - 4. Abbt Reasons (b.1913;d.1933)
    - 4. Marshall Reasons (b.1916;d.1966)
    - 4. Genrose Reasons (b.1919)
    - 4. D.W. Reasons (b.1922;d.1992)
    - 4. Gladys Reasons (b.1924)
    - 4. Dorris Grey Reasons (b.1927)
- 3. Elizabeth Taylor (b.1892;d.1974)
  - sp: John Nelson (b.1895;m.1920;d.1972)
    - 4. A.J. Nelson
    - 4. Paul Winston Nelson
    - 4. Juanita Nelson
    - 4. Mary E. Nelson (b.1921;d.1922)
    - 4. Charles Nicholas Nelson (b.1924;d.1924)
    - 4. Herman Taylor Nelson (b.1926;d.1951)
    - 4. Jerry Duane Nelson (b.1934;d.1935)
- 3. Alton (Alta) Taylor (b.1898;d.1993)
  - sp: Cleveland S. (Joe) Lloyd (b.1894;m.1914;d.1969)
    - 4. Blondell L. Lloyd (b.1915;d.1998)
    - 4. Jimmy Taylor Lloyd (b.1918;d.2006)
    - 4. Steven H. Lloyd (b.1920;d.2007)
    - 4. Ernest N. Lloyd (b.1922;d.1996)
    - 4. Mary R. Lloyd (b.1925)
    - 4. Betty Joe Lloyd (b.1928)
    - 4. Bobby Zane Lloyd (b.1934;d.1993)
    - 4. Jessie Vernell Lloyd (b.1937)
    - 4. Abraham Prince Lloyd (b.1939;d.1939)
    - 4. Wendell R. Lloyd (b.1940)
- 2. William Taylor
- 2. Martha Taylor
- 2. Mary Catherine Taylor
- 2. Albert Prince Taylor
- 2. Pricilla Taylor

1. Richard Bailey (b.1620;d.1677)

  sp: Unknown

  └─ 2. Samuel Bailey (b.1665;d.1728)

      sp: Elizabeth Rogers (b.1677;d.1728)

      └─ 3. Sr. Jeremiah Bailey (b.1709;d.1779)

          sp: Unknown

          └─ 4. Richard Bailey (b.1740;d.1830)

              sp: Millie Fuller (b.1747;d.1860)

              └─ 5. Alsey Bailey (b.1792;d.1855)

                  sp: Matilda Ray (b.1803;m.1819;d.1860)

                  └─ 6. Martin Luther Bailey (b.1821;d.1863)

                      sp: Dizey Washington Craig (b.1826;m.1846;d.1877)

                      ├─ 7. Emily Cynthis Bailey (b.1847;d.1912)

                      │   sp: Thomas Wilson Kenner (m.1868)

                      ├─ 7. Sarah Ann Bailey (b.1849;d.1919)

                      │   sp: William A. Winn (m.1866)

                      ├─ 7. Nathaniel Columbus Bailey (b.1850;d.1919)

                      │   sp: Sarah D. Emison (b.1859;m.1880;d.1943)

                      │   ├─ 8. John E. Bailey (b.1872;d.1905)

                      │   │   sp: Bettie Elizabeth Forsythe (b.1872;m.1900;d.1974)

                      │   │   └─ 9. P.H. Bailey (d.1904)

                      │   ├─ 8. James Arthur Bailey (b.1881;d.1968)

                      │   sp: Lou Myrtle Forsythe (b.1890;m.1907;d.1980)

                      │   ├─ 9. Marion A. Bailey (b.1909)

                      │   ├─ 9. Buhrl J. Bailey (b.1910;d.1968)

                      │   ├─ 9. Olive G. Bailey (b.1912)

                      │   ├─ 9. Mamie Elizabeth Bailey (b.1914;d.2002)

                      │   sp: Cyrus L.(Buster) Leggett (b.1911;m.1932;d.1951)

                      │   ├─ 10. Myrtle Rose Leggett (b.1937)

                      │   sp: Joseph (Joe)Silas Emerson (b.1937;m.1955)

                      │   ├─ 11. Mame' Emerson (b.1961;d.1977)

                      │   ├─ 11. Jody Vann Emerson (b.1963)

                      │   │   sp: Kristi Kay Hart

                      │   │   ├─ 12. Kayley Mame' Emerson (b.1992)

                      │   │   └─ 12. Silas Austin Emerson (b.1994)

                      │   ├─ 11. Elizabeth Shane Emerson (b.1965)

                      │   │   sp: John Fenner French

                      │   │   ├─ 12. Rebecca Emerson French (b.1998)

                      │   │   ├─ 12. John Fenner Jr. French (b.2000)

                      │   │   └─ 12. Flora Elizabeth French (b.2003)

                      │   └─ 11. Milley Ann Emerson (b.1967)

                      │   sp: ?? Hart (b.1965)

                      │   ├─ 12. Maggie Leigh Hart

                      │   └─ 12. Olivia Rose Hart

Descendants of Richard Bailey

```
            └ 10. Betty Leggett
                    sp: Russell Cooke (d.2010)
         ─ 9. James M. Bailey (b.1916)
         ─ 9. Lawrence O. Bailey (b.1921)
         ─ 9. Edith C. Bailey (b.1924)
         └ 9. Dorthy F. Bailey (b.1926)
              sp: James Harlin Lowery
      ─ 8. Conrad O. Bailey (b.1887;d.1959)
      ─ 8. Donald Harrison Bailey (b.1891;d.1915)
      ─ 8. Ira McKinley Bailey (b.1892;d.1908)
     sp: Martha M. Thomas (b.1855;m.1870)
      └ 8. John E. Bailey (b.1872;d.1905) ** Printed on Page 1 **
   ─ 7. Mary Elizabeth Bailey (b.1855)
     sp: George Winn
   ─ 7. Samantha(Addie) Adeline Bailey (b.1858;d.1940)
     sp: James Owen Harvey (b.1854;m.1878;d.1929)
      ─ 8. Nora Fair Harvey (b.1879;d.1883)
      ─ 8. Lillie Browne Harvey (b.1881;d.1958)
      ─ 8. Ethel Harvey (b.1883;d.1958)
         sp: Horace Leon Carter (b.1881;m.1904;d.1945)
          ─ 9. Virgil Leon Carter (b.1904;d.1986)
          ─ 9. James Wesley Carter (b.1906;d.1906)
          ─ 9. Halbert Leroy Carter (b.1910)
             sp: Esther Virginia Hillsman (b.1909;m.1937;d.1988)
              └ 10. Dixie Virginia Carter (b.1939;d.2010)
                    sp: Harold (Hal)Rowe Holbrook (b.1924;m.1984)
                    sp: Arthur Lloyd Carter (b.1932;m.1967)
                     ─ 11. Rosalin Helen Virginia Carter
                     └ 11. Mary Dixie Carter
          └ 9. Melba Ethel Carter (b.1917)
      ─ 8. Virgil Harvey (b.1886)
      └ 8. Bertie Estelle Harvey (b.1893;d.1979)
   ─ 7. Newton Warren Bailey (b.1860;d.1916)
     sp: Dora Hartsell
   └ 7. Thomas Jefferson Bailey (b.1862;d.1916)
     sp: Ella Jones
```

Descendants of Sampson Leggett

1. **Sampson Leggett (b.abt. 1770-England)**

  sp: Unknown McKerman (b.1775-England)

    2. Samuel David Leggett (b.1810-Martin County,NC;d.1851-Madison County,Tennessee)

      sp: Lavenia M. (Davis) Byrd (b.1810-NC;m.8 Jan 1849;d.1861-Madison County,Tennessee)

        3. Francis Marion Leggett (b.10 Feb 1850-Madison County,TN;d.1 May 1932-Crockett County,TN)

          sp: Charlonas Ann (Lony) Emison (b.11 Sep 1855-Madison County,TN;m.23 Dec 1874;d.7 Jul 1933-Crockett County,TN)

            4. Ella Mae Leggett (b.28 Mar 1876-Crockett County,TN)

            4. Walter Columbus Leggett (b.5 Apr 1878-Crockett County,TN;d.9 Jan 1965)

              sp: Rosa Belle Webb (b.Feb 1888-Crockett County,TN;m.1 Feb 1914;d.26 May 1937-Crockett County,TN)

                5. Louise Leggett (b.26 Oct 1914-Crockett County,TN;d.31 Jul 1937)

                  sp: Wilson H. Woodson (b.27 Jan 1909-Crockett County,TN;d.28 Nov 1988-Crockett County,TN)

                5. Clarence Leggett (b.17 Mar 1917-Crockett County,TN;d.12 May 1985-Crockett County,TN)

                  sp: Virginia Spragins (b.19 Jun 1919-Crockett County,TN;m.2 Jan 1937)

                5. Elvin Leggett (b.1922-Crockett County,TN)

                5. Lilley Belle Leggett (b.1924-Crockett County,TN)

                5. Howard Leggett (b.1927-Crockett County,TN)

            4. William Arthur Leggett (b.31 Aug 1880-Crockett County,TN;d.1 Jun 1931-Crockett County,TN)

            4. Dorsey(Dorse) Leonard Leggett (b.12 Aug 1888-Crockett County,TN;d.17 Nov 1964)

              sp: Erin Bedwell

                5. Garland Leggett

                5. Nathalie Leggett

                5. Joe Leonard Leggett

                5. Merlin Leggett

                5. Clifton Leggett

                5. Madeline Leggett

                5. Bennie Faye Leggett

            4. Homer Cyrus Leggett (b.Aug 1890-Crockett County,TN;d.1912-Crockett County,TN)

              sp: Rosa Belle Webb (b.Feb 1888-Crockett County,TN;m.22 Dec 1906;d.26 May 1937-Crockett County,TN)

                5. Raymond Leggett (b.4 Oct 1907-Crockett County,TN;d.Feb 1978-Crockett County,TN)

                  sp: Eunice Mary Crochet (b.1909-Louisiana)

                5. Mary Jewell Leggett (b.1 Aug 1909-Crockett County,TN;d.10 Nov 1993-Crockett County,TN)

                  sp: Arthur Bailey (b.26 Feb 1909-Crockett County,TN;d.27 Mar 1999-Crockett County,TN)

                5. Cyrus L.(Buster) Leggett (b.11 May 1911-Crockett County,TN;d.1 Aug 1951-Crockett County,TN)

                  sp: Mamie Elizabeth Bailey (b.12 Oct 1914-Crockett County,TN;m.26 Dec 1932;d.11 Nov 2002-CC,TN)

                    6. Myrtle Rose Leggett (b.23 Aug 1937-Crockett County,TN)

                      sp: Joseph (Joe)Silas Emerson (b.21 Mar 1937-Crockett County,TN;m.23 Oct 1955)

                        7. Mame' Emerson (b.8 Aug 1961-Crockett County,TN;d.21 May 1977-Crockett County,TN)

                        7. Jody Vann Emerson (b.27 Sep 1963-Crockett County,TN)

                          sp: Kristi Kay Hart

                          8. Kayley Mame' Emerson (b.15 Nov 1992)

                          8. Silas Austin Emerson (b.12 Sep 1994)

                        7. Elizabeth Shane Emerson (b.4 Jun 1965-Crockett County,TN)

                        sp: John Fenner French

                          8. Rebecca Emerson French (b.17 Nov 1998)

```
            ┌── 8. John Fenner Jr. French (b.23 Jun 2000)
            └── 8. Flora Elizabeth French (b.27 Jan 2003)
       └── 7. Milley Ann Emerson (b.27 Jun 1967-Madison County,Tennessee)
            sp: ?? Hart (b.1965)
            ┌── 8. Maggie Leigh Hart
            └── 8. Olivia Rose Hart
  └── 6. Betty Leggett
       sp: Russell Cooke (d.Sep 2010-Crockett County,TN)
─ 4. Florence B. Leggett (b.Oct 1892-Crockett County,TN)
─ 4. Norma Irene Leggett (b.13 Feb 1896-Crockett County,TN;d.3 Mar 1970)
sp: Nancy Ann Emison (b.20 Mar 1842-Madison County,Tennessee;m.11 Aug 1867;d.Apr 1871-AR)
─ 4. Margaret Lavenia Leggett (b.23 Jul 1868-Lauderdale County,Tennessee;d.31 Jul 1913-Garvely,Yell County,AR)
   sp: Tillman Erastus Poindexter (b.21 Oct 1860-AR;m.29 Mar 1884;d.12 Feb 1939-Rockwall,TX)
   ─ 5. Viola Poindexter (b.12 Feb 1885-AR)
   ─ 5. Theodore Poindexter (b.13 Aug 1886-AR)
   ─ 5. India Mae Poindexter (b.7 Jun 1888-Pope,AR)
   ─ 5. Thomas Marion Poindexter (b.12 May 1890-Pope,AR)
   ─ 5. Librum Erastus Poindexter (b.26 Dec 1891-Pope,AR)
   ─ 5. Lilly Equilla Poindexter (b.13 Dec 1893-Pope,AR)
   ─ 5. Borce Franklin Poindexter (b.11 Nov 1895-Pope,AR)
   ─ 5. Dewey Lee Poindexter (b.18 Jun 1898-Pope,AR)
   ─ 5. Maxi Poindexter (b.13 Oct 1900-Pope,AR)
   ─ 5. Susan Frances Poindexter (b.23 Jun 1903-Pope,AR)
   ─ 5. Bonnie Irene Poindexter (b.10 Dec 1905-Pope,AR)
   ─ 5. Tilman Ernst Poindexter (b.25 Nov 1907-Pope,AR)
   └── 5. Aubrey D. Poindexter (b.27 Apr 1908-Pope,AR)
─ 4. Mary Susan Leggett (b.12 Jan 1871-Lauderdale County,Tennessee;d.8 Feb 1904-Crockett County,TN)
   sp: Joseph LaFayette Gaba (b.13 Sep 1870;m.3 Aug 1891;d.17 Feb 1904-Crockett County,TN)
   ─ 5. Sarah Ann Gaba (b.30 May 1892)
      sp: E.G. Johnson
   ─ 5. William Robert Gaba (b.16 May 1894)
      sp: Addie Lee Love
   ─ 5. Jesse G. Gaba (b.30 Aug 1897)
      sp: Gracie Howell (m.21 May 1916)
   ─ 5. Francis Marion Gaba (b.19 Mar 1899-Crockett County,TN;d.14 Sep 1952-Crockett County,TN)
      sp: Lillie Taylor (m.11 Sep 1920)
   └── 5. Bessie Pearl Gaba (b.1901-Crockett County,TN)
      sp: Claude Gourley (m.16 Oct 1923)
      ─ 6. Hester Laverne Gourley (b.1924)
      └── 6. Frances Janita Gourley (b.1926)
─ 3. George Washington Leggett (b.10 Feb 1850-Madison County,Tennessee;d.24 Feb 1925-Dyer County,TN)
   sp: Amanda E. Griffin (b.1850-Dyer County,TN;m.26 Apr 1880;d.1881-Dyer County,TN)
   ─ 4. Clyde Wilson Leggett (b.18 Jan 1881-Dyer County,TN;d.4 Apr 1962-(Bonicord) Dyer County,TN)
      sp: Josie G. Gibson (b.1889-Dyer County,TN;m.28 Dec 1903;d.1931-Dyer County,TN)
```

        5. Ella May Leggett (b.1905-Dyer County,TN)

        5. Clyde W. Jr. Leggett (b.1910-Dyer County,TN)

        5. Maywood Leggett (b.1912-Dyer County,TN)

        5. Christine Leggett (b.1913-Dyer County,TN)

        5. Woodson Leggett (b.1916-Dyer County,TN)

        5. Clara F. Leggett (b.1918-Dyer County,TN)

        5. Marion Leggett (b.1920-Dyer County,TN)

sp: Ruth J. Milligan (b.Jun 1863-Dyer County,TN;m.26 Nov 1884;d.1909-Dyer County,TN)

4. Clyde Wilson Leggett (b.18 Jan 1881-Dyer County,TN;d.4 Apr 1962-(Bonicord) Dyer County,TN) ** Printed on Page 2 **

4. Alvin Glenn, Sr. Leggett (b.7 Apr 1885-Dyer County,TN;d.19 Mar 1965-Dyer County,TN)

  sp: Cready M. Esprey (b.14 Sep 1889-Dyer County,TN;m.8 Jan 1907;d.22 Nov 1972-Dyer County,TN)

      5. Wilma L. Leggett (b.1909-Dyer County,TN)

      5. L. Zula Leggett (b.1911-Dyer County,TN)

      5. George William Leggett (b.19 Jul 1912-Dyer County,TN;d.25 Mar 1994-JMCGH)

        sp: Flora Proctor

      5. Alvin Glenn, Jr. Leggett (b.26 Dec 1917-Dyer County,TN;d.8 Apr 1989-Carl Vinson Medical Fac. Dublin,GA)

        sp: Minnie

      5. Leonard G. Leggett (b.1918-Dyer County,TN)

      5. Gordon L. Leggett (b.1925-Dyer County,TN)

4. Benton E. Leggett (b.5 Jan 1887-Dyer County,TN;d.31 Oct 1918-Dyer County,TN)

4. Sarah Viola Leggett (b.Apr 1889-Dyer County,TN)

  sp: Rufus King (m.1 Mar 1914)

4. Mary L.(Jettie) Leggett (b.Sep 1891-Dyer County,TN;d.24 Feb 1932-Dyer County,TN)

  sp: William T.,Jr. Nash (b.23 Nov 1890-Dyer County,TN;m.6 Apr 1921;d.14 Jan 1962-Dyer County,TN)

4. Gus M. Leggett (b.14 Feb 1894-Dyer County,TN;d.31 Mar 1922-Dyer County,TN)

  sp: Hattie L. Conder (b.1897-Dyer County,TN;m.25 Sep 1917;d.Aft 1922-Dyer County,TN)

4. Elizabeth B. Leggett (b.Apr 1896-Dyer County,TN)

  sp: Carlie Hammons (m.24 Mar 1920)

sp: Emma Watson (b.1870-Dyer County,TN;m.24 Dec 1911;d.1921-Dyer County,TN)

3. D. Byrd (b.1833-Tennessee)

3. William Byrd (b.1839-Tennessee)

3. Dicey Byrd (b.1844-Tennessee)

Main Street Publishing, Inc.
206 E. Main Street, Suite 207
P.O. Box 696
Jackson, TN 38301

Toll Free #: 866-457-7379
or
Local #: 731-427-7379

Visit us on the web:
www.mainstreetpublishing.com
www.mspbooks.com

E-Mail: editor@mainstreetpublishing.com